Aussie Ties

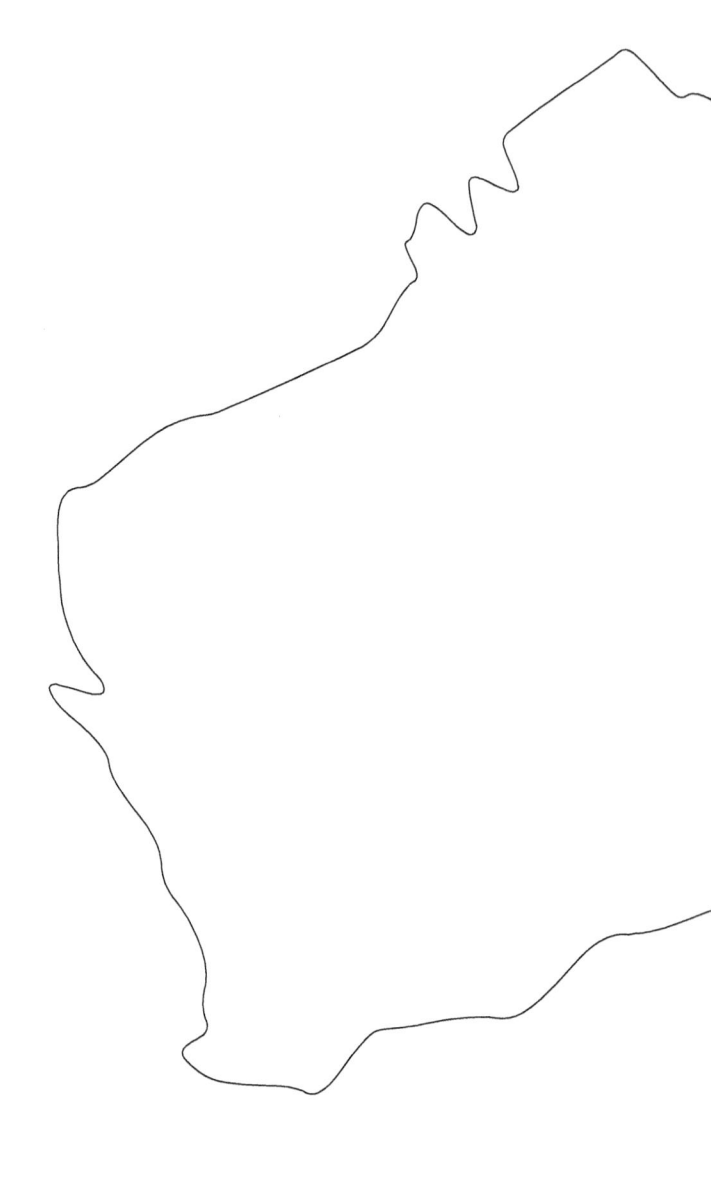

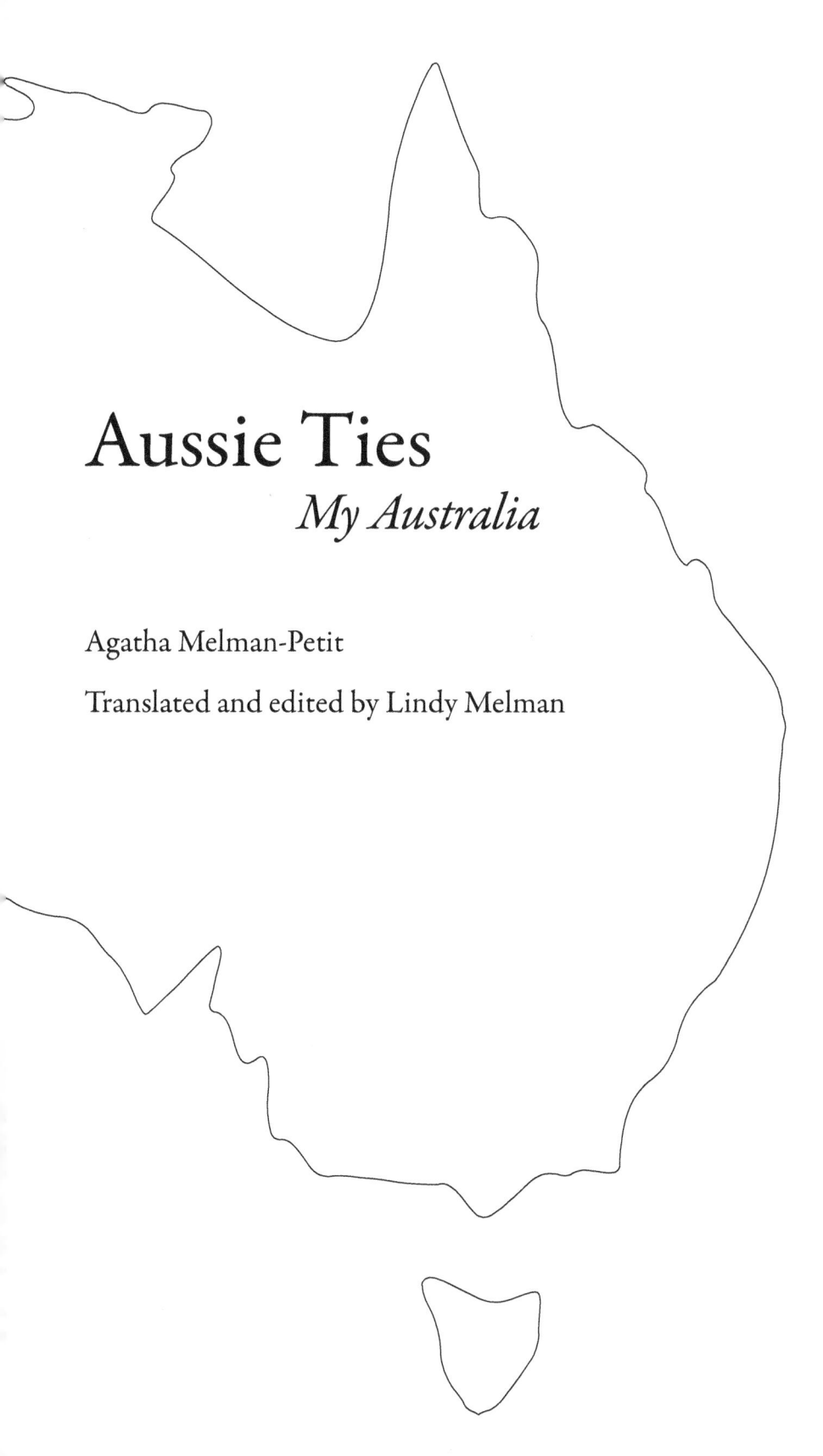

Aussie Ties
My Australia

Agatha Melman-Petit

Translated and edited by Lindy Melman

Copyright 2019 Agatha Melman-Petit and Lindy Melman.

All rights reserved. No part of this publication may be reproduced, stored in a retrieval system, stored in a database and / or published in any form or by any means, electronic, mechanical, photocopying, recording or otherwise, without the prior written permission of the copyright holders.

Published by Slide Books, The Hague/London.

ISBN 978-94-9-186804-7

Note from the translator: My mother's original, Dutch-language memoir was entitled *Waltzing Matilda and I: A Memoir*. The title of the current English version was devised by my brother, Bob, and was enthusiastically adopted by our mother.

To Janneke, Lindy, Paul and Bobby

Preface

SIXTEEN YEARS AGO my mother finished a memoir written in her mother tongue, Dutch. It recorded what she felt were the most formative years of her life: her emigration to Australia after the Second World War and her subsequent eighteen years there. She had been working on the text, on and off, for over ten years. Along the way, she even published excerpts in a Dutch women's magazine (albeit, a little airbrushed). Once her final, "uncensored" version was completed, we printed and bound it for her. She gave copies to Dutch family and friends who hugely enjoyed reading it. But her real hope, that it would be published as a book, was never fulfilled.

She is now ninety-one years old. She and my father (who is 94) live in a comfortable apartment in Breda, the city in the south of Holland where my parents settled after they returned from Australia. Both are still remarkably sound of mind and even of limb, though the latter do creak ("Growing old," my father often says ruefully, echoing Bette Davis, "really, really isn't for sissies!"). They live quietly, enjoying friends, family, children and grandchildren, and especially each other. Last year they celebrated their 65th wedding anniversary and the birth of their first great-grandchild. In hindsight, their decision to move back to Holland fifty years ago for the sake of my father's health was clearly a sound one.

About a year ago, my mother asked me to translate her memoir into English so that friends and family in Australia could read it. She accepted my initial, aghast refusal philosophically enough: I would never have the time alongside a fulltime job! But on reflection I decided to do it anyway. I wanted to grant her her wish while she and my father could still enjoy it.

With my mother's permission, I did not simply translate, I edited too and so, I hope, gave the text a new pace and coherence. My mother writes with a journalist's clarity, but she wrote for a Dutch audience. For English-speaking readers, less needs explanation; the sunburned country sings easily; the conversations flow naturally as this is the language in which most of them were held.

Of course, like every memoir, the story is not complete. Nor is it objective, despite my mother's determination to tell the unadulterated truth. The facts and occurrences she relates are certainly true and the people she describes were real. But there are many events, good and bad, major and minor, she only touches on or skips, and multitudes of people she ignores. And the occurrences and conversations she does describe are not based on recordings or diaries, but on memory, and solely on her memory at that. But as she herself asks: what is truth, after all? Her memories – even if selective and subjective – are no less valid for being that. If all we can ever do is make sense of the world through our own perception, then subjective memory is also truth – perhaps, some might argue, the only truth.

To my surprise, my offhand favour became a great deal more to me. Translating my mother's memoir meant inhabiting it. I found myself making a journey of discovery I had never expected to make, and sometimes a painful and emotional one. I became immersed in my mother's (and my father's) experiences, and my and my siblings' early youth (traumas and all), but also in a past that had meant little to me before: Holland after the Second World War; being a penniless immigrant, with no social safety nets, dependant on resourcefulness and grit; discovering a – literally – new world; being a young woman at a time when gender inequality was routine.

And I came to realise that my mother's story does offer what she always hoped it would: something of interest to readers outside our family. There are snapshots of life in the 1950s and 60s; there are colourful characters aplenty; there are often hilarious, sometimes tragic, sometimes inspirational events. There are loves and betrayals, successes and failures, births and deaths: entertainment and drama enough for any reader. And there is also, of course, Australia. Above all, my mother wanted to share her love for her strange, new, beautiful adopted country.

Underpinning all this, there is something more. Lightly and unconsciously, what this story lays bare are the foundations of a marriage that has weathered the upheavals of a lifetime – internal and external. So in the end, it may simply be a love story or at least a story about the beginnings of one. And in our fast-paced, narcissistic, anguished age, it is good to read how real love is forged and good to be reminded that it can and does endure.

Lindy Melman, January 2019

Contents

Preface   vi

Part 1

1   How to begin?   3
2   Passage to Australia   15
3   New Australians   27
4   Meeting Gerard   35
5   Auburn and Katoomba   43
6   My world changes   49
7   Burwood, Henk and Odette   65
8   Ellamatta Avenue and the tie factory   71
9   First pregnancy   77
10   Janneke   83
11   Dr Maine and asthma   89
12   Lindy   99
13   Father Pierce, Paul Albers and Binalong   107
14   Home decorating   117
15   Catholics, Seaforth and Josie   121
16   Middle Head Road   135
17   New jobs   145
18   Picnics and discussions   149
19   Patsy, Laurel and Bobby   159
20   New kitchen and thunderstorms   171
21   The locust tree   185
22   For better or worse   193
23   Weddings, divorces and babies   203
24   Paul   215

Part 2

25 Globe Commercial   223
26 Norman   237
27 Christmas and a new home   245
28 Upheavals   257
29 Turramurra and Torron   271
30 Torron success   281
31 Life in Turramurra   291
32 Hill End   301
33 Losses   311
34 An unexpected journey   321
35 Departures   333

PART 1

CHAPTER 1

How to begin?

NOT THE WAY *I began twenty years ago, in any case; not determined to write a publishable book. Twenty years ago I filled 400 pages with light-hearted stories about our eighteen years in Australia. I called it "a report in novel form." I gave it the title "Waltzing Matilda and I." I firmly believed that I could find a publisher for it as long as I wrote a bright and breezy book. Write it like a story for a glossy, I thought, stick to a light, magazine-reporting style.*

I now look back with compassion on that hardworking me. I wrote and rewrote, deleted adjectives, mutilated the original (it no longer exists, only the three later drafts) and it all led to nothing. I also look back with some embarrassment. Did I even think about a reader? I must have had have a reader in mind. One always does. Who is it this time? Why am I sitting here?

I can't answer that. All I know is that it keeps tugging at me, our story. I want to write our story. My story. But this time I want to write it without self-imposed rules and without anxiety. This time I will use real, not fictional names; this time I won't mix fact with fiction. To the best of my ability I will tell it how it was. How I remember it. So this time I will not make two men into one. I must give Charles the place he deserves. He existed. He was very important.

How to begin? Twenty years ago my first sentence was: "This is 'now', this is the 80s." Now as I write "the now" is the year 2000...

... and "then" is 1949. The Netherlands, the city of Deventer: huge chasms between hastily patched-up buildings. Wet, broken streets. "*The spring of 1949 is the colour of ash,*" I wrote, and "*It is four years after Hiroshima. In September 1949 the Soviet-Union will detonate its first atomic bomb. The ruins around us have barely been cleared away. And following the cold, the hunger, the darkness and the whispered stories of horror from our teenage war years a new, incomprehensible threat hangs in the air."* True, all true. But was this really the reason we wanted to leave, Charles and I?

I need to go further back, to 1946/1947, I think. In any case, to shortly after my school finals when I ended up at the editorial office of the newspaper *Het Vrije Volk* in Arnhem as a proof reader and fledgling reporter. In those days, you learned the profession on the job. I had written stories for as long as I could remember. Our Chief Editor – I have forgotten his name – quickly realised that I could write. A year later I was offered a job as *Vrije Volk* correspondent in Deventer. And there, on a summer's day, I met Charles.

Since yesterday the opening sentence of a famous English novel has been running through my head: The Go-Between *by L.P. Hartley. "The past is a foreign country, they do things differently there." It made me think about how I view "the past." Like a giant exhibition space in which countless panels are set up, large and small, forming hallways and rooms where you wander, lost, amid endless series of dusty paintings; here and there, one suddenly lights up. Silence. I hear nothing. Sound must come from another part of my brain or perhaps I need to add this myself? The first time I met Charles is such an image.*

I am sitting on what someone has called "the press platform." A row of chairs behind a long table on a low, raised platform placed against the back wall of the council hall of the village of Diepenveen, which nestles against Deventer. Reporting on council meetings in the surrounding villages is part of my job. I am "the little lady from the newspaper," the only female reporter ever to arrive in Deventer and therefore something of a curiosity. I have a few male colleagues whom I encounter regularly – from *Het Deventer Dagblad*, for instance, the local newspaper, and a man who represents Reuters and a few national newspapers.

Het Vrije Volk, then the largest newspaper in The Netherlands as it's sub-title proclaims, is the only national newspaper that has its own small office in Deventer where I am solely responsible for the reporting side of things. I am a small part of the Enschede desk; this is where I send my stories, by train-letter during the day and by phone after 6 o'clock in the evening. My newspaper is the only morning paper in Deventer so especially in the case of council meetings we are always one step ahead of *Het Deventer Dagblad*, at least if I can phone through my story before our midnight deadline. I live a full and busy life.

Diepenveen wanted sports fields. There is a heated discussion about the plans. I make notes. And then someone moves into the seat next to me, a tall, broad-shouldered, bony man, with wildly curling blonde hair and clear blue eyes. He grins broadly. He is a bit like a satyr. He is wearing a sweater, not a suit like everyone else. He says something. What? Probably "I'm Ruys." He takes hold of my hand. He mumbles something about the fact that he writes for a sports magazine. And I become aware of an intense astonishment that continues to last for years.

And then we are cycling together back to Deventer. He has a racing bicycle! The sun is shining. Suddenly life is no longer serious. Life is absurd, giddy, fun – full to the brim of exuberant idiocy. I have never met anyone who is so verbal, so witty, funny, quick and bold. I never stop laughing. And I am proud that he is so different, so scandalously different from everyone I know: a buccaneer on a racing bicycle. He says he is a freelance sports journalist.

And who was I, then? I was 20, as green as grass. I had never had contact with boys. Catholic schools and the war made sure of that. I only became aware of that opposite sex when Nijmegen was liberated: young men, all at least six feet tall, all of equally athletic build, all with broad grins on their tanned faces. Our liberators were breathtaking. The men whom I later met through my work were measly in comparison; until Charles turned up.

I had a friend in Deventer – friend in the old-fashioned sense of the word. Henk was an engineer and he had a limp. He dragged his right leg heavily, that is about all I remember about him, except that we talked together about Henri Bergson and philosophy in general. I also remember Henk as being bitter for some reason. And then Charles appeared.

Charles was 30. He had been a member of the underground resistance. He had been arrested twice by the Germans and had escaped both times. If I am not mistaken he had ended up in England by way of the Pyrenees. He had become a marine and had been in America where Dutch marines were given training. He told me he had become fed up with this after a while and so had gone on a trip through the US together with a mate, out of pure boredom, after which he had been sent back to Holland in disgrace, at least in the eyes of the Dutch marine corps. Holland didn't suit him, so he left for Brazil where the same mate owned a sugar plantation. Unfortunately, the mate had been killed in an accident by the time he arrived, so the good job he had been hoping for failed to materialise.

He had returned to Holland, completely broke, as a stowaway on the cruise ship *Willem Ruys*, after having enlisted the help of a few members of the crew. A day after the ship had sailed, he had dutifully presented himself to the captain. He was set to work washing up the dishes. He swore to me that after that experience he had never done any washing up again. The Dutch actor Cor Ruys was his uncle. His father was also an actor. The whole family had theatre connections, except him. As a toddler he had been sent to stay with a farming family, I have forgotten why. The profession of house painter was chosen for him, why is again a mystery to me. He was apprenticed to a painter. His great passion was sport, especially cycling, hence the racing bicycle, and hence also the sports writing. He wrote well. He talked even better. I was enchanted. He saw life as one huge adventure. He saw limitless possibilities.

But not in Holland: Holland is far too small. Holland is full to bursting with people who can't see beyond their own noses! Who can't appreciate grand ideas, without the slightest sprit of adventure. And so is the whole of Europe. Smothered in provincialism; everyone bickering, squabbling, exhausted. Europe was finished. But the United States, on the other hand! There was space there, space to breathe. A shame it was so difficult to get into though, especially if you didn't have a penny. There must be a way to get a little money quickly; enough to pay for the trip at least. The rest he would talk his way into.

I believed him. I believed every word he spoke. I agreed with him completely. I suddenly realised that I too had always wanted to leave this small, claustrophobic Holland. He was the rebel that I had always wanted to be, deep down inside. That I was! I too was sick of all the old norms and values. I too wanted space. I too wanted to be different.

I lived in a boarding house on the corner of a narrow street that ran from the Brink to De Heuvel. *En famille*. The newspaper had arranged this. Charles lived with friends. His sports writing barely earned him enough to live on. He quite rightly remarked one day that we could both save money if we could share a room together somewhere. Together as a married couple, that is. Otherwise we would not be accepted anywhere. And we would then even be entitled to part of a house, one of the "requisitioned" sections of houses that young married couples were housed in at that time.

"What do you think?" he asked. It was a brand new idea for me, getting married. It sounded eminently logical, sensible, and at the same time adventurous, daring and therefore fun. We were already a couple. I was convinced that we loved each other. Charles had initiated me in his room, a few days before, with tact and tenderness, into the secrets of sex, which had left me with an "Is that all?" and at the same time a "Now I am finally an adult" feeling. He was so familiar now; it was so normal to have him around. I did not hesitate for a second. I was delighted. So we got married, as unconventionally as possible. A quick trip to the town hall to pick up the document we needed to claim a place to live. Absolutely no "fuss." I felt proud and free. Especially free. Even though Charles rightly remarked that evening that we would only be really free if we left this *"pokkenlandje,"* if we could lead a new and completely different life. And that was what he was now going to work hard to achieve.

But first there needed to be money, money to pay for his rent arrears and then money to pay for our passage. Freelance writing earned far too little, but he had a few other ideas. He wanted to set up an advertisement newspaper, a weekly, to be distributed free door to door, for which he would also write a few articles. Not many: advertisers would pay for the costs and ensure a pretty profit. It was perfectly possible. He had already made a few enquiries here and there and drawn up a cost calculation. He had already found a printer who was interested, who was prepared to print the first edition for free if he, Charles, could bring in enough advertisers. It would all take a little time of course, something like that needed time, but luckily he could pound the pavement every day, had no other obligations. Of course it would succeed! Now that the war was over, now that rationing was ending...How fortunate that no-one else had had the idea yet and that I had a good job and therefore a steady income! It gave us a bit of breathing space. I was deeply impressed. I was wildly enthusiastic. As a kind of wedding gift, I bought him a winter coat the next day. He did not own one and it was getting increasingly colder.

Back to the painting exhibition: there are large shards of mist in that mysterious room. I mustn't try to hurry. I must do this very calmly. It is still there, that Deventer of almost 70 years ago and Charles is there, so much larger and stronger than I am. The born story-teller to whom everyone listened breathlessly; the man of ideas who never had a problem persuading other people, getting them to share his dream; the always-laughing performer who constantly produced an inexhaustible arsenal of jokes and anecdotes. And the man who could not stand routine, drudgery he called it: "There is nothing more deadly than getting in a rut!" Who always wanted something new, something different, a fresh horizon. Who always threw away his old shoes before he had a new pair...

Deventer 1949. Still wet broken streets and provisionally patched-up buildings, but not as bad as Nijmegen. Nijmegen, my home, had had its heart torn out by bombs. Seven months of daily artillery raids when the front lay on the opposite bank of the Waal River had smashed countless holes into the city. We had slept for seven months in a tiny cellar under the stairs...

But Deventer too still carries the scars of violence and is dark, so dark. I hate gloom. I peer through the swirling mist and there we are. We are the boarders of a stately, child-less couple in a dilapidated room in their damaged mansion. We do indeed have a "requisitioned" room with "cooking facility." That facility is situated two flights of stairs up, an antique stove next to a tiny washbasin in a small space where the temperature is always below zero. I only cook soup there, sometimes. I can't cook at all. We sit in front of a small iron stove on two second-hand, straight-backed chairs, the only furniture we acquired when we moved in here. There was already a table and a bed. I had to buy a few domestic things like a pan, some plates, knives and forks, and a wooden breadboard. (I still have that wooden board! It is round and has a drip channel that I was always very proud of. "You can also use it for meat!" In the course of the years a deep round hole emerged in the middle, you could put your finger through it. But I still love that wooden board).

We have to adhere to strict rules: no visitors after nine o'clock, no noise on the stairs (our room is on the first floor), no electrical appliances and especially, no babies, not now or in the future. Our room looks out over a square called the *Beestenmarkt*, where every Monday morning a cattle market is held. Our Monday mornings begin with loud mooing, which starts at an impossible hour, and are full of manure and mud (it always rains on Mondays) and weather-beaten farmers in blue smocks who wade through the slush in black cogs, patting cows and horses, and bellowing hoarse, incomprehensible instructions.

Now (is it the weekend?) our square is empty. It is already almost dark. Behind our high window wet snow swirls down. I think it is March. I have a heavy cold. I blow my nose every few minutes using a grey, threadbare hand towel. I went through all the hankies in the house long ago. My nose is red and sore, my eyes are streaming, my head is throbbing. On our little round stove our saucepan filled with water is gently steaming. Charles intends to pour menthol oil into it soon; he has promised it will help. Charles is bursting with good health, as always, and with optimism. "You'll feel a whole lot better once you've inhaled this steam, you'll see!"

He puts a comforting arm around me. "Rotten climate, rotten country. It really is high time we pack our bags. We need to get out of here!"

"Yes, but how?" I have practically lost my voice so croak like a frog.

"I've got an idea. I met someone this afternoon who wants to go to Australia. The man who has an office supplies shop on the corner of the Nieuwstraat. His name is Bijl. We had a long conversation about it. His idea is to get a group of people together who are willing and able to turn their hand to anything and to start a kind of building cooperative over there, to build their own houses. Not a bad idea, I think. He already has quite a lot of people interested. He asked me to come and tell them about living in a foreign country, when they next get together."

I am astounded; the towel falls to the ground. "Australia?!" I envisage a black native holding a spear, standing on a hill on the edge of a desert with a blood red sun setting in the background. And children on unsaddled horses galloping by. Where these images come from God knows, but they represent the total sum of my knowledge about Australia. "At least it will be warm there," I add, with resignation.

Charles and I, our life together: was there loneliness already? I try to adapt to a completely different lifestyle. I accompany him to cycling races that I don't understand a thing about, even though he tries patiently to explain the tactics and technique to me. I go with him to visit his cycling friends where we always accidentally end up at dinnertime and are asked to stay for dinner. It takes a long time for me to realise that Charles does this on purpose and then I do not have the energy to protest. I just let it go. I have been tired for months, have been suffering from severe headaches for months. I even see a doctor about this, but he can't help me: "Nervous headaches."

The embryonic advertising paper turns out to be stillborn. Charles manages to get the printer to commit to a verbal agreement. For every customer he acquires he receives a small fee. I am no longer enjoying my work. Can no longer cope with it. It demands too much time, too much attention. I realise that a normal job, with regular hours, would be much better for me, preferably something requiring me to use my hands, not my head. I quit and end up in a bookbinding company, a kind of factory, where I need to be at 8 o'clock every day and which is vaguely reminiscent of a nightmare. Pounding machines into which you place the spine of a book.

The cold and dark of that winter: on the bike in the pitch-black mornings and evenings. Books are as always my greatest comfort. And Charles, who always sees solutions, who expects the future to be glorious, and manages, no matter what happens, to bring home some money. He is now also organising sporting events. He still tells wonderful stories, laughs and makes me laugh. I adore his recklessness, his unbreakable spirit, his sense of freedom.

Charles also teaches me how to play bridge. He is an excellent bridge player. And then there is the evening at Jan Bijl's house. A group of hopeful potential immigrants who want to hear from an experienced world traveller what it is like to turn your back on your fatherland and what the customs and usages are in "foreign parts." I have no idea where Charles gets his information from, but he actually has things to tell about Australia, which he does with great conviction. We learn that the passage there is free. All you need is 50 guilders per person, so-called landing money. Of course you will have to undergo a medical check. You need to be healthy and preferably have a good trade. You will have to go to a few assessment interviews, all in The Hague. On that evening, Charles becomes a member of the group. He declares that in Australia he will be fully prepared to take up his old, long neglected profession of house painter. This fits perfectly with the building cooperative plan.

That evening we also meet Hieke and Jan Anink. I talk to Hieke for the very first time and have the feeling that I have come home after a long journey. No, a different feeling: as if we have known each other for years. As if we had been talking together for years. As if very little needs explaining, a kind of semi-conscious recognition. The same loneliness? But there was also an indomitable joy to be alive, an almost palpable radiating of warmth and optimism, a love of other people.

Hiek, Hieke, Hiekje. The group clearly adored her. She was very calm and did not say a great deal, but when she did speak, everyone listened. Should I try to describe her? Black hair, blue eyes and a snub nose. She was only small, she wasn't pretty but she was attractive in the literal sense of the word. She was about ten years older than I was. Had two small children, little boys of 5 and 3. She lived, we discovered, quite close to us, in a rented house behind the barracks. They rented out rooms to supplement their income. She already had a lodger, full board. She could easily handle that, she said, a nice, gentleman-like man. Had become a friend.

She and Jan had definitely decided to emigrate. Jan was a sales representative in office supplies, but did not enjoy the job. "He's a very good carpenter," Hiek said, "And he does enjoy that. He should have become a carpenter but his parents didn't approve of that. It wouldn't do as a profession at all. Well, I think that over there he can make it his profession, don't you? Moreover, there is the future of the children to think of. It seems wonderful to me to be able to make a completely new start, to get a second chance."

Of course, I completely agreed with her. I looked at Jan with some surprise: he was already starting to go a little bald and was a little deaf and looked permanently anxious. He struck me as kind, but somewhat nervous. Not exactly the type of man born to succeed. But he was meticulous and precise, well-organised. He told us that he had already submitted the first application and that they had already had their first assessment interview. "All this red tape takes about a year," he said. "There will also be a medical check-up and x-rays and a few more interviews. And then there needs to be space in a boat. It can all take a long time. You are placed on a waiting list and there aren't that many boats."

"Oh, aren't there?" said Charles, "I bet there's a way to short-cut the whole procedure." We cycled home with Jan and Hiek that evening and talked with them deep into the night. About what it would be like to emigrate…

Hiek became my support and my anchor. She was always around. She taught me to cook a little. She took me cycling in the woods, to look for cuttings. She knew a lot about flowers and plants. She had a tiny garden where she dug and weeded. I could talk to her about books. She listened. She often asked us to dinner and I could accept that from her.

When we discovered that she and Jan used to play bridge when they lived in Amsterdam, Charles decided to give us bridge lessons together, which resulted in hilarious and very late nights in Hiek's living room. And in the meantime we fantasised wildly about what was needed to become an emigrant. You have to be able to speak English, Charles told us, so he gave "the group" English lessons. He had learned English on his travels, not the way I had at high school ("High schools are a complete waste of time!" said Charles). He had taught himself German and French in the same way, as well as a few words of Spanish and Portugese. All this impressed me hugely.

Charles went to The Hague on his own and returned with a pile of papers, which had to be filled out. "They ask you a million questions," he said, "But we really can go there without it costing us a penny. This is the opportunity of our lives!"

"And somehow we'll get the 100 guilders landing-money together that we need for the two of us," I added sensibly.

I had to take a day off so that we could go to The Hague together to be assessed and later again for a series of interviews. We received a letter. We had been accepted and were now on the waiting list. At which Charles took another trip to The Hague to find out how long the waiting list was. He was vague about this when he got back. "But I now know a few people at the Australian Embassy…"

"You'll have to wait at least another year," Jan predicted. And then Jan and Hiek received a letter, which told them that they could leave in the middle of January 1951, on the *Sibajak*. Charles immediately rushed off to The Hague the next day and arrived home late that evening. "Surprise! We're now on the stand-by list for the *Sibajak*!"

"Stand-by list?" I had never heard of such a thing.

"That means that they will take us if there are people who can't go at the last minute. And that always happens! You wanted to go on the same boat as Jan and Hiek, didn't you? I've just arranged that for you. You should quit your job just before Christmas and I'll arrange things here so that we can leave in January." My all or nothing gambler: it made me slightly drunk.

Jan said we were mad. "And what if it all doesn't come off? You don't have anything in writing. You'll never find another place to live if you can't leave."

"Of course we'll be able to leave," said Charles, "Do you really think they'll send us away once we turn up on the docks with our suitcases? There are only two of us. They'll always be able to find space for us. You never get anywhere if you don't take a few risks, old man!"

"I bet it will work," Hiek giggled.

I can see us packing. All our belongings in a small chest, which Charles had found somewhere: our two plates, two cups, two glasses, our pan, our breadboard, sheets, blankets, books. I refused to leave behind a single book. Another suitcase each and that was that.

Jan and Hiek left for Amsterdam to be with family in their last week. Two days before the ship sailed Charles rang The Hague, but no one could give him any definite information about cancellations. He remained buoyant. On the last night we slept on mattresses on the floor in Jan and Greet Bijl's house. On the day of our departure we took the very first train to Rotterdam.

The train: I can still see us in the pitch dark trudging through dirty slush and snow. I can see our fellow travellers, all pale men, wasted away, in shapeless, dark coats. Our chest stands forlorn in the aisle.

I am standing in the customs warehouse near the harbour, a vast, dimly lit, wooden temporary construction full of people who smell of wet coats. Charles deposits me together with the chest and suitcases outside a brightly lit, glass office. "The boat doesn't leave till five this afternoon," he says, encouragingly, "If only I can find someone I know, then everything will be fine. You'll be okay here, right?"

"Fine," I say in a strangely high-pitched voice. Sitting on the chest, I watch him walk away. He saunters into the office as if he belongs there. I am alone in the world. I stare at the suitcases at my feet. People continuously come and go; people with children; people without children; people talking in nervously loud voices and people whispering in deep disappointment. Laughing people and people silently crying. It is icy cold in the warehouse. I am chilled to the bone. My teeth are chattering. An odd little melody is playing in my head, tonelessly, monotonously: *We have burned our bridges – we have burned our bridges.*

How long did I sit there? An age. I am sitting underneath an invisible glass dome, slowly diminishing. Soon there will be nothing left of me. And yet I do not feel the least surprise or even relief when Charles suddenly materialises, broadly grinning. "Come along, pussycat!" I find it difficult to stand up. I hobble stiffly behind him into the office, teeth still chattering. Behind a desk full of papers sits a round, rosy-faced, grey-haired man. "This is my wife," Charles says, triumphantly.

"Your husband is a persistent man," the man says affably, "I like that. They can use such dynamic men over there. Here are your tickets. How much luggage?"

"Two suitcases and a chest," I reply anxiously (will it be too much?), "but it isn't a very big chest."

"Can easily be carried by one man," Charles adds, and he should know as he has carried it all the long way from home.

"Oh, I think we can handle that," the man says, laughing, "Leave it on the dock, you'll see where. And the very best of luck." He shakes both our hands.

Two hours later, standing next to each other at the railing of the ship, we see Jan and Hiek come up the gangway, each holding a little boy by the hand, Jan with Frank, and Hiek with the youngest, Paulie. And then suddenly I know for sure that this is real. That we are really are going and that I am alive.

I see lead-coloured water under a leaden sky. I hear gulls screeching. I feel my hair blowing in the icy wind. The glass dome has gone. Over there, where we are going, the sun is shining: I know that for sure. I start jumping up and down like a madwoman. My voice rings out: "Hiek! Hiekje, we're here! We are here!"

Jan. 1950 Begin van het grote avontuur. Met de "SIBAJAK" naar Australië. Lijsseth en Charles Ruys

Aankomst Port Said

Hiek Conink

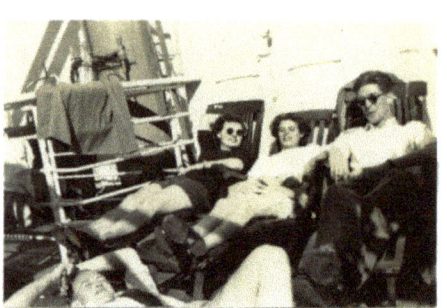

Met Mies en Jaap Kofman

Achter Jaap Kofman, Charles Ruys

CHAPTER 2

Passage to Australia

THE *SIBAJAK* HAD been used as a troop transport ship in the war. Thinking back to that crossing of so long ago I see dark, brown hammocks hanging in steel frames, three on top of each other. Rows and rows of brown hammocks in a brown cargo hold, deep in the bowels of our ship. There are sleeping quarters for women and children, and one for men and older boys. There must have been more. Did the *Sibajak* not transport about 1200 emigrants on that crossing? It doesn't matter; all I see now are the women's quarters, giving access to a long row of showers and toilets.

I am lying somewhere in the middle of the hold, in a middle hammock into which I climb by means of a small step. Underneath me sleeps Hiek's little boy, Frank, and above me hangs an anonymous female hump, alarmingly close. If I stretch out my arm and Hiek does the same we can shake hands across the aisle. She sleeps opposite me, with Paul underneath her. Oddly enough, we slept quite well.

Our mess is also down here. I see countless rows of long wooden tables with equally long rows of wooden benches underneath them. We are served by dark brown *djangos* who shuffle by us noiselessly. Down here our boat resembles a gigantic tent, constantly teaming with masses of people, where, nevertheless, everything somehow runs perfectly. Everyone quickly learns where he or she needs to go and I can't remember that anyone grumbled. We laugh at everything. What does it matter how we get there? We are on our way! And for six weeks we are very well looked after.

Above decks everything is light. There is a recreation hall full of small bamboo tables, which are always crowded with parents and children, and there is an "adults only" lounge: leather armchairs and large portholes behind which the sea heaves. And then there are small, packed decks with here and there a few deck chairs, and finally the sports deck where during the day we can almost always be found – that is, Charles and I, and Jaap and Miep.

Jaap and Miep Kofman are fellow passengers, the only ones I remember clearly. Miep was born in Indonesia and there was something undeniably Indonesian about her enormous, black eyes and patient mouth. She was tall, thin and shy. Jaap was even thinner and so tall that he always had to stoop slightly to get through a door. He had a long, narrow, hollow-cheeked head. Two deep furrows ran from his nostrils to the corners of his mouth. From behind his glasses light eyes observed the world somewhat sadly. But what tumbled out of his mouth was far from sorrowful. Jaap drily supplied a witty commentary on the ship, the passengers, the world and life in general, to the great joy of Charles who immediately recognised a kindred spirit. Jaap had lived in Indonesia for a few years where he had met Miep. They had been married a week by the time they boarded the *Sibajak*.

The six of us, Hiek and Jan, Jaap and Miep, and Charles and I very quickly formed a bridge club. We played bridge day in day out. In the afternoons, Jaap and Miep, and Charles and I played (Hiek and Jan were then busy with their children). In the evenings we often swopped partners so that Jan and Hiek could take part. Not every evening though. Jan regularly decided that he and Hiek should attend the information sessions or the so-called "cosy gatherings" in the large recreation hall: group entertainment, which the rest of us carefully avoided, something that caused Jan to frown in worry. "You really have no idea what's waiting for you over there! Shouldn't you prepare yourselves a little? You're just messing about as if you're on holiday!"

"We are!" said Charles, "Jan, old chap, we'll cross that bridge when we come to it. Everything will be fine."

"But don't you think you should be making plans?"

"We're definitely not going to a transition camp," said Jaap, "Miep has just spent a few years in a camp."

"You won't have any choice," Jan said, grimly, "unless you can find somewhere to stay straightaway and that's extremely difficult, so I hear. You really should come and listen to people who know about these things."

"We're going to start our own business," said Jaap dreamily, "an Indonesian restaurant. We can make a fortune that way."

"Oh?" Jan said, "Do you have such a lot of capital, then? Start a business? Ha!"

"We'll have to acclimatise," Jaap said, looking down his long nose at Jan, "We'll wait and see how the land lies. But don't worry about us, old chap. We veterans roll with the punches, don't we, Charles?"

"Anyone for bridge?" Charles asked, grinning broadly.

Yesterday I pulled out my oldest, most well-thumbed and worn photo album, and carefully removed a handful of neglected-looking photographs, which I had at some point stuck in messily and in random order: Sibajak *photos. Most are tiny and square, and you need a magnifying glass to read the names on the lifeboats or to see faces well. Two of them are rectangular and are not so bad. At least you can see what they capture: Charles, Jaap and I in a dingy (on the way to Port Said) and Jaap, Miep and I on deck chairs in summer clothes. Who owned the camera? Jaap? A very inexperienced photographer, in any case.*

I looked intently at the faces: young, happy, beaming with limitless self-confidence. For the first time in my life I have curly hair. I had had my hair permed just before we left, at someone's recommendation. "It makes life so easy, love! You won't need to do a thing to your hair." That feeling of "how did all this happen?" The photos don't help. I need to go back to the painting exhibition in my head.

The Suez Canal: we sail slowly between ochre shores, which seem oddly close. We glide through water that is of exactly the same colour. The four of us are standing at the railing for the first time in summer clothes. Oh, that wonderful sun on your skin!

"It actually looks like the Wilhelmina Canal," Jaap says, "You just need to ignore those camels. I wouldn't mind wearing one of those Arab dresses." We reach Port Said and the four of us wander around there. No pictures, just heat and a feeling of unease.

Fremantle. We have arrived in Australia, but that doesn't mean a great deal. The first immigrants leave the ship here, on their way to Perth. We must have wandered around Fremantle for a whole day. I see masses of multi-coloured flowers, a sun-drenched park and Hiek who keeps trying to stop Paulie from jumping into a gigantic fountain. "Look! They're still right in the middle of the 'New Look' here," she says, pointing to two girls in ankle-length skirts. We must have landed at Melbourne, but I recall nothing. Impenetrable mist.

At six o'clock in the morning of the first Sunday in March we arrive in Sydney. We have all got up early. I feel hollow inside. I am standing next to Charles at the railing and I don't believe this is Sydney. We are sailing slowly past a hilly, quite low coast covered in darkly wooded hills, and here and there something that looks like a building. And then I see a huge mass of rock rising up out of the sea. "That must be one of The Heads," Charles says, "Look, behind us there's another one. Can you see it? This must be the entrance to the harbour."

Entrance to the harbour? I turn around and stare at another mass of rock far away, misty in the early morning light. I don't see a harbour, just sea and more sea. "In a minute," says Charles, "Let's go and have some breakfast first."

And then, half an hour later, I am face to face with Sydney, the harbour, the heart of the city. The world has become blue and silver. Everything around us sparkles and glistens in the blindingly white sunlight. The harbour is an inland sea of unimaginable proportions. There are countless bays, coves, inlets, and the coast along which we sailed (still hilly) is littered with houses with red and blue roofs, and later with glass and steel buildings, which I, at the time, and with great reverence, called skyscrapers. There is a huge, silver, one-spanned bridge, which we sail under with ease. "Do you see how big the city is?" asks Charles, "About as big as the whole province of Utrecht." I am breathless. I do not have an answer. That morning I fell in love with Sydney Harbour, deeply in love. I still am.

"We need to go below," Jaap says behind us, "They're already checking landing cards and passports. You need to be in the recreation hall." The recreation hall has been transformed into an immense office. Official looking men whom we have never seen before sit behind long rows of tables. Everywhere there are already suitcases and packages, and crowds of people.

"Clearly more than high time to pack," Jaap says drily, "See you later, okay? They won't throw us off the boat within ten minutes of docking, right?"

"This will take hours," says Charles, "No need at all to hurry." And to me: "Will you sort out our packing? I want to look around here. Need to find out a few things." Below decks in the sleeping quarters I find Hiek with her arms full of clean washing and two excited sons who are running up and down between the hammocks, shouting. "Oh, hallo," she says bending over an open suitcase, "Jan's upstairs."

"Charles too," I say in a shaky voice. We look at each other.

"Let's get this done first," Hiek says, calmly, "And then we'll dive into the men's quarters, pick up their suitcases, so that we have everything together." And at that moment the motors stop and the ship becomes quiet beneath our feet. "We've arrived," Hiek whispers. "Yes," I say, which sounds idiotic.

Later we climb up the stairs together with difficulty, wrestling our way through our nervous fellow immigrants, each holding the hand of a wriggling little boy. We discover our men in a corner of the control hall. Charles is deep in conversation with a tanned stranger wearing a white pair of shorts and a pink sports shirt. Jan takes Paulie from me and murmurs something to Hiek, which I can't hear.

"We are *not* going to the camp," Charles says decisively, "This is Piet Verkerk. He has been living here for a year and a half already, and he has a job for us, here in Sydney."

"Married couple with a doctor's family," Piet clarifies in a friendly way. He does not look particularly bright, I think. "My wife and I did it for a year and we liked it. You'll have your own flat, you eat with the family and you even get two pounds salary."

"Married couple," I repeat, staring at him, stupefied.

"You do the housekeeping," says Piet, "And the cooking and so on. And your husband looks after the garden, but that isn't a lot of work. He can look for a job in the meantime. I did that too."

"But I can't cook," I stammer, latching onto that one terrifying word.

"Of course you can cook!" Charles intervenes impatiently.

"Oh, you'll quickly learn whatever you don't know," says Piet, "Every woman can cook. You speak English and that's more than we did when we arrived here."

"We'll do it, right?" says Charles, his eyes gleaming, "It's a huge piece of luck! We can go there right now. Think of it, pussycat, to have a flat immediately, the day we arrive and in the most beautiful part of Sydney, Piet says!"

My heart is somewhere in my throat. I feel nauseous. I am staring into a bottomless pit.

"Of course you'll be able to do it," says Hiek at my elbow. I turn to her. "And what about all of you? Where will you be going?"

"To the camp, of course. We won't be travelling on till this afternoon," says Jan. He doesn't yet know where it is exactly, somewhere outside the town in any case.

"You'll see, you'll be fine. If we didn't have kids..."

"I'd much rather go with you."

"I'll write to you," says Hiek, "Ask the man for the address, write it down. We won't lose touch, don't worry. I'll write as soon as I can."

Charles pulls my sleeve, "Piet has just told me that friends of the people we are going to are looking for a married couple too, and would like to have a Dutch couple. They live in the same neighbourhood. Wouldn't that be perfect for Jaap and Miep? Where is Jaap?" Both of them are standing behind us. Jaap is silent for once. Charles is talking quickly and intensely, "We don't have to stay there if we don't like it. It will be a roof over our heads, a breather, a way of avoiding the camp! That isn't our thing at all, a camp."

And then it is all arranged. I am told that we are going to Wahroonga, and Jaap and Miep to Warrawee. "About five minutes further. Both on the North Shore Line," Piet says.

"A railway line!"

"Yep, everything goes by train here. Wahroonga and Warrawee are North Shore suburbs. As soon as you're ready we can go. I need to make a phonecall, will be back in half an hour."

I needed every second of that last half hour to recover from my fright. To have explained to me what suburbs are; that – logically enough – the North Shore is the part of Sydney which lies to the north of the harbour and that I can always explain away my lack of cooking skills by blithely claiming that, "We do that very differently in Holland!"

Hiek and I hold each other tightly. "We'll keep in touch," she says softly, "I bet we'll meet each other again very soon! Lots of luck, love, it's bound to be a fun job and you'll be able to do it easily, you really will!"

Charles gives me a suitcase, "Let's go." The first image that comes to mind when I think about our first steps on Australian soil is Sydney's Town Hall, which stands in the centre of town and in the middle of George Street. How we got there from the harbour I don't know – by train, perhaps? I see a huge sandstone building that in 1960 a historian would call a "Victorian grotesqueness." It boasts a square tower over 55 metres high, crowned by an Italian-looking cupola. Underneath, there is a huge clock-face, in blue and copper. I only register that clock-face, despite the multitude of columns, arches, vaulted ceilings and domes. We are standing in the middle of a large intersection in the sun under a blue sky. There is not a great deal of traffic.

"It's Sunday," Piet says, "It's usually very busy here. Come on, we're going into the Underground." He shepherds us down a broad stone staircase, into the underworld. We find ourselves in a huge hall and then in a wooden train with gleaming wooden benches. First an ink black tunnel, then we rise up through grey walls. It grows lighter and lighter. Suddenly we are driving along the Harbour Bridge. The sky and the immense blue expanse of water deep below us are both equally blue. My eyes can't get used to the bright, shimmering glitter. The four of us, we newcomers, can only stare. "It's big, huh?" says Jaap.

And then on the other side the overwhelming feeling of grandeur disappears. We are driving through low hills, which are packed with flowers and behind which we glimpse thickly wooded streets where people in summer clothes are strolling. Every fifteen minutes we stop at doll-house-like stations, which are all connected to the street by means of a wooden bridge. Later I will know the names of these stations by heart, but now they sound wild and exotic when Piet reads them out to us: "Chatswood, Pymble, Killara, Waitara, Turramurra, Wahroonga and Warawee." I know so little, absolutely nothing. "Abo language," Piet says, "Aboriginal."

"What?"

"Native Australians," says Jaap, "The Australian natives are called Aborigines. Aboriginal is the adjective."

"Good old Jaap," Charles says happily, "How much further, Piet?" Piet, Charles and I get off the train first. "Next stop," Piet says to Jaap, "You'll be met. Oh, and Mr and Mrs Wilson don't have any children. That job of yours there will be a cinch."

"Look after yourselves," Charles says, slapping Jaap on the back.

"Will do," Jaap says laconically. Miep just nods, smiling, as calm as a smooth lake. Piet starts to walk briskly.

Another week has passed since the last time I sat here. The "here and now" has asserted itself with a vengeance. Back pain, which makes sitting a torture; tiredness; depression. I am so very old now and if I continue at this pace I will need years to finish this book. And yet...

She is still here, that girl of so long ago. If I make a conscious effort, shut my eyes, I remember what it felt like to walk down Fox Valley Road in Wahroonga for the first time in my life, going to the house of the Stathams, which stood right at the end of the road on the edge of virgin bush.

I can feel the sun, which is so very different from the Dutch sun. I can feel the heaviness of my suitcase and the droplets of sweat on my face and arms. I can feel the afternoon stillness around me, the dreamlike quality of a long, empty, hilly road of broken asphalt without footpaths, which I found so strange then. On either side of the road there is only a narrow strip of reddish earth with here and there patches of weeds. Tall, grey-green trees stand motionless in the white afternoon light. We walk past the gardens of enormous houses encircled by hedges, yellowish, tough-looking grass and yet more whimsically shaped, grey trees. You can smell the spicy heat. The road meanders.

"Are you hot?" Piet laughs, "This is a cool day! The summer is drawing to a close. You should have been here in February. 105 in the shade! That's Farenheit."

Charles is unusually quiet. His blonde head is dark with perspiration.

The final house at the end of a short drive is white, a broad, white house with a long veranda in front behind an imposing row of pillars. "That's the front door," says Piet, pointing to the double glass doors behind the pillars, "but we'll go around the back, come with me."

Next to the house is a double garage. We follow the tiled path, which goes around it. And discover that the house does not have only one floor, but three, at least at the back. It is built against a hill. Our path leads down past an ample terrace, past the open glass doors of a cool, dark space on the second floor ("That's the ballroom," Piet says) and comes finally to a small stone stairway, which leads to the entrance to the souterrain and the back garden. The back garden dips sharply, clearly the valley of the foxes after which the street has been named. Piet points downwards, "That's where they grow a few vegetables; it's where you usually work on Saturdays," to Charles. "Hum," Charles says, wiping his forehead.

"We go inside here, through the laundry." We go through a green door and find ourselves in a large, grey, concrete space with a concrete floor. In a corner is an enormous boiler, as high as the ceiling. Next to it stands a shiny, white, washing machine and next to that two large square basins of cement with double faucets above them.

"Your flat," says Piet, opening a second green door directly opposite the boiler. We shuffle into a large bedroom. There is a double bed, a table with two chairs, a deep couch, a huge wardrobe and a low cupboard. It is quite dark and everything seems to be brown. Daylight comes through two small, screened windows next to each other above the bed. They look out over the back garden.

"Nice and cool in here, huh?" Piet says, "And here is your bathroom." He pulls at a sliding door and shows us a long, narrow shower space, tiled in brown, with a toilet on the one side and a shower curtain on the other. Charles suddenly comes to life. "It's a bloody palace!" I put down my suitcase.

We meet Piet's wife briefly when she comes to report that Mrs Statham is waiting upstairs for us. I only remember that she did nothing but giggle nervously and was quite plump. Piet escorts us upstairs. We go up a wooden staircase, through a screen-door and into the kitchen. The kitchen is large, ultra-modern, radiantly white and blindingly clean. Mrs Statham is small and slim. Her dark blonde hair is impeccably styled. She has a large mouth, lipsticked bright red, and cool blue eyes. She wears a brown silk dress and looks a little like a picture on an expensive biscuit tin. She looks at us thoughtfully. "You do speak the language, don't you?" she asks.

"We most certainly do," Charles says, cheerfully, "My name is Charles and this is my wife Agatha. How do you do? Nice to meet you," shaking her hand, completely at his ease. I follow his example, not at all at my ease, despite the fact that she, clearly relieved, is smiling at me in a friendly way.

"It's okay, Piet. You want to leave, don't you? Best of all possible luck and look after yourself," at which Piet disappeared. Literally disappeared. We never saw either Piet or his wife again. I hear Charles talking to Mrs. S. while I take in the terrifying kitchen. Cook? Me? Here? Oh God! I vaguely hear "Room and board, pocket money and Sundays off. And if we need to go out we expect you to look after the children." "Yes, of course," says Charles.

And then suddenly directly to me: "I think I will call you Anne. It's less old-fashioned. And I would like you to wear a uniform. Looks so much neater, don't you think? I think you are the same size as me. I'll have this taken care of first thing tomorrow." I am so astounded that I can only nod speechlessly.

We are given a tour of the house. The kitchen is on the second floor. The dining room is next to the kitchen. It is decorated in quintessentially English style with a large, shiny, mahogany dining table in the middle and eight matching petit point chairs neatly tucked underneath. With an immense mahogany sideboard and a mahogany, glass-doored cupboard in which porcelain and glassware glitter; with heavy, velvet, dark brown, floor-to-ceiling length curtains framing the high windows and in between the windows a dark painting, featuring a hugely moustached ancestor. The floor is covered in shiny, dark brown parquet.

A few stairs take us from the dining room to what is called the lounge, the living room, a space that looks almost empty at first glance. A vast way away from where we have come in stands the glass front door and equally far away on the opposite side are high, gothic, arched windows. In the middle, a very large, thick, antique pink carpet with nothing at all on it. Under the windows stands a long, black couch with antique pink cushions and there are matching armchairs on either side, also with pink cushions. There is a large fireplace and a long, low bookcase, which takes up almost a whole wall. An abstract painting in bright colours hangs there. The walls are not wallpapered and are white.

Dr. Statham is sitting on the couch. He stands up when we come in. He seems almost twice as tall as his wife, is thin and dark-eyed, with romantic grey sideburns. He is clearly looking amused. I remember that I immediately stared, fascinated and longingly, at all those books and that he suddenly said to me, "Feel free to borrow whatever you like," for which I will be eternally grateful to him.

On the other side of the lounge, reachable by a small staircase, are the bedrooms. There are three: the master bedroom at the front of the house and the children's rooms overlooking the back garden. The walls are covered in thick, leathery wallpaper in white and gold. Then we meet the children, Virginia who is 10 and is called Ginny (small and dainty, shy, long blonde hair) and two little boys, both just as dark as their father. Robert is still chubby and cuddly, and Nigel is skinny and quick. The three of them never make a great deal of noise. They all three go to school for full days.

Next to the boys' room, a stately stairway, covered in thick pink carpet, leads downstairs to what Piet had called "the ballroom." And it is literally a ballroom: an empty room with a parquet floor, which covers the whole width of the house. It is split in two by a wrought-iron, double balustrade with three broad stairs in between. The section behind the balustrade is raised. A piano stands there and in the middle a table-tennis table. Along all the walls hang gilded candleholders, with real, gold-coloured candles in them. "The children play here when it rains," says Mrs. S. "And that door over there leads to the laundry. Makes babysitting easy for you two. You can stay in your own room as long as you come and listen every now and then. All the floors need polishing once a week, Anne, but the Hoover makes that simple."

"The Hoover?" I stare vacantly at the endless floor, envisaging ladies in crinolines and gentlemen in knee breeches and long, brocade coats.

"The polisher?" says Mrs. S., looking at me, enquiringly.

"Oh, oh yes, of course," I stammer.

"I think we are going to get on together splendidly," says Mrs. S. "You can go downstairs through the house now. I'll see you tomorrow morning at half past seven in the kitchen, Anne."

"Thank you," I say, and scurry out through the door she is indicating. It leads to a storage room at the top of a high, dark staircase, which in its turn leads to the laundry. Behind me Charles is crowing. Our room is virginal, as if no-one has ever lived there. Our suitcases stand next to each other in front of the bed. "Hugely nice people," says Charles, "don't you think? I told you, what a piece of luck! We couldn't have found a better solution. We're sitting on roses!"

"Do you really think so?" lifting my suitcase onto the bed.

"Yes, of course!" he throws his arms around me and we waltz around the room. "Pussycat! We're going to make it big here!"

"Don't mess about," I wriggle free, "We need to unpack. And I'm terrified of this cooking business. What am I supposed to do?"

"What about me, in the garden? I haven't the foggiest idea about gardens! Just act as if everything is completely normal and keep your eyes and ears open, and everything will turn out fine. You don't need to clean windows or do any heavy house work, they have a cleaning service for that. I'm going to take a shower in our very own bathroom. And we finally have our own bed again. Our own bed! Aren't you happy?"

"Yes," I say doubtfully, "It was all a bit strange, don't you think? They don't know anything about us."

"They know enough! They know perfectly well we were screened before we ended up on the boat and that we're perfectly healthy. That's why they wanted immigrants, fresh off the boat, you can't go wrong that way. And I told them a little bit about us, didn't I? Are you hungry? You got the message that the staff need to remain invisible on Sundays, right? Not a chance of joining them for dinner. Close to the station there's a milk-bar and next to that a Chinese restaurant. Shall we take a look there later?"

"Okay," I say, feeling about two hundred years old.

We are standing hand in hand at the edge of the bush at the end of Fox Valley Road. It is almost seven o'clock and it is already completely dark. Twilight does not last long here. We are standing in the light of a lonely streetlight. The night is warm. The breeze is made of black velvet. There is an unbelievable silence here, behind the sounds of the bush, the shrill high noise of innumerable cicadas. We are alone in the world. The stars are enormous and very close. When was the last time I looked at the stars? I find the Southern Cross. "Can you smell the eucalyptus?" Charles asks, "Those are all eucalyptus trees. Gum trees, they call them here."

What is it that is so different here? There is an almost palpable presence here that lives and breathes, something primeval and eternally patient; something that waits and waits, for what? All of a sudden I am no longer afraid.

CHAPTER 3

New Australians

THE ALARM CLOCK went at half past six on my very first Australian Monday morning. The sun! Outside our small windows the sun was shining! And there was silence, a deep silence; the fragrance of trees and moss: a summer smell. And then, just outside our window, a bird began to sing. It sang a complete melody, a whole raft of notes! "Charles! Do you hear that? Charles!"

He turned over, gently snoring. I carefully slid out of our new bed. The morning was a light, gloriously translucent blue. A vague mist still hung among the trees on the other side of our valley. The bird was nestled in the branches amongst the thickly packed bushes under our window, a small, multi-coloured bird. I saw electric blue, yellow, green and a bit of red. I never discovered what kind of bird it was, but I will never forget how happy it made me feel. How light and brave, how glad. A flat of our own, a shower of our own, life was a party!

I felt a little less celebratory when I climbed the stairs to the kitchen. The screen door stuck to my clammy fingers. Mrs. S. was waiting to welcome me, all cool, fresh, amiable professionalism. From the minute I entered I started to learn. Firstly, I learned how to make sandwiches for the children's school lunches. These had to be paper-thin slices of bread, with cold meat and peanut butter in between, placed on a bed of fresh salad, which did not look at all like our Dutch salad. I then learned how to operate the coffee percolator and was told all about Australian eating habits.

I learned that tablecloths were seldom used; placemats were usually used instead. In the morning the white, starched placemats and in the evenings those made of thick brown lace. I learned that the children ate cereal in the mornings, that they wore school uniforms and that they had to leave the house at exactly eight o'clock. After this Mum and Dad enjoyed a leisurely breakfast reading *The Sydney Morning Herald*, which was thrown into the garden, rolled up, every morning around six from a fast driving car, ending up somewhere in the damp bushes. It was my job to retrieve it. I was glad to hear that Mum and Dad only drank coffee and ate toast every morning, not a full English breakfast.

I learned that lunch was always a light, warm meal and "dinner" a more extensive affair with at least three kinds of vegetables, one yellow, one green and potatoes, which were scarce and of which no more than one was eaten per person. I learned what lamb chops were and that pork was a delicatessen. I also learned that dessert had to be a homemade work of art, and that Mrs. S. had the patience of a saint, and a great faith in my culinary abilities. (Misplaced, alas, but a lightning course in Australian cooking worked wonders).

On the first day, I discovered that Mr. Statham was a dermatologist with a practice in Macquarie Street in the heart of Sydney, the equivalent of Harley Street in London. I also learned that Charles and I were "New Australians," and that we should call ourselves that. I was instructed about how to use the vacuum cleaner, a contraption I had never seen before. It was called a Hoover and could be transformed into a polishing machine. And then there was the washing machine and the dryer, which I had originally not noticed in the laundry. We were allowed to use them ourselves too, Mrs. S. told us amiably.

During the first few days, I was coached intensively. But Mrs S. very quickly left me to my own devices, and in this way I discovered that I could do much more than I had ever imagined in my wildest dreams. I grilled, baked and roasted – although I had never grilled before and had never used an oven – and learned how to deal with the gigantic spinach and football-hard pumpkin that came from the garden. I learned how to compile menus, as it was expected that I would order all the food by phone, which was subsequently home delivered. I can't remember that shopping was ever done in the normal way. Prices were never discussed. We just ordered what we thought would be needed and if I am not mistaken Dr. S. received a bill once a month. (I quickly learned that Mr Statham had a PhD, and belonged to the top tranche of specialists).

The floors I had worried about turned out not to create any problem whatsoever. They required putting liquid wax in the Hoover and pressing a button. I then walked through the ballroom, lounge and dining room, humming a tune and throwing the occasional satisfied glance at the immaculately gleaming floor, which appeared behind me. Even the washing machine worked as it was supposed to.

My "uniform" turned out to be a pink apron coat with short sleeves under which I did not need to wear a dress. I was given three, new and well fitting. They lasted for years.

After the first week, Mrs. S., resumed her usually busy social life. Almost every day at 10 am, she jumped into her grey car and disappeared, to return after the children had come back from school. When I also started to read *The Sydney Morning Herald* I saw her name regularly in the so-called social column. Sometimes, but not often, she received guests at home for lunch for which she herself had devised the menu. Usually this was my quintessentially Dutch vegetable soup, which I had once cooked for her because I could not think of anything else to cook that day. To my great surprise, the soup was regarded as exceptionally tasty and exotic, the ideal winter dish. Not that I minded that, on the contrary. It was about the only meal that I could make without inner trepidation.

I was home for the children in the afternoons. It is difficult to recall the three of them. I can't remember any upsets or difficulties. They were polite and sweet. There was a great aloofness, I think, no emotional involvement whatsoever. I can see myself making dolls for them from pieces of cloth and embroidery cotton. The arms and legs were made of matchsticks rolled in cloth. They loved them. My mother did that when I was small. I think I vaguely thought that this kind of thing was appropriate for children.

The ballroom was only used once officially in the eight months that we lived with the Stathams. Charles and I were both on duty. Charles was dressed for the occasion in a pink waiter's coat. He manned the bar while I struggled in the kitchen with an unending stream of washing up. Was there no dishwasher? This is a black hole in my memory.

Charles. He devoted the first days to exploratory expeditions into town. During dinner in the evenings (we had dinner together in the kitchen) he reported on his findings. My responses were lukewarm. I was concerned with other things. What I very much wanted to know was how Jaap and Miep were and what had happened to Hiek. The latter remained a mystery for the moment, but Jaap and Miep were contactable. On our first free Sunday we took the train to Warrawee and paid the Wilson house a visit.

Jaap and Miep were also living in the basement, like us, in a similar kind of flat. The house above them was just as grand as ours. Miek was as calm as ever; Jaap already had a job. In a factory, but that was only temporary. He worked in Hornsby, a suburb at the end of the North Shore line, quite close by, in fact. He had started on Tuesday and it wasn't too bad. "I'm also working on our real future," he said, "Come and have a look." He led us into the garden into an open space in the back.

The garden was a real jungle, much worse than the garden in the S's house. Gum trees and pine trees intermingled amongst masses of low, grey bush and scrub. There were no flowers. In the open clearing stood an old, grey caravan. "I bought this," said Jaap, "From the people here, for a song. I'm going to renovate it completely. There'll be a large awning on the side and I'll build a counter behind it."

"You're going to turn it into a stall!" said Charles cannily.

"Exactly! And when it's finished we'll set it up along a large road. We'll sell sausages or something to start off with. You can do that here. I talked all about it with Mr. Wilson. It'll be the beginning of our own restaurant, you'll see."

"Not a bad idea," said Charles. He strolled around the caravan, frowning and knocking at it here and there. "Let me have a look inside." It was completely empty. All four of us fit inside, though Jaap still needed to stoop. "Not a problem. Once the awning is installed I can stick my head out there. Don't you feel like helping, Charles? We could work on it on Sundays. I'm allowed to use all the tools in the garage, makes a huge difference. At least we don't have to buy them. You know what, we could do this whole project together. What do you think?"

"I'm in," said Charles. We devoted the rest of the afternoon to making plans: sausages and sandwiches and my soup and Miep's sateh. And every Sunday we would hammer and saw. Jaap waved a drawing he had made about, and Charles made a few expert changes to it. "I won't look for a job. I'll freelance, painting. I'll take a look with Statham at the neighbour's house and give them a quote. It seems finding good painters isn't easy here. The outside needs painting. That should take me about a month, I guess. And with luck, I'll make a nice bit of money." I couldn't believe my ears. "Oh, I discussed it with him yesterday when we were working in the garden." That had been on the first weeding Saturday, with Dr. S. and Charles working side by side.

"We could share the renovation costs," said Jaap, "The purchase costs I'll pay. Partners, Charles!" Hands were shaken, and off we went again. Would Dutch meatballs be a success here? "Nasi," said Miep, "Indonesian food will work in this climate."

Three days later a letter arrived from Hiek. The camp wasn't that bad, it was actually quite nice. They had a tiny room. Jan hadn't yet found a job, but the children were having a good time and she herself was helping in the camp shop, and getting paid. "We can stay here for a maximum of four weeks."

I wrote her back the same day and two weeks later a second letter arrived, postmarked *Woodford*. "We're living in the Blue Mountains now. It's beautiful here. We've been able to rent a small house, a bit primitive, but very cosy. Jan has a job at the sawmill, just outside Katoomba. That's a mountain town in the neighbourhood and the children are going to school for the first time tomorrow not far from here. When are you coming to visit us?"

"The Blue Mountains!" I crowed, "Charles! Hiek and Jan are living in the Blue Mountains. It isn't far away at all." I had just read Eleanor Dark's *The Timeless Land*. It was my first serious attempt to find out a bit more about the history of Australia. I now knew how the Aborigines had lived before the white man arrived. Who Bennelong was, what convicts were and how the penal colony had arisen. I knew who Captain Cook and Captain Arthur Phillip were. The year 1788 meant something to me. And I knew that the mysterious blue mountain range west of the first settlement was called the Blue Mountains. I had eagerly followed the first failed attempts to go beyond the wall of rock and I knew that success had finally been achieved in 1813. I knew the names of Blaxland, Lawson and Wentworth. I traced them on the map of New South Wales as small white dots among masses of black. I found Woodford. It would be many months before Hiek and I saw each other again, but we could now write to each other, and we did this regularly. We kept each other constantly informed about all our ups and downs.

Charles and I settled into a peaceful routine. While I ran the Statham household, in a fashion, Charles painted the houses in the neighbourhood. One neighbour after another asked for his services. He was good. First, just the outside; later also inside the houses. He railed against his work every now and then, kept on telling me that he wanted to stop doing it as soon as possible, but he kept on at it. And every Sunday we made our way to Warrawee to work on the caravan.

The awning did indeed appear and a tap materialised in the counter. I paid little attention to the discussions about where the water tank and drain should be installed. I usually tidied up and cleaned a bit while Miep helped with the painting work, and somehow fabricated little red and white curtains and hung them up.

By way of relaxation we occasionally went into town on a day that all four of us were free. We usually ended up in a cinema of which there were many in the centre of town. Jaap always knew exactly which films were worth seeing. Our regular station to alight was Wynyard. Wynyard was the largest and busiest underground station in Sydney, about half a kilometre from the Town Hall and also in George Street.

I can still see the dark blue tiled walls of all those platforms with the words *"Wynyard"* in bright yellow brick letters. I can smell the soot and old wood. I can hear the rattle of the high, wrought iron gates you had to pass through at the ticket counter. And then you found yourself in a massive circular underground hall full of flickering neon advertising and hurrying people, with exits from tunnels, which went every which way. And shops all around you. Wynyard was a miniature city where you could buy anything and everything, and which offered whatever services you could possibly imagine. There was also a clean, hugely proportioned washroom, which smelled exuberantly of disinfectant.

George Street, deep as a canyon and straight as an arrow, as if drawn by a ruler. It starts at the harbour at Circular Quay and ends – where? "Past the Town Hall," said Charles, "That's where the Western Suburbs start. There are only about six or so major city streets, and they all run parallel with each other, from the harbour to the Town Hall, simple as simple can be."

It would take me a while to find my bearings, to stop staring at the vast city buildings (Georgian? Victorian?) and the immense rows of shops, and wondering where on earth I was exactly. But there were always people ready to give directions, friendly, helpful people; happy people. There was a permanent holiday atmosphere here. I felt at my ease, in a Lilliputian kind of way.

None of us realised at the time what a secure and protected spot we had found there on the North Shore and that what we were doing was playing. Playing in a paradise-like garden far from any ugliness. We just lived from day to day and carelessly spent all the money we earned, mainly on the caravan, of course. Did we talk to the Stathams? We certainly did and I believe they gave us good advice every now and then. All I can remember is an atmosphere of friendly, aloof interest and absolutely never a word of criticism.

And then it became winter. At least, that is what Audrey and Clive Statham called it. The days became shorter and chillier. The children started to wear sweaters to school and I wore a cardigan every now and then, but the sun continued to shine and I continued to eat my lunchtime sandwich outside on the terrace. No snow, no ice, no night frost. I didn't believe it would ever rain, as it had been predicted to do.

The rain came. No decorous showers or misty, gentle drizzle, but a deluge, which continued for a full week. It rained in thick, hard streams that crashed with a furious drum roll onto roofs and windows. We lived behind a curtain of rain. The garden was transformed into a pool of mud. The stream in the valley became a raging torrent. All the paths became streamlets and everywhere water gushed and gurgled. Charles worked exclusively indoors and came home early, and one afternoon I met my very first Australian spider. A hairy, dark, grey monster that, I think, with its legs spread out was the size of a small saucer. It emerged from behind that one painting in the lounge. I screamed loudly and long. It scuttled along and down the wall, and ran across the pink carpet out of the front door, which, thank God, was almost always open. The children materialised from nowhere. "A tarantula", said Ginny.

"I want to catch it! I want to catch it!" Robert crowed, at which I grabbed hold of him tightly, "No!"

"They're not dangerous!" Nigel called, running after the insect. We saw how it crossed the veranda and jumped into the bushes. I was trembling.

"I could have caught it," Robert said indignantly, "It wasn't a funnel-web."

"A funnel-web?"

"A funnel-web is a big black spider," Ginny explained, "And if it bites you, you die."

"Also if a red-back bites you," Robert chimed in again.

"No you don't!" said Nigel, "It just makes you very sick."

I listened to all this in horror. Poisonous spiders! That same evening I noticed for the first time the sign about spiders in our local station waiting room, which had clearly been hanging there for years. It showed unmistakably clear pictures: "Funnel-web spiders" with a jet black, huge body, and creepily fat legs; and "red-back spiders," which are much smaller with a bright red spot on their back. "It seems that the North Shore is notorious for its funnel-webs," said Jaap, "It seems that in the rainy season they regularly turn up indoors. And there are poisonous snakes here too."

"Oh God!" I said.

"Don't tease her," Miep said, "It was much worse in Indonesia. I bet nobody is bothered by such things here." Which was the exact truth.

After the rain there was a long succession of cold, sunny days. At night a fire now burned in the fireplace in the living room, fed by huge tree trunks. In all the other rooms, small portable electrical heaters appeared. We were also given one for downstairs. Once we moved into June we actually needed it. It could be very cold here especially in the mornings. July was even colder and August brought a strong wind, which bellowed around the house for days. But on the first day of September masses of blooming freesias suddenly appeared and the garden smelled of spring again. The winter was over.

CHAPTER 4

Meeting Gerard

OH, MY BACK. *I still get stiff if I sit here too long, am still moving with difficulty. Will it stay this way? Every now and then I look down from our balcony at the elderly people who also live in this building and who need a stick to move about. We too are "elderly", I sometimes think. It doesn't feel that way. It feels as if I still have all the people I have ever been freely at my disposal, all the people who live inside of me. Only when something begins to falter, like my back, do I begin to feel uncomfortable. Who or what am I now? Is there really an inexorable process of erosion going on? Something happening which I cannot control, even if I stick faithfully to my back exercise regime every day? I should ignore those questions, just as Tante Cor does, she is 81! Back to half a century ago and the first distant rumblings of a coming landslide.*

Sydney's airport is called Kingsford Smith Airport, but was (and still is) generally referred to as "Mascot" after the suburb in which it is located. Why Charles and I went to Mascot on that day in September is a mystery I can't solve. The reason has disappeared from my memory. I know that we were there in the evening and that we had decided (that is, that Charles had decided) that the best thing to do would be to spend the night there on the empty rows of benches in the main hall. This must have been because whomever we were picking up or meeting was due to arrive very early the next morning. There were no night trains to or from Mascot. In any case, it was an indisputable fact that we were there.

I can see myself in the mirror of the ladies bathroom: sleepy eyes in a dishevelled face. I yawn. I stretch. We are adventurous and resourceful, I feel. It is quite fun to have the whole Arrivals Hall of the airport almost to ourselves. I pass a surprised cleaning lady when I leave the toilet. It must have been about six in the morning.

Charles is talking to someone. A young man dressed in khaki trousers and a white shirt with rolled up sleeves. A very handsome young man with blonde hair, a square chin, a long, slightly upward turned mouth and blue eyes. His face is a little furrowed. Did I stand there, as if struck by lightning? Well, no, not really, but there was something special. Briefly, something inside me became very quiet.

They were talking enthusiastically, Charles and the young man, whose name turned out to be Melman, Gerard Melman, an ex-marine. They knew each other from America, from the training camp. Gerard told me how he had seen Charles returning from his AWL escapade, between two MPs. "He was an O&O (Relaxation and Entertainment) sergeant and we rookies in officer training looked up to him greatly."

"I immediately lost my stripes then," said Charles, grinning, "Did you go to Indonesia?"

"Yep. First back to Holland. Swearing in, in Rotterdam, then to Indonesia. Was there for three years, the best years of my life! Couldn't stand Holland after that. Did you know that a whole bunch of our old mates are here? Give me your address. I'll call you. We must get together."

I can't recall that Gerard paid a great deal of attention to me. I do remember that I looked at his broad shoulders. He was slim, shorter than Charles but just as muscled. The way he moved, walked…He told us he had a removal company. Owned a Morris panel van and was at the airport to convince immigrants to let him take care of their transportation. I think he left with a few customers that morning. What we did has disappeared into the mist of the past.

He did indeed ring us a few days later, and Charles asked him over for drinks (not that we drank much at that time, I don't think I drank at all). That evening in our flat I heard his life story. Born in Wassenaar, he had always lived in Leiden. Secondary school (HBS); war; had left home on foot with a friend and crossed enemy lines into Belgium after it had been liberated. Spent a short time in Brussels and signed up for the marines there. Training in England and America. Then Indonesia, and now Australia. He had come to Australia together with two old friends, both ex-officers just like he was, on the cargo ship *De Annakerk*. Had also left in early January. Had taken the train from Melbourne to Sydney. Had already had a variety of odd jobs, such as at Mark Foys a large department store in the city where he had sold sheets and blankets and about which he told hilarious stories.

His removal company was a new venture, but had a lot of promise, he said. Being his own boss was much more fun (something with which Charles heartily agreed). I listened with round eyes. He came from a large family, he told us, seven brothers and seven sisters. He was one of the youngest and the only one who had left the country. I warmed to him. Recognition? He lived with a group of friends in Kings Cross. "We've rented a house together. You should come round soon."

A week or so later we did go round, on a Sunday evening. Kings Cross was and is Sydney's entertainment district, a noisy, colourful crossroads on the hill at the end of William Street: a melting pot of nationalities, as well as of nightclubs, sex clubs, theatres and restaurants. A fountain which, spraying constantly, resembled a huge dandelion: the El-Alamain fountain. Shops that were open day and night, a rarity in the fifties. In short, a little bit of Europe is what I thought at the time.

The old mates welcomed Charles with much shoulder slapping, and naturally plunged straight down memory lane. Gerard, whose nickname I later discovered was "Flip" (a much nicer name, I thought, and one I promptly adopted), took me under his wing. He introduced me to Henk van Eendenburg. Six foot tall and athletically built. Mild, smiling blue eyes and very good manners. Henk talked without raising his voice. Got me a chair, filled my glass and asked about my background with interest. I found it difficult to imagine that this well-dressed young man had ever been part of a helmeted, sweaty group of landing troops, crawling on their bellies through a jungle of blood-sucking insects or waving hand grenades about. Not so Gerard/Flip. You could see that he had been a soldier.

Who else were there? Joop and Hans Jansen, who were brothers; and a man called Jacometti, tall and blonde with a long, curly beard which, for some reason, he was not allowed to shave off, I was told, despite the fact that he worked the night shift in a sugar factory and returned home every morning with a snow white beard, sticky and covered with powdered sugar. There was also a restless young man with a sharp, quick tongue whose name I have forgotten.

That evening we discovered that Flip also did an ice run in the Northern suburbs, to top up his income whenever there were no removals. And that he could sometimes do with a bit of help in the house-moving business, should Charles be able to take the occasional day off? (Of course Charles could, he said!). I laughed heartily at all the mad stories, but was secretly glad that we lived in Wahroonga and led a calm and well-regulated life with a clearly defined future. Or so I thought.

How many weeks has it been since I typed that last sentence? Six or seven. I am again just as nervous as I was when I typed my first sentence on this computer. It is now mid-October, autumn, and in the drawer of my desk are two Qantas tickets, a present from Joel M. We will be going to Australia again on 25 January.

The reason for this drastic interruption: my back, for starters. The back misery became deadly earnest when I tumbled off our bed and could no longer move my arms or legs. Indescribable pain. The doctor prescribed two weeks of rest and valium. After that I could walk and move again, but could not sit. Thank God I can now. And after the back: migraine. I had no idea what migraine was. It is awful and mysterious. It suddenly strikes, out of nowhere: first the aura, then pain, nausea, dizziness, everything in superlatives. Have now read various books about migraine and understand a little about what is going on, but nothing about what the real cause could be. It puts your life on hold completely. It is as if you are outside of yourself, alone in a vacuum.

That too is now behind me, I hope. Have been free of migraine for about four weeks now and hope to be able to get on with life despite the fear of another attack. Have almost reached the point that I can forget it. Can ignore the sense of turmoil.

I re-read the first pages of this manuscript yesterday, and think that I can now continue.

They are here again, those figures from the past. Charles, with his blonde curls and broad grin; Flip, before he became Gerry, and before – much, much later – he took on his old Dutch name, Gerard, all sunny optimism and intoxicating plans.

And me, so happy that we were leading a regular, civilised, well-ordered life in Wahroonga. The caravan was nearing completion and Charles felt it was high time to take things further, to find the best spot to set it up. Flip, who was deeply interested in our hot dog project, who wanted to be part of it, whom we all four regarded as naturally belonging to our team, offered to drive us around. We drove to a spot recommended by the Wilsons, close to a small town outside Sydney called Rouse Hill on the road that eventually led to the Blue Mountains. We needed to find somewhere close to a farm where we could get water...

What I can draw from the shadows is so vague and bare. A dusty spot among meagre bushes with a few, unhealthy looking eucalyptus trees in the background alongside an unpaved road. A small, unpainted wooden house glows in the midday sun. Whether this is a truthful recollection is not really important. I think that day we all subconsciously came to the conclusion that this was not for us, that the caravan project was a dream, which could never become a reality. We drove back without having achieved anything at all.

"We need to consider carefully how to approach this," said Charles.

"Something like this will only work along a highway," said Flip.

"We need time to prepare it properly," said Jaap.

A kind of lethargy promptly descended on all of us. Our Sundays became less and less productive, and Jaap became increasingly more melancholy. Miep became quiet. She did not look well, and then: "We'll have to give up on the caravan idea," said Jaap. "I'm going to try to sell it. Miep's pregnant."

We gaped at him. Jaap shrugged. "Can't be helped. This wasn't what we planned. You'll understand that I now really need to earn more money quickly. And I need to find somewhere for us to live. We can't stay here. Once I've sold the caravan, of course I'll pay you back the renovation costs."

My first, unarticulated reaction was a sense of relief. How long had I already known that Charles was fed up with messing around with the caravan? "You don't need to pay us back," he said cheerfully, "We were all in this together. Just place an ad in the newspaper tomorrow. Who knows what you'll get for it."

"It will be nice, a baby," I said, tentatively, "How do you feel, Miep?"

"I would have preferred to wait a little while longer," she said with a shy smile.

Unfortunately, only one odd character responded to the ad. He wasn't even prepared to pay the original purchase cost. It was very depressing. But shortly afterwards a letter arrived from Hiek, to whom I had naturally immediately written all the latest developments. "We'd love to take over your caravan," she wrote. "We'd like to set it up alongside the road here and open the stall in the weekends. How much does Jaap want for it? You need to ask him whether we can pay for it in instalments. We can't raise a large sum all at once."

A sudden ray of light in the darkness: Jaap was thrilled. And two days later Charles came home asking: "How would you feel about renting a house with the whole gang? Flip and Jaap and I went to see a house in Auburn this afternoon, in the Western suburbs. It was advertised in the paper this morning. It's big enough for all of us and if we share the rent, dirt cheap."

"What?!"

"We can't stay here for ever, you know. I think you've played housekeeper long enough and I'd like to do something else than painting too." How long had I known that he was fed up with being a house painter?

"Yes, but what about the Stathams?" I protested feebly, "We can't just…"

"Of course we can! It's a free country, isn't it? Relax. I'll tell them. Oh, and we've already rented that house, from next week onwards. You have to grab these opportunities otherwise they pass you by. An elderly couple lives there, in one of the front rooms. They will stay. They are the parents of the owner. We needn't have anything to do with them. The rest of the house is ours; we can do with it what we like. Oh, and there's also a large workspace with a couple of sewing machines. We're allowed to use them if we want to. It seems there used to be a kind of textile factory there."

"Sewing machines?" I stammered.

"Oh well, you never know what you can put to good use. Flip will move us and as soon as we're settled we'll take the caravan to Woodford. Will you write to Hiek? So she knows she can count on us. I'm going to talk to the Stathams. Don't worry, pussycat, everything will be just fine!"

Reunion of Dutch Marine Brigade, Sydney, 1952. Charles Ruys, crouched (1st left); Gerard Melman, standing behind Charles, with hand on his shoulder; Paul Albers next to Gerard (on right); Henk van Eendenburg in back row, 3rd from left.

CHAPTER 5

Auburn and Katoomba

WE MOVED ON a Saturday, a Saturday in the spring. It was glorious weather. Flip turned up very early. And once Flip had arrived, all my doubts disappeared. Why, I did not understand at the time, but I suddenly felt as if I belonged again; there were limitless possibilities, we were pioneers again. There was something very reliable about Flip, and a sunny, stubborn optimism. If he thought this was a good idea, then surely…

Perhaps it had something to do with the fact that he was a driver. I sat in the front with him and secretly admired his hands on the wheel, the confident, relaxed way he drove. Have I already mentioned that he had been giving Charles driving lessons for the past week?

We picked Jaap and Miek up in Warrawee. Just like us, they had all their belongings in suitcases and chests (we had two, they had four). We drove from the affluent North Shore, with its luxurious houses, its giant flowering rhododendrons, purple jacaranda flowers and masses of exuberant, yellow acacias to the dry, bare, colourless desert of houses, which was the Western suburbs.

Once we had crossed the Harbour Bridge and had left the centre of town, we drove along Parramatta Road, a road that offered nothing on either side but second-hand car shops. Cars as far as the eye could see; cars in all sizes and colours, neatly parked in rows, glistening in the sun, with the asking price boldly written in red on the front window. And then came the car wrecking yards, with cars piled high, hundreds and hundreds of cars.

The traffic around us was indescribable. Immense rows of trucks and cars thundered past us. It was the first time I had been in this part of the city. After the car wrecks, there followed a sea of houses; small houses, each with a minute veranda and a tiny, dusty garden. Low buildings, with flat roofs, built of wood or weatherboard, usually painted in a pastel colour. And in the meantime it grew hotter and hotter. It felt as if we had driven into an immense oven. Our fresh, bright, spring day was gone and so was our idyllic life on the green North Shore.

Harrow Road, Auburn, was a respectably paved street with a narrow pavement on either side. Our house was what I would now describe as a classic Australian, brick, middleclass house, built to keep out the heat. There was a wide, red brick-covered front veranda under three brick arches. At the back, on either side of the front door, which stood in the middle and was always open, were the windows of two bedrooms. The front door opened onto a long, straight corridor, which ran right through the "lounge." Our communal living room therefore consisted of two deep, square alcoves. Further down the hall, on either side, were the doors of two large rooms and a kitchen and laundry. There was a shower in the laundry. Behind the kitchen was a tiled patio and beyond it a neglected garden.

When we arrived the elderly couple we were to share the house with were sitting on the front veranda. He was sitting in a rocking chair and she was in a wheelchair next to him. He was small and scrawny, and as dark as if he were made of old leather. He wore a white, sleeveless singlet, a dark pair of trousers with braces, and was wearing slippers on his feet. She had an oddly smooth, large, round face and was completely shapeless: a large, heavy, amorphic body in a flowery dress. She was smiling vaguely (I had never heard of dementia at that time). On the ground between the two chairs stood a transistor radio from which emerged, almost without pause, a voice devoid of all personality. A hard, flat voice, which spoke without intonation, without variation, a monotonous, endless monologue in a barely comprehensible code: the typical voice of the racing commentator. The Paisleys had only one, all-engrossing hobby. They listened to the horse races day in day out.

We did not know it at the time but that voice would be with us every moment of the day for the next 18 months. We would even become almost fond of that unintelligible sound, in the same way that you can become attached to the hum of traffic if you live close to a highway. If it fell silent, even for a little while, we became vaguely anxious.

On the first day Mr. Paisley spoke the only complete sentence, which I ever heard him utter. "You can park your car round the side, mate. Take the back door." To which Flip responded with a friendly, "Okay, mate," and manoeuvred his panel van to the side of the house where there was a wide, dilapidated drive.

From the moment we moved into the house Mr. P. pottered through our lives noiselessly on his slippers without interfering with us in the slightest or attempting to have a conversation with us. I discovered later that the Paisleys had their own bathroom at the front and their own telephone. Mr. P. would sometimes appear suddenly in the garden, smoking a pipe, staring thoughtfully at the washing line or would glide like a ghost through the middle of our living room (by means of the corridor, of course). Sometimes he appeared in the kitchen, with a saucepan in his hand, though never when we were cooking or eating. I think that in his own way he kept an eye on us, though he tacitly accepted us the way we were, just as we accepted him. We always greeted each other in a friendly way.

Our house in Auburn: I try to conjure up an image of it, but it isn't clear. It remains dark. It was a dark house, in fact. Every room had a few small, stained glass windows, which you could only open with the greatest difficultly. Fresh air came in through the open doors. There was almost always a breeze blowing through our corridor. Coolness was a precious commodity.

Charles and I slept in the middle room on a mattress on the floor. Had we bought it? I assume we had, just as we must have bought sheets and blankets. We probably thought a bed was too expensive. I remember that we used our chest as a bookcase and our suitcases as extra storage space. There was a small wardrobe.

The house was supposed to be furnished, which meant that Jaap and Miep had a real bed in the largest bedroom (which they needed, we all felt, because of the coming baby) and that the kitchen was well-provided with a stove, plenty of pots and pans, a table with four chairs and more than enough kitchen cupboards. The living room, however, was almost completely empty. There was a divan, I think, or was it a sofa? In any case, Flip regularly slept on it. And there was also an old, worn armchair. In the workspace stood two black, industrial sewing machines and a long, solid worktable, various chairs and a filing cabinet. I found this room imposing and slightly daunting. I had no idea how a sewing machine worked.

In the laundry we found, in addition to the normal cement washbasins with faucets above them, a large, copper vat, somewhat green, with a faucet above it and a gas burner underneath it. This was "the copper," which Flip turned out to be familiar with. "You boil the washing in it." I have always thought the copper to be a very clever Australian invention. In our pre-washing machine era, I contentedly used one for years.

The kitchen also contained a mysterious, large, brown, wooden chest of which the lower section was covered with something that looked like a layer of zinc with underneath a removable drawer, also covered in zinc. "The ice box," said Flip, "I'll find out from the Paisleys when the ice man comes by." This turned out to be every Friday morning. A man then brought an enormous block of ice, which fit snugly into the bottom half of our icebox and slowly melted in the course of a week. We drained the water regularly by means of the drawer. In the top section we stored everything that we would normally put in a refrigerator. It worked beautifully and was dirt cheap.

Miep and I became increasingly more enthusiastic until it struck me that we had not come across a toilet anywhere. "They don't have a toilet here," I said, "What are we going to do?"

"Yes, they do," said Charles, "In the garden!" In the garden, next to two ancient, crumbling wooden poles across which three washing lines had been hung, stood a square, wooden hut with a sheet-iron roof that was built to shoulder height of stone; above the stone were widely spaced wooden slats with vegetation sprouting through them. Behind the wooden door that had no lock was our toilet. Huge, blue blowflies buzzed busily above the old-fashioned wooden throne with a cover. "Spiders," was the only word I could utter when I had recovered the use of my voice.

"Nonsense," said Charles, "Just a matter of keeping things clean."

"At least it's a real toilet, not a tub," said Flip, "There are plenty of houses here that aren't connected to the sewers. They have a tub in the garden, which is emptied every week by the city poop collecting service." He was completely serious. The things I didn't know about Sydney!

We started to unpack. Jaap produced a large batik rug, which he hung like a curtain in the opening of our lounge alcove. "At least we'll have a little bit of privacy here." His smallest chest turned out to be a perfect coffee table. Later, he would fabricate a chair with a backrest from his larger chest. We all agreed that we didn't need any floor covering. There were dark brown, varnished, wooden floors everywhere, which looked quite respectable. Moreover, all you needed to do was sweep them and give them a mop every now and then. We didn't need a vacuum cleaner.

After we had finished unpacking and "decorating" we held a council of war in the kitchen. Flip was there too. He stayed over that night. We were going to take the caravan to Woodford the very next day. "We" were Flip, Charles and I. The journey was too long for Miep, and Jaap would not hear of leaving her on her own. That day, Jaap took on the role of administrator, and it always stayed that way. He calculated that we could survive, even if we couldn't find work for a little while, for about four weeks at least. Easily. "But we're going to look for a job first thing Monday, aren't we, Charles?"

"Will be a cinch."

And then the Paisley daughter appeared. A hefty young woman whose name I have forgotten. She came to collect our first rent, something she would do in person every Saturday from then on. She also gave us a prophetic piece of advice to which we paid not the slightest attention at the time. "You could make ties in the work space. Tie factories use lots of home workers," to Miep and myself.

At the crack of dawn on Sunday we were on the road again, first to Warrawee. Flip had found a slightly rusty hook with which he attached the caravan to his van. A few pieces of rope were also deployed. He nevertheless did not seem to regard the construction as completely reliable, as he stopped regularly to inspect it, when either he or Charles would jump out of the car. Behind us there was a constant squeaking and groaning.

In the distance the Blue Mountains resembled an undulating mass of kale. We were in fact driving along steep, winding, unpaved roads with naked rock face on the one side and dizzying precipices of rock mass and virgin eucalyptus jungle covered in a copper glow on the other. Breathtaking. The loneliness was astounding: we never met another soul during all those hours. No cars, no people, no animals. Only sharply teethed rocks, heat and silence. We descended into deep valleys, and struggled up again, creaking and whining. We crept past gaping holes in the road alongside dizzying ravines. We bumped over loose rocks at the foot of yellow and grey sandstone walls.

Every now and then we would pass a weathered sign, testament to the fact that humans had actually visited this wilderness. And Flip remained firmly cheerful, although he occasionally drove with grimly closed lips. Charles supplied the accompanying commentary.

Mid afternoon we came across a large wooden arrow with *Woodford* written on it. We turned into a parched, hard, sandy road, the surface of which resembled the ridged washing board in our laundry. The squealing from behind became more tortured still and I realised what marbles rolling around in a marble bag must endure. But we had left the precipices behind, so had something to be grateful for.

Hiek's house was made of wood and was square, with a broad veranda running around the whole house. It consisted of a living room and two bedrooms. The kitchen, bathroom and laundry were located in a separate rectangular annex. Water came from an immense corrugated iron water tank on stilts, painted bright green, which was fed by rainwater. In the living room there was a fireplace where a large fire was burning; two petroleum lamps had already been lit. In the bathroom there was a rusty cast-iron bath and a wood-fuelled water-heater. The immense kitchen stove was also fed with timber, as was the copper. I can see myself wandering around speechlessly, suddenly realising that in Auburn we were living in outrageous luxury: we had gas, water and electricity!

Hiek had not changed in the slightest. "Cosy, isn't it? And so cheap! We get all our wood from the forest around here. Wait till we go for a walk tomorrow. We've just discovered a waterfall close by, so pretty."

The atmosphere in that quintessentially Australian bush house could not have been more Dutch: Dutch chairs around a Dutch table and a coffee table with a Persian carpet on it. There was an antique Dutch cupboard, there were side tables with lace tablecloths, there were paintings on the wall and there was a vase with wild flowers in it. In the kitchen hung a dozen multi-coloured coffee cups and soup mugs on a wooden rack.

Jan materialised from the wilderness carrying an axe, dressed in an Australian singlet. Two little boys, brown as berries, each dragging a bundle of timber, followed him closely. Jan now resembled a contented, self-assured gentleman farmer. "We're leading a healthy life here! I've just bought a car. It's old, but good enough to drive me up and back to Katoomba. That's where I work. I've had to hitchhike till now. Worked fine, actually, but this is a lot better. I've found a great spot for the caravan, not far from the road. We're going to start with just selling hot water, lots of people do that here."

The car turned out to be a pre-war, black monstrosity, a bit rusty, but otherwise in prime condition. While we were inspecting it, darkness descended, incomprehensible darkness, and in a very short space of time. Nowhere was there the tiniest point of light, except in the little house we stood alongside. The chirping of the cicadas in the trees around us seemed to intensify the silence. It was suddenly very cold.

How Hiek managed it I will never know, but she placed piping hot plates of Dutch *hutspot* (carrot stew) in front of us. "Nice and warm, isn't it, a wood fire?" said Hiek, "We've been so lucky, love. Isn't it a paradise here?"

CHAPTER 6

My world changes

THE TREES ALONG the street of our apartment building have turned the colour of burnished gold. The sun is shining. It is October 2000. I am finding it hard to return to Auburn. That must have been October too, spring in Australia, the world down under. I let myself get distracted so easily and seduced into putting my energy into other things. Is that because what comes now is hard to describe?

My memories are fragments: Miep and I, sweeping and mopping the floors; Miep and I, lifting scalding washing out of the copper with a broomstick and moving it to the washbasin to scrub on the washboard; Miep and I, sitting on the patio, drinking Nescafe, watching the washing flutter in the wind as it dries. It is always dry in no time. I see us finding a large "public" hospital in the middle of Auburn, walking distance from Harrow Road. Jaap and Miep discovered that public hospitals offered their services free. To our great relief, Miep can have her baby there as long as she is registered and turns up for monthly (later, weekly) check-ups.

I also see Flip, very early in the morning, sleeping on our sofa. I am completely overwhelmed, helplessly, hopelessly in love, for the first time in my life. There can be no one else for me now. When did it start? I have tried to find the exact moment: that day in the kitchen at the stove, when I was cooking? At a certain moment, he stands behind me and I turn around and there is a kind of recognition, a knowledge. This is it, for both of us: a word-less and will-less crossing of a boundary, an acknowledging of each other. I walk into his arms.

And from that moment I live in a gold-coloured, silk cocoon. The rest of the world no longer exists. With respect to everyday life I become an automaton, a robot. I am perfectly aware of what is happening around me, but it no longer matters. Charles is a vague figure on the edge of my consciousness. That Jaap and Charles, after various visits to employment agencies and frenzied attempts to respond to ads in the paper (they always arrived too late), cannot find jobs is no longer important; that our financial reserves are steadily declining means nothing. I am deeply, intensely happy. I sleepwalk through the days. This does not last long.

The confrontation: Charles, who asks me whether I still love him and the heart-stopping effort it takes to look at him and say "No." He suddenly looks old, a little defeated, tired, but not surprised and not particularly upset. After that, we talk very calmly, Charles, Flip and I. No, not I: I am there, but only on the outside. Charles talks to Flip, asks him what his intentions are. And Flip says we love each other, that he wants to look after me, that I am the woman he has always longed for and how sorry he is that things have gone the way they have. This was not planned, it is just chance...Charles shrugs. "If you don't look after her, I'll come back and break every bone in your body."

I see us later, Flip and I, at the railing of a veranda (where?). I am crying. I am crying and don't know why. I feel alone and adrift. What have I done? And Flip puts his arms around me, holds me tightly, and then there is an overwhelming sense of inevitability, of security, of coming home.

I seem to recall that Charles left that same day. Flip gave him his van. It had been decided that Charles would take this; that is, he took over the down payments that still needed to be made, and that was that. There was no scene. Everything happened very quietly and calmly. We had talked to Jaap and Miep, who did not appear to be surprised. They tacitly accepted the new situation. "I'll take over Charles' share of the rent and other things," said Flip.

"We don't have anywhere else to go," said Jaap.

I suspect Charles took Flip's place in the marines' house for a little while. Flip heard from "the mates", whose reactions weren't positive. Only Henk van Eendenburg refused to comment. "It's not my business." He remained a good friend.

Later, when Charles had remarried, he came back into our lives with Joke, who suited him much better than I, I thought. He returned as an old, trusted friend and always remained one. In the course of time, we sometimes lost touch, but always found each other again, in the seventies, in Holland. He continued to lead a restless and adventurous life to the bitter end. He died in 1986, of a sudden heart attack. His son let us know.

Flip brought a few books with him. He had found them in antique shops, he said. We still have them. Three stories by Joseph Conrad in a small, classically bound blue volume; *The Artamonov Business* by Maxim Gorky; *The Malay Archipelago* by Alfred Russell Wallace, Darwin's friend; and from Holland *De Geschiedenis van de Mariniers Brigade* (The History of the Marine Brigade). I respectfully placed them next to my Marsman and Adriaan Roland Holst in our bookcase chest: a world to yet be discovered. I was back in my golden cocoon again, this time, together with Flip. We had embarked on a journey of discovery. We roamed hand in hand through Auburn. And we slept in each other's arms. We were extremely happy, and so very, very young.

After two days, Flip resolutely took over the management of our Auburn household. "We need to do something about our income, Jaap."

"I completely agree," said Jaap, "But what?" We had just handed over our weekly share of the rent and the housekeeping budget to him. (Miep and I took turns to cook, with the help of our partners. Her cooking was considerably better and more varied than mine).

"Make do with what we have," said Flip, "Finding a job in the neighbourhood isn't going to work. There seems to be a kind of depression going on. God knows how many people are out of work. We should make use of the workspace, the sewing machines. It's ridiculous that those things are just standing there and not being used. Didn't that lady who picks up the rent say something about making ties? Surely that can't be too difficult." He promptly pulled off the tie he was wearing, turned it inside out and studied it. "Look, there are only three sections and then there's the lining in the point and so on."

"But we don't know how those machines work!" I squeaked, "Have you ever looked at them? They look far too heavy for Miep and I to operate."

"Not you and Miep," said Flip, "Jaap and I! Come on, guys, let's see what the workspace has to offer. Who has a pair of scissors?" The scissors were used to undo all sorts of seams and the result was again examined. "Simple. Piece of cake."

Then it was the turn of the sewing machines. Flip and Jaap tried one each and started experimenting with old rags. "It's a cinch," Flip concluded triumphantly, "Don't you agree, Jaap? They're a bit rusty, but a drop of oil here and there..." The machines were almost dismantled and their wheels and cogs were oiled. Then Flip went to borrow the telephone book from the Paisleys. To phone, we needed to go to the phone booth on the corner of our street. Flip flipped through the pages. "Necktie manufacturers, a whole list of them. And there are two close to Wynyard. Jaap and I will go there tomorrow. And if that doesn't work we'll go to Leichhardt or Glebe. All reasonably close. With a little bit of luck..."

"Only if what the daughter said is true," warned Jaap.

But Flip was adamant. "Of course they use home-workers! Much cheaper than hiring staff."

The next morning at half past eight they left in the direction of the station. By lunchtime they were back. Jaap was carrying a small cardboard box under his arm. "Two dozen," he said, tapping the box, "We have to deliver them tomorrow. If they're up to scratch, we can get as much work as we want."

"Klipper Ties: they're in Clarence Street, just behind Wynyard Station. Couldn't be better," said Flip.

"We'll get five shillings a dozen," beamed Jaap, "That's 25 pounds per 100 dozen. Between the four of us we should be able to make 400 ties a week. We looked at how they did it there. It's a small factory. They use a kind of assembly line system. A few girls sew and a few others cut and iron. That's what you two will do."

"Cut?!"

"Easy does it," grinned Flip, "They're pre-cut. The seams just need to be ironed and the end product needs to be ironed flat a bit too. You'll get the hang of it, it's easy." The box turned out to contain six, neat piles of wine-red tie parts: a front section, a middle section and a bottom. Plus two piles of pink lining and some strips of unbleached cotton. "To put in the middle," said Flip.

And so we set to work. The sewing machines were placed opposite each other so that Flip and Jaap sat almost nose to nose. Miep and I found scissors and an iron. "Okay," said Flip, "I'll first sew all the front and middle pieces, one after the other, in a long string. Miep can cut them loose, put them on a pile and give them to Jaap. He'll sew the back sections onto them, also in a string. Miep will cut them loose again and you'll iron the seams. After that, I'll sew the front lining in the same way, and Jaap can do the back lining. Miep will cut these and turn them inside out, and you'll iron them again. Then we'll fold, add the inside lining and close things up. Turn them around, iron them and they'll be right as rain. That's the way they do it over there, so it must be the most efficient way. If we really want to make money we'll have to produce large quantities very quickly."

Miep and I decided to test-run one tie first, which immediately made clear that the artificial silk pieces of cloth had a mind of their own. They were slippery and difficult to handle; the tension of the thread needed constant alteration; ironing the seams was simple enough, but the lining required a different temperature; and the edges refused to peak. A knitting needle didn't help; it was far too sharp. After deep thought, Jaap produced from somewhere a long, blunt, copper rod, which became part of our standard equipment; we promptly christened it "The Pointer."

The cotton reinforcement strips had the tendency to curl. Our first tie turned giddily on its own axis. I ironed it with all my might, but it continued to curl stubbornly and the artificial silk lining began to crease. So Jaap cut a small triangle from cardboard and fit it snugly into the pointed front. After a final iron, something that resembled quite a respectable tie materialised.

"Okay," said Flip, "Now we've got the technique down pat, let's work more systematically."

"We'll stick that one in the bottom of the box," said Jaap.

We worked furiously all afternoon and evening. It was almost midnight by the time we could place our first 24 ties tenderly in the box. We were exhausted.

"So that's 10 bob," Jaap remarked, dourly. "Ten hours work by four workers is three-pence an hour." The silence was deafening.

"Oh well," said Miep, "When we're more experienced we'll work faster. And it's still better than nothing, isn't it?"

"We need to let them know tomorrow how many we can handle," said Flip, "Shall I say about 100 dozen to start off with?"

I groaned.

"It's the ironing that takes the most time" Flip pointed out, "We'll need to get a steam iron like the one they have over there. Can't be helped. A small investment…"

"Small?!" Jaap said, appalled, "We're down to our last 100 pounds, old man! Can't we wait a little while?"

"Absolutely not. If we get work tomorrow we are going to order a steam iron straightaway; we're bound to be able to pay in instalments. We have to generate an income from all this, so company costs can't be avoided…"

"Let's go to bed," I said nervously, "and just pray that man is satisfied." He was! The next day we had 100 dozen, pre-cut, artificial silk ties, neatly packed in suitcases that Flip and Jaap, with great forethought, had taken with them to Clarence Street. "And tomorrow a steam iron will be delivered," said Flip.

Production Phase 1 was initiated immediately. Miep was installed with a pair of scissors and I was dispatched on shopping errands, as my job could wait. "Bring back something nice so we can celebrate", said Jaap, hugely elated, "We've got 25 pounds of work, that'll feed us for at least two weeks!"

When I returned to the workshop half an hour later I discovered a glistening, rainbow lake undulating through the room. In the middle sat Miep. These embryonic ties were red with blue stripes, green with yellow spots, brown with copper dots and dark blue with golden squares. From Flip's fingers flowed a slippery stream of coloured silk from machine to floor to Miep's lap. Miep was cutting furiously and shoving disobedient piles towards Jaap. He was feeding the rainbow lake on her other side. They all three looked wild-eyed, and were covered in sticky, glistening bits of coloured thread. A shimmering cloud of threads hung in the room, and the machines purred like giant cats.

"What a mess!" I said, "How are we ever going to get all this sorted!" Both machines stopped abruptly. "It isn't a mess at all!" Jaap said indignantly, draping his colourful string over his arm. "Look how even the piles are."

"Lousy material," Flip grunted, wiping his forehead and smearing threads through his hair. "The cheapest of the cheap. Just look at it!" He lifted up his string and started to sneeze exuberantly, "Can somebody get me a handkerchief?"

"It frays like mad," said Jaap, "They've clearly given us the inferior line."

"I'm coming to help cut: how far have we got?"

"Far?! Look at the suitcases – we haven't even touched suitcase two. 100 dozen is 1000 ties."

That day Miep and I did nothing but cut. We cut till our fingers froze, and until Flip came up with the idea of using a razorblade. This was much faster though had its drawbacks: we needed a lot of band-aids. We cooked quickly, and held a long dinner break. But after the washing-up we marched back into the factory. Midnight was bedtime.

The next morning the steam iron indeed arrived. Miep and I found it astounding. It looked exactly like a blood-transfusion machine. There was a large, glass cone that needed to be hung up, and into which water had to be poured regularly. Jaap built a contraption to hang it up on. From the cone a thick, clear hose led to the iron, which was very heavy and sported a thick electric wire, and a daunting selection of buttons and arrows. But the result was impressive and it steamed with gusto! I now had my own private cloud, a warm grey one. And I ironed with a speed that gave rise to admiration all round. "You see what a difference it makes?" Flip said triumphantly, "Now we're getting somewhere!"

With the arrival of the iron, our factory began to steam ahead in earnest. We started at 7.30 in the morning and only stopped when we could no longer see straight, around eleven at night. Nevertheless, it took us a full ten days to finish the first 100 dozen. But by then we had become masters at our trade! We had overcome all the teething problems. The future was looking bright.

For the first two months, the flow of work remained constant. The tie man in Clarence Street gave us as much work as we wanted. Flip cleverly found a wholesaler in thread, which lowered our costs. Moreover, he was fearless enough to negotiate a higher wage for us. First 6, then 7 shillings a dozen, but that was the absolute highest rate, declared Mr. Klipper Ties. No one in Sydney paid home-workers more than 7 shillings! Our factory buzzed like a beehive from morning till late at night. We lived like contented hermits, and dreamed of making a fortune.

And then one Monday morning, the men returned home with empty suitcases. No work. "Ring me in a fortnight," Mr. Klipper Ties had said. We were deeply hurt. How could he abandon us like that? But we weren't defeated. Flip and Jaap made a lengthy visit to the phone booth on the corner. The seventh attempt was successful: a Mr. Eddy Zimmermann in George Street could use us: 50 dozen.

Eddy's ties resembled wet tissue paper. They were plain wine-red and had the tendency to spilt slyly. They irritated us hugely. After a difficult week, we had earned all of 15 pounds; and the week after that, absolutely nothing. We tidied and swept, polished and oiled. We counted the days until we could ring Clarence Street again. But Clarence Street had nothing to offer us: "Maybe in a month..."

Jaap proposed an emergency financial measure. Our housekeeping pot had been replaced long ago by a general fund into which we deposited all our income and from which we drew the weekly housekeeping money and pocket money. We introduced a drastic cut in both household expenses and pocket money: 10 pounds for domestic needs – an absolute minimum – and a pound pocket money per couple.

Flip succeeded in getting Eddy to give us another 50 dozen ties, this time navy blue. Amid Eddy's blue ties, we celebrated our first Australian Christmas. Miep baked a cake, which we solemnly ate together in our lounge-room on Christmas Day, after which we felt we could respectably return to the workshop. There was a lot of work to do!

After Christmas, there followed a depressing period of unemployment. At his wit's end, Flip contacted Klipper Ties yet again. Did we know how to make woollen ties? Of course we did! Flip told him, recklessly. Instead of a pointed lining, the woollen ties required a tiny hem along the front and back points. Flip installed a new foot in his machine, and proved so proficient in the delicate operation of hemming he quickly became our hem specialist. Jaap took care of seams and closing up. A label also needed to be added, which cost extra time, though it never occurred to us to charge extra for this. We were too relieved to have work. Ten days later we delivered our first batch of woollen ties.

Only much later did I meet the Clarence Street man myself. A small, stockily built, grey-haired, business man, with sharp, brown eyes and a heavy, Eastern European accent. He actually struck me as quite nice. I had expected a much more sinister character.

On the blistering January day that Flip and Jaap deposited their suitcases in the cutting room of Klipper Ties, he was yelling at his foreman. The foreman usually collected our ties. This time it was the boss himself who grabbed Jaap's suitcase. He placed a pile on the cutting table and pulled out a tie, which he examined carefully. Then he took hold of the top and the bottom ends, and pulled. "Snap!" went the woollen tie. "That was the thread," the man said belligerently, "Broken. Your thread tension is wrong. Look, that's where the breakage is," sticking a large finger into our handiwork, and violently splitting it open. "I want quality work! My label is on the inside! This tie will fall apart in no time. Not acceptable!"

And we had been so proud of our magnificent-looking woollen ties. The perfect hems, the beautiful ironing. We thought they looked so refined. Jaap was struck dumb. "We just need to use different thread," Flip muttered.

"No, you don't!" the man bellowed, murdering two more ties, "It's the thread tension. The tension! Do them again, the whole lot!" and he disappeared into his office. The foreman wisely kept his mouth shut.

"Nine hundred and sixty ties," Jaap groaned, when, bathing in sweat, the two of them came tottering back through our backdoor, "We have to re-do 960 ties!"

"That man should be locked up," Flip snapped, "Bloody perfectionist!"

"Oh well, it's only that one thread, after all," said Miep with resignation, and began to turn all the ties inside out, an immense job, as was getting the flaccid fabric to stay put on the sewing machine. When we cut them loose, Miep and I subjected them to a ruthless test: we gave them each a firm tug and almost every time the thread broke again.

The men moved heaven and earth to get the thread tension right, but the ties kept snapping, and in the end the old status quo turned out to be the best solution.

"That's the way they'll have to stay," Flip said bitterly, "There is no way they'll fall apart. They each have two threads that can't possibly be broken at the same spot. Let's just iron them."

Pre-snapping the threads proved to be the only way: what had already been snapped couldn't break again in the hands of the tie man, that much was clear. Miep and I introduced a small, clever change to our process: we tested the ties after they had been turned inside out and ironed, just before we folded them neatly.

The repair operation took a week. After delivery, our men returned with full suitcases and in the best of moods. "He tried six of them!"

"From the bottom of the suitcase!"

"And he couldn't have been nicer. Not a snap to be heard."

"We have 100 dozen here," Jaap gave each suitcase an encouraging tap, "Not a problem, right?"

"These will also have to be snapped," Flip informed us, "From now on, snapping will be part of our method: a double final seam and then a good tug. That's clearly the only correct way to make woollen ties." We never again had complaints about our woollen ties.

After this undeniably low point our little factory began to flourish. We worked 10 and sometimes 14 hours a day, but we took every Sunday off. Then we each went our own way: Jaap and Miep usually stayed home, but Flip and I always went out. We needed to leave Auburn and the ties as far behind us as possible. And, to be honest, we also needed to leave Jaap and Miep. In the tie factory and the household we were comrades, and everything was fine. But comradeship born of necessity isn't friendship. We were relieved to be able to shut the door behind us on Sundays and step effortlessly back into our own, golden, carefree world. Being together, in love, with the whole of Sydney at our feet, waiting to be explored.

Flip knew so much about the vast city. He had traversed it often and had read much more about it than I. There was so much he wanted to show me and there was nothing I wanted more. With arms around each other or hand in hand, we always started by strolling down to Parramatta Road, the closest large road. Because we had so little money, we usually tried to hitch a ride there, sometimes into town, sometimes in the other direction. Flip decided the route. We always succeeded and sometimes got very far. I have a vague recollection of a trip to the Eastern suburbs. I see water planes landing in Rose Bay; the bay is blue and gold. I see us ambling through Vaucluse, where the elite lived and still does in Victorian splendour: steep streets and very few people. And I am sure we must have visited Bondi, the beach situated, as it were, in the heart of the city. Just to have a look. It didn't occur to us to swim. We didn't even have bathing costumes then.

I remember best of all my first view of Manly, all the way near the North Harbour. I can see The Corso, Manly's famous, always busy, shopping street with at the one end the piers of Manly Cove, a white, harbour beach, a large, open-air swimming pool and calmly lapping water. Far in the distance, shrouded a little in mist, the South Head is visible. On the other end of that same Corso, behind a long boulevard fringed by pine trees, lies the Pacific. The beach is gold-coloured. I can see us sitting together on a bench under a tree, just looking, speechless. I can feel the fine droplets of sea-foam on my cheeks. I can hear the waves, the great, lazy, ocean waves that rise up high, curl and shatter into fields of pearly white foam. The sea is a deep, heartrending blue.

Manly Beach lies between two rock masses and is literally a surfers' paradise. I am enchanted. We eat fish and chips wrapped in newspaper on our bench, for once not sandwiches taken from home. And as the height of reckless luxury we catch a ferry back to Circular Quay in the heart of the city. We sail for half an hour through the harbour. First past the entrance to the Heads, a strong swell here, then past the thick vegetation of rocky inlets, luxuriant parks, mansions with swimming pools and also past the historic prison island called Pinchgut, from which no convict had ever escaped. The sharks and merciless current were effective prison guards.

That day we run into Henk in town. He takes us to his office somewhere in the middle of the city, high up in a somewhat dilapidated building. There is a squeaky lift, an old-fashioned, cast-iron cage from the thirties. Henk has just set up a support agency for immigrants, a one-man company, which is going very well he tells us. He teaches new immigrants the ropes and helps them find somewhere to live, a gap in the market. We promise to keep in touch.

When the weather begins to get colder, two radical changes take place in the world of ties. Miep's baby is born and Jaap purchases a transistor radio.

Miep went about having her baby with her usual sedateness and reticence. From one day to the next, she simply disappeared. Jaap shuffled into the kitchen on his own one morning. "Miep's gone to hospital", he announced blandly, pouring himself a cup of tea, "I took her there at four this morning."

"Jaap! Why didn't you wake us?"

"No need," he shrugged, "We walked over there together. I'm going to ring now, see how things are going," and he disappeared out of the backdoor. Flip and I looked at each other. Compared to Jaap and Miep we were maniacs. Jaap was back within five minutes and was beaming. "We have a daughter! I'm going over to look at her, I'll be back soon."

That afternoon I also went to visit Miep. To my amazement she looked exactly the same, although her tummy had slunk somewhat. She had very little to tell about the birth: "It went fine. The sisters here are very kind." She stayed away for a week. In the meantime we decided that Miep would do the housekeeping from then on and would only come to help in the factory in the evenings, if she was needed. I was promoted to fulltime factory worker, to be deployed for any and every task. The baby was the spitting image of Miep and was as good as gold. We barely noticed there was a baby in the house. Life went on.

Jaap's transistor arrived a few weeks later. Jaap placed it on the corner of his machine and relished in it from morning till night. In the mornings we were forced to listen to light music, interrupted occasionally by chirpy commentary. In the afternoon there followed a never-ending stream of radio soaps, clearly the highlight of Jaap's day.

Poor Flip. The music he loved (primarily Mozart, he confided to me), which he had had to do without for years now, was never broadcast. Never. He endured his fate without complaint. There was nothing we could do about it, we felt. Later, when we had saved enough…

The afternoons were long and sleepy: the machines hummed, the iron steamed, the radio chattered. The days ran into each other like links in a chain. We continued to live as frugally as possible. We now knew that we would have to get through a few slow months at the end of the year.

Our second Christmas brought us the bowtie affair. In mid December Clarence Street abandoned us again, but our old standby Eddy came to the rescue. "I've been able to get hold of a small batch of real Italian silk, ideal for bowties. Can you make bowties? Not a whole lot, just a few hundred."

"We'll do it," said Flip, "Anything's better than doing nothing. And he'll pay double for these." We had never looked at a bowtie carefully before and I don't think we ever discovered the correct sewing technique for them. But we cut, sewed, turned and pressed until we had created two strange, long shapes, with curves in the middle and connected by a cord.

"How on earth do you tie these things?" It was a very hot day, and Jaap and Flip were working in nothing but shorts. Bare necks and legs served to try out the results, which looked undeniably like bowties. I still had a sinking feeling, however. "Shouldn't they all look the same?"

"Oh, they'll each go into a separate box, who cares if they look different?" But my premonition proved correct: all the ties were returned for repairs: their curves were all wrong. "I thought Eddy was going to burst into tears," Flip suddenly started to laugh uncontrollably, "You should have seen his face!"

"And we'd put the best ones on top!" Jaap said dourly and then began to chortle, "You should have heard him!"

"Goddamit! My best silk!" Flip guffawed.

"Are they all like this?!" Jaap hiccoughed with mirth, "And the bottom layer, the bottom layer!"

"He never even saw the bottom layer!" Flip, roaring with laughter.

"He never got the chance!"

"I'm glad you both find it so hilarious," I said icily, "But what are we going to do?" Flip wiped his streaming eyes: "It isn't so bad, darling. His wife took a look and said that if we trim the sides a bit, and redo the sewing here and there…"

Three days and nights later we delivered the ties, now looking more uniform, but still not perfect. We were hugely relieved when Eddy paid us for this fiasco. We were even more delighted to receive two telegrams a few days after Christmas, one from Clarence Street and one from Eddy. "Please contact immediately," which was code for a rush job.

We received black ties, black on either side, from both suppliers. For some reason both Eddy and Clarence Street seemed convinced that the market was desperate for black ties, in the middle of the summer! Our factory became a funeral parlour. We swept fat black flakes daily from underneath the machines. Working constantly with black thread on black material caused our eyes to burn and water. Tiny black trimmings filled the air.

And it became hotter and hotter. Sydney was suffering its annual heat wave. Day in day out, the newsreaders on Jaap's radio brightly announced that there was no sign of a break in the weather; that the soil in heavily afflicted New South Wales was cracking; that water restrictions had been imposed and that it was again expected to be 104 in the shade.

The ties stuck to our fingers, and sweat poured down our foreheads, arms and legs. Even our hall no longer offered respite. The corridor breeze had become a hot desert wind. We realised that the Paisleys had shut their doors and windows, and that their curtains were shut day and night. We followed their example, which gave our factory an even more funeral aspect. Miep provided us with cold drinks; no one wanted to eat. We barely spoke. The heat hung around us like colourless syrup. The world became soundless and seemed to stop.

The end came abruptly. The radio suddenly erupted in excited announcements: "A Southerly is on its way. Tonight around seven the Southerly will hit Sydney!" From that moment the wind's progress was followed carefully, a bulletin was issued every half hour. And at exactly seven o'clock a miracle happened. We heard a murmur that grew steadily into a loud rustling. We heard windows and doors open everywhere. We heard voices, footsteps. We ran into the back garden and oh, the glorious, indescribable relief! A cool breeze washed over us: the wind from the South Pole. The wind sang, trees and bushes swished, our hair fluttered. Within ten minutes the temperature had dropped by more than 15 degrees. That night we finally slept again.

A week after we had delivered our black ties and were once again working on coloured ones, King George VI of England died. It was February 6, 1952. On their next journey into town, Flip and Jaap spotted our ties around the necks of many of the men they saw and more were displayed in the shop windows. "They're more British than the British here!" said Flip.

A wintery Sunday morning: we are finishing off a batch of woollen ties when Miep puts her head round the door of the workshop: "The Paisley daughter wants to talk to you guys, can you come?" "I'll go," says Jaap, uncurling like a snail from its shell. He stretches and trudges out. Ten seconds later he is back. "You should come too, Flip."

"What's going on?" I look up from my work. "They don't have any complaints, do they?"

"No," says Jaap. "But we are going to have to leave. She says we need to be gone by next week Saturday."

"What?!" Flip jumps up from his machine, "She must be out of her mind!" and they are both gone. I am staring into nothingness, petrified. I have forgotten why we had to leave at such short notice. It doesn't really matter. Our rental contract is brutally clear: mutual termination of contract at a weeks' notice. We are losing our house, our sewing machines and our factory.

"So this will be our last batch," I hear Jaap say, resignedly.

"This can't be legal," Flip is white-faced, "They're robbing us of our livelihood! I'm going to ring Henk. He'll know what we can do about it." Henk is hugely sympathetic. He consults a friend who is a solicitor, but there is nothing to be done. We have to leave whether we want to or not.

Two days later Henk found a workspace for us in Roseville, a suburb on our old North Shore Line, much closer to Wynyard than Auburn. Unfortunately, it was only a first floor workshop, in a commercial building where a dentist was located on the ground floor. Flip went to take a look. "We have our own entrance," he reported, beaming, "And there's a small office and a toilet. We can move in almost straightaway. Shall we go shopping for sewing machines this afternoon, Jaap?"

"And where are we going to live?" asked Jaap.

"Oh, there are plenty of houses for rent, old man. We'll find something. First we need to get machines. We can afford something more modern now, good machines that we can really...."

"To be completely honest," Jaap said slowly, "Miep and I are a bit fed up with all this."

"Fed up?!" This was a new, unexpected thunderbolt. "But we're doing so well, old man, we're finally making headway! If we persist now we'll have a flourishing company within a year, you'll see."

"Sorry. We just don't think it will work. If we have to go and live somewhere else, Miep won't be able to work in the factory anyway. No, I'm quitting. We talked it through with Jan and Lucy last Sunday. I can probably get a proper job through Jan and we can move in with them for a little while. I have a family now; we can't keep on living like this. I really am going to stop."

Jan and Lucy Vermeulen were an older, child-less, immigrant couple with whom Miep and Jan had become good friends in the last year. Miep had first met Lucy in Auburn hospital, where she worked, when the baby arrived. Slowly but surely, Lucy and Jan, who lived close-by, had become Miep and Jan's Sunday outing. To us, the Vermeulens were nice enough people, but boring. We treasured our own Sunday expeditions, the only times we could really be alone together.

"We aren't going to stop," Flip said resolutely, "Even if you get out, we'll keep on going, on our own. How do you want to arrange things?"

"Well, let's just split the pot. Seems the most honest way to me."

"We'll take the iron, and we'll pay for it."

If I think back to our last days in Auburn, all I can recall are grey confusion and rain. It must have rained then, day in day out. I see us finishing off our last ties, in silence. We don't have a great deal to say to each other, which is strange. Flip is gone a lot. He tells me he has bought two sewing machines, on instalment of course, and that we will hire a girl to take Jaap's place. That I will like Roseville a lot and that he has taken a flat for us, unseen, so that we will have somewhere to go on Saturday. "In Burwood. That's reasonably close to here. It's furnished. At least we'll have a roof over our heads. As soon as we're up and running in Roseville I'll find somewhere for us there, in the neighbourhood."

I am inwardly torn between excitement and fear. We will be on our own at last, Flip and I, and have a place of our own at last! But, oh God, can the two of us really keep the business running? At the same time I am so very proud of my knight in shining armour. My very own pioneer. He finds solutions for everything, no matter what!

Saturday is cold and wet. Jan and Lucy come to pick up Jaap, Miep and the baby. Jan and Lucy have a car. Flip and I will march on foot to the station

MY WORLD CHANGES 63

with our suitcases later, on our way to Burwood. Our parting is very calm and practical.

"Well, good luck and all that! We'll have to keep in touch," we say, though I think we all know that we won't.

CHAPTER 7

Burwood, Henk and Odette

"Now" is November *2000 in our apartment in Breda. Daylight saving has just started. Our days grow steadily shorter. I hate the wintery darkness with a vengeance. Yet I know that our life here, in this flat, has many advantages: safe, warm, comfortable; close to the shops; no worries about maintenance. We are so lucky.*

And I remain split. Writing this is schizophrenic. I live in two worlds. Is Gerard doing that too? In a different way, I think. A few days ago he started to put our oldest photographs into albums. He wants to make a new album, a chronological one, as complete as possible. He has found a box of old slides and wants to have a small selection made into photos. We often talk about "the old days."

I wonder if writing this is a way of distancing myself from the here and now? Or is it a return to something I deliberately pushed away a long time ago? I can hear myself complaining to Charles. "Everything I see I start to describe in my head! I don't want to do that any longer. I just want to live!" He couldn't help. Did he even hear what I said? I assumed it was an occupational thing and that, since I was no longer a journalist, it would disappear. But it never disappeared; it just changed.

Burwood is a red, velvet tablecloth; wallpaper scattered with blue roses; a fiercely flowered carpet; and plastic flowers under a glass dome on the mantelpiece. There is also a double bed with a dip in the middle and a landlady with a black bun on the back of her beady-eyed head. She wanted "key money," which I had never heard of before. Flip had. Ten pounds in addition to the first rent of 15 pounds: a fortune! "It's a guarantee in case we damage anything. If all goes well, we'll get it back once we leave."

CHAPTER 7

While we were living in Auburn we had made enquiries about how to get a divorce in Australia. We wanted to get married as quickly as possible. We discovered that this would be a costly affair. First, you needed to hire a solicitor, who then appointed a barrister, a lawyer who had access to the courts. All the barrister did, after all the relevant papers had been deemed satisfactory, was to ask the judge for permission to grant a divorce. The judge then pronounced the verdict that had been established long ago. It took all of ten minutes. For this the barrister was paid a tidy sum and of course the solicitor had to be paid too. We were determined to get the money together somehow, which we did do, though it took a lot of time. Even though we scraped and saved as much as we could, it took almost two years before we were officially married.

The Sunday after we had moved to Burwood the sun shone. The day turned into a holiday. First, we went to our new factory in Roseville. The trip by train was quite long. To get onto the North Shore line, we had to change at a busy station called Strathfield, where there were connecting trains every ten minutes. Roseville station was hidden behind rose-covered walls. When we had crossed the inevitable wooden stairs and bridge across the train tracks, Flip pointed out our front door to me. "Great, huh? We're right opposite the station." We bounced down the stairs and crossed the narrow, two-laned and traffic-infested Pacific Highway. "It runs all the way to Brisbane."

Flip opened a green door adjacent to a shop window, which was covered by grey blinds: a long, narrow corridor with the dentist on the right. We went up the stairs at the end of the hall. Our workshop was large and elongated, with windows on either side. In front of the front-facing window stood a long table and a few chairs. A corner of the other side of the room was partitioned off to shoulder height, and a gap between the partition and the wall functioned as a doorway. Our office. There I found a desk with a phone on it and an electric heater. Next to the back window in the main area was a glass door. This gave access to a narrow balcony with a door at the back, which opened onto a neatly kept toilet with washbasin. I was thrilled and speechless.

"We don't need to buy anything much," said Flip, "I think we should get an electric kettle and cups and things, we have to be able to offer that to our staff. I want to have a good seamstress and a junior whom we'll teach the trade. The sewing machines will arrive tomorrow. They're a great deal better than those dinosaurs in Auburn. Have you seen that there is a neon light above the table?"

"It's just perfect," I said, "And all ours? I can't believe it."

After Roseville, we journeyed on to Mosman, where Henk lived together with his girlfriend Odette, whom we had never met. Henk had told us to take the train to St Leonards, and to catch the bus from there.

We had never been to that part of the city. We had studied the map and discovered that Mosman was located on the water of Middle Harbour. And that the street in which Henk lived was called Ellamatta Avenue, and was close to the peninsula "Bradley's Head." St. Leonard's was no more than three stops from Roseville, in the direction of the centre of town. Next to the station stood a large hospital complex, The North Shore Hospital. The Pacific Highway here was considerably wider.

Sitting in the bus, we drove uphill through broad, shining streets. Every few minutes we glimpsed strips of glittering, blue water through downward sloping side streets. There were trees and neatly kept gardens. This was my own familiar Sydney again: light, open, with the harbour and ocean nearby. We got off at a bright, green bowling field, surrounded by vigorously flowering pink and purple plants. Ten or more elderly ladies in blindingly white outfits (complete with white shoes and white linen hats) were using wooden hammers to hit heavy black balls through tiny wooden hoops: croquet.

Behind the field, was a sloping sea of red roofs and behind them blue water and the harbour bridge, shimmering as if it were made of silver. You could smell the sea here. Ellamatta Avenue was a dead-end street containing at that time four or five stately sandstone villas. Shoulder-high balustrades made of stone, topped by thick, gnarled trees enclosed the first two. It was indescribably quiet. The only sounds were the rustling of leaves and chirping of birds.

Henk was standing waiting for us near the dilapidated wooden fence of the third house. "All faded glory," he remarked, in answer to my jubilation, "Most of the houses here are split up into flats and are pretty neglected." This did not dampen my enthusiasm.

Henk took us through the back garden – yellow, parched grass and weeds, and the same washing line as we had in Auburn – to an open double, front door at the top of four grey stone steps at the side of the house. We entered a large, marble hallway, not particularly clean, and covered in a woefully threadbare, red carpet. To the right was a long, dark, empty hall with a row of closed doors and at the end a light rectangle, which framed a washing line far in the distance. To the left was a black, ornate, Victorian door, which led to a nice, spacious flat, Henk told us.

We went up a flight of stairs, also covered in a threadbare carpet with ornate balustrades, which turned abruptly halfway up. We found ourselves in a long, carpeted corridor. It looked a good deal more respectable than the hall below. Another row of doors with here and there a nameplate and at the end another flight of stairs. "We have two rooms and use of the bathroom and kitchen," Henk said, opening the first door.

Henk's living room is high and light and has a built-in balcony. The floor creaks ominously there, but behind the glass back wall the light dances on the copper treetops, which look so close you could touch them. The whole room is beige, the walls, the floor, the wicker chairs, the blonde table.

Against this décor Odette stands out like a flaming hibiscus flower. She is wearing an ankle-length housecoat of flaming red with wide sleeves, fringed with gold tassels. She has ebony hair tied in a bun low in her neck. She has huge, shining eyes, which are so black you cannot see the pupils, fringed by impossibly thick eyelashes. Her eyebrows have been shaved and redrawn in thin, black lines and she wears deep blue eye shadow with a hint of gold in the corners. Her mouth is bright red and she has beautiful, even, white teeth. She is tall, much taller than I am and quite plump.

She immediately envelops me in her exotic arms, all welcoming warmth and sympathy. Henk has told her about our Auburn woes. Odette is French; she works at the French consulate. She was born in Egypt, in Cairo, and talks about Cairo with such worldly-wise wit and animation she makes me feel like a toddler, glimpsing an adult's world. How and where she and Henk met remains a mystery. But that there is a strong, mutual and fiery attraction between them is blindingly obvious.

We are served a delicious meal (silver and crystal, embroidered linen napkins – I had almost forgotten there were people who lived this way!) and drink golden Australian wine. And later that evening we discover that Odette plays bridge with great skill and shrewdness. Henk's ability is on a par with ours.

CHAPTER 8

Ellamatta Avenue and the tie factory

T**he experienced seamstress** whom Flip hired was called Della. Della was sturdily built, bespectacled and of indeterminate age. She had a large mass of pepper and salt curls. She was married, but had no children, and she called her husband "me old man." She had a sunny temperament. She hummed while sewing. From the start, she clearly felt at home with us. She mothered me and became an adviser to Flip. Did we need a junior member of staff? She could get someone for us straightaway! She had a young, next-door neighbour who would be perfect for the job. The next day, she brought Lizzie along, a scrawny, shy 15 year-old who followed Della's order without complaint.

At exactly ten in the morning, Della stopped sewing and loudly announced the first tea break, a signal to Lizzie to drop whatever she was working on and grasp the kettle. While Lizzie made tea, Della would, every morning, take a strong headache powder, called a Bex Powder: evil-looking stuff in a garish yellow box. This was preventive, she explained, because you never know… The tea break lasted exactly half an hour. At 12 o'clock it was lunchtime. Then Lizzie would again make tea while Della shoved her work aside in a decided manner and deposited a package of sandwiches on the table. At three o'clock the second tea break would follow and at exactly 4.45 everything would be tidied up. Lizzie was presented with the broom that we had found in the balcony cupboard and would sweep the factory energetically. The fact that Flip and I would work on for a few hours was irrelevant. At five o'clock our staff would leave and our workshop would always look spick and span.

Every Monday morning Della would pack Flip's tie suitcase and wave to him from the window as he crossed the street. Della liked order and regularity. It was her idea to deliver whatever was ready every Monday morning and then to pick up new work. No more irregular batches. And Klipper was happy to comply. There was more than enough work; we were given more than we could handle.

We decided to take work home in the weekends. Cutting, trimming, and turning didn't need to be done in Roseville, after all. It seemed to us the only sensible way of increasing our output, and ever since we had moved to Burwood our Sunday expeditions had stopped.

The third Friday: I see Flip and I hoisting our full suitcase of ties into the net above the heads of two newspaper-reading commuters. The train is packed. We are standing, squashed amongst other long-suffering passengers. I see us on a damp platform in Strathfield, drowsily waiting for our connection. We are too tired to talk. We watch the train from which we have just alighted chug slowly into the rocky tunnel on its way to the city.

"The suitcase!" I scream.

"Damn it!" Flip roars, sprinting pointlessly down the platform in the direction of the departing train.

"Fifty dozen Klipper ties!" I am running after him, weeping. What if we are going to have to pay for the loss? "The station master!" We race to the station office, and find a mountain of a man with hands like coal shovels. He listens, ponderously shaking his head, while Flip explains the enormity of the disaster that has befallen us. He languidly picks up the phone: it seems that the train has already left the next station.

"I'll call Central," he says. He is quite sympathetic, but so slow! I am almost hopping with impatience. He mumbles into the phone and turns thoughtfully to us.

"They'll ring me back. It'll be another ten minutes before the train arrives there," and he placidly turns his attention to some paperwork.

Ten minutes become fifteen, then twenty. "It takes time to search a train," he says, "We'll just have to be patient." At Flip's desperate urging, he rings again, half an hour later. "You're in luck," he announces benevolently, "They found it. You can pick it up on Monday morning. Lost Property Department in Central Station."

"Monday!!" we moan in chorus. "Monday," he repeats ruthlessly, "They are shut over the weekend." And that was that. All our pleading has no effect; we return to Burwood empty-handed.

"I've had enough of this!" Flip announces, the minute we sit down, exhausted, at our red, velvet-covered table, "This little farce is going to cost us a fortune. We'll lose two whole days! You know what? We're just going to live in Roseville, in our workshop, it's perfectly doable."

"But we're not allowed to, the contract says that explicitly."

"How will anyone find out? I'm going to rent a van tomorrow and we'll take our mattress and other things over there. We just have to hide the bedclothes every morning before Della arrives. Think of the money it'll save us. No more rent, no more travel costs. And of course we'll try to find a place in the neighbourhood as soon as we can." I may have become a numb wreck, but crises do wonders for Flip. He is beaming with optimism again. "I'm going to give notice straightaway!"

The very next evening we slept in our office. We had to improvise a bit. We washed very early every day using the washbasin in our toilet. This is also where I did our washing in the weekends. I hung it up on Saturday evenings, as soon as the blinds of the front window were hermetically closed, on a line that Flip hung through the factory and took down late on Sunday evenings. We didn't cook. We had fish and chips or ate steak and eggs in a shady little café on the opposite side of the station bridge.

I never discovered whether Della knew. I wouldn't have been surprised. She continued to be the same cheerful, loyal employee, well versed in workers' rights, which, she once explained to me, had been so hard won in the past. We did tell Henk. He had helped us find the workshop, after all. He laughed: "If you can keep it a secret, good luck to you!"

"Only till we've found somewhere else." But finding somewhere else wasn't easy. The weeks passed. How long we camped in Roseville I can't remember exactly. What I do remember is that shortly before Christmas, on a warm summer evening just as I was folding the washing, Henk rang. "Okay, kids, the downstairs flat is going to be empty soon. The rent is very reasonable. Half of what you paid in Burwood. There's a kitchen and use of the shower and laundry. If you're quick..."

At nine o'clock Monday morning Flip arrived on the doorstep of the realtor who managed the house on Ellamatta Avenue, in Mosman. It became the most exciting Christmas of our lives. One afternoon, we bought a few second-hand pieces of furniture, a table with four chairs and a vast, somewhat shaky wardrobe with a large oval-shaped mirror on the outside of the door, and a bed, our first bed.

Ellamatta Avenue: the haven behind the left door of the downstairs hall. A one-room flat as large as a ballroom! There is a high, dirty grey ceiling with cherubs and bunches of grapes adorning the four corners. There is a broad, bay window, which looks out on the part of the garden housing the trees that touch Henk's balcony. There is an arched opening to our kitchen, which must once have been a red-tiled veranda. The old, waist-high banisters are still there. A wooden wall with a row of small windows has been built along them. Under the windows there is a sink with a worktop where four gas rings reside. Rows of planks serve as kitchen cupboards.

The shower we share is right at the end of the empty corridor, opposite our front door. It is a long, narrow room with a boiler into which you have to put coins. Directly opposite the shower is an extravagantly large laundry; miles of worn cement. In addition to the essential copper, which is for general use, there is a large, ancient and indescribably dirty stove.

I have never felt richer than when we moved into the flat in Ellamatta Avenue. We put the table in the bay window, the wardrobe against the wall dividing the kitchen and main room, and our bed in the corner opposite, so far away that it was almost as if we had a separate bedroom, we thought. Later, when we had a little more money, we would buy easy chairs and create a lounge area. There was more than enough room, we agreed. In the meantime we revelled in what we had: a real flat. A cool, spacious dream of an apartment close to the sea, where we could forget the ties, where we could cook and wash, and finally take a shower whenever we felt like it.

Henk explained that we shared our floor with a couple with a grown-up son who had a living-room, kitchen and two bedrooms (all connecting to the empty corridor); and with Tom who lived in the last room in the hall and who used the stove in the laundry to cook. Tom, Henk told us, was the legal owner of the house.

Above us lived Adrie and Frans Schillmoller, Dutch immigrants of Indonesian descent, whom we met through Henk and Odette. He was small, clearly Jewish and worked in the jewellery trade, and she was tall, blonde and did something in cosmetics. She always wore strong perfume. The perfume is what I remember, the woman wearing it remains vague. But we liked them. On Henk's floor lived an old lady called Miss McGillicuddie, whom I would later get to know well. On the attic floor there was also a flat in which a young English couple lived, whose name I have forgotten.

We spent the Christmas holidays exploring our surroundings. We discovered that Taronga Park Zoo, Sydney's beautiful zoo, built against thickly wooded hills, was situated on Bradley's Head. Walking distance from us. We discovered that under the dark trees at the end of the dead-end part of Ellamatta Avenue nestled a private hospital, a small, extremely expensive private hospital. And behind this were sports fields, on the top of a windy plateau of rock, which gradually descended, stairway-like, into a park and tree-lined streets. These meandered into the depths like corkscrews towards a wide harbour beach called Balmoral. The view was breathtaking. Balmoral Beach lies opposite the entrance to Sydney Harbour. From our sports fields, around which a path had been created, you could see the Heads: misty giants surrounded by deep blue water.

On Bradley's Head Road, around the corner, stood a modern, redbrick, stone Catholic church. The house opposite ours, to which the washing line belonged, turned out to be its presbytery. Behind the garden that our bay window overlooked was a dead-ended alley. This started in a street called Effingham Street, which led to Middle Head Road, a street that would later become very important for us. Middle Head Road was the tail end of a busy road that ran straight through the nearby shopping centre (and still does). The shopping centre housed only small shops, but these supplied everything we needed, and we loved them. We also discovered that the quickest way to get from Mosman to the city was to travel by ferry, over the water, from Mosman Wharf or to take the zoo ferry from Taronga.

Once we were settled in Mosman, we made our last payment to our solicitor. We had made an arrangement with him while we were in Auburn. For a year we paid him a small amount every month until all the costs were covered. Only after that would he set the legal machinery in motion, which would eventually lead to my official divorce from Charles Ruys.

CHAPTER 9

First pregnancy

It must have been the end of February. It is impossibly hot. I am bent over our kitchen sink, early in the morning, being violently sick. I had realised a while ago that I had missed a period. Ever since we had moved here we had been taking less care. Flip is ecstatic. I feel his hands on my shaking shoulders. "Oh, sweetheart. You are really going to have to go and see a doctor," he says, "Hospital," remembering Miep Kofman, "North Shore, don't you think?"

We pass the North Shore Hospital every day on our way to work. I see us, walking hand in hand, up the broad driveway for the first time, past long, well-watered flowerbeds. We follow the arrows "Maternity" to a square, red-bricked building with large, high windows. We are nevertheless promptly directed to an old, wooden building a considerable distance away.

We enter a large waiting room with long, wooden benches where it smells overwhelmingly of disinfectant. In the corner stand old-fashioned, waist-high scales with sliding weights. A row of wooden doors that, it turns out, give access to examination rooms and, behind glass, a small office containing a friendly young woman who does her best to make us feel comfortable. We fill out a form. Shortly afterwards I enter just such an examination room and am examined by a young doctor. I am declared "pregnant." The girl in the office tells me that I need to come back here once a month with a little bottle of urine. She encourages us to go together to the first information evening and to register together for pregnancy gym classes (we do.).

"The morning sickness will pass," the doctor says airily, "Some women suffer more from it than others." Clearly, I am the kind that suffers from it! I throw up violently every morning at our kitchen sink. After that I feel normal for a while until we get into the bus, when the nausea starts rising again from somewhere in the region of my toes, reaching my throat by the time we arrive in St Leonards. Usually, Flip, who is constantly urging me to breathe deeply, succeeds in getting me off the bus without mishap. In the fresh air, the nausea subsides – except for the one time that it doesn't, and an irresistible wave erupts onto the pavement of the station. Flip tenderly wipes the sweat from my forehead, ignoring with dignity the curious glances of passers-by.

The last part of our journey in the train is the worst: the smell of the tightly packed bodies, the heat. Flip always wrestles through the crowds until he has found a place beside a window where I can sit. "Not long now, darling, just another five minutes, just keep on taking deep breaths."

As soon as the train arrives in Roseville, we fly down the stairs and across the road to our front door, where I can collapse in our office bathroom, unutterably grateful to be on my knees, leaning against a cool, porcelain toilet seat. After that I am usually free of nausea for a few hours, until lunchtime. In the afternoons I often need to dash to the sanctuary of the bathroom.

Della feeds me dry biscuits and holds my hand. Flip reminds me regularly of the North Shore doctor's final remark: "It almost never lasts longer than four months." But after my fourth month has come and gone I am still throwing up with gusto, in the mornings, afternoons and even occasionally in the evenings. Moreover, I have developed a strange oversensitivity to the smell of roasting meat and to everything that resembles perfume (I have to make a quick getaway whenever I encounter Adrie Schillmoller).

Poor Flip is forced to become a vegetarian. He scours the shops to find a bar of soap that has no smell, and scrubs our kitchen floor on Saturday evenings when I am safely tucked in bed with a bucket. He steers me, taking a wide berth, past cafes, fish and chip shops and chemists, waving a folded newspaper to keep me cool. He grows thinner and thinner as my tummy expands.

One Tuesday morning, after a particularly turbulent Monday, he suddenly announces briskly that I am going to stay home from then on. I burst into tears. "I can't! The factory can't do without me!"

"We'll be fine without you. I've already talked to Della about it, you're not travelling to Roseville for the next little while."

I feel betrayed and abandoned, like a piece of ballast that has to be thrown overboard. I get back into bed, weeping, feeling totally alone, and promptly fall asleep. I wake up with a strange feeling of liberation. I am no longer nauseous; it must be about ten in the morning. I contemplate the long, glittering winter day ahead of me. What does a normal housewife do with such a day? Washing, I decide – there is still a basket full of dirty washing.

That day I meet Miss McGillicuddie for the first time, in the laundry. She must have been about seventy. She is tall, extremely thin and straight as an arrow. She is dressed in a dark, pencil skirt and a white, frilly blouse with a dark blue cardigan. She wears a string of pearls around her long, wrinkled neck. She has silver grey, carefully styled hair with a blue sheen. Her face is a network of wrinkles covered in a thick layer of powder that is a shade too light; she wears red-purple lipstick and has lacquered nails in the same colour. In her shaking fingers she holds a watering can. Miss M. is a passionate gardener. In a small corner of the garden next to the washing line, bordered by little palisades, she grows sweet pea in rows that are marked by tiny poles against which the flowers climb. Clouds of butterfly flowers in fairy colours…I would see her there every day, watering her flowers, tying them up and spraying them, while she talked to them gently. Sometimes she would be on her knees, weeding, or she would just stand quietly observing or walk with small, elegant steps amongst the rows.

That morning my sudden appearance gives her a start. She looks at me with large, appalled eyes and dashes into the dark hallway, without saying a word. Miss M. was as shy as a bird and always stayed that way. Later she would occasionally offer me a bunch of sweet pea, with never more than a few mumbled words, after which she would immediately slip away like a shadow. If she wasn't holding garden implements she rubbed both her thumbs incessantly against the tops of her index fingers, as if she was testing an invisible piece of cloth. According to Henk, Miss M. was the last of an old and once extremely wealthy colonial family.

I then encountered the mysterious Tom. He was just exiting his room as I was walking to the laundry. A short, stocky, middle-aged man with arms that seemed far too long for his somewhat squat and hunched body. He had thin brown hair, which grew far back on his large skull. He had broad shoulders and almost no neck, a large, red nose and elongated, brown eyes, which blinked vehemently. He was wearing pants that had seen better days and that were held up with a rope around his waist. Above this he wore a singlet that had once been white. I startled Tom too. He scuttled back into his room like a mole, but at least he answered my "Good morning" with a vague murmur.

I would later discover that Tom slept till midday almost every day. After that he would potter about, yawning and complaining loudly, doing mysterious things on the back veranda that was crammed full of old junk and where, when dusk fell, occasional possums would drop down along the veranda railings. Tom filled his days waiting for the pub in the shopping centre to open. Then he donned a respectable suit and disappeared, to return after closing time, usually singing and somewhat dishevelled. He would prepare a warm meal for himself on the stove in the laundry, which took a large part of the

CHAPTER 9

evening, and would then dive back into bed as happy as a lark. This same Tom would often, when I was highly pregnant, take the basket of wet washing out of my hands and carry it downstairs for me.

Miss M., Tom and I formed the home front in Ellamatta Avenue. All the other occupants left the house at the crack of dawn. It took me a while to get used to that. Instead of enjoying myself, I felt guilty. I had the luxury of time to go shopping at my ease, to walk, to cook, to read in the afternoons and even sometimes take a nap if I needed one; to listen to the radio (the first thing Flip and I had bought when we left Auburn). It took me over a week to start feeling happier. I still felt nauseous, but I vomited a great deal less. And in the evenings when Flip came home I usually felt quite reasonable and we could have dinner together. Flip too began to look better.

On the 27th of April 1953, my divorce decree came through, the so-called "decree nisi." The "nisi" meant "unless," indicative of the fact that you could still change your mind. It was presumed that you would try to find a solution for your marital problems in the period between the "decree nisi" and the "decree absolute," which under normal circumstances was filed a full year later. Only then were you completely free and could you remarry if you wished. In our case, because I was pregnant, our solicitor submitted a request for the decree absolute to be accelerated. As a result, it was pronounced one month later, on 27th May 1953 and on the 30th of May we were married. The registry office in Sydney where the civil marriage took place was at that time located in Macquarie Street, not far from St. Mary's Cathedral.

The sun is shining; it is a glorious day. I am wearing a new, brown, woollen dress and a corsage of white orchids, an unexpected gift from my husband-to-be. Flip is dressed in the only tailor-made suit he owns (originally from Holland) and is wearing a white carnation in his buttonhole. He has bought, with the help of Frans Schillmoller, real wedding rings, a luxury I had not dreamed of. When I had married Charles, there was no question of wedding rings, it did not occur to us to buy them. The rings are not engraved, this would have been too expensive, and they are slender, but they are wedding rings! I am so proud of them. Our names, incidentally, were engraved in them on our wedding day last year. To commemorate...

Henk and Adrie Schiffmoller are our witnesses. It is a short, succinct ceremony. We nevertheless emerge from the office beaming. We are intensely happy. I seem to recall that Henk and Adrie then had to dash off to their respective places of work. Wasn't it around lunchtime? Flip and I strolled down to Circular Quay, Flip having taken the day off. We take the ferry to Manly. This is our honeymoon, we laugh! I remember the sun on the water and leaning together over the railing and no trace of morning sickness. At the end of the afternoon we return to Mosman.

It was Flip's idea to split our kitchen into two and to turn the half without the sink into a baby room. "Just two wooden partitions with an opening in between where we can hang a curtain, so that the baby has its own space. I'll ask Della." Henk suggested we ask the Englishman on the attic to help, as he was in the construction business. I'll call him Jim, though I'm not sure that was his name. I can't recall his face, just his amiability and warmth. Jim acquired wood for us and one weekend he and Flip set about hammering. The result was a small, light, happy room with a window in the back wall; all the other walls were yellow. Just before Janneke was born we added a baby bed and a commode, they fit beautifully. The arched opening between the kitchen and room was indeed closed off with a heavy green curtain with golden stripes, an excellent muffler. We felt as rich as kings.

And then Flip came home with a car. We had fantasised for a long time about having a car again, our own means of transport. How often had our conversations ended with "When we have a car again…."? I don't know how much he paid for it, not much, I believe. He had found it on Parramatta Road. It was an ancient Morris Oxford and it was green. It changed our lives. Flip no longer needed to race in the mornings to catch the bus. And in the weekends our action radius increased vastly. We roamed around Sydney, visiting its far-flung suburbs. We discovered that Manly could be reached easily by land too, via the Spit Bridge, which spanned the narrowest part of Middle Head. The Spit is an odd, low-lying peninsula, fringed by water sports shops and jetties for pleasure yachts.

We discovered Kuringai, a vast nature resort that is part of the city, where you can walk, fish and picnic. The winding road that led to it, traversing steep hills and passing naked walls of rock, offered breath-taking views. My favourite outing became driving all the way to Palm Beach along a long ocean road, which twisted and turned past rocks as large as fortresses. You drive past grapefruit-coloured beaches with fairytale names like Collaroy, Narrabeen, Warriewood, Mona Vale, Newport and Avalon (all Sydney suburbs) and end at Palm Beach and Barren Joey Head where, on the one side, the ocean pounds the rocks and on the other a gigantic cove nestles called Pittwater, calm water and innumerable sailing boats. The colours are dazzling, ranging from sapphire to ice green. White crests of foam swirl around dark brown and grey masses of rock. And shimmering over everything is that silvery light. No matter how far we went, there was always more to discover about Sydney.

CHAPTER 10

Janneke

Henk turned up unexpectedly at our front door one evening in late August. "I'm going to move. I've been offered a job at the Dutch consulate. Time to move on. Odette and I are splitting up. She has decided to go back to Cairo," with a faint smile.

I am devastated, but Flip tells me later he is not surprised. It is true that Odette could react quite sharply during our regular bridge evenings; that she was always finding fault with Henk, who never reacted to her barbs, who always maintained the same sunny demeanour. But Odette's opinion of men in general wasn't very high. She saw them, I think, as oppressors, as dim potentates who deserved to be opposed. And yet, there was that electric spark between the two of them..."No tragedy," Henk said soothingly, "We're splitting as good friends. Friends of mine whom you'll like are moving into our flat. Oh, and the downstairs flat, the big one, will be free soon too. Any idea what we can do with it?"

I don't think it occurred to us to move in ourselves – too expensive, too ambitious. But I did immediately say: "Hiek! Hiek and Jan. They want so much to move to Sydney. Wouldn't it be wonderful…?" "I'll send them a telegram," said Flip.

The next morning Hiek rang us (there was a coin-operated phone for general use in the downstairs hall). Hiek and I wrote every week. We followed each other's ups and downs closely. I knew that the caravan was proving a disappointment. That Jan wasn't very happy in his job in Katoomba and that despite the beauty of their surroundings they were getting a little fed up with the Blue Mountains; they weren't making any headway, they felt.

A day later Jan came to Sydney to take a look at the flat. Flip came home and went with him to the real estate agent. Two weeks later Hiek and I were hugging each other, overjoyed.

From that moment Ellamatta Avenue was transformed. Hiek was bursting with energy and clever ideas. For starters, we made clear agreements: every other week we would each clean the hall, the shower and the toilet. Hiek and Jan tided the back veranda and suddenly the back of the house, including the laundry, became considerably lighter. The little patch of lawn was mown and a few garden chairs materialised along with a small table. The door of Hiek's kitchen, with its high, old-fashioned mantelpiece displaying her jaunty Dutch *boerenbont* mugs, was always open. It became a kind of meeting place for the occupants of the house on their return home. Everyone came to say hello at the end of the day. Hiek soon knew a great deal more about all those people than I did. Miss M. actually talked to her and she also quickly became good pals with Tom. Within a week, Jan found a job as a furniture maker. Frank and Paul went to the local primary school and Hiek herself began to explore the options for an office job somewhere in the neighbourhood. Life was good.

I became heavier and heavier. My navel turned inside out. I slept with an extra pillow under my tummy. I was hideous; no pregnant woman had ever been as hideous as I was!

Sunday 1 November is a blisteringly hot day. There isn't even a cool corner in the house. I drag myself around, grumbling and sweating. I still have fifteen days to go! "Let's go to the beach", says Flip, "Avalon."

"But I look so awful!"

"Don't be silly, I'm proud of you." We go. We sit in the shade between the rocks. It is indeed cooler here, but I am still envious of the children splashing in the shallows, shrieking with laughter as they escape from the waves. We stroll a little through a mist of heat and sea foam, I leaning heavily on Flip's arm. When the sun begins to go down, we drive home.

Hiek is cooking eggs and tomatoes in her kitchen, cheerful as always. "Hallo you two, was it lovely and cool at the beach?" She and Flip had become fast friends long ago; she, too, had not been surprised by our relationship. At that moment I feel water start to flow down my legs. I look down astonished at the pool, which is starting to form around my sandals.

"Well, love," says Hiek, "It looks as if your baby is coming; your waters have broken."

"But my book says it doesn't happen like this!" I am very indignant. "And I don't feel anything. Oh Hiek, your kitchen floor is a mess, give me a mop."

"Oh no, you don't," says Hiek, and to Flip, who is speechless, "I would call the hospital if I were you." He dashes out of the room. Hiek takes me by the arm and leads me to our flat. "We have to go to the hospital immediately," Flip reports. He is uncharacteristically nervous. "Do you feel anything yet?" "No," I say, grumpily, "I need to get changed first. I'm drenched."

Under Hiek's watchful eye, I change my clothes. Flip grabs my suitcase, which has been ready for the past week and we march in procession to the car. The baby is no longer kicking, it is being completely quiet; and nothing else is happening either, absolutely nothing. Hiek waves goodbye to us.

We are allowed to go straight to the maternity building. The porter calls for a nurse who takes my arm as if she is my best friend. "Say goodbye to your husband," she instructs, when we have reached the lift. And to Flip: "You can phone whenever you want, but it will be a while before we have any news." Flip puts his arms around me and kisses my forehead. "Well – see you later." "See you," I say gloomily.

Upstairs in "Delivery" everyone I meet is cheerful and relaxed, nowhere is there a hint of panic or haste. My file is found, papers are filled out, there is some chatting. It all proceeds in the most leisurely way. Finally I am assigned to a ridiculously young girl, who takes me to the showers. "Why don't you take a nice shower? I'll wait here," says the girl.

A shower? Oh well, if she isn't worried, why should I be? I shower. I am given a hospital robe. I am taken to a delivery room and placed on a high bed. On the bars above my head hangs a black mask on a long black cord. I am shaved. Then the head nurse comes to examine me, she listens at length to the baby's heartbeat and finally she nods at me, looking pleased. "Just keep on lying there quietly. How does it feel inside?"

"Fine," I say, feeling like a three-year-old.

"Well, all you need to do is relax. It'll all take its own course in a little while." Now it is my turn to nod. I had read Grantley Dick Read's book *Natural Childbirth* thoroughly and thought I knew exactly what was going to happen and how important it was to stay relaxed now. I know for sure that my muscles are well trained: I hadn't done my series of prenatal exercises day in day out for nothing, after all!

"Do you know what this is for?" she asks, showing me the little black mask, "If it starts to hurt you just put it briefly over your nose and mouth and take a deep breath. It helps. You don't need to do anything else. Just take the mask and breathe. Okay? We're very busy this evening, but we'll come and look in on you regularly." She disappears.

It is all rather disillusioning. No army of doctors and nurses; just me, the bed and the mask. "Relax," I tell myself strictly. That is the magic word that I have been repeating for months now: re-lax. A little while later a definite something starts down in my belly. I try to remember the drawings from the book. "Just muscles contracting and releasing," I whisper. And then, without warning, it becomes extremely violent. I grab the mask and do exactly what I had been told, I breathe deeply and suddenly I become two people. Myself, who have become fluid and float somewhere near the ceiling, and the other person below, whom I look down on with interest: the woman having a baby. I feel the baby pushing its way into the world. I "listen" to it, but there is an immense distance between the ceiling and the bed.

I know I am very busy and must concentrate at all costs, that this needs my full attention. I hear myself, somewhere in the region of the ceiling, giving encouraging instructions to the woman below: "Just relax, go with the flow, don't fight it." Pain? Yes, there is pain, but it stays behind glass, a veiled pain, a dark, mysterious ebb and flow of pain. I have no idea of time. And then it becomes a relentless, astounding primal force. Something completely outside my control that picks me up and raises me higher and higher.

Suddenly there really is an army of people around me. I can't see them, but I hear their hurried footsteps, voices. My bed is being shifted. Above me a blinding lamp is switched on. Someone takes the mask out of my hand and pushes it down hard over my nose. "Well done, love. Take deep breaths." I try to push it away. What on earth is this person doing? Someone else is doing something with my legs. I feel them being pulled up and I feel cold steel around one ankle. I swim through a sea of light and sudden, intense, very real pain. I am deeply indignant. I have suddenly become a thing, an object under a microscope. "Get away, leave me alone!"

"Very good, love. You're doing very well. Come on, push." I push. I hear myself groaning, pushing. A man's voice: "If you feel the urge again now, don't push – do not push, do you hear me? Try to take a deep breath, but don't push. OK? Here it comes. Now." I feel rubber-coated hands between my legs, and a powerful, all-consuming pressure. And then an explosion: a warm, fast flowing something, which leaves my body on a long sigh; for a moment, an indescribable feeling of pleasure, a delicious, soft, wet warmth. And almost at the same time I hear a baby cry.

"You clever little thing," that same male voice says, "That was beautiful. You have a little daughter." I hear myself laughing and crying at the same time.

"Do you know my name?" I ask, suddenly fearful, "You won't give her to the wrong mother, will you?"

"Don't worry, Mrs. Melman. We'll give her an identification bracelet straightaway. But we still have a few things to finish up here. You were almost too quick for us!"

I don't remember what happened after that. I only recall the baby in my arms. A soft, warm, tiny mound of humanity with a head fully covered in pitch-black, furry hair. The little mouth yawns and makes sucking movements. There is a tiny white strip with the word "Melman" on it around her wrist. With the baby in my arms, I am placed on a stretcher and suddenly Flip appears; just like that, upstairs in the delivery room corridor.

"Half past nine!" he cries, "She arrived at half past nine already! Hiek said it was far too early to ring, but I couldn't bear it!"

"Didn't we do well?" I am suddenly wide awake, "Isn't she adorable?" My nurse places the baby in his arms and he looks down at her with such tenderness in his eyes that tears suddenly begin to stream down my cheeks. "I am so happy," I sob, "I am so happy."

CHAPTER 11

Dr Maine and asthma

WE CALL HER Marianne. "Marjanneke," says Flip. "Janneke," I suggest, and Janneke she stayed. We remain in the secure, happy cocoon of the hospital for a week, after which we are sent home.
And then, without cause, terror strikes; an irrational panic, which wells up from somewhere deep inside me. Here I am, with a tiny, new being in my arms, and she is totally dependent on me! I can't cope. I don't know what I am doing; I am completely unprepared, incompetent. And somewhere out there is a vengeful god waiting to pounce without warning at any moment. I need to be vigilant at all times, alert and constantly on my guard. My baby could catch a cold, get pneumonia, choke, be bitten by a spider or snake; she is utterly defenceless. "Take her outside straightaway," the hospital nurse had said on saying goodbye, "Isn't it wonderful to have a summer baby?"

Wonderful?! I hate it. But I nevertheless obediently place her in the pram, tightly packed in a little blanket. I seal the mosquito net as hermetically as I can with rows of clothes pegs so that no gruesome insect can slip through a miniscule hole. And then I peer through the net, fearful and helpless. Is she still alive? Is she still breathing? Is she really lying on her side the way she is supposed to? My instinct is to lie down beside the pram under the trees in order to keep hostile nature at bay. But I force myself, heavy-hearted, to go inside, only to run back outside every ten minutes. I peer through the net with tears in my eyes.

I quake whenever anyone wants to take a look at her. I see Miss M., Tom, all our upstairs neighbours and even Hiek as sources of potential, awful infections, as clouds of harmful bacteria on two legs. I am even relieved when Hiek finds a job and disappears like everyone else from 8 to 6. I don't trust her well-meaning, calming counsel. This isn't Holland, after all! I carry this little life on my shoulders as if I am Atlas bearing the world. Alone.

My baby promptly develops a rash and cries a lot. I am in despair, until I remember the baby health centres I was told about in the hospital. Every suburb in Sydney has a baby health centre: free check-ups and advice. We drive there, me with the baby in my arms, swaddled in a far too hot blanket.

The health centre nurse is small, as round as a tub and, in my eyes, frighteningly old. She has sharp, dark eyes and thick, grey curls. To my horror, she starts by undressing the baby and placing her, completely naked, on the scales without even holding her in place. It is all I can do not to snatch her out of harm's way. "She is wearing far too many clothes!" The nurse says, severely. "That" pointing to the rash, "is Prickly Heat! Just dress her in a thin singlet and a nappy, that's more than enough in this weather. And no blanket!"

"But then she won't stay lying on her side!" I lament.

"Oh yes, she will." She places her in our travel cot, and I watch her competent, wrinkled hands with envy. "Just a sheet. Like this. And after every feed, place her on her other side." The baby stops crying. She does indeed remain obediently on her side. I heave a sigh of relief.

"Keep her in the fresh air as much as possible," the nurse instructs, "And let her lie in the sun every day for one minute, without any clothes on; keep her head in the shade. She needs to sunbathe for a short while. This is very good for babies," with extra stress.

Sunbathe? Is she insane? But I have no other choice than to do what she says. She is the source of all baby wisdom; an all-knowing oracle, a priestess. I am given an orange card with the baby's name, birth weight and the date on it. The first, accusatory sentence reads: "Prickly Heat," and "Sunbathe, 1 minute." The orange card begins to dominate my life. It stands above the kitchen sink, glaring at me reproachfully. It is updated every week: "Weight increase insufficient." "Cries too much."

Terrified, but obedient, and holding a watch tightly in my sweaty hand, I place my naked baby in the sun every day for one minute. And every morning anew I am indescribably relieved when the ritual has been completed and I can replace the clamps of the mosquito net. For about eight weeks I live like a hermit, in complete isolation. I am deaf, blind and mute. The baby, the nurse and I are the centre of the universe.

Flip is a vague, concerned shadow; he performs excellent services, but has no substance for me. He discovers that our baby loves to drive! As soon as she is inside the moving car she stops crying and falls into a deep, ecstatic sleep. We therefore take her for a drive at the strangest times, like midnight when we are close to despair because she keeps on crying even though she has just been fed. We drive around the block and afterwards carry the baby bassinet into the house, gently rocking it. Usually, she keeps on sleeping.

We have in the meantime acquired a different car. Flip has traded in our old Morris and bought a tiny, brand new Renault, a so-called Thriftmaster, on instalment. I barely notice these developments – in my deaf, blind and mute state, as long as we are mobile, I don't care.

"She really isn't getting enough to eat," the oracle tells me, "You're going to have to top up your breastfeeding with a bottle." And I had had such good intentions. To feed her myself, for at least nine months! I become even more depressed. But from the moment we start to bottle-feed her, the baby stops crying. She starts to laugh, gurgle and grow. And I crawl out of my isolation like an embarrassed snail, and finally take a look around me.

That must have been about the time that Flip decided that his career as a tie manufacturer had to end. He had seen an advertisement in the newspaper for a salesman at Ira L & A.C. Berk, the company from which he had bought the Renault 750. He went to talk to them and was promptly hired. How he managed it I don't remember, but he subsequently transferred our tie factory, including the equipment and staff, to someone who was also prepared to pay us "goodwill." Only after all this had been arranged did he tell me what he had done.

I was stunned, but not sorry. Since the arrival of the baby I couldn't have cared less about the ties. And I hadn't the slightest doubt about Flip's abilities as a salesman. I was sure he would quickly become one of the best salesmen they had (and he did!). Moreover, he was given a company car in exchange for the Thriftmaster, another Renault 750, but a more luxurious model. And we suddenly had money! We could buy furniture and (much needed) clothes and lovely things for the baby and baby room. Flip found brand new Swedish furniture, a few easy chairs and a coffee table, a real bookcase, and a couple of standing lamps. Our flat became a real house.

And our baby underwent a metamorphosis. The wiry, black hair disappeared and golden curls framed her head. She had little, golden brown legs and round, pinkish-brown cheeks, bright blue eyes and a mouth like a rose petal. She was soft as velvet and smelled of sunshine, sweet milk, freshly mown grass. She began to pull herself up, to sit, to play. She started teething and eating solid food. "Brains," the nurse instructed, "Only a tea spoon to start off with. And mashed, fresh vegetables." So I bought lambs brains at the butchers and spent hours pealing the creepy, grey mass, mashing spinach and carrots, and squeezing fresh oranges. At that time there was no such thing as tins of baby food.

I think that the time has come to turn "Flip" into "Gerard." It feels more appropriate, now. He had already become "Gerry" to outsiders for some time by then, and the name "Flip" seemed to belong to our early, carefree time together. Things were changing now.

Asthma. The time has also come to write about asthma. While we were still living in Auburn, Gerard would always dismiss his recurrent sneezing as "a little touch of hay-fever, nothing to worry about," until the sneezing turned into a heavy cold which developed into what he himself called "a little bronchitis." Vicks in hot water and inhaling sessions in the evenings followed.

After much urging on my part, and a lot of resistance on his, we finally went to a doctor. Although all my pre-natal care and delivery in a public hospital had been free, a visit to an ordinary GP had to be paid, cash, on departure, to the girl at the desk. The (female) doctor gave him a thorough check-up and told us that he did indeed have bronchitis, but was also suffering from asthma. She sent us home with an expensive dose of penicillin. We did not believe this at the time. "Nonsense," said Gerard, "I just have a tendency to develop bronchitis." The penicillin did the trick. And yet, every now and then there would be a wheezing in his chest, though he shrugged his shoulders at it.

When Janneke was about nine months old I began to get seriously worried. Gerard looked worse; he had lost a lot of weight, moved like an old man and the wheezing in his chest occurred almost constantly now. He was very busy, and often worked in the evenings and sometimes also in the weekends. It was no wonder he was always tired, and yet....

"I really want you to go and talk to Dr. Maine." Dr. Maine was the GP whom I visited, at the recommendation of the baby health centre, for Janneke's shots. He was part of a group practice in the Mosman shopping centre, which consisted of three doctors. He was young, tall and dark, and comfortingly calm. I trusted him unconditionally. Gerard refused: "I don't have the time. It'll pass."

A few days later he came home with lips that were whitish blue. He held tightly to the windowsill, gasping for huge breathes of sea breeze. His fingernails were blue too, I saw. "I'm calling Maine!" I raced to the phone. He turned up a few minutes later. He took one look at Gerard, panting at the window, placed his bag next to our bed and began to prize his fingers off the windowsill. "Come and lie down for a little, mate. I'm going to give you an injection and it will make you feel a lot better very soon." He listened carefully to that heaving, wheezing, squeaking chest. He took out an injection needle. Very slowly, one hand on Gerard's wrist, he injected a colourless fluid and very slowly Gerard's breathing became a little easier, his lips turned a normal colour again and his fingers began to relax.

"Well, well," said Maine, piling pillows behind Gerard's shoulders, "That was quite an impressive asthma attack. I'll give you something to help you sleep. And if you start feeling breathless again, ring me immediately. Okay? Even if it's the middle of the night. I live just round the corner, on Bradley's Head Road. I'll leave you my telephone number," this last remark was directed to me. I nodded gratefully.

I did indeed ring him that night. He arrived within two minutes, wearing a coat over his pyjamas. He again gave Gerard an injection, calmly and without any haste. He talked to him comfortingly. He asked after the baby. He assured me again that I could ring at any time if necessary, day or night. By seven the next morning he was back. Another injection, and he left tablets behind and strict instructions. A few days of rest in bed, leaning up high against the pillows. And if another attack occurred, we were to ring him immediately. "And once this is all over, I want to see you in my practice."

Gerard, extremely pale, and as weak as a baby, did not protest. A few hours later, however, he whispered to me that he could not afford a few days rest: "I don't get paid a cent of salary if I'm sick." "So then we won't have any salary," I said, dauntlessly, "But you are going to do what Maine has ordered!" with brand new authority.

The minute he felt better he became recalcitrant. "I don't have the time to see a doctor. I have asthma, we know that now, right? I just need to learn to live with it."

Two weeks later he suffered another attack, worse – if that were possible – than the first. This time Maine called an ambulance to take him to the North Shore where he was placed in an oxygen tent. He returned home three days later white and shaking, but breathing freely. If I am not mistaken, this happened a second time too. The hospital stints are a vague memory now: didn't I visit him there, by bus, together with Janneke?

What I do recall is that after all these experiences, Gerard was more than willing to subject himself to regular checkups and studied everything that was known about asthma at the time. He was tested for allergies. Dust, feathers, down, animal fur, pollen and a multitude of other airborne seeds were the primary culprits. (I sometimes wonder now what damage the ties did; weird that this did not occur to us at the time). We promptly bought foam rubber pillows and a good vacuum cleaner, which we couldn't really afford. As I have already said, doctor's bills and medication were very expensive, and the bills never seemed to end.

Under the watchful eye of Dr. Maine, Gerard experimented with all kinds of medication and slowly, very slowly, the terrible attacks stopped. Only years later when the first asthma sprays came onto the market, which we called "medihalors" and which he always carried with him, did he learn how to anticipate and prevent every attack. But in those early days we would lie awake, night after night, holding each other like frightened children, listening together. Would the quiet wheezing in his chest change into a raging attack? Would those air passages suddenly become blocked again? Would I need to ring Maine again? Our nights were full of ghosts.

Blissfully, morning would always come, and Janneke would creep giggling into the big bed, falling all over us. An azure sky would appear at our bay window and we would set off, whenever we could, for Balmoral Beach, our own, quiet, neighbourhood beach at the foot of our hill.

Balmoral, with its mighty fig trees lining the boulevard; with its Rocky Point, a mass of rock that split the beach in two and where you could always sit in the sun, protected from the wind, even in the middle of the winter; with its two swimming pools – one large official pool, where you had to pay an entrance fee at that time, surrounded by a walkway on high wooden poles. And a section of beach protected from sharks by a net, near Rocky Point. And the kiddies' pool, which Janneke adored, that had been cut out of the rocks right at the other end, and where the water was knee high. Balmoral, where the dancing water was transparent green and where there were never towering waves that made swimming impossible; and where the Heads stood sentinel eternally, far away in the distance, shrouded and insubstantial, like a half forgotten dream. On Balmoral Beach Janneke stood all on her own for the first time.

Hiek and I together kept the downstairs area of the house clean. We took turns to vacuum and sweep the hall, laundry and back veranda, and scrub the shower and toilet. One wintery Saturday morning I ran through the hall, shivering in my bathrobe, with a towel over my shoulder, on my way to a hot shower. Gerard was still in bed playing horsey with Janneke on his knees.

I open the door of the shower and am met by a penetrating stench. I switch the light on. In the middle of the cement floor lies an enormous pile of soft, evilly shining excrement. A trail of brown droplets, which my bare feet have just missed, leads into the hall. It was my week to clean and I had scrubbed the shower the evening before and had left it sparkling. I gag, squeal and back away, which brings Hiek running out of her kitchen.

"Oh no!" she gasps, "Tom! He got the door wrong. He was pretty drunk last night, didn't you hear him?" I had, but had paid no attention. I run back to our flat, throw Gerard's bathrobe at him, grab Janneke, and point down the hall: "You have got to see this!"

In the meantime a small group of interested onlookers has collected at the shower: Hiek, Jan and the two boys are studying the evidence. Gerard takes a long look, follows the trail of drops to Tom's door and glances at our expectant faces. He squares his shoulders grimly and hammers on Tom's door. This results in a faint groan from inside, but nothing more. "TOM!" Vague mutterings, then silence.

"What the hell does he think he's up to?" Gerard says, and wrenches open the door. A musty, night smell envelops us. Six pairs of astounded eyes survey the interior. Every more or less horizontal surface in Tom's room – table, chairs, floor and bed – is covered with dirty clothing, innumerable shirts, underpants, trousers, coats, sweaters. Littered among the mess are empty beer bottles, overflowing ashtrays, newspapers and towels. A huge brown wardrobe stands next to the bed, its doors gaping, also overflowing with clothes. In the bed lies Tom, blankets and clothes pulled up to his chin, his sparse hair sticking wildly up from his head. He gapes at us, eyes wide and appalled.

"Tom!" Gerard bellows, "Out of that bed! Now! I'm waiting for you." He slams the door shut. Two seconds later Tom materialises clutching, oddly enough, a reasonably clean red, silk bathrobe around himself: "What, what??"

Gerard almost grabs him by the collar: "This is what you did, Tom! You should be ashamed," pointing to the trail of droplets, "And here!" the shower. "Clean up this mess. Now!"

"I couldn't help it," Tom moans, "I'll clean it all up."

"You had better," Gerard says, suddenly breathless. "I will be back to inspect everything in half an hour. And don't let it happen again!" whispering now, which seems to have an even greater impact than the bellowing before.

"Never, never again!" Tom is almost in tears, "It was an accident." Hiek hands him the Dettol we always use and Jan appears with a bucket and mop from the back veranda. "Good luck, Tom!" he grins. At which the six of us beat a retreat.

When Gerard came to take a look half an hour later Tom had indeed cleaned everything up, more or less. He promised again, all abject humility, that something like this would never happen again. Gerard sent him back to bed. Hiek and I quietly cleaned everything again, just for good measure. "That room!" she sighed, "Actually, it's terribly pathetic. We should do something about it, you and I."

I wasn't all that keen, but I knew it would probably be wise. "I've read there's a flea epidemic in Sydney. If we aren't careful..."

"If we give the whole room a thorough spring clean, and wash and tidy all his clothes, it'll be easier for him to keep up with everything after that. I'll talk to him."

The next Saturday was devoted to Operation Tom. Tom himself was delighted, at least to start off with. When he realised how merciless we intended to be (we had started by completely emptying his room and throwing all his dirty clothes on the laundry floor) he began to wring his hands and protest. "Oh my God, if my mother saw this...."

"Never mind, Tom," I said, soothingly, "Everything will be spic and span by this afternoon, you'll see. All of this has to go to the cleaners." He went, as obedient as a child, with his arms full of trousers and coats.

We packed the copper with his underwear and then pulled the table, chairs and a large antique desk into the corridor. We discovered that the wooden floor was covered with a dust-faded, but clearly expensive carpet that it took the two of us to sling over the washing line. Hiek then attacked it with a carpet-beater. Brown clouds of dust engulfed her kerchief-covered head. Miss M. abandoned her sweet pea and fled past us, also wringing her hands. "Unbelievable! But he is still a good boy. You are doing such a good deed, a very good deed."

I emptied a bucket of suds, generously laced with Dettol, over the wooden floor and scoured with abandon. I then scrubbed the wardrobe while Hiek cleaned the windows. We washed masses of sheets, shirts, socks and handkerchiefs, singlets and shorts. The skin of our hands looked white and shrivelled afterwards. But by six o'clock we stood, exhausted but satisfied, in an impeccably neat, sweet-smelling room with Tom at our side, beaming with shy joy.

"You'll keep it like this, won't you Tom? It's much nicer to live in, isn't it?" He swore on his mother's grave that he would mend his ways. And we did indeed find him every Saturday morning busily cleaning, with the door of his room wide open, just as we were. He became Hiek's most devoted slave. He would lie in wait for her in the afternoons so that he could open the gate for her when she came home and could tell her he had done laundry and ironing. He accompanied her to her front door, but never crossed the threshold, not even into the kitchen.

He continued to live his strange life and only asked for a few crumbs of attention every now and then, less from me than from Hiek. But we were good friends and we stayed that way for the six odd years we lived in what was essentially our one-room flat in Ellamatta Avenue.

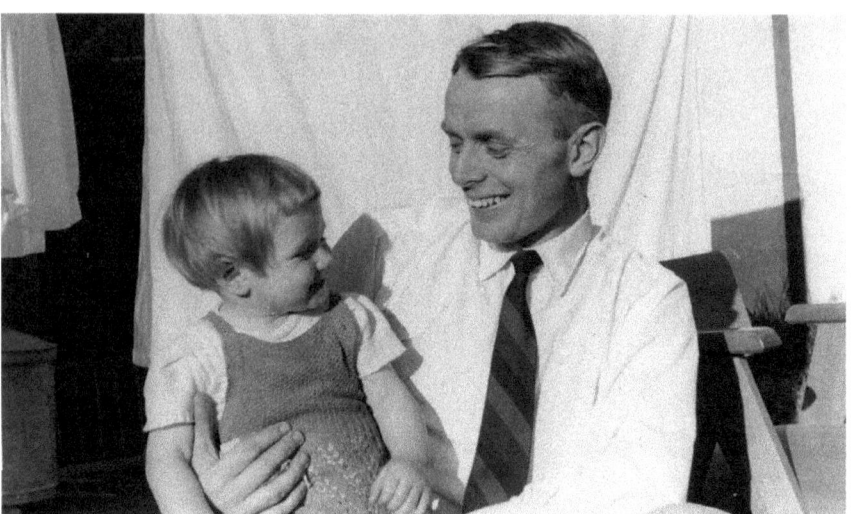

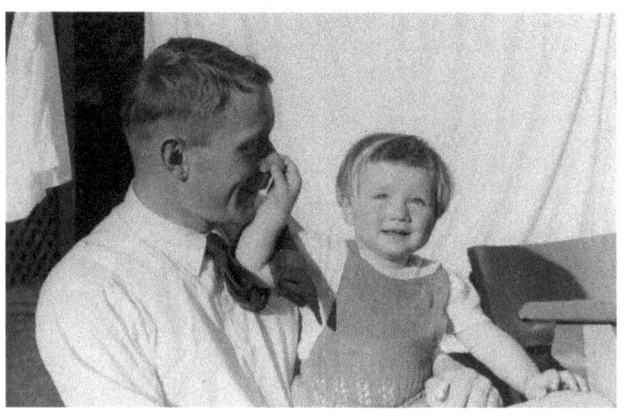

CHAPTER 12

Lindy

I AM NOW 73 *years old and find I am becoming increasingly more insecure. How could I ever have believed the fiction that "the older you get, the more serene and wise?" There are a few exceptions of course, but if you look around you all the evidence points to the contrary. Clearly, I never used to pay enough attention, certainly not to elderly people.*

Why does it make me anxious that Gerard needs to be out unexpectedly for a morning? Is it because I like order and predictability? He plays tennis every Tuesday morning. Why do I feel a vague sense of panic if a phone call heralds a switch to a Thursday morning? Am I suffering from a fear of abandonment – at my age?! Or am I afraid that something might happen to him, he is 76, after all?

It is late November and it is raining. The trees I look down on from the back of our apartment are becoming bare. The autumn foliage is threadbare.

Life in Ellamatta Avenue glowed with sunshine. We were happy and brimming with confidence. We never wondered how we were going to cope, Gerard and I, despite the asthma. (Oddly enough, Gerard would only start worrying about this much later: what would happen to us if he couldn't work?). And despite our modest means. We couldn't save a great deal even though we doggedly tried to. Gerard was a successful car salesman. He received a salary and commission. He seemed unstoppable. He persuaded hesitant customers to buy with the promise of a few free driving lessons, which he would give them himself in his spare time. He came home every day full of funny stories. He was clearly a popular man.

I can't recall rainy days in Ellamatta Avenue. We lived outside. We were the only ones to use the garden, which was sun-drenched, but the trees offered shade when it was hot. I remember strolling peacefully with Janneke in the pram, shopping in a leisurely fashion. I even had time to write letters at the table in the bay window. And in the evenings we could usually eat together quietly and listen to the radio. Music…

And there was Hiek, the best neighbour anyone could wish for. We talked every day. And Henk visited us every now and then. He had a new girlfriend but it wasn't a bed of roses. He usually came over to pour his heart out.

A sunny autumn morning in May: I am vacuum cleaning. Janneke, now a blonde toddler, two and a half, is giving her teddy bear a ride on the vacuum cleaner. I am seven months pregnant. We are delighted with this second baby. A child needs a brother or sister, we felt. And you shouldn't wait too long with that.

I switch off the vacuum cleaner. "We're done! We'll tidy everything up and then go shopping." Janneke tugs at the hose enthusiastically. As I bend down to pull out the plug, I feel something warm dripping down my legs: blood, a large clot of dark blood. I freeze; another clot, and then another.

I am completely on my own in the big house, alone with Janneke. "Leave the vacuum cleaner alone, darling," trying to keep my voice steady, "Mummy has to make a phonecall."

"Teddy can come," Janneke says and skips to the door. She can just reach the doorknob.

Very slowly and with great care, I shuffle into the hall. I sit down heavily in the wicker chair next to the phone. I put a coin into the machine and with trembling fingers ring Maine's practice. I keep my thighs tightly clamped together. "I'm bleeding," I tell the girl at the other end of the line, "I am seven months pregnant and I'm bleeding. Is Dr Maine there?" To my indescribable relief, he comes to the phone. "Lie down immediately. I'm on my way."

"But I'm here on my own, with Janneke. I was just vacuum cleaning," My lips begin to tremble.

"Don't lift anything," he says, "Just lie down on the bed. And don't worry about a thing. I'll be there in a jiffy."

Janneke is jumping up and down impatiently, waving her bear who is bald and scraggly from her constant sucking. "Come on, Mummy!" I take her hand and shuffle carefully into our room. "I have to lie down, sweetie. I'm a little bit sick."

"A little bit sick."

I lie down with great care. "Why don't you put Teddy to bed too? He's a little sick too." She looks at her bear thoughtfully. "Sick too," she decides and runs to her own room. Five minutes later Maine appears at my side. "How much blood have you lost?"

"I don't know," pointing to the trail on my recently cleaned mat. "But I'm still bleeding, I'm soaked."

"I'm not going to examine you. I'm just going to listen to the baby's heartbeat. It's excellent. That's good. I'm going to give you an injection and ring an ambulance. North Shore hospital."

Large tears begin to run down my cheeks. "I can't go to hospital! What about Janneke? What's wrong with me? What is it?" He ties something around my arm and gives me an injection. "I think a piece of the placenta has broken off. Not fatal for the baby, but we do need to be careful now. The longer you can keep the baby with you, the better. Seven months is a bit too early. Just stay lying quietly now." He disappears into the hall. I begin to feel sleepy.

"Mummy," says Janneke. She leans her head against the bed, her thumb in her mouth.

"You need to be a good girl, dinky," I say dreamily, "The doctor will be back soon."

"The ambulance is on its way," I hear Maine's voice, "I also called Ira Berk and left a message for Gerry. And Janneke is going to come with me." He stretches his large hand out to my little, blonde daughter and she puts her hand in his, without hesitation. "I'll bring her to my wife. She can play with our Jimmy. How do you feel now?" I feel euphoric. "I'll give you a letter," says Maine. While he is writing, the ambulance arrives. Two men in white coats move me onto a stretcher. I just glimpse Maine lifting Janneke up into his arms.

A hospital room: more injections; doctors, nurses. The bleeding has stopped. "Your baby is fine. Just keep on lying quietly." And then Gerard appears. With my hand in his, I fall asleep. When I awake, I am lying in a large ward with a dozen or so women around me who have just produced healthy babies.

That evening Gerard and Hiek come to visit me. "Janneke?" She is just fine, they assure me. I only learn days later that she sits on the steps of the back veranda every day waiting for Mummy to come home. By then I have also learned that I will only see her again when I am allowed to go home. Children were banned from the maternity ward in those days. I also know that for the time being I will not be allowed to go home. That I have to stay lying flat on my back if I wish to bring a second, healthy baby into the world. I cry tears of powerless rage.

"In a little while, when you're allowed up," Gerard says, "I'll bring Janneke anyway, so that you can see her through the window."

"What if they never let me up?" I wail.

"We'll see," says Gerard, "Everything is going fine at home. It's all sorted." He has made an arrangement with old friends whom we used to see occasionally. A Dutch couple Gerard had once moved in his van. They live in Lindfield, a suburb adjacent to Roseville: Miep and Carl Gerke. Miep is at home during the day. She has a son of the same age as Janneke. Gerard takes her to Miep's every morning when he goes to work and picks her up at the end of the afternoon. They then have dinner together (sometimes at Hiek's). She sleeps in her own little bed. I am very grateful to Miep, but am counting on this being a very short-term arrangement.

I am allowed to sit on the edge of my bed. I am allowed to take a few, careful steps from chair to bed and back again. I am allowed to go to the toilet on my own.

The baby kicks lustily and I do not lose another drop of blood. I am allowed to stay out of bed for a few hours, to walk around, to shower. "I'm proud of you," the doctor, who visits me twice a day, says.

"When can I go home?" He shakes his head "Not yet." I keep hoping.

That Sunday I stand at the corridor window staring at the parking area, at our little blue car out of which Gerard, Hiek and a tiny figure in a pair of long, blue dungarees and a red sweater emerge. Gerard lifts Janneke up high and points. She waves. She waves with two hands. Hiek takes her and puts her on the ground. She laughingly starts to play catch-me-if-you-can with her, every now and them looking up at me and waving.

Gerard comes upstairs, and stands next to me. "She looks great, doesn't she? Believe me, she's having the time of her life." I don't believe a word of it. I want to go home! I am given piles of books, masses of wool. I knit, I read, I read and knit. And the days pass.

On a cold Monday the head nurse appears at my bed. She is holding my suitcase. "You're going to the cottage," she says cheerfully, "You'll have the company of fellow sufferers there. We simply can't let you go home, it would be far too risky."

Both my left-hand and right-hand neighbours, who predicted this would happen, had told me about "the cottage." A separate building in the hospital grounds where maternity patients with prenatal problems were housed. I do not want to go there, I want to go home!

Our head nurse is tall and stately, all blue-eyed, controlled authority. Protest is unthinkable, tears are pathetic; I have to submit to my fate like an obedient child.

I am not allowed to walk. I am put in a wheelchair, with my suitcase on my knees. A bright, young girl pushes me outside. The sun is shining, but there is a chilly wind blowing. She pushes me past long paths bordered by late-flowering rose bushes to the other end of the hospital grounds, far from the highway.

There, surrounded by bushes, covered with ivy and hidden under high trees, stands a long barracks, painted white and brown, with tall, wide windows framed by deeply pleated, white curtains. Inside is a hospital ward. There are two rows of empty, but clearly inhabited beds, their head ends placed under the windows; in between is a wide corridor, which ends in a large, grey desk with a telephone on it. That is our only link with the main building. Our lifeline, I discover later. I am assigned a bed close to this desk. My nurse helps me unpack and place my things in the chest of drawers next to my bed. "So, come along."

At the far end of the ward, next to two large bathrooms, there is a spacious kitchen; a normal kitchen with a countertop and sink with hot and cold water taps; with a fridge and a stove; with a glass cupboard full of cups, glasses and plates, and kitchen cupboards with pots and pans. In the middle stands a large, square table and around it are sitting seven or eight women, as round-bellied as I am, and all dressed, just like me, in dressing gowns and slippers. They are drinking tea and the kitchen smells of fresh toast. There is laughter and chattering, both of which stop when we appear.

"Is there any tea left for this lady?" my nurse asks, "Dawn, you're not eating toast are you? You'd better not be, because I'm going to weigh you later, and you're not supposed to have put on an ounce."

"Me?!" asks one of the women, all surprised innocence, "You know I only live on lettuce!" Dawn is twice as large as I am and not much taller. She has a face like a smiling currant bun. She has short, bristly, ebony hair, which frames her face like a curly halo. She pushes a chair out for me. "Don't be shy, love. Have a cuppa. What are you in for?"

How to describe the cottage? Looking back, I see it as a version of the famous Australian "mateship;" that unquestioning loyalty doesn't only exist amongst men.

We were a kind of ship without a captain, a closed community, with an ever-changing mother superior (in my time, it was indisputably Dawn). And yet, we were also very democratic. Everyone said and did exactly what she wanted. The only rule was that we looked out for each other.

I was immediately included, without any reservations, in this curious community. I felt from the first day as if twelve pairs of protective wings were enfolding me. We were a group of ordinary women, huddled together, with nothing in common except the fact that we were all in the last stages of pregnancy. We depended on each other and were in the most literal sense responsible for each other.

That first night I was woken up by Dawn switching on the desk lamp. It must have been about four. She picked up the phone. "Mary-Lou has started, nurse. Yes, for sure. Okay," and a little while later the quick rustling of starched skirts and a sister bending over a bed in the left row at the back. A stretcher. More nurses. Here and there a head popped up. Someone sighed, "Damn, I wish it were me." From somewhere else came gentle applause, "Good for you, Mary-Lou!"

We exchanged pregnancy stories. We encouraged each other. Sometimes we would sit half the night in the kitchen, talking, drinking tea. Some of us had such a gift for producing endless streams of gallows humour that we laughed much more than we cried. And some of us had more than enough reason for tears. I have forgotten their names, but I can see their faces: a middle-aged lady who slept propped up against piles of pillows and had great difficulty breathing, she had severe asthma; a lady with a kidney complaint; a lady with a rhesus baby; a woman who, after four miscarriages, was fighting to keep this pregnancy safe.

We were allowed to sleep in as long as we wanted, but everyone was up around seven anyway; whoever wasn't on a diet made her own breakfast. For the dieters, breakfast arrived at seven, together with fresh bread, in neatly labelled dishes, which were always met with a groan. Warm meals arrived in a closed trolley, each dish bearing its own label.

Twice a day two nurses dashed in to take our temperatures, weigh us, collect urine samples and make our beds if we hadn't already done this ourselves. They were followed shortly afterwards by a parade of doctors, the head nurse and a long row of students. We all had our own gynaecologist who brought his own students. We were examined, instructions were given; we could ask questions.

Visiting hour was at 7 pm. Then we all sat neatly turned out in our beds and our men were allowed in, a kind of dream that ended far too soon. Back to reality and the night, which always brought surprises. People came and went. The kitchen light stayed on all night. Sometimes, if most of us couldn't sleep, conversations were held in the semidarkness.

"Do you feel anything? Do you have a contraction?" "I bet there isn't a baby at all, just wind!" "If you were really in labour…" "Shouldn't you ring, Dawn?" "No, no, wait a little longer. It'll probably be a false alarm. I'm so fed up with it." "Well, it shouldn't be your turn for ages yet! I'm almost two weeks overdue. It's just so unfair."

13 June: I am woken by fierce pain in my belly. It is two o'clock in the morning. I break out in a cold sweat. This doesn't remotely resemble what I had experienced when Janneke announced her arrival. Ease into the pain? Absurd. Find a rhythm? Not the slightest chance. I toss and turn. Dawn stands next to me. "Hey, Dutchy! Don't tell me you've started?"

"I don't know. Oh God, it hurts so much!"

"Well, I do know, matey," she says decisively, "You lucky thing."

Then a hand on my forehead and a gentle voice that says, "Atta girl, here you go." I am placed on a stretcher and carried out, amidst cries of "Best of luck, sweetie!" and "How dare you, it isn't your turn at all!" I am laughing and crying at the same time, and look up at the stars in the dark sky outside.

It doesn't go as fast and smoothly as the first time. After six weeks of complete inactivity my muscles have clearly become lazy. This time I am not left alone for a second. At eight o'clock, our second daughter is born, a healthy, six-pound baby. At half past nine, just after I arrive back in the ward, exhausted, Dawn and two other cottage-dwellers appear, supporting their enormous bellies with their hands. My jaw drops. "We got special permission," she says smugly, "We thought we ought to check up on you. You deserter! You traitor! You were at the bottom of the list!"

"Oh, no! Don't make me laugh, everything hurts too much!"

"Dawn is going to be induced tomorrow," one of the other women tells me.

"What's it like?" Dawn asks, visibly anxious for the first time since I had met her.

"It's not so bad," I say weakly.

"We miss you. The cottage isn't the same without you."

The next night Dawn was safely delivered of a 12-pound son. She made so much commotion in the process she promptly became a hospital legend. She was moved into in a bed, three beds down from me and gave us all a blow-by-blow description.

My new baby is as pretty as a picture. She has a little, round, serious face. "We're going to call her Lindy," I tell Gerard, with great conviction.

CHAPTER 13

Father Pierce, Paul Albers and Binalong

Before I was rushed off to hospital, Hiek and I had often talked about how I would manage with two children, and she suddenly hit on an idea: "Why don't we ask Tom whether you can use the laundry as a kitchen? I bet he won't mind. The stove works perfectly, it just needs a good clean. We could clear out the laundry together." When we put the idea to Tom he began to beam, all helpful generosity: we could count on his help when the time came!

My sudden departure thwarted these plans. The laundry was still in the same state when I returned. Not for long, however. As soon as I was settled at home, we devoted a weekend to "Operation Laundry." Gerard and Hiek did most of the work, with Tom acting as an inept assistant. I was only allowed to decide where I wanted things to go. Our fridge was moved. Extra shelves were put up so that I could store my pots and pans, and we decided that the washing up could easily be done in the washbasins next to the copper. It was a brilliant solution. Now we had two little children's rooms behind our green curtain. My trek from the laundry to our front door carrying trays full of bowls, plates and cups felt a bit like a North Pole expedition, but I quickly got used to it. I was the most contented young mother in Mosman, until Janneke decided to explore the wide world.

Janneke quickly became fed up with the new baby who did nothing but sleep and required all my attention when she was awake. She had, moreover, developed her own little routine during my absence. Every morning, first thing, she set out to visit the rectory opposite the back of our garden. This was where Father Pierce lived, together with his housekeeper. A greying, squarely built Irishman with grey, jutting, bushy eyebrows and a somewhat morose demeanour. I barely knew the man, but Janneke clearly regarded him as a trusted member of her family. Every morning, while he was having breakfast on his shady veranda, she deposited herself at his feet on the top step of the stone veranda stairs, and helped him finish off his toast and marmalade. In the meantime, she engaged him in lively conversation.

Once the toast was finished she would skip, singing softly, straight through our garden, past the front door and through the gate that led into the alley, which our bay window overlooked. At the end of the alley stood a house where a child-less couple lived whose name I have forgotten. I never discovered what ailed the wife, but she was always home and lying on a sofa bed on her veranda. She did not look particularly well. She and Janneke must have met while I was in hospital. She adored Janneke. She had set up a corner with toys for her next to her bed on the veranda and Janneke went over every day to play for an hour or so. When I discovered this I accompanied her once to meet our neighbour, but did not see any reason to interfere. Janneke would always come home afterwards to report faithfully on her activities. By that time Lindy would be sleeping in the pram and we could go shopping.

On Janneke's third birthday her newfound friend gave her a beautifully spruced up tricycle. A very sweet gesture, but it put an end to my peace. Janneke saw no reason to restrict her bicycle rides to the garden and alley. She launched into the world with gusto and I would regularly need to run out looking for her, calling her name, my ponytail flying in the wind, around the block of houses to which our house belonged. I would usually find her there, and made her promise always to stay on the pavement…

But there came a day that I ended up wringing my hands and crying at the gate behind the washing line after a futile search around the block. No Janneke. Not a sign of a small, blonde child on a red tricycle. Nowhere.

This was the first time Father Pierce spoke to me directly. I hadn't noticed the black shadow on the shady rectory veranda. "What's the matter, dear?"

"Janneke!" I cried, fighting my rising panic, "She's gone! On her tricycle. I've looked everywhere!"

He shook his weather-beaten head and put down his breviary. "I'll get my car." We drove first in the direction of the shops, me still wearing my worn apron dress (a farewell present from Mrs. Statham), he in his shiny black habit with its innumerable black buttons; then in the other direction, towards the zoo. And all the way at the end of Bradley's Head Road sat a small, inconsolable heap next to a capsized tricycle, crying her eyes out. "I didn't know where you were!" she wept, clutching me tightly. And then, in immense surprise: "That's Father Pierce!" And she promptly began to beam.

We put child and bike in the car while I thanked our benefactor profusely.

"It's high time she went to kindergarten," Father Pierce growled, "I'll talk to the nuns. How old is she?" Nuns? School? There was a school behind the church on Bradley's Head Road. "She's only three," I said hesitantly.

An incident like this turns out later to be a tiny cog in a vast, constantly rotating set of cogs. They are of decisive influence on the course your life takes. Which doesn't mean you do not make choices. Of course you choose. But those cogs, those tiny, interlinking cogs: aren't they the reason for at least half of what happens to you?

How Father Pierce ever discovered that we were "lapsed Catholics," I do not know. But it was no coincidence that within a short period of time after this incident we received a visit from two Catholic lay missionaries from his parish, members of the "Legion of Mary."

At that time I knew nothing about the Catholic Church in Australia and the role that the Irish played in it, and possibly still do. Most priests were of Irish descent. Australia was viewed as a missionary country. Irish Catholics have played a very important role in Australia's history (having supplied, among other things, four Prime Ministers). I saw Father Pierce as the prototype of an Irish missionary. Highly conservative (as was the whole Catholic Church in Australia at that time, without a trace of modernity, not the tiniest spark of rebellion); a father figure endowed with God-given authority, which could not be questioned. Actually, I don't think it ever occurred to anyone to question it. He was who he was, a gnarled old Irish tree under which you could shelter. I liked him and still think he was a deeply compassionate man. The Legion of Mary movement was a kind of Catholic version of the Jehovah's Witnesses. The members went from door to door, in twos, in their spare time, trying to generate interest for the Catholic faith. As far as I am aware, the Legion of Mary still exists, worldwide.

Our two visitors, who suddenly materialise on a Sunday afternoon, turn out to be an Australian and a Dutchman, Kevin Goodson and Paul Albers. Kevin is red-haired, tall and gangly. In the beginning he is painfully shy. He almost whispers when he speaks, and is gentle and tolerant. Paul is the opposite. He is straight as an arrow, implacable and zealous, a fighter who saves souls with fire and sword. He is also an ex-marine, had fought in Indonesia, and is even an old schoolmate of Gerard's from primary school in Leiden.

Gerard is astounded when he sees him. He pulls him inside, welcoming him as heartily as he would any of his old comrades in arms. Tells me that they had seen each other a few years ago when he still had his transport company. Paul had just got off the boat then, fresh from Indonesia. And now here is he, standing in front of us, and he makes immediately clear that he is here to induct us, seasoned materialists that we are, into the "life is not bread alone" aspect of existence, to show us the way back to our old flock.

Of course, on that first afternoon he and Gerard spend their time dwelling on old memories and catching up. Paul, like Gerard, comes from a large Dutch, Catholic family, most of whom appear to have moved to Australia and are spread around the country. He himself lives in Mosman and works in a bank. His parents and youngest sister live somewhere else in Sydney. He has another sister in Sydney, Tessie, who works as a physiotherapist in the centre of town. (Tessie will later become a dear friend of mine.)

Paul is a handsome man; a little distant, square chin, military bearing, commando voice. But he turns out to be very kind; he makes me feel as if I have acquired a concerned elder brother. Admittedly, one who is of the view (I would later discover) that he always knows best with respect to philosophical and religious matters, but we learn to live with that. Luckily, he also has a good sense of humour. I like Kevin too. Gerard and I are fascinated by this habit of going from door to door, which especially for Kevin must be real torture. That first Sunday afternoon is the beginning of a series of discussion afternoons. We argue a great deal, and also become real friends.

I can no longer recall how the plan was born to go, together with Paul, on a visit to the youngest Albers offspring. His name is Phons and he lives in Binalong, a tiny town in the neighbourhood of Canberra. He has a chicken farm there, Paul tells us. I think it started with a conversation about Canberra, the capital city of Australia, where I had never been. "It's about four hours drive from here," Gerard said.

Gerard and Paul had recently gone fox hunting together, for a few days in the Snowy Mountains, in the neighbourhood of a place called Thredbo. We have photos of them standing with rifles leaning against the car, real pals. They had talked so much about Canberra, which they had driven through on their return, and had decided that it was high time I had a break too, a few days of country air. "We can all spend the night with Phons," said Paul, "He'd like that! The poor boy never sees anyone."

Gerard now has a Renault Fregatte, courtesy of Ira Berk, of course. All of us, including luggage, fit into it easily. I sit in the back with Lindy in a travelling cot and Janneke next to me. The men sit in the front. I am fascinated by everything I see. Once we leave the city we drive through a peaceful, pretty and fertile landscape, which resembles a chequered, undulating tablecloth made of green, yellow and brown squares, a landscape with grazing cows. I suddenly realise I haven't seen a cow for years. These do not resemble Dutch cows. They are brown and skinny, but cows nevertheless. We drive down long, silent, tree-lined, blue-grey asphalt roads full of dancing circles of shadow. I see trees in autumn colours amongst the gum trees. I can't believe my eyes. "Just wait till we get to Canberra," says Paul, "They planted two million European trees there when they decided that Canberra would become the capital."

We drive through a small, Wild West town with only one, broad, sunny street, totally deserted, along which low wooden shops with swinging signboards are ranged along a wooden walkway.

Canberra lies in a valley surrounded by wooded hills, in a kind of amphitheatre almost 200 feet above sea level. To my eyes, it looks as if it was set up, ready made, on a huge, flat plate, which was subsequently picked up and deposited in a European park. All those straight, smooth tree trunks are unsettlingly un-Australian. There are neat streets running in a circle, with wide pavements and decorous stone houses. It even smells European, of freshly mown grass, mushrooms, moss, dying leaves. I am driven past the embassies: square buildings in pastel colours – hard white, soft grey, pink, sky blue. I do not feel at ease in Canberra. I am glad when we finally take the road to Binalong.

It is already beginning to grow dark. We are stranded, after hours of trying to find the nameless chicken farm, at the end of an almost impassable sand road full of potholes, which ends abruptly in a sticky looking pool of mud. We are parked next to a completely pointless piece of fencing: rusty iron wire hanging between crumbling poles. A line of sombre hills stands starkly against the sky, which is still light, framing an almost treeless landscape consisting solely of fields full of stubble.

Beyond the mud stands a rickety wooden hut with a water tank next to it. The hut has a corrugated iron roof and is flanked at either end by mysterious corrugated iron extensions. "This must be it," says Paul, without conviction, and remains seated in the car.

Then a broad-shouldered figure in wader's boots appears around the corner of the house. A true-blue, old school pioneer in a frayed safari jacket wearing a broad-rimmed, extremely dirty felt hat. He holds a stable lantern in one muscled hand and casts a huge shadow ahead of himself. "Hallo there!" a deep, dark voice, "Hang on a minute." The boots wade with slow, giant steps through the mud.

"That's him! That's Teun!" grins Paul, "How are you doing, old man?" He jumps out of the car (he had told us the family nickname for its youngest son was Teun) and slaps the bushman enthusiastically on the back. Gerard gets out of the other side of the car and does the same. "Hey, Phons, good to see you!"

"I've just butchered a lamb," the pioneer remarks blithely. He puts his lantern on the ground. "Had a good trip?" Is there really a huge, bloodstained, butcher's knife hanging from his belt? My stomach turns. I hold a sleeping Janneke in my arms. I have remained in the car.

"Do you guys want coffee?" Phons asks, "Mind you, I need to get cleaned up first."

"Is this your homestead?" Gerard asks, critically surveying the construction, his hands on his hips, "A bit meagre, isn't it? Or does it just seem that way?"

"This," says Phons, not in the least put out, leaning an elbow on the car door, "This is only temporary. I built it with my own hands! In a year or so there's going to be a real house. Not here, further down. I've already started clearing a piece of land."

"Um," I say to the elbow, "Um, where, what? The babies…".

The elbow disappears. The felt hat replaces it. "Oh, hi!" says the hat, peering into the dark car, "Oh, yes, well, you see… I don't have many home comforts here. Pretty makeshift, really. I thought you'd probably be happier staying in the pub in Binalong. At least you'll get a real bed there." The hat disappears from my view, "You can sleep on the floor here, Paul," is the last thing I catch.

"Let's do that, Gerard!" I call to him, "Let's drive there now!"

"We're not in a hurry."

"Yes we are!" I can barely keep my voice steady, "The children are exhausted and so am I."

"Turn the car around," says Phons, "Once you're back on the main road it's very close. They know you're coming. Tomorrow you can have coffee here and lunch of course. Fresh lamb chops, man! Fresh off the land, the best quality!"

"Mummy," a sleepy voice murmurs in my ear, "Are we going home, Mummy?"

"Ssh," I say unsteadily, "Just a little bit further. You'll have a lovely bed soon." I am furious, absolutely livid. A farm?! I hadn't really given it much thought, but a ramshackle shepherd's hut and a knife-wielding, mud-covered host who couldn't possibly put us up were the last things I had expected.

"Never again!" I hiss to the back of Gerard's head, once we are on our way again. "We are never doing something like this again! You two and your hairbrained schemes; this is what they lead to. We're stuck out in the wilds, in the middle of the night! What are we going to do?"

"We're going to the pub, aren't we?" dumbfounded, "What are you complaining about? It isn't that late." He clearly has no idea that he has a livid, scratching, rebellious mother cat in the back of his car.

"Wow, what an achievement," he continues, "Clearing a piece of land with your bare hands. That's a far cry from selling cars!" Do I hear a note of nostalgic envy in his voice?

"It didn't look very cleared to me," I snap, "It's a chicken farm isn't it? I didn't see a chicken anywhere. Did you? Oh God, if I had known..."

Binalong seems to be deserted. The bumpy main street boasts one crooked street lamp, which sheds very little light. The pub doesn't even have a sign. We initially drive past it. When we drive back slowly we see the faded letters of the word "Hotel" on the only two-storey building in the street. There is, as far as we can see, no light burning inside. When we get out a chilly wind greets us. Large balls of weeds roll along the street ahead of us.

We clatter onto the wooden front veranda. The front door is shut but not locked. Somewhere in the back of the building a light is burning. We march inside, Gerard carrying Janneke in his arms and I carrying Lindy in her basket. We are welcomed by a morose, weary young woman. We are given a large, square room on the first floor. There are two wooden beds plus a child's bed, a cupboard and two chairs, all perched on a bare wooden floor. The floor and beds are dark brown. Everything is dark brown. A single bulb hangs from the middle of the ceiling, yielding a paltry amount of light. "The bathroom is directly opposite," says the woman, "If you want I can make you steak and eggs."

The bathroom is also dark brown, but very large. Everything works perfectly, to my relief. Together we bathe the children. Afterwards, we go downstairs for steak and eggs. I ask for milk for the children and am given, after a lengthy interval, a bowl of hot water and a tin of powdered milk. "We don't have fresh milk here." No fresh milk? I am speechless. My first visit to the Australian countryside and they don't have fresh milk.

"They only breed cattle for meat here," Gerard says authoritatively, "Oh well, it won't kill them. The steak is very good, don't you think?"

After dinner, we both take a bath, which warms us up. It is cold in our room, but the sheets are clean and we have piles of warm blankets. We all four sleep like babies.

The next morning Binalong, drenched in exuberant winter sunshine, looks very different. The street with little pioneers houses is actually quite sweet. I see grass and flowers, tall trees and an old wooden church. Phons too looks very different. He isn't as tall and large as he appeared the previous night. He is actually quite small, though his shoulders are impressively broad, farmer's shoulders. His skin is brown and sunburned, and his eyes are young and blue. And he is an excellent host. He serves us a lunch he has prepared himself; lamb chops of inordinate size and fresh salad. The hut appears to have a long sofa bed, a generous coffee table, a pair of old armchairs and a large, old sideboard with glass doors. And is even equipped with electricity. One of the enormous extensions turns out to be a vast deep-freeze unit containing frozen chickens, neatly packed, ready to be delivered to various embassies in Canberra. "They're my best customers," Phons tells us. The other extension is his shower. You pull a rope to release a flood of cold water. "Terribly healthy!"

What else do I remember? A number of chicken runs, fields with grass and corn, and a freshly burned stubble-field on the top of a hill. "This is where my house is going to be built," his arms making a wide, sweeping gesture, "What a view, huh?" I see him standing there. Chin up, eyes screwed a little shut, blonde curls waving in the wind. He has Janneke on his shoulders.

I can't claim that I already had a premonition of how important Phons would become for us. Nor that he really would one day own that large house in the country in New South Wales, on top of a hill surrounded by fields and hills that change colour every minute of the day. He has lived there now for over 40 years. What I do know is that I made him promise that if he ever came to Sydney he would visit us.

My last recollection is of a large wooden house not very far from Phons' hut. That is where the owner of most of the land around us lived (Phons leased from him). He was, if I remember correctly, a vet. He had a large number of children. We were invited to afternoon tea: a vast room, with large, high windows, thrown wide open. I see children tumbling in through those windows, and jumping out of them again, a constant cascade of children, one of whom is our Janneke.

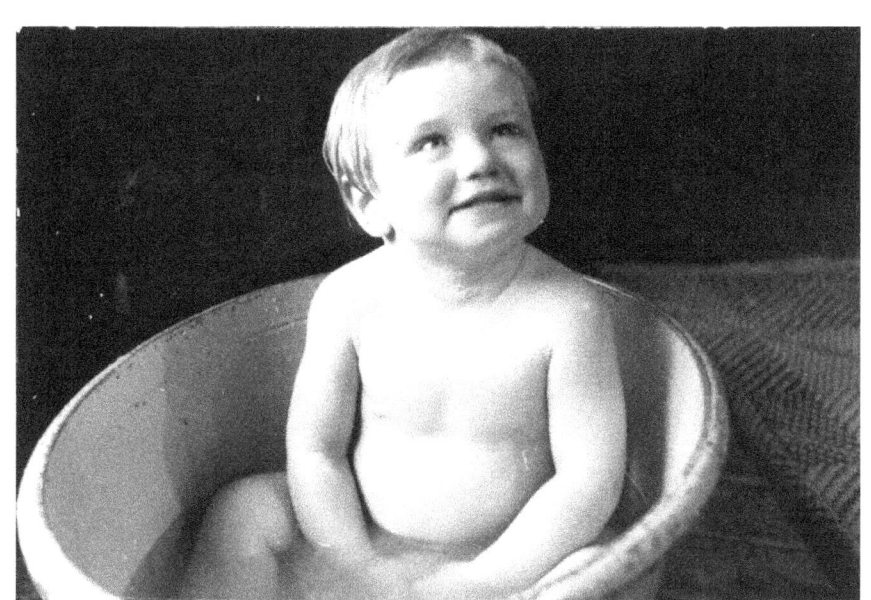

CHAPTER 14

Home decorating

A DIRECT CONSEQUENCE of this excursion was that our Mosman flat underwent a transformation. Our brief experience of pioneer life had clearly made Gerard restless. He had a week's holiday and he announced to me that he intended to put his time to good use. Our flat needed sprucing up. "Do you really think that's necessary?" I asked, weakly.

"Look at that ceiling! Look at the woodwork!" I peered up, which I never normally did, at the stained, brown cherubs and bunches of grapes way up above us. "Nobody notices that!"

"I do! I'm going to see if I can't get hold of some cheap paint."

Sighing, I resigned myself to the inevitable. I dragged as much of the furniture as I could into the corridor and covered our bed and the mat with old newspapers. We borrowed Tom's rickety ladder, which stood on the back veranda. After which I was urgently requested to go out with the children.

I lifted Lindy into the pram, took Janneke by the hand and went shopping. We then headed for the sports field and played games. After that I sat for a while on a bench and daydreamed, staring at the sea above which wisps of chilly afternoon mist were rising. That wild, tough life in the countryside was not for me, I decided. Mosman, on the other hand: just enough tamed nature and the big city within easy reach. Ideal! I sniffed with pleasure the typical Mosman autumn air: eucalyptus, sea air and the sharp tang of garden waste burning somewhere.

I waited until the sun had disappeared, leaving behind stripes of pink, soft yellow and green, and then went home; high time to bathe Janneke, whether Gerard was ready or not.

When I entered the laundry hall I saw, all the way at the far end, a poppy red rectangle. Our front door had taken on a psychedelic aspect. "Oh, my God."

Hiek came out of the kitchen. "What do you think?" grinning, "That paint was on special, he said. He worked on it for hours." I took a deep breath. "I hope to God he hasn't done everything in that colour."

Immediately behind our front door stood Tom's ladder, festooned from top to bottom with bright pink rags. Next to it stood open pots of paint down the sides of which bloodstained paint dripped onto newspapers. Gerard was lying on our bed, dressed in shorts that were as stained as the rags on Tom's ladder. Across his forehead ran a smear of pink paint. His face was ashen. He was wheezing audibly.

"Hi!" he gasped, "I had just started on the ceiling (*wheeze*); you need to bring a high ceiling like that down," he ended on a whistling gasp. I looked up and was struck dumb. A quarter of our ceiling, a large corner, had acquired the same hippy aspect as our door. On the white expanse next to it was a large, pink palm print, surrounded by specks of pink paint. "I couldn't go on," whispered Gerard, apologetically. "Antique pink" (*wheeze*) "Great colour, huh? Was dirt cheap."

"Antique pink," I repeated, flabbergasted.

"Oh dear, are you having such trouble breathing?" Hiek asked, with concern.

"I bet he's allergic to paint," I said.

"Nonsense," said Gerard, "I'm feeling a lot better already. My tablet's starting to work. I'll finish it in a little while" (*wheeze, wheeze*).

"No, you won't," I pushed Janneke in Hiek's direction, "Can she stay with you for a little while? There isn't going to be any more painting today." I started to gather up the newspapers, "I'm not really crazy about the colour, are you?"

"It's just a bit different. Don't be so conservative."

"Oh – that hand, ..." looking up.

"Working above your head on such a rotten ladder isn't easy. I have to get a proper ladder next week." The wheezing was already becoming considerably less.

"Are you feeling better? Why don't you take a shower, I'll tidy up." He went. Later he admitted that painting and especially painting a high ceiling wasn't the best of occupations for an asthma patient. Finishing the job was postponed for an indefinite period. We lived for months with a quarter of a red ceiling and a red painted hand above our heads. Lying in bed we had the best view of both.

Paul and Kevin finally finished painting our ceiling for us on condition that Gerard would not lift a finger. It became, after mutual consultation and to my great joy, grey. Our front door, however, remained until the day we moved out, both on the inside and the outside, poppy red.

CHAPTER 15

Catholics, Seaforth and Josie

It has taken me five days to overcome a feeling of resistance, an unwillingness to continue. This is because of what comes next. I tell myself that a few days of rest will help me get over it. That I then won't find it difficult to write about the reasons why we became Catholics again. The respite has helped a little, but not much. I don't really know what I am going to write. In my old manuscript, I skipped this episode altogether. I wanted to keep things light. This is a different book.

There is no short, clear answer to this why. I can only write about my own feelings then, although in the end it was a shared decision. At the time it seemed to us to be the best decision, the only possible decision. I look back on it now with astonishment: all that God stuff. Was there really a time that I thought "faith" so important? What difference does it make? There is only one, real – for want of a better word – sin: cruelty, deliberate cruelty. All those religions that claim to be the only truth; all that searching for answers, all those attempts to regulate through rules and laws the endlessly complicated network of human relationships...

Mornings in our flat here start with breakfast and each of us reading a part of the morning newspaper. Then my back exercises in the hall, which take about twenty minutes, while Gerard reads a bit more and washes up. I stretch and bend, and try to anchor myself in the here and now, as I am convinced my exercises will be more effective if I do them with full focus. I have been doing this for many years now. Counting helps. Though I don't often succeed in keeping my focus. That whirlwind in my head, the endless stream of images. I jump from past to future, from what has happened to what still needs to be done. I wonder if deep concentration results in inner peace, concentration on anything at all?

Back then, in Ellamatta Avenue, we were given the assurance that it was the Catholic faith we had grown up in that would bring us inner peace. Returning to the order and security of our youth when life was regulated down to the smallest detail. Good and evil, sin and punishment, heaven and hell, all indisputably clear, for eternity.

And they were such lovely people. Paul had brought us into contact with Father van Houten, a Dutch priest who was part of St. Mary's Cathedral. He came from a village in Zeeland, and his origins were clearly visible, I thought. There was something square and sturdy about him, something that reminded me of a solid chunk of earth. He was incredibly kind and understanding, always happy to listen. Father van Houten often came to talk to us. He explored our doubts, refuted our objections. To surrender yourself, to have faith in divine providence: it was all enormously appealing (though the Catholic church's adamant rejection of birth control was a serious stumbling block). No need to weigh everything up oneself anymore. Being embraced. Belonging. It felt like being touched by gossamer butterfly wings. Everything would be so much easier; our life would be so much richer. An immutable, infallible authority would accompany us every step of the way. And Paul and Tessie had become such good, dear friends. We had almost become family.

We married again, quietly, in Father Pierce's church. The Catholic Church did not recognise our "civil" marriage. And as my marriage to Charles had also only been a civil marriage that marriage had never existed either. In Catholic eyes, therefore, I was still single and had never been divorced. Our daughters were baptised after this short service. Paul and Tessie were witnesses.

In the meantime, there were still our other friends. Hiek was not a Catholic, but was full of understanding; and "live and let live" Henk, who had troubles of his own. He had a new girlfriend called Winifred who owned a clothes shop in, of all places, Lindfield where the Gerke's lived. According to Gerard, Miep Gerke worked in her shop. All I can recall is that Miep and Win were friends. Win owned a house in expensive Lane Cove and shared it with two dogs, a cage full of parakeets and two brightly lit aquaria full of tropical fish.

She was slim, blond and utterly Australian; and she played bridge, as cannily and fanatically as Odette did. We were regularly invited over to play bridge, children and all. Win adored our children. She was very tolerant of them, even though she was extremely neat and tidy. Eerily tidy. Later, after having lived together for a while, she and Henk got married. Gerard was their best man. On the wedding photo we own Miep Gerke is sitting behind the bride. Was she a witness? I no longer know, I wasn't there. Was I pregnant with our third baby?

Around that time a whole set of changes occurred. Both Kevin and Paul came to say goodbye; Kevin, because he had accepted a job at an American university (he was a physicist); and Paul, because he had decided, after careful consideration, to heed his late vocation to become a priest. He was going to a seminary somewhere in the interior of New South Wales, hundreds of miles from Sydney. Tess came to tell us that now that Paul was leaving she was going to move back in with her parents. They needed her financial support. And Hiek and Jan suddenly made a down payment on a house.

"It'll be ages before we can move," Hiek said, soothingly, at my distressed reaction. "The house isn't fit to live in. It needs complete renovation. But the location is glorious and we got it very cheaply. You'll come and take a look won't you, next Sunday?"

That location turned out to be Seaforth, on the other side of the Spit Bridge, not so far from Mosman. Which didn't mean it was situated in the urban part of Seaforth. We were led down a dusty, abandoned, hilly road and all we saw when we got out of the car that Sunday was a weather-beaten wooden pole on top of a mass of rock with "Lot 24" written on it in tar.

Next to the rock mass were rough stairs, cut out of the rock, about half a metre each, leading downward: a kind of goat's path that twisted and turned through wildly growing brushwood. At least twenty metres below us we could see something that looked vaguely like a roof; miles below that shimmered the sea.

"Isn't it marvellous here?" Hiek cried, joyfully. The goat's path ended in a small terrace, covered in rough brick. The rock we had clambered over appeared to contain a shallow cave. "This is going to be my workshop," said Jan, "There's loads of space! I can store wood here and my tools. I'm going to buy a carpenter's bench. I can keep it here too. I'm going to renovate the house myself."

The house was a weatherboard and wooden shed, with a sheet-iron roof. In between the house and an outbuilding was a paved and covered patio. Behind the house was a small, sad-looking veranda. There were two rooms and a kitchen, and added to the veranda a sloping roof, which Jan called the "lean-to." He intended to turn this into an extra room, the boys' room. The sheet-iron roofed shed on one side of the patio was the bathroom, which contained an old bath and a boiler.

A considerable distance away, in the back garden, under a mandarin tree, stood a sheet-iron hut: the toilet. The back garden was enormous, sloping down from top to bottom and ending in a kind of jungle through which a small path ran into the depths and to the beach. "All ours!" crowed Hiek, "This piece of land alone is worth twice what we paid for it."

"A great plot," Gerard said, with admiration.

"But do you think you will ever be able to live here?" I asked tentatively.

"It'll take a while," Jan said, "But if we can work here every weekend…I already know exactly how I'm going to go about it. First, I'll close in the lean-to and make a door. And then I need to deal with the living room floor." This was completely warped. The gaping floorboards were humpbacked. You had to climb to get to the middle of the room but then slid inevitably back again to one of the walls along the side of the room. In between the gaps you could see the foundations of the building, neat piles of bricks.

"A huge amount of work," Gerard said pensively.

"Once the floor is fixed we can move in," Hiek said, "We can camp out here for a little while. It'll be fun."

"After that, the roof," said Jan, looking upwards with anticipatory glee. "There are holes here and there. Not surprising, really. It used to be an old holiday home." He was clearly itching to get started. "And one day we'll have a proper bathroom and inside toilet. The estate agent assures us that it won't be long before we can be linked to the sewerage system."

"Even if it takes years!" said Hiek, "We're not in a hurry. But it's ours! We finally have a house of our own! We can already sit on our own veranda in the sun. And once the garden is tidied up…"

"Heaven forbid!" said Gerard when we were in the car on our way home. "Him rather than me. He has bought a disaster if you ask me, impossible to renovate. The whole thing should be bulldozed, it would be the only solution."

"They could never afford that. But the land…"

"Yes, the land. But would you want to move in there if it had been fixed up a bit?"

"Not if you paid me!" I said, shuddering at the thought of the toilet. And yet: a house, your own house. We still had a negligible amount on our savings account. We could only manage with a great deal of effort to put a few pounds aside. Would we ever be able to afford our own house? And baby number three would be arriving soon.

We now had actual health insurance and Gerard announced to me that he had booked me into the Catholic Mater Misericordiae hospital in Crow's Nest for the birth, not far from the North Shore hospital. The Mater was a semi-public hospital, which meant that if you were insured you could make use of your own doctor, something that wasn't possible in the North Shore.

And that meant that I could now go to my own Dr Maine in Mosman for check-ups and that he would do the delivery. Which was a happy thought. But the whole adventure would cost us a great deal, a reason for Gerard to take an extra Saturday morning job. He became a weekend taxi driver. And he assured me that when Hiek and Jan left we would take over their flat: much more greatly needed space.

I promptly became depressed. My nausea began to play up as usual and I suddenly discovered that I actually thoroughly disliked Ellamatta Avenue and its inhabitants.

April 1958, about six weeks after the beginning of the Australian school term. We had succeeded, with Father Pierce's help, in getting Janneke a place at the little school behind the church even though she was still a little too young for it.

Janneke herself did not see why there was any necessity for this. When we went to take a look at the school, she liked it well enough and the prospect of "going to school" made her very proud. But when she discovered what it actually entailed she was deeply indignant. To be left behind every morning on her own with a group of strange children and a couple of nuns? Were we out of our minds? Every morning anew she protested loudly, at which Lindy, sitting in her pram, would also begin to cry woefully, out of pure sympathy. Weeping heartrendingly, Janneke would clamp herself tightly to me, one hand grasping my arm, the other grasping Lindy's pram, while Lindy pulled, lamenting loudly, at my skirt. And all the time my stomach lurched…

Usually one of the nuns would intervene, firmly picking up my anguished, resisting eldest child. "You should go home. As soon as you are gone she will stop crying." I can't recall that any of the other children made so much noise. "Just stick with it," said Gerard. "It'll pass."

In the afternoons when I came to pick her up Janneke would be bouncing with sunny contentment and would tell me that she liked school. But in the mornings, as soon as school loomed on the horizon, her bottom lip would begin to tremble and the tears would once again roll down her cheeks.

On the fourth morning, I suddenly found another mother at my side, with a second child in a pram, just like me. "Awful, isn't it? But it really does get better. Some kids need longer to settle down than others. Do you feel very bad?" She was tall, slim and dark, with radiant brown eyes and a narrow face. She had shoulder-length, curly brown hair and a large, smiling mouth.

"Morning sickness," I said.

"Thought so, you look so very white. I noticed it yesterday too. Do you feel like a cup of tea? I live close-by. Walk with me, a little distraction will do you good."

"Oh, I can't," I said sadly, "I throw up all the time."

"So what? You can do that at my place! I know all about it, I've gone through it three times. Just come along." She talked incessantly. Her name was Josie Braun. She had a son, Michael, who was already in second class, so her daughter Katie, a little older than Janneke, had got to know the school well before it was her turn that year. "Tomorrow Katie will take your little girl inside with her. You'll see, it will go a whole lot better then." Sally, in the pram, was the same age as Lindy. "I bet these two will get along very well. Just look at how they are staring at each other."

She told me her husband, Monty, worked for a transport company and was away a great deal. That he was a Catholic, but she wasn't. And who was I? A New Australian, she could tell from my accent. How wonderful! I was the first New Australian she had met. Fascinating! Where did I come from? What had made me immigrate to Australia? As we walked along, she got me to give her a brief autobiography and as I talked I began to feel better. My nausea subsided.

We passed Ellamatta Avenue. We walked down Effingham Street and crossed Middle Head Road. We turned a corner and went down a dead-end alley between garden fences. Josie explained that she lived in a flat, which was really part of her parents' house. "We're perfectly private though, completely independent. What do you think of my garden?"

Josie's garden lay behind the last garden fence. It wasn't big, but it was colourful: a man-sized poinsettia in full bloom with fire-red blossoms; hibiscus flowers, red, pink and purple; rows of golden daisies. "I love gardening. Do you?" Her flat wasn't much bigger than ours but she had three bedrooms. Two narrow rooms with bunk beds and one a little larger. She also had a narrow kitchen and a tiny bathroom, with all the mod cons. And there was a large living room with wall-to-wall carpets and a real lounge. It was cool and dark inside; the windows were shuttered to keep out the heat.

Josie lifted Lindy and Sally out of their prams, and deposited them next to each other amongst a pile of Lego blocks on the kitchen floor. "Play, my darlings." Both babies sat perfectly still. Then Sally, who was dainty and slight, put her hand out and Lindy, after some consideration, put a Lego block into it. "You see!" Josie said, triumphantly, "The beginning of a beautiful friendship! Morning-tea time. Shall we stay in here? I love kitchens, don't you? Where exactly do you live? Do you have a garden too?"

I began to tell her shyly about how we lived, while watching those thin, brown, overwhelmingly capable hands, moving unerringly among the kettle, the teapot, the milk and cookies for the children. And I listened to that ceaseless stream of words. Josie talked and talked and talked. About Australian flowers and plants, about bush flowers. "Do you have any idea how many wonderful plants grow here? My mother has a holiday home in the Blue Mountains, right in the bush. There are wild orchids! Glorious!" She picked up a book and suddenly we were talking about books in general, about writers. We mentioned authors; we clearly had the same taste. She told me her father was a publisher. "He publishes journals for cattle and sheep farmers, though. Not our kind of thing," and that her mother worked in newspapers, which interested me greatly.

And suddenly it was 12 o'clock. "Oh Lord," I said appalled, "my washing!"

"Why don't you just stay?" said Josie, "You can do the washing tomorrow. Just look how happily those babies of ours are playing with each other. How do you feel?"

"Very well," I said surprised. Amazingly, my stomach was behaving like a normal organ. "But I really do need to go. I'm messing up my whole schedule."

"Okay, we'll see each other tomorrow. I'll come and have tea at your place. I'm so happy I have found you!"

"Me too!" I said, from the bottom of my heart.

The next morning she was waiting for us, holding Katie who looked exactly like her mother, by the hand. That morning was the first time Janneke entered the school, together with Josie and hand in hand with Katie, without shedding a tear, and waving her little lunch box just like Katie.

Josie. Looking back I see a sharp dividing line. Not until I had met Josie did Australia become my "home", become – for good and forever – my country. My adopted country, admittedly, but I belonged there. I had arrived. Everything that happened before that time had simply been an initiation.

Josie was like an Australian southerly wind that puts an abrupt end to a heat wave. Whatever she undertook she did with style. She threw herself into everything with heart and soul. I was immediately enlisted into the small army of her friends, among whose ranks were representatives of all ages, from very young to over sixty. She had time and attention for everyone, and took us all to her large, warm heart. At the same time she studied and analysed everyone who crossed her path and never tired of describing her findings. She was generously endowed with the gift of the gab. She loved to talk, categorise and play the psychologist. She did it with passion. Other people and their quirks were her biggest hobby. I was a unique specimen, a European immigrant who was in more or less the same situation as she was herself (we were the same age) but who clearly had a lot to learn. For starters, she took my education in hand, with great enthusiasm.

She herself was frighteningly quick and competent, much quicker at everything than I was. She was also very creative and tirelessly adept at inventing games for the children. And she made children's clothes and games from bits of cloth and beads. She was a genius at concocting cheap but nourishing meals and could whisk together exotic dishes using minimal ingredients. She taught me to shop sensibly, to try out new foods. She forced me gently to become a little more flexible and to live a bit more in the moment. She would burst into the house at the oddest times: "Come on, love, let's go to Balmoral, the weather's much too nice to do housework!" She inspected our flat and examined the whole downstairs floor. She then announced to me, shaking her head, that it was high time we bought a house. Moving into a bigger flat simply wouldn't do. A real house was what we needed!

And then one lovely spring morning: "I've had a brilliant idea! There's a house for sale on Middle Head Road, directly opposite Effingham Street. It's only a semi, one half of two houses sharing a roof, so it can't possibly be very expensive. And you know what? Your backdoor would be opposite my front door!" She has run over and is out of breath with excitement. She is beaming with eager entrepreneurship.

"Oh, Josie, you're out of your mind. Do you know how much money we have saved? Exactly one hundred pounds. How can you buy a house with that?"

"I bet there's a way! I've heard that you can take double mortgages and things, as long as the deposit isn't too high. It can't be, it's only a small, old house. Think about it: you wouldn't have to buy anything new. You have all you need. And I'll help you with everything. I'll be your back neighbour!" She dances around me, like a large bird with flapping wings. I am a nervous sparrow. I sit down heavily on the edge of our bed. "Josie."

"Don't be scared, love. Just ring up the estate agent and ask for the key. Here, I wrote his name down. Shall we do it? We'll take a look. I'll go with you! And if we think it looks interesting, we'll ask for an option. Doesn't cost a thing. They'll keep it for you for a week or so. That way it won't get sold to someone else."

I keep shaking my head.

"But you have to do something!" she says, while she sits down on the bed next to me. "You can't just wait passively for something to happen. I would move heaven and earth if I were in your shoes. You can't go on like this here."

"I need to talk to Gerard first," I say weakly.

She jumps up. "Don't you need something from the shops? I do. Do you want to come? We'll walk past it on the way. Just take a look at the outside. I've got a hunch it has three bedrooms. And there's a front garden and a back garden."

We walk past the house. The front garden is below street level. You enter through a small gate and then walk down stone steps to the path that leads to the front door. There is a red brick front veranda. We stand together in front of the gate and look at it. I sigh; this is an impossible dream, a fairy tale.

"Where there's a will there's a way," says Josie "We could do so many things together. Our kids could play together from morning till night. Wouldn't that be fantastic? It's just meant to be!" pointing to the "For Sale" sign in the garden.

"What if a hundred pounds really is enough for a deposit?" I ask Gerard that evening, starry-eyed, "It would be ours!"

"Impossible," devastatingly blunt.

"But we could at least find out? Josie said something about two mortgages…"

"What does she know?" He is less impressed by Josie than I. "And do you have any idea what other costs there would be?" I don't, not the slightest.

"Just asking and taking a look wouldn't cost us anything," I say stubbornly, "What harm would that do? Why don't we just take a look, please?"

He looks tired, a little pale and listless. "Okay, ring the estate agent then if that's what you want. We'll go and have a look. I could take an hour off work tomorrow afternoon." The estate agent's office is nearby. The next day Josie and I go to pick up the key together with Lindy and Sally; this is handed over to us without the slightest problem. I can't remember that anyone from the office went with us to view the house. What I do remember is my first impression of what would become our very first house.

The front door opens onto a narrow, dark corridor with a blind wall on the right side and on the left a row of doors. Bedroom doors. The first bedroom, which is large, has windows that look out onto the front veranda. The next two, smaller in size, look out onto the path that encircles the house and leads to the back garden. All three rooms have old-fashioned, open fireplaces, each with a cracked, yellow- marble mantelpiece.

Then a side corridor that leads to the narrow bathroom with toilet, a battered boiler and a bath on three, ornate, curled, copper supports and a pile of bricks where the fourth should have been. Then the lounge room: the same bay window as in Auburn with the same stained glass windows. It is dark and cool. There is a door to the kitchen. The kitchen is large. There is a rusty stove in a niche, which must have been an open cooking area in the past. The chimney shaft above the stove is immense. "They must have roasted half a cow here once upon a time," says Josie. "And look! You have a scullery. A real, old-fashioned scullery!" This is a deep, narrow walk-in area, with a window under which a sink and counter are located. Opposite these are kitchen cupboards and shelves. The door leading outside is on the other side, in the extension of the corridor.

That door opens onto a square, wooden veranda, with a long, narrow, wooden staircase leading to the garden, with a sturdy banister, thankfully. Under the veranda we discover the laundry, complete with copper, washbasins and electric light. And next to that a second toilet: a real, flushing toilet, in a small, stone hut. The back garden consists of little more than a plot of withered grass with a tree in the middle. "A locust tree," says Josie, "The fruit is edible."

The three of us are standing next to each other on the veranda. We are looking down on layers of copper-coloured treetops, on red roofs and streets like corkscrews. My hand is resting on my enormous, undulating belly. "You can see Balmoral from here! Look!"

"And that's my garden gate," says Josie, "Directly opposite. We'll be able to shout to each other!"

"If only we could," I say dreamily.

"I'm going to try to make it happen," says Gerard, who has been uncharacteristically quiet while walking through the house in our wake. "I'll ask for an option. God only knows how we'll manage after that, but I'm going to try."

"Atta boy!" Josie says, with a broad grin.

Of course the deposit required wasn't a hundred pounds, it was a terrifying multiple of that. In the last week before our Paulie was born, Josie came over every day. The girls were to stay with her as soon as the baby announced its arrival. No problem at all, she said, she had everything arranged. She could always use her mother's large house if need be. And Monty was fine with it. (Monty remained hidden in Josie's shadow, a kind of benevolent ghost who rarely appeared).

I loved having her around. It wasn't that she had taken Hiek's place. Nobody could do that. But Hiek and Jan and the boys were always gone in the weekends now, they were working hard on the house in Seaforth. Josie was always there, endlessly energetic and inventive, and so good with the children. She had been, I discovered, a kindergarten teacher, which must have suited her down to the ground, I thought. She helped me to organise Janneke's fifth birthday party in our piece of Ellamatta Avenue garden. That is to say, she helped with the preparations and then took over the management. I was allowed to enjoy myself and not lift a finger to help. "That baby of yours. Any tick of the clock now! You simply must take it easy!" She was passionately interested in our attempts to acquire the house on Middle Head Road. "I have a stake in it too!"

While I brought our first son into the world on 20 November, with Maine's help, Gerard moved heaven and earth. He received help from unexpected quarters. Father van Houten and an unknown benefactor supplied us with an interest-free loan, which served as a second mortgage. When our Paul was two months old, we signed the contract of sale and were owners of a house.

We had an immense debt. We would need to scrimp and save to be able to pay the instalments, but we were starry-eyed. Reborn. Weren't we seasoned and resourceful veterans in this country of limitless possibilities? Hadn't we weathered worse storms than this? We both discovered reserves of energy we never knew we had. Gerard could also work as a taxi driver on Friday evenings. We could rent out a room. Hiek could get me a second-hand typewriter and typing work to do in the evenings. Typing envelopes to start off with.

"I'm my own boss at the office," she said, "I can farm work out if I want to. I have more typing work than I can handle and I can get more. I'll pass it on to you. It doesn't pay much, but every penny helps." Hiek's job, her third, I think, since she had arrived in Sydney, was then still a mystery to me. She referred to it breezily as "running a duplicating service." Whatever it was, I wanted nothing more than to become her home worker.

Even the nest of red-back spiders I discovered on the front veranda when I set about scrubbing the red tiles during the cleaning spree Josie and I embarked on didn't give me an immediate heart failure. They were unusually big and had the tell-tale bright red spot on their black backs. About ten of them: father, mother and kids, undoubtedly. I pushed Lindy and Sally who had come after me back into the corridor and shut the front door. Then, terrified and shaking, I trod on the two largest. After which I called Josie, who got rid of the nest with great efficiency using a bucket of boiling water. "That's how you do it."

Josie, longer-legged than ever in white tennis-shorts and wearing a bright red handkerchief around her brown curls, worked miracles that day. She scrubbed and polished, cleaned windows, cleaned the stove, brought provisions and took the children shopping with her while I gave the baby his bottle. And she sang all day.

The next morning, on a glorious summer Saturday morning, we moved. Monty turned up with a large van. Jan and Gerard used their own cars and whatever wasn't too heavy we simply carried. It was a stone's throw away, after all, at the end of Effingham Street, and even downhill.

That evening. A warm summer's evening. The six of us are sitting in a row, on the veranda floor of our new home: Jan and Hiek, Josie and Monty, Gerard and I. All the children are asleep. Our girls together in their own girls' room; the baby in his travel cot in the big bedroom at the front, our first, real bedroom; Josie's kids in the flat opposite us; Hiek's boys in Ellamatta Avenue.

We are too tired to talk. I should tell them how grateful I am, but I can't utter a word. My bones have become liquid. I am transparent, as transparent and as boneless as a jellyfish op the beach. I gaze at the stars, which are so close that I could pluck them out of the velvet sky if I had the energy.

"Another fortnight and it'll be our turn," Hiek sighs, sitting next to me.

"You always have more stuff than you think," says Josie, "But it went well, don't you think?"

"Guys," says Gerard, "How can we ever thank...?"

"Time for bed," says Monty, scrambling up and stretching himself.

"And sleep in tomorrow," Josie stands up too, and Jan pulls Hiek up.

We all stand together and look down at the lights twinkling below us. A hill covered in glow-worms, stretching into immense space and peace. "It's nice, huh?" says Hiek, "Yet another milestone." All I can do is put my arms around her.

CHAPTER 16

Middle Head Road

WHEN I THINK of our house in Middle Head Road what I always see first is the back veranda. We never used the front door; we always entered and left by the back veranda stairs. The veranda, not the living room, was the heart of the house. The kitchen was also part of this. The kitchen door was always open; from inside it was an inviting rectangle of light. Behind it lay my beloved treetops, roofs and view of the sea, and the safe enclosure of the veranda, with its worn, but smooth wooden plank floor.

The veranda was our living area and our playroom; it was where we received guests and threw parties. In the summer a cool breeze always blew there and there was shade, and in the winter it was dry and, when the sun shone, warm. And even if a sharp wind howled on occasion, it always blew around the side of the house and could never reach us there.

The rest of the house was a kind of dark cave into which we withdrew in the evenings and at night. Our days were spent on the veranda. Paulie grew from baby to toddler there. He slept there in the mornings and afternoons. We set up his playpen there. He learned to crawl there, to walk and to climb the stairs.

From the veranda, Janneke left for school every morning, now without me, but together with Katie; she and Katie returned there again every afternoon. Lindy played with the dolls she loved on the veranda until, usually around eleven o'clock every week-day, Sally would clamber up the stairs. The play area would then move to the garden below or sometimes to the lane behind our fence. Sally was more adventurous than Lindy. Luckily, they always remained within hailing distance.

Sally's mother usually followed her; she claimed that my veranda was the ideal place to lounge and that I was an incorrigible workaholic. "You need to take a break, love. Let's have a quiet cup of tea. If it weren't for me you'd wear yourself to the bone!" And there we would sit, on the veranda. And talk and talk. Or rather, Josie would talk and I would listen.

Josie's maiden name was Neville. It was only many years later, when we had returned to the Netherlands in fact, that I realised that the Neville's were actually a very special Australian family. By that time, Richard Neville had become famous, or at least infamous, as the publisher of *OZ* in London, a rebellious magazine that he had started in Sydney. And Jill Neville had already published a few novels and made contributions to the *Times Literary Supplement*.

Richard was Josie's younger brother, Ricky, who was still at school when we were living in Middle Head Road. (He was a boarder at the renowned Knox Grammar School). He came home every now and then, at which times Josie would usually look after him. Jill was Josie's younger sister who left for England when she was eighteen (1950) and about whom her mother worried a great deal. Josie talked about Jill with some nostalgia and a little envy. Jill had thrown off the chains of her upbringing. She was forging her own path through life. She was free. She was living the life of an artist in London. She was so brave. She wrote poetry and had contacts in the literary world.

"Jill is so different from me. All I'm good for is running the household. My mother always used to say that I would end up married to a truck driver." I now think Josie underestimated herself grossly. She was a natural storyteller and I a fascinated listener. (Jill died in London in 1997 at the age of 65. I have an obituary from the *Sydney Morning Herald* with a photo that I look at every now and then. She didn't look like Josie, but does have unmistakable Neville features. Did she look like Ricky?).

I met Clive and Betty Neville, Josie's parents. We even stayed once in their famous house in the Blue Mountains but I don't have a clear recollection of it. I remember Betty vaguely as small and skinny with intelligent eyes.

Josie showed me around the house that her flat was attached to, a grand house with the front door opening onto Wolseley Road, one of the circular roads that led to Balmoral Beach. Her parents were gone every weekend and often also for weeks on end, and then she could use the house as she pleased. It was roomy and comfortable. There was a piano. I remember her sitting at the piano surrounded by all the children. She would play traditional English nursery rhymes, and everyone would sing along. Those songs still play in my head every now and then, especially one of them, a winter song:

The North wind doth blow,
And we shall have snow,
And what will the robin do then, poor thing?
He'll sit in the barn
To keep himself warm
And hide his head under his wing, poor thing.

I loved it and I loved talented Josie. She was my window into Australian society – both the present and the past. She opened my eyes to all sorts of things. She described everything so well, painting pictures in words. She described people especially, her old friends who regularly turned up. She unravelled their past for me and so gave their present a colour and shape. She offered wisdom and grown up knowledge, and every word she uttered I naively took as the absolute truth. If she encouraged me enough, I would talk too. My vocabulary expanded by leaps and bounds. I imitated her. I also began to imitate her style. I felt I was acquiring insight, making discoveries, forging an identity.

Our talking sessions belonged to the mornings and the veranda (I wonder what we sat on? We didn't have very many chairs). The rest of the day was devoted to domestic duties and children, and the evenings to typing. Gerard wasn't home a great deal. He was working as hard as I was, now trying to sell cars in the evenings as well if he wasn't driving his taxi.

And then there was Fred. Fred was our boarder, our full board lodger. We had found him thanks to Father van Houten, who had sent him to us with the assurance that he was "a good Catholic boy." Fred was skinny, pale and lanky, and had thin blonde hair that hung wispily down from his round skull. He wore a small pair of round spectacles. He worked in a factory somewhere. He got up every morning at six o'clock and returned in the afternoons around four, only to disappear again every evening, immediately after dinner. He was docile and shy, and rarely spoke. He shuffled when he walked. He reminded me a little of Tom. Even though he was in his late twenties, I regarded him as an extra child whom I had to look after as best I could. Josie thought I should find out what he was doing every night, so I asked him when he came up the veranda stairs one afternoon at four as usual: "What is it that you do in the evenings, Fred?"

The pale eyes blinked at me from behind his spectacles, but he seemed perfectly happy to enlighten me. "I practice," he told me amiably.

"Practice?"

"Yes. At my ballet school."

I couldn't believe my ears. "Ballet school? Do you mean that you take ballet lessons?"

He nodded earnestly. "In North Sydney. It's a good school. I think the jumps are very difficult. But I'm allowed to practice there whenever I like. Well, I'm going off to rest now. Good afternoon." And he shuffled through the kitchen door in the direction of his room. I looked after him, open-mouthed. Ballet? Fred? In my eyes, everything about the boy was awkward. He walked heavily, without the slightest trace of natural grace and his movements were almost clumsy.

When I reported back to Josie, she burst out laughing. "You should ask him to give us a demonstration. During your housewarming party! I'd love to see him jump!" For some reason this idea gave me the shivers.

"I hadn't intended to invite Fred."

"But you can't give a housewarming party without inviting your boarder! Leave him to me. I bet I can get him to agree."

Our housewarming party was also Josie's idea. She had explained to me at length that this was a good Australian tradition and that I shouldn't worry about a thing. It wouldn't cost us a fortune. All I needed to do was make the house available. She would do the rest.

I suspect my memories of our housewarming party have merged with those of a few of the other parties we threw in Middle Head Road. I can see our veranda decorated with Christmas lights (Josie's). I see candles placed everywhere in empty bottles. I see Josie dragging around an old-fashioned record player and piles of records. There is a wide selection of alcoholic drinks on my kitchen counter and my kitchen table is full of festive party food. Australian tradition dictated that every male guest turned up with a bottle (or more than one) and every female guest with a plate of food. While our children slept peacefully in the front room, we drank, ate, danced and talked in the back of the house and on the veranda.

And we sang. There was always someone sitting on the top stair of the veranda strumming a guitar and constantly changing choirs would form there. I see crowds of people. In the shadowy light of the candles they all look equally exciting and romantic. There is a constant flow from living room to kitchen to veranda and vice versa. And a constant changing of groups, a standing still and moving around, coming and going. Only much later in the evening do people sit, usually on the floor. By then the music has been turned down, the voices are muted and the candles almost burned out. Here and there, the ends of cigarettes glow red in the dark.

Where did they all come from? Josie, they were friends of Josie's who brought their own friends along, also an Australian tradition. Everyone was welcome. Josie had prepped me thoroughly. She had told me stories about almost everyone.

Like Seth Frith, a name it was almost impossible for me to pronounce, an old school friend who had a mundane job of some kind, but was in fact a frustrated musician. He was as thin as a rake and looked slightly grubby. One of his front teeth was missing. Through this hole he could, on request, miraculously whistle whole symphonies. The tunes sounded improbably beautiful. He had a wife whose face was thin and pointed. But according to Josie the marriage was in trouble. "She has no idea what goes on in his head. She hates music! No wonder he drinks so much" (he did).

And then there were Tony and Yolande. Tony was an Englishman with an Oxford accent and a sardonic grin. He was quite small and limped a little, but was extremely witty. He supplied a humorous running commentary on life in general and party incidents and people in particular, through a permanently slanted mouth.

"He was seriously ill as a child," Josie told me, "he feels disfigured. That's why he's so bitter. Not easy for Yolande" (Yolande was an old school friend, tall, dark, glamorous). But Tony never struck me as bitter: he always made me laugh so much. I liked him hugely.

Another school friend of Josie's was Patsy Morgan. Josie called her "the girl with the biscuit tin face." She was very beautiful, in a vaguely Victorian way: blonde curls, blue eyes. I was told she also had a bunch of children.

And of course there is Kenny. Ken Neville, Josie's youngest uncle who behaves more like her elder brother. He seems messily built somehow: long arms and legs, and a square torso; broad swimmers' shoulders and a weathered, brown face, furrowed with laughter lines. He has a vague job at the Sydney Symphony Orchestra, Josie tells me, something to do with taking care of the instruments. Uncle Kenny is very musical. He always carries his ukulele with him and a harmonica, buried in one of the deep pockets of his permanently drooping trousers. He loves to organise what he calls singsongs. Old English tunes and nursery rhymes are his favourites. He has been married twice and divorced twice. "Women adore Kenny," Josie tells me, "but they can never stand living with him. He's a darling, but he has never grown up. He sees the world through the eyes of a child."

Yet Kenny is one of the sunniest, most evenly tempered men I have ever known and to my children he is a fairy tale uncle who fills in for all the real aunts and uncles and grandparents they lack. When I think of Uncle Kenny I see him with a baby on his lap, and a toddler leaning against his shoulder and a whole group of children breathlessly listening to his gentle voice. He could tell the most wonderful stories. About a green fish who lived at the bottom of the sea and with whom he regularly conversed when he went swimming every morning; about old Aboriginal legends from the Dreamtime when all the animals could talk. And of course he would get the children to sing while he played his ukulele and harmonica simultaneously.

Most of the guests who came to our parties lived in Mosman and its neighbouring suburbs. I now wonder whether Josie hadn't launched a noble "Let's integrate the New Australians" campaign amongst her friends and acquaintances. But it could also have been "Look what I've found!" She was so proud of us. Gerard was a sparkling host. He enjoyed himself hugely. He was tireless, and always danced with every woman there. "Your gorgeous husband," Josie called him, "Such beautiful manners! So European!" She had huge admiration for everything European.

Back to that first housewarming party: of course Jan and Hiek were there and Win, and Phons was there too: Phons from Binalong! A week or so before we finally left Ellamatta Avenue Phons suddenly turned up. He had come, as he had promised, to visit us. He was travelling with a sleeping bag en route to a farm in Queensland (bananas or pineapples, I don't recall), which was run by yet another brother. The chicken farm had given up the ghost, he told us. In part because of a financial calamity due to an exotic chicken disease and in part for personal reasons, which he did not want to talk about. He was nevertheless as cheerful and optimistic as ever. He was going to start a new life, a brand new life.

"Why don't you stay in Sydney?" Gerard had asked, "More opportunities, more room to manoeuvre. Country life doesn't have all that much to offer, all that primitive living. You know what? If you don't like it there, just come back here. We'll have our own house soon, you can always stay with us," with which I agreed completely.

They resembled each other, I thought, Gerard and Phons. They had much more in common than Gerard and Paul; they understood each other wordlessly. They laughed at the same things; they talked in the same way and clearly dreamed the same dreams. A week before our housewarming party, Phons was back in Sydney, completely broke, but still as upbeat as ever. Gerard had been right. Life on the farm hadn't suited him. He had looked around Brisbane for a bit but it did not appeal to him either. Brisbane was such a boring, provincial town. Here in Sydney there were many more possibilities.

When we moved we had acquired an old sofa bed from Josie's mother, who no longer needed it. "You're going to come and live with us," Gerard had decided, "You can sleep in the living room for the time being." Phons fit into our household as if he had always been a part of it. Within no time, he became indispensable. Whenever he was around, he helped with the cleaning, tidying and washing up. He made coffee and tea. He washed dirty children's faces and lifted gurgling babies onto his shoulders. He played Daddy on taxi evenings and Mummy if I was behind with my typing work. He found a job almost immediately at a firm that installed alarms in factories and told us the most alarming stories about welding jobs, high up on ceilings, while mobile cranes swung around beneath him. He insisted on paying us the same rent as Fred although Fred had his own room. So I had, at the time of our housewarming party, two lodgers or boarders as Josie kept on calling them. "Can't you rustle up a few for me? It's such a pity I don't have a house with extra rooms to rent out."

Fred is indeed at the party that evening, and, true to her nature, Josie persuades him to give us a ballet demonstration. I enter the living room at one point to discover Fred standing ready, in ballet tights and ballet slippers, his feet splayed in the first position. A space has been cleared for him to perform. A small group of people are watching. He takes a short run and launches himself into a giant leap. But he slips as he comes down and lands with a thud on his bottom on the floor. He scrambles up immediately, shakes his head and starts again, this time with his arms spread wide, his head thrown back. He takes three hesitant steps and launches himself anew. He falls again. "Every beginning dancer falls a lot," he declares, sitting on the ground, looking earnestly up at Josie.

"Of course they do!" she cries, with dancing eyes, "And it's a bit too cramped in here, isn't it? You really need a larger space."

"Much too cramped," I say decisively, "Thanks so much Fred, it was very sweet of you to try."

"I don't mind trying again," he says, getting up.

"No, better not. Maybe another time, don't you think?" He looks intensely sad, and sits down on the corner of the sofa bed. I quickly put on a different record. The spectators have disappeared, as has Josie.

I find her a little later in the kitchen with Phons, wiping tears of laughter from her cheeks. "Wasn't that incredible?! Oh God, Fred's secret passion!" For the first time in our friendship I actually don't like her. She flicks Phons' cheek. "And then there is your other boarder! This one is all blonde manliness. If I wasn't a respectable married mother with three kids…"

Phons laughs and I join in nervously, but wonder at the same time whether there isn't something obsessive about her chatter, something hungry. I immediately banish this disloyal thought. There is no better, more loyal, more warm-hearted neighbour than Josie.

Very late on that same evening I share with her something that I have suspected for a while. That baby number four is on the way. Too quickly, too soon, I think. Our Paulie is only six months old.

"You should first find out whether you're right," says Josie," And if you are... well, four children is an ideal number, isn't it? And it's better to have them in quick succession, while you're still young. It's also much better for the other kids. They'll grow up together. You've got a house now, love, don't you? You just need to make absolutely sure that this will be the last one. You have to raise them after all, those four! You should forget all that Catholic rubbish and so-called safe periods. Go and talk to your doctor. It's high time you took your own decisions about such things, matey."

She was right, of course. But I realised that for the moment there were no decisions to be taken. There was no point in thinking about any of it yet.

Upjohn Conference 1961

Harry Todd
John White
Ross Whidden
Ron Tobin

CHAPTER 17

New jobs

CHRISTMAS 2000 IS *the first white Christmas in many years. It is now December 2000 and it is snowing outside my window. I haven't sat here for days. I'm not happy with the image my writing projects. I try to be as honest as possible but what emerges has a kind of Pollyanna ring to it, a stereotype. Is that because I am using my old manuscript as a guide? I need to. I need that memory prompt. But I am only transcribing very little, this is a different book, although the chronological order is the same and for some reason this imparts a particular flavour. Clearly I need not only to change the language I used in my previous text, but also amend the lack of insight underlying it. Moreover, I manipulated things a bit then in order to create a certain pattern. I am trying not to do that now; I am writing to gain insight not impose order. Not that I am being very successful...but I think now that then, in our Middle Head Road time, I was surrounded by a conspiracy of silence. That I was protected, shielded from the all too brutal facts of life and human nature, if such a thing exists. By everyone I met, at least to a certain extent; and that I, consciously or otherwise, adapted myself to that.*

Gerard and I were delighted with another child, even though this addition to our family meant even more financial pressure. We nevertheless decided that he should give up his taxi job. It was too much of a burden for him, I thought. He was getting too tired and had lost far too much weight. We had already paid off our smaller debts. We could now handle the monthly mortgage payments easily.

When Fred came to tell me that he had found a room in North Sydney closer to his ballet school, I wasn't sorry about this at all, on the contrary.

Phons took his room so we still had a little extra income and life was a lot nicer that way. No strangers in the house.

"You see how it has all worked out!" said Josie, "And this pregnancy will be a breeze. You now have two handsome men around you to look after you and I'll be around too. I'll be responsible for the essential relaxation. My mother is going to buy a television and she has promised that we'll all be able to watch it. Films in your own home! Just imagine!"

I can't really imagine it. I had read about televisions on occasion – the miracle of the century – and had caught vague echoes of them. Janneke had recently started to disappear every Saturday morning to a friend's house further down the street. "Louise's house," she said. She would come back with stories about someone called "Annie Oakley," whom I had never heard of. "On TV," she explained.

It never occurred to me that this unheard of luxury would ever enter my orbit. And here it was all of a sudden, almost within reach. Now Josie would regularly charge up the veranda stairs saying, "If you have time and feel like it we can watch TV tonight!" Which meant that Betty and Clive were gone. Once the children were sound asleep, we would dive into the television room in the big house together and stare breathlessly at the screen. We never went out. Now we suddenly had access to the wide world. Films! And a series called *Route 66* that we became addicted to and could talk about endlessly. Of course this was a black and white television. Our men were completely uninterested.

Yet another earthquake, the full meaning of which we barely realised, began with a vague rumbling one Saturday afternoon. Our Saturdays were always a little festive. After the morning whirlwind (Saturdays meant shopping by car, getting supplies and groceries. But all the shops shut irrevocably at 12.00 and we always had great difficulty meeting that deadline!), we would have coffee and cake on the veranda. Phons always made the coffee and Gerard organised the cake (with meringues for the children) after which the three of us would swap stories from the *Sydney Morning Herald*. Paul would sleep, and the girls would play with Katie and Sally below in the garden. Peace.

"Upjohn," Gerard suddenly reads, "Pharmaceutical Company. American, Medical Representatives wanted. Academic background preferred. Oh well, I seriously considered that once upon a time. Didn't happen because of the war. And I've always been interested in medicines."

"I haven't," says Phons drily.

"Here's another one. This company is called Nicolas. Veterinary medicine. That's perfect for you, old man, with your country experience! Excellent salary, both of them and a company car! We should try this. We're going to apply straightaway. We'll write letters they can't possibly refuse. Phons, old man, this is the chance of our lives!"

Gerard and Phons have been talking for months about the fact that something needed to happen. That there needed to be more money. A good idea and they would be millionaires, they thought. A pity you always needed capital to make an idea into a concrete product, though. It was a vicious circle, without a product no mountains of money and without mountains of money no product; this fact gnawed at them. They both also thought they should be able to find better jobs. Every Saturday the job section of the *SMH* was thoroughly scanned therefore. Hence, this Saturday....

Letters are written. A whole weekend is devoted to writing and re-writing. Three days later Gerard receives an invitation for an interview and Phons receives an invitation the day after. Four weeks later they have both been hired. They both disappeared in succession for a week of intensive training. And then we are suddenly a household with two cars and our financial future has become distinctly rosy.

January 2001. 15 January 2001 to be exact: a cold, sunny winter's day in Breda, a cloudless sky. In ten days' time we fly to Australia. I am not going to try to add anything more to this manuscript. When I get back...

CHAPTER 18

Picnics and discussions

27 APRIL 2001. *We are back. We have been back since 21 March, but I find myself as intimidated by our Mac and this project as I was when I first started and have been avoiding both. I had meant to describe Australia as it is now, as we have just experienced it during the past two months, but find it impossible. The country now and our old Australia are different worlds. And that "now" is coloured by a deep feeling of loss. There is still the sense that "I have come home;" and the embrace of the sea, the warm wind, the space. But at the same time there is the knowledge that it is all over, that this was a last leave-taking. "This is really going to be the last time," Gerard kept on saying and I think he is right. I just want to pick up the old thread and keep on writing about the way it was back then, but why? And does the why even matter?*

Back to 1959 and a household with two cars and the promise of a great future ahead of us. Gerard celebrated the turn in our fortunes by buying what was then called a radiogram: a combination radio and record-player in a big red, Bakelite box. And Phons' first pay contributed to the festivities in the form of a record by the *Dutch Swing College Band*.

That whole Saturday afternoon clouds of jazz music wafted from our open back door while inside solo-swingers gyrated about. Grinning from ear to ear, my men danced around each other, Gerard bent almost double, with his nose in the air, index fingers stretched up to ear height, Phons snapping his fingers to the beat. Janneke jumped around with them, screaming with pleasure. Lindy sat, with her thumb in her mouth, watching them earnestly, and Paulie, who had just taught himself to stand, bounced gurgling to the beat, holding himself up with two little hands clasped firmly around the railing of his playpen.

Life was good on Saturdays. Life fizzed and frolicked on Saturdays; actually, life fizzed throughout the winter of 1959. Admittedly, I was once again dragging a pregnant tummy around and the men would disappear regularly (especially Phons, Gerard luckily less so) for a week into the interior of New South Wales for work. But I nevertheless felt liberated, relieved of a yoke. I knew everything would be alright. It felt as if after many wanderings we had once again found an oasis of tranquility. We belonged here. We were home. (And it helped that this time I did not suffer from my usual pregnancy nausea).

I can hear myself proclaiming deeply felt convictions, on the veranda, in the mornings. (Some of these convictions I still have, and some I met again during our recent two-month trip to Australia). How wonderful it was that so many things were upside down and back to front here compared to Europe, just like the seasons!

For instance, in the weekends everyone, whether rich or poor, walked around in their oldest clothes, preferably barefoot. Then there was the fact that no-one would dream of making disparaging remarks about someone else's appearance. That no-one cared how much money you earned, what occupation you had, where you came from, who your parents were. That melting-pot feeling, that welcoming "Come and join us, and show us what you're worth, here and now!" I called it classlessness then. At which Josie would smirk and point out just how important it was in this classless society which schools you had attended (the most expensive!) and in which rich suburbs you lived, and whether you had a few million in the bank. And the mighty unions weren't easy to live with either. But then, Josie adored Europe and was greedy for anything European.

It must have rained in that first winter in Middle Head Road. That harsh Australian rain which could freeze you to the marrow must have fallen, but I can't remember it. I can remember the sea breeze on Balmoral Beach when we picniced there among the rocks. And the winter sun. I can also remember winter picnics in the bush in Kuringai Chase National Park. In that vast expanse of protected bushland, within the borders of wider Sydney, narrow asphalt roads wound through dark, mysterious valleys, crowded with wildly twisting gumtrees. You drove past ravines where water glistened way below in the depths and alongside lead-coloured rock faces, zigzagged with red and yellow zebra stripes. Or past rocky outcrops, sprouting thick clusters of exotic flowers and plants, with small eucalyptus trees clinging valiantly to the strangest places.

We would take two cars: Gerard (and sometimes Phons too) and I with the kids in one car and Josie, often with Kenny, but never Monty, and her children in the other. We sometimes drove to Bobbin Head, a low plateau along the Hawkesbury River surrounded by forests, where there were often sailing boats and where you could fish from the pier; we once drove all the way to the mouth of the Hawkesbury to see the ocean, which was indescribably blue. Endless.

Our normal routine was to stop at one of the first wooden signs, which indicated "picnic area" and "water." We would then traipse into the bush in procession, laden with picnic baskets and our "billy." We would look for and always find a sun-warmed, flat rock with camp-fire possibilities. To our children, the camp-fire was the highlight of the day. They would dance around it, crowing and jubilant. In the meantime, our billies would hang above the fire on a contraption made of strong branches and tea would be brewed. Uncle Kenny was an expert at this.

And then we would eat, and trees and rocks would be discovered and climbed, and every time anew I would become aware of the immense wilderness surrounding us; of the strangeness of this country; of the indifference of nature and the vulnerability of small children in its midst. How I envied Josie her carefree nature, her optimism, her talent for laughing away anxiety and care. The only anxiety we all shared was making sure at the end of our picnic to stamp out any trace of slumbering fire and cover it with sand. This was a solemn duty. Under no circumstances did we want to start a bushfire, Kenny explained to the children each time.

Just as my memories of our Middle Head Road parties have fused, so too have my recollections of our picnics. We have photos of children dancing round a camp-fire, and Bobby is one of them, as are Phons and Patsy with Julie and little Luc. That was years later. Nevertheless, I always associate bush picnics with Josie and Uncle Kenny, who introduced us to them.

Another idea of Josie's during that winter was our discussion group. Following one or two accidental evenings of discussion, which arose spontaneously, she proposed that we get together regularly with a group of friends, exclusively to talk, to philosophise, to discuss important issues of the day and life, to devote ourselves to anything but evenings of mindless fun! And we should do this at our house, because we had the most space.

I was immediately wildly enthusiastic. I did my best to give our living room a Parisian flavour on the evening of our first session: candles on the table and a solitary lamp, and cushions and folded blankets on the floor to sit on. We were all deeply serious. Later, these evenings became a little more frivolous when the discussants began to bring red wine along, but they remained evenings of discussion. And our discussions remained general; there were no cozy one-to-ones as far as I can remember, even though we did not have a chairman. We decided in advance what we would talk about, which did not mean that we did not discuss the most diverse topics.

And almost everyone always advanced his or her own hobbyhorse with gusto. Josie's was breaking taboos, making yourself vulnerable, taking risks in relationships. Tony's was rebellion against the establishment, free love and open marriage (even though he readily admitted he would avoid all this like the plague, "I hate confrontations!"). Mine was a plea for clarity and defining terms. Gerard? Phons? Theirs have disappeared into the grey mists of time. And those of all the other members of our group? The group evolved every time we met. I remember the evening that Tony brought Peter and Jane along.

"This is the most beautiful girl in my office. Unfortunately, we'll have to put up with this fellow too. They're two souls twinned together or something..." Jane had huge shining eyes that were sometimes sea green and sometimes as brown as a deer's. She had narrow, graceful hands and almost translucent skin. Peter had a black beard, was Jewish, and looked exactly like the traditional figure of Christ. His shoulders were slightly stooped and they seemed to bear invisible burdens. He had velvety dark eyes, which were both melancholy and fierce at the same time. Jane and Peter sat next to each other on our couch, hand in hand.

First, they listened for a little while, and then Peter informed us that all we were doing was talking on a purely emotional level and that he had so hoped this would not be the case. At which Jane threw him an adoring look and nodded in agreement.

"Do you see this cup?" Peter picked up an empty coffee cup, and suddenly directed himself exclusively to me. "Can you really see this coffee cup?" I stared in fascination at the cup and the others stared with me. Deathly silence. "What is it?" asked Peter, "Is its coffee-cup-ness its fundamental essence? Does something like a coffee cup really exist? Don't you see how your own subjectivity determines your view?" The black eyes released me and turned heavenwards, "Oh, the deadly barrenness of subjective perception!"

"Oh really!" Tony snapped, "And here I was thinking that objectivity is impossible. That it's only possible for me to see through my own eyes. Aren't you a member of Push, Peter – that beatnik movement? If those people aren't steeped in subjectivity then no-one is!"

"I have some contacts in Push circles," Peter said haughtily.

"Young artists," Jane explained, "Don't you agree that art is finally developing a unique style nowadays? I think representation is gone forever, at long last." Peter and Jane resembled an antique wood cut, their hands intertwined, their dark heads close together.

Peter had been smuggled out of Vienna to England as a baby during the war and then on to Australia. He had just ended his studies in forestry, which he never completed. He wrote and experimented with the visual arts, designs in copper and mosaics. Every now and then he would take a freelance job. Jane wrote too, but claimed she was not in Peter's league. She also had less time for writing, as she had a steady job. Peter was so gifted, she would say, he needed space, couldn't tolerate rules, had to have room to improvise and experiment. And so Peter Adler very quickly assumed the leadership of our little group: no more fuzzy, confused aberrations....

And then Patsy and Paul arrived: Patsy Cairns and Paul Gundry White, the latter of English descent. Patsy was small and fragile, and very beautiful. She had large green eyes, framed by enviably long, dark eyelashes. She had a thick mane of long, red, curly hair, which danced around her small, pointed face every time she moved. She had the cream white skin of all redheads. And she was always well dressed and carefully, though never excessively, made up.

Patsy was an old school friend of Josie's. They had lost touch for many years until a chance meeting with Kenny on the Mosman Ferry. (Josie told me that Patsy and Kenny had once been briefly engaged, which astounded me). Josie promptly rang her and invited her to dinner, and then invited us over to meet her. When we arrived Pat was sitting at the piano singing, accompanying herself. She had a beautifully clear soprano voice. She also danced. She told us she had worked at a dance institute briefly when she could not find another job. (She was now working for an advertising agency). She offered, laughing, to teach us the cha-cha-cha. She moved like a natural dancer.

Inevitably, our discussion group came up. "May I come too? I yearn for more spirituality and depth in my life. I know I seem to be frivolous, but deep down I'm a very serious person. I'd like to bring a friend along, an Englishman, quite an intelligent man, would that be okay?"

Patsy's friend Paul turned out to be twice as tall as she was. He had a narrow, slightly triangular face and a very long neck. He had gentle brown eyes, which always looked slightly surprised, and a delicious BBC accent. He called himself an "efficiency expert," though whether he had his own company or worked freelance I can no longer recall. He was clearly moneyed. He drove an old, but well-maintained red Ford with an open roof and he never locked his car, on principle. He left his expensive leather jacket, gloves and camera lying on the back seat. He believed in the goodness of mankind. "We have to rid ourselves of distrust and suspicion, we need to trust our fellow men, that's the way to foster honesty."

Josie quickly discovered that Pat and Paul were in a casual relationship. "At least, that is what she tells me. She's had loads of flings, that one, and this is nothing serious. He doesn't interest her hugely, she says, but he takes her to good restaurants and values her company. So she lets him take her out – not good form, in my view," frowning.

In the meantime, Pat and Paul had become keen members of our discussion group. Paul's view was that the good of the group, society, should always take precedence. That individual ambition should be subservient to that. Pasty, on the other hand, passionately defended the individual, the strong individual of course, who consciously chose his or her own path. When at one point the topic of ancient Sparta came up and the custom of leaving deformed babies on hilltops for the vultures, all hell broke loose.

"Not a bad idea," Patsy said coolly, "Mankind might be much better off if a kind of selection took place."

"That's pure fascism!" But Peter did not get the chance to continue, as four or five voices attacked Patsy at once: didn't she realise what she was saying? Couldn't she see where views like those could lead and had led?

She defended herself with spirit, and this became one of our wildest evenings.

"What a woman!" said Phons afterwards while he helped me collect the glasses.

"Who?" I asked absent-mindedly.

"Patsy, of course! What an interesting and courageous woman." I saw an expression in his eyes I had never seen before. Phons always treated every woman he met as if she were a fun but troublesome sister, someone amusing to have around, but generally: "Why couldn't a woman be more like a man?" Until now. "Couldn't we ask Patsy to dinner? Just Pat? Couldn't you ring her? It would be great fun."

It is the middle of May and summer at last. All at once the trees in our neighbourhood are bursting with leaves. The fruit trees are flowering exuberantly. The lawns suddenly look luscious. I have never seen that shade of green anywhere else: that essence of freshness, of manicured fertility.

I have been working so little on this manuscript. It sometimes seems such an impossible task. At times the figures from the past are only frozen shapes, trapped in glass, incapable of movement. But they are always young, even though some have already died. Already? Some died in the course of growing old, as old as I am now.

Is what I am writing now too much like my first attempt? Too much of a stab at writing a novel? Oh, what does it matter: I still want to try to put down on paper how we were then, how things were then. The group of friends around us, the interactions, the fun we had and the problems we battled, of which the most pressing was lack of money – something we never stopped to think about at the time, but which determined our whole lives, which ran like Ariadne's thread through all our decisions. The effort it always took us to make ends meet, to survive. Did something like the dole exist for hopeless cases? If it did, I never saw it in practice. We were the way we were then. Or rather, I can only write what I see, hear and experience when I look back, even though I know full well that memory is selective.

Snippets of conversation: Gerard: "You aren't under the illusion that all these things haven't been said before, and much better, are you?"

Me: "So what?! The main thing is that we are being forced to think, not just accept everything as gospel truth. And I like these clashes of personalities, they're fun."

Gerard: "Cackling roosters and chickens. Waste of a good evening, right, Phons?"

Phons: "Well… I think it's quite worthwhile. It can't do any harm to spend time thinking about really fundamental things every now and then."

This must have been after Patsy's arrival. Normally, Gerard and Phons agreed wholeheartedly about everything.

Patsy came to dinner. And enchanted us. She looked so pretty in a green dress with a wide skirt and tight waist that begged to be circled by two male hands. She told us that she was responsible for compiling a catalogue for a mail order firm. She thought that our children were very photogenic, especially Paul. She adored him. Would we be able to bring him to her office one afternoon to be a model for baby clothes? She could pay us, even though it wasn't a great deal, and we would get to keep the photos for free.

"I'll go along," Phons immediately offered, "I'm much less busy than Gerard!"

Pat helped me to put the children to bed. "You've no idea how much I envy you. You're doing something really worthwhile. Raising children. I'm nothing compared to you." And: "I can't bear to be alone. That's the only reason I go out with Paul. I wish I were more like you. You're so calm, so sensible and patient."

"Me?!" Even then I thought this was over the top, although I promptly did my best to appear serene, sensible and patient. It suited my size! I could no longer sit on the floor during our discussion evenings. I had to sit on a chair. "Our Earth Mother," Josie called me.

When Patsy announced to us that she had to catch the ten o'clock ferry to town ("working-day tomorrow"), Phons offered to drive her home.

"All the way to town? Oh, you angel, are you sure?"

"Not a problem, easily done," he mumbled.

"May I come back?" Pat asked me, "Next Wednesday I have a day off. I'd love to come here. I have the feeling you and I are on the same wavelength somehow."

I hear Gerard say: "Phons needs to be careful. She's a handful." And I: "Oh, don't be silly. She's lovely." I see Phons walking through the house, whistling. He takes Patsy out. He meets her at least twice a week, somewhere in town. She still takes Paul along to our discussion evenings. He gives her a lift, she says. "They've never been anything more than good friends," Phons assures me, "They both believe in giving the other complete freedom and so do I. She can go out with whomever she wants."

"Do you really think that?" I ask.

"Well... of course I hope things will change one day," Phons tells me with a shy laugh. "But it's too early now, still far too early. Once we know each other better, in a little while..."

CHAPTER 19

Patsy, Laurel and Bobby

My Mosman kitchen became a kind of jetty where friends moored regularly. I was always receiving unexpected visitors, which I loved, as long as I could continue with what I happened to be doing. Feeding Paulie, folding washing, ironing, washing up, sometimes cooking. My visitors usually helped out a little while we talked.

Patsy came often. She told me about her youth. She and her sister had been raised by her grandmother, whom she still called "Dearest." Somewhere in the country, until her grandmother died, much too young. She then went to live with her father who had just remarried. Her real mother had been and still was an alcoholic, who trailed from town to town and from treatment to treatment, and who would suddenly turn up every now and then to beg Pat for money. Her sister had left for England at a young age, as so many young Australians did – first a European tour, then settling there for good. And Patsy? She shook her head and launched into her views about men and women. "I'd like to be the power behind the throne. But for someone who has something to offer the world. And who is capable of taking decisions completely independently, also from me; an elite man. Someone who stands above the crowd."

And then more dreamily: "I knew someone like that once. I was still at school. He was twenty years older than me. His eldest daughter was a friend of mine. The ideas he had were so different from all those dusty rules. He wanted to create a different kind of world, a natural world. Untainted; without a concept of sin and without remorse and regret. And also without all those pesticides we use nowadays. He grew his own vegetables and the flowers in his garden were indescribably beautiful. I have never seen flowers like that anywhere else." She looked up, and looked straight at me. "He was my very first lover," she said, "I'm still looking for someone like him. Even if only a little bit like him."

I could find nothing to say to this. "His wife had cancer," she added curtly, "He looked after her to the bitter end." And then I heard Josie on the veranda stairs: "Yoo-hoo! Are you home?"

Jane turned up, unexpectedly on a weekday. She had been to the doctor. She was pregnant. She looked slightly stunned. She was extremely happy, she said. And so was Peter. They had discovered natural childbirth. "I'm going to do it all completely on my own."

"To the extent possible," I added.

"Of course it will all be possible. We just need to get to know and trust the processes taking place in our bodies. We need to consciously return to nature. This is the most important task I have ever had to fulfill." She was bubbling with enthusiasm and so brimming with hope. I didn't tell her how I was feeling that day. Tired. Fed up with being pregnant and only being able to move with difficulty. With all that eternal waiting, which even after the baby had been born remained a part of you.

I nodded, smiling, and made encouraging noises. I listened. She had had a Catholic upbringing, a nun's school: dancing lessons and a debutante's ball; and then Peter Adler and full-scale rebellion; rejection of all those narrow-minded values, of materialism, of ownership. But all that had calmed down a little now, she admitted. She and Peter had got married in the traditional way. She had a half-sister. "Nina is only eighteen, but very bright. She reads everything she can get her hands on. She is very different from me, but we're very good friends. I'd like to bring her along sometime if that would be alright."

Paul came for tea, in the afternoon. He brought an enormous watermelon with him. He watched me iron. He told me about his work. How he analysed factory processes and then re-organised them. We talked about efficiency in the household. And about the importance of sending birthday cards, which I thought was an excellent custom: "You're telling someone you are happy they were born, that they exist," at which Paul declared he had never looked at it like that and that he loved talking to me. He let me know he liked Phons hugely and felt some empathy for him. And he shook his head about Patsy: "A mixed-up kid if ever I met one."

Phons too came to pour his heart out in my kitchen. And he too talked about Patsy, endlessly, how beautiful she was, how funny, how special. He tried to cheer himself up: "I just need to hang on in there. She hasn't dealt with her past yet. She doesn't know me well enough. She needs time. But I would so much like to look after her. She needs someone to look after her."

And of course Josie had a vast amount to say about everything that was going on, and especially about Patsy. When one day she discovered Patsy in my kitchen, she asked breezily how the budding romance was going. Frowning surprise was the answer.

"Oh, Pat, come on! Phons adores you. And he's such a lovely man. He'd make an ideal husband, believe me."

"For someone else," Patsy said coolly, "Not for me. Phons puts women on a pedestal and then kneels down in front of them in hope and expectation. He isn't a leader; he wants to be led. I find that irritating."

"What?!" For a moment Josie was speechless, "But you're going out with him! Why? He's spending a fortune on you. He isn't doing that for nothing. He's clearly hoping things will work out between you, anyone can see that."

Patsy shrugged. "He's a grown man. I've told him loads of times he shouldn't take us too seriously because it will never lead to anything more than a few cozy dinners. I have to go, gals. If I hurry I can make the 4 o'clock ferry. I have a meeting tonight." And she was gone.

Josie: "How unreliable and selfish she is! And she's always been that way. She just uses people. I don't understand what he sees in her. I feel so sorry for Phons, don't you?"

Now, almost forty years later, it all sounds so Victorian: the ideas and opinions we had, how we viewed everyone's actions. How I viewed them: I didn't agree with Josie. I thought Pat was trying to be honest and that Phons was good for her. I assumed that she came by so often to find out more about Phons and his background...

Josie came to tell me that her mother had asked her to take a young, lonely, Austrian immigrant under her wing, the protegé of good friends. A young writer, a poet: "Still terribly young, just turned twenty, but he looks much older and is so handsome! You'd swear he had stepped out of a movie!" She brought him along to our next discussion evening.

He was indeed very good-looking – tall and broad-shouldered; thick, black, curly hair and shining, deep black eyes. He introduced himself as Christopher Nonveillier. He told us that his first name was actually Heinz, but he never used it to avoid pronunciation problems. He also told us that he had recently managed to have a short story and a poem accepted by a small, literary magazine. He worked as a proofreader at the *Sydney Morning Herald*, but that was only temporary. He wanted to become a full-time writer as soon as possible. This made a big impression on me, as did his good manners and how eloquent he was. He had come to Australia with his parents, had lived on a farm somewhere deep in New South Wales and moved to Sydney when he was 16. He owed his remarkable vocabulary to reading a great deal, he said. He was anything but shy, took over Peter's leadership role almost as a matter of course and commented on everyone's arguments.

That first evening, Patsy sat at his feet, literally. She was strikingly subdued.

He left early, had a night shift, he said. His office was in the centre of town very close to Circular Quay where all the ferries docked.

I can hear Gerard and Phons: "The fellow talks such nonsense, it's unbearable," Gerard said.

"Just a babe in arms," Phons said, "No life experience whatsoever."

"That babe," Patsy snapped, "Could run rings around you both! He is the first man I have met for a long time who is worth listening to. He is a natural talent, mark my words."

"Oh, come on," I said, "Let's read what he has published first. He talks a lot, but what exactly did he say?"

Her green eyes flashed, "You wouldn't recognise a real artist if you fell over him. You and your eternal, what exactly do you mean?" Clearly, there was interference on our shared wavelength...She turned to Paul: "Shall we go? There's been enough talking for one evening. I want to think quietly about everything I've heard."

When Phons rang Patsy a few days later she had no time to have dinner with him. A week later she still had no time. Paul brought both Patsy and Christopher along in his car to our next discussion evening. I must admit that Christopher displayed remarkable erudition for his age, also on that second evening. He referred repeatedly to examples from world literature, art and history to lend weight to his arguments. He really must have read a remarkable amount, I thought, impressed. And when he asked me whether I realised how beautiful I was, pregnant – the essence of the eternal feminine – I promptly took him to my heart!

Pat made very clear that she relished every word he spoke and announced much earlier than usual that she would take the ferry home together with Heinz. There were things she needed to do. She had called him Heinz from the beginning, which he had smilingly accepted.

"She can't possibly take that boy seriously, can she?" Phons asked me, after they had left. He tried to ring her for two days, but she wasn't at home. He tried her office. Patsy had taken a few days off, and couldn't be reached. After two more days she was still incommunicado. Phons began to be seriously worried.

"Maybe her mother turned up unexpectedly," I suggested, "Didn't she say that that always turns her life upside down? We just need to wait patiently. She'll turn up one of these days." Which she indeed did do, unannounced, on a dark, rainy afternoon in November.

We are camping out in the living room, probably because it is cooler there than outside. Every now and then the rain clatters against the stained glass windows, a summer rain. Paulie hangs onto the rungs of his playpen, bored; Lindy sits next to him, also in the playpen. She is building something with Lego blocks. Next to the playpen, in a low, easy chair sits Paul Gundry White, long legs stretched out in front of him, arms folded. On the couch sit Jane and Peter, hand in hand as usual. Josie is there too and I can see Phons standing with a brown teapot in his hands. Gerard is attending to the record player; something by Bach is playing. Then the bell rings: the front door. Gerard and I look at each other in surprise; our bell rings so rarely, no-one uses the front door. Gerard walks down the corridor. I hear talking and laughter. Phons looks up: Patsy and Christopher, in dripping raincoats. "Good Lord!" I hear myself say, "Pat! Where have you been all this time?"

Pat throws her coat over Christopher's arm, and shakes her red curls. She straightens the pleats of her blue skirt and raises her chin: "We got married. Heinz and I got married two days ago." Bach suddenly stops.

"Oh no," says Josie.

"Well, well, well," says Paul, studying the two with deep interest, but not getting up.

I slowly sit down on a straight-backed chair, and do not dare to look at Phons. And then I do. He is as white as a sheet, and holds the teapot tightly to his chest.

"It took some doing," Patsy says sunnily, "Do you have any idea how much paperwork is involved in doing something so simple? But we were determined. I thought you should be the first to know. You are my dearest friends."

Jane jumps up and hugs them both. "Oh, good luck, mate! I think it's fantastic. So…so brave."

"Congratulations," Peter says, without getting up, and for some reason he sounds sarcastic.

"Ditto," says Paul, still from the depths of his chair, "And the best of all possible luck."

"We found a flat," says Pat, "In Turramurra. We moved in yesterday. You're all invited to visit, any time. I quit my job. Heinz doesn't want his wife to work," with a quick look at her brand new, silent husband. He looks a little dazed, does Christopher, as if he is just waking up from a drunken stupor.

"Congratulations, old man," Phons says and slaps him on the back. His normal colour has returned and he has put the teapot down. "Thank you," Christopher says, looking at him. He seems a little more at ease now.

"So that's that," says Phons, later in the kitchen when I am washing up the cups. He is standing next to me, with a tea towel in his hand. Inside, behind us, the record is playing again and there is animated talking going on. Patsy's high voice can be heard above everyone else's.

Josie appears at my other side. "She's nine years older than he is!" she hisses, "She is out of her mind."

"Oh Phons, I'm so sorry…" I feel about a hundred years old. I think we held one more discussion evening after that, but it was a lacklustre affair. I suddenly realised I couldn't handle any more organised evenings. I felt as large as a dinosaur. Monstrous. And was constantly tired. Moreover, Dr Maine had told me at my last check-up that I might be carrying twins. "Here is a head," he said, placing his hand just below my stomach, "and if I'm not much mistaken, this could well be another one. I want you to have a photo made. Then we'll know for sure what we're dealing with."

Twins? I didn't want twins! What on earth would I do with two more babies?! Gerard too blanched at the idea. We went together to have an X-ray taken and heard a week later that – to our immense relief – I was only carrying one baby. "But this little fellow is sitting straight up," Maine said, showing us the photo, "A classic breech. But don't you worry about a thing, we'll let him come out with his legs first, Mother Nature can run this one."

I know it is high time I wrote about Laurel, whose influence on me was so very great, but I find it almost impossible to capture her in words. Her name was Laurel Gidley King. That historic Australian surname was her husband's, but she herself came from an old and distinguished Australian family. Her maiden name was Cox and the Cox River was named after her ancestor who helped to map the Australian interior. She must have been around fifty when I first met her. But Laurel was ageless, generation-less and class-less. Everyone, young and old, always called her Laurel, which is exactly who she was: just Laurel.

I strolled into Josie's garden one sunny winter afternoon and there she was, with Josie, amid the flowering daisies. A tall, slim, dark-eyed woman with thick, dark hair, cut short, with golden streaks in it. This was long before the arrival of Christopher. Laurel had eyes that burned with light, eyes that observed. When I think of Laurel I think of pure, selfless attention.

There was an immediate and natural rapport between us; it was almost as if we picked up the thread of an old conversation after many years that afternoon. As if we had known each other for a long time. I remember that we talked about modern French writers, and that it seemed the most natural thing in the world that when she left she took my hand and said: "I want you to come and look at my books. I live close by. In Raglan Street. Why don't you visit me on Thursday evening? I'll be on my own then and we can talk in peace."

I hear Josie's cheerful voice, calling us bookworms who have finally found each other, telling Laurel that if Gerard can't babysit that evening she will. She thinks it will be very good for me to do something on my own for an evening.

Once Laurel has left I receive an avalanche of information about her. She is, Josie tells me, a very special woman. Married to a French wool-buyer when she was only 18 and mother of a little girl by the time she was 19. She lived in France for a few years. But came back to Australia with her child when the war broke out. Her first husband died shortly afterwards. She remarried an Australian. A second baby soon arrived, but the little girl had a serious heart problem, and lived only for nine months. "Those pine trees in the middle of the lawn at the back of Laurel's house, she planted those just after Deirdre died." Then she divorced. The man to whom she is currently married returned from the war more or less an invalid. They have two children together, Rosemary and Phillip, who are both at boarding school.

That Thursday evening was the first of a whole series of evenings, which I spent with Laurel. There was so much to talk about. So many writers, so many ideas, so many famous books I needed to read. After which she expected to hear my views. The evenings were far too short. I remember we would ring each other the following day to continue our conversations and share new ideas. I can see myself sitting on the floor in the hall near our bathroom where our telephone stood on the floor, for want of a telephone table, excitedly talking about some new discovery.

Laurel's house was a stately villa surrounded by trees. There was a low garden fence and then a long path leading to the front door, under a tiled archway that was thickly overgrown with laburnum. There was also a low veranda with wicker garden chairs. The house had high, elongated windows with many small panes in wooden frames. The front door had heavy, old-fashioned copper fittings.

When Laurel opened the door that first evening she took both of my hands in hers. Her eyes were very clear. "I'm so glad you've come," she said. She led me through a dark, panelled hall, past two enormous connecting rooms (thick carpets, cupboards full of gleaming porcelain), then through the TV room with bookcases along two of the four walls (from which she took a pile of books) to the kitchen. Her kitchen was very spacious. Under the large window that offered a view of the garden (lawn with trees) stood a huge, brown, wooden table. There was also a large, wooden glasses cabinet and a low wooden sideboard, a granite sink, a gleaming black stove and a wooden butcher's cutting block, with a worn, but shiny top.

"Next time you must come through the back," said Laurel, "My personal friends all come to the kitchen. Why don't you take a look at those books while I make coffee?" We sat at the large kitchen table. We talked about Sartre, Camus, Simone de Beauvoir (she lent me *The Second Sex*); about modern (at that time) literary and philosophical movements; about English writers, like DH Lawrence and Aldous Huxley, whom Laurel admired greatly; about theatre. Theatre was Laurel's real love. Later, she would regularly take me to the Sydney University Theatre. We saw Ionesco there together. I remember *The Chairs* and Samuel Beckett's *Waiting for Godot,* examples of the Theatre of the Absurd. We went to literary lectures together.

She leant me endless piles of books and I read and read. I used every free hour to read. There was so much to learn, to discover. Laurel shaped and refined my literary taste. She opened doors, which I did not know existed until then. Over the years, she taught me to see connections – science, philosophy, literature. That first evening I met her husband, whom everyone called Gidley. A thin, tall, grey-haired, extremely polite gentleman, who, after a short greeting, disappeared again. I never got to know Gidley well. He remained one of the shadowy figures in the background.

Laurel on the other hand created a place in my life that was very special, where I could breathe freely, that had nothing to do with Gerard and the children. And nothing with our discussion group, oddly enough. She remained outside it, although she became familiar with the people who inhabited my world from the stories I told her. She listened to these with interest, but rarely commented. She never judged, she did not analyse. Nor did she advise. She met Gerard and Phons, and got on with them well. She sometimes came to visit me, but not often. I went to her.

She never talked about her own social life: a stream of cocktail parties, meetings, official dinners and bridge afternoons, if Josie was to be believed. She belonged to the Mosman upper ten, Josie claimed. That did not interest me a great deal. The only thing that interested me was keeping our own private corner carefully protected, which Laurel did too. I was prepared to share her, though. Following the Patsy-Christopher drama, Phons, who rarely talked about anything private, talked to Laurel, which I was happy about. She was, I felt, exactly the person he needed.

I knew that Josie turned to her if she had a problem: "I go to Laurel if I have an emotional problem," she said, "And to Patsy Morgan if I have a practical one." I actually did the same with Hiek. Hiek was my dependable Dutch rock in a choppy Australian sea. She continued loyally to organise typing work for me, she rang me regularly and every few weeks we took the family to spend a Sunday in Seaforth. Though we were fast becoming Australians, Hiek and Jan held steadfastly to their Dutch origins. They had a circle of Dutch friends; they read the *Dutch Australian Weekly* and they occasionally attended Dutch Club evenings. No big life issues were discussed at Hiek and Jan's, there were no passionate arguments. It was all just simply "*gezellig*" (cozy). We were just good, old friends, spending time together, and Hiek always had advice about practical issues.

She maintained all sorts of Dutch customs. She knew where there was a Dutch shop in Sydney where you could get salted licorice (*drop*) and *appelstroop* and she taught Janneke and Lindy to sing old, Dutch nursery rhymes. Our children were entranced by Seaforth, by Tante Hihi's mandarin tree in the back garden and Oom Jan's handyman cave; they were always given tea with *speculaasjes* and were deeply impressed by Hiek's great big sons who knew everything about surfing and fishing, and who were fixing up an ancient car. Life without Hiek would have been unthinkable.

Hiek and Jan's house remained a source of wonder too. Every time we visited it had grown a little bit. They devoted every free hour to renovating it, and it had, thanks to the devotion of its inhabitants, already survived a few potential disasters. Such as when the lean-to they had built and which was to become a bedroom for the boys lost one of its walls in a mild, winter hurricane...

The last weeks of my last pregnancy weren't easy. Not for me, and not for those around me. Ever since the "almost twins" episode I felt weighed down by a vague sense of anxiety. Was it my imagination or had Gerard changed too? It was as if he was around less, less present. As if the underlying stream that always connected us was interrupted again and again. Was that my fault? I know I was difficult. I moped a great deal. I found it hard to move. I slept very badly and was tired all the time, and felt lonely for some reason; that sense of no longer being protected; of no longer belonging.

I stared enviously at Josie's long, brown legs under her short, white shorts, her daily attire. And how athletically she ran up and down the stairs. I began to dislike her teasing laughter, which was primarily aimed at Gerard and Phons (Phons made it his task to go for a short walk with me every evening, "Come on. Mother Melman. Let's stretch our legs. It will be good for you."). It felt as if I was being lied to.

It is 23 December. Every day the temperature rises higher. Gerard has just met a Dutch emigrant called Henk Beukers, who has his own painting company in Mosman. He has offered to paint the outside of our house for a friendly price. I don't agree with this. I think we can wait another year. We are having such difficulty making ends meet as it is.

"We'd be mad not to grab this chance," Gerard had said, and "Your eternal worrying drives me crazy."

So Henk Beukers has arrived and is painting. It is two days before Christmas and blisteringly hot. I am standing at the kitchen table. I am as round as a tub, and feel sticky.

Janneke is at school. Lindy and Paulie are playing together on the floor. Josie has gone to town, Christmas shopping. My back hurts. It is about eleven o'clock. Gerard left very early. Phons is making a country trip, and will come home tomorrow evening. I drag myself to the phone and call Laurel. "I'm coming round," she says. She looks impossibly cool and slim. She looks at me and says: "The baby's coming, isn't it?"

I nod. I am not due for another fifteen days, but all my babies have arrived early and there is certainly something going on. "This will go on for hours and hours. Gerard should be home at four."

"You're going to ring the doctor right now," says Laurel, "Let's see what he thinks." I go, obedient as a child. It is a relief that someone else is taking over. "Go straight to the hospital," says Maine, "I'll meet you there."

Back in the kitchen Laurel has asked Henk Beukers to help. And three minutes later I am sitting in the front of his painting truck. Laurel has promised to look after the children until either Josie or Gerard get home.

"The Mater?" Henk asks with a broad grin. "They won't believe their eyes! I dropped my wife off there last week, also in this truck, and she gave birth to our fifth baby in the lift. And her name is Agatha too! You aren't going to do that too, are you? I'd never be able to face those sisters again!" And then to Laurel: "Just joking, don't worry, I know about these things, we'll make it in plenty of time." He drives carefully and slowly, and the paint tins rattle gently in the back.

At a quarter to twelve, I stumble into the hospital lift, holding my stomach with two hands, and barely an hour later I hear Maine's voice somewhere behind a red mist telling me that I am now going to sleep a little: "I need to make a little more space for this fine fellow, he's coming out back to front, remember? And he seems to be in a great hurry."

Peace: dark, blue peace. After what seems no more than five minutes, he is shaking me awake again. "Don't you want to see your new son? Here he is. Five centimeters longer than his brother when he was born." I hold the warm, little bundle in my arms. I kiss the little face. I sleep again.

When I finally wake up again, I am lying in a ward and Kenny is standing at the foot of my bed with a large bunch of roses. "Everything is fine at home," he says, beaming. "The children are at Josie's. We haven't been able to reach Gerard. Laurel rang me. I've been here for a while, but you were sleeping so peacefully."

"Oh, you angel," I say. I feel as if I am in an oasis of peace. "It's a boy and we are going to call him Robert Kenneth, after you. Sounds nice, doesn't it?" I had had Robert in my head for a long time, and Kenneth had just come to me, spontaneously.

Gerard materialises a few hours later. He looks a little dazed. "Well, you certainly took care of this one all on your own. I couldn't believe it when I got home! I tried to ring you, around two. It had all already happened by then. You've done such a great job."

"This was the easiest of them all," I murmur.

CHAPTER 20

New kitchen and thunderstorms

7 JUNE 2001. *Cold. Rain. Heavy clouds. A sense of being confined. That distance between living in an apartment and living in a house with a garden, even if only a small garden, a Dutch garden. That even vaster distance between our Australia then and Australia now...*

Of course we value the comfort of our flat. Warm, spacious rooms, no stairs (I hear Paul's excited voice when we arrived in Leiden in 1969 and he had his first view of Dutch staircases: "A double-decker house!"). A cozy, secure and pleasant home. And yet... it would be so wonderful to go out of the front door and feel earth underneath my feet instead of concrete.

I had intended to write about small children as a beginning to this new chapter. How moving I find them, especially in recent years: the body language of little ones who are trying to walk or of two and three year-olds who yearn to explore the world on their own. The courageous, determined gait of their little legs, how they place their feet on the ground. I saw it in my own children when they were small, especially Paul and Lindy: that resolute setting out, with a little fear, but with eagerness too, pushing through a vague unsteadiness. And children's voices, their tears, which break my heart, their words which move me. Was this always the case? I suspect that when I had four little children of my own I yearned only for adult voices. Though there were also moments of perfect happiness because the children existed. Of deep, intense astonishment at their being, of complete fulfilment.

They all came to visit me in the Mater Misericordia Hospital after Bobby was born, all the members of what Josie called "the inner circle."

Tony and Yolande, Tony with his crooked grin: "How can you stand it here, surrounded by all these post-natal women?" handing me a book which I have always kept (Colin Wilson's, *The Outsider*, the literary bestseller of that year).

Jane and Peter with a huge bunch of white roses. Peter like the figure of Christ, dispensing blessings; Jane like a shy Madonna: "Oh Agatha, I can't wait till it's my turn. It won't be for ages yet."

Paul Gundry White with a single white orchid in his hand: "I think you're wonderful." Christopher and Patsy. Christopher seemed a little depressed even though, looking about him, he murmured "The great ebb and flow of life," and held my hand much longer than was necessary. He then sat, silent and lost in thought, next to my bed while Patsy chatted, too fast and too much. She smiled constantly. I did not think she looked well. When Josie came in, they left immediately. Hiek and Jan came too, bringing a homemade romper suit and a wooden rattle. And Laurel came, bringing me a pile of books.

After five days in the hospital, Gerard picked me up on a Saturday morning and drove me home, with my new son in my arms. I was still having difficulty walking as I had had quite a few stitches. So we went in through the front door. No children's voices, everything was quiet. "Where is everyone?" I asked surprised.

"Why don't you put the baby down first?" said Gerard, "We have a surprise for you."

I obediently took the first door on the left, our bedroom, and placed the sleeping baby in his cot. I followed Gerard through the long corridor. The living room door was shut. I heard muted music and then a strange voice. I opened the door.

In our living room stood a television set. On the couch opposite it sat Janneke with Lindy curled up beside her. Paul sat, thumb in mouth, on the ground at their feet. Three pairs of eyes were intently watching the moving image in front of them.

"There's Mummy," said Janneke, looking up briefly, as if I had just come home from doing the shopping.

"*And then the little princess found herself alone in the forest,*" said the television.

"Second hand," Gerard told me, "My Christmas present to the children." I was completely dazed. It was a very different homecoming than I had expected. "They're so quiet. Shall we make a cup of tea? I'm dying for one." The kitchen door was shut too, which was very unusual. Everything was strange, as if this was no longer my own house. "Er, well, the kitchen is still a little bit of a mess," Gerard said, as I opened the door.

That nightmarish feeling of deja vu. The kitchen was unrecognisable. It was a building site. The entrance to the pantry had been given a new brick arch. Monty was standing on top of a ladder, hastily trying to finish this off. Next to him, on the ground, stood Phons with an old sheet tied around his waist, hurriedly painting the wall. The stove had been moved aside, and its alcove newly painted. The stove and the kitchen table were marooned in the middle of the kitchen, like props in a Jan Steen painting, covered in towers of pots, pans and storage canisters. The sink and countertop were full of dirty plates and cups, bowls with leftover food, empty beer bottles and glasses. The kitchen floor was covered in a thick carpet of muddy and paint-spattered newspapers.

"This is the real surprise," said Gerard, "A completely new kitchen. We're renovating it from top to bottom. Now that the outside of the house has been painted, I thought we should do the kitchen too. It was high time. Only we couldn't get it done in time."

"Oh no, no! Oh no!" I wailed, tears streaming down my cheeks. Monty almost fell off his ladder. He scuttled down, threw me an appalled look and ran out of the back door. Phons put his brush back into a paint pot and pulled off his apron, and Gerard turned white, not out of remorse, but with anger. "What kind of a reaction is that?! We've been doing our best, we've been working like slaves through the Christmas holidays!"

"The baby," I sobbed, "What am I supposed to do? I can't even get into my own kitchen. Look at this disaster area! How am I going to feed the baby in this mess?!"

"Why don't you have a little rest?" said Phons, "We'll have all this cleared up in a jiffy. It's just unfortunate timing, that's all; we thought you wouldn't be home till this afternoon."

"I wanted to come home early!" I wailed, "Everyone wants to come home early! And now look at what I find. Oh God!"

Behind me, the television suddenly erupted with music. Phons took my arm and led me sobbing back into the living room. Our children were still sitting on the couch, though Lindy now had an arm tightly around her little brother. All eyes were glued to the screen where Mickey Mouse jumped up and down crazily. "We can turn it down a little, I think!" Phons yelled over the noise, and turned down the volume. "Wasn't this a great idea? They've been as good as gold since we bought this thing. Why don't you take a nap? There'll be coffee in half an hour, I promise.

"I will never forgive you two! I bet there isn't a clean cup in the house. And all this must have cost loads of money. It wasn't necessary at all!"

"That's all she ever thinks about," I heard Gerard's bitter voice behind me, which caused a fresh bout of tears.

"I've just had a baby and I don't even have a kitchen tap!!"

"Ssh," said Phons, "Calm down, it's all going to be fine, there's nothing to get upset about. It will be bad for your milk if you make yourself so upset. Just get under the blankets and have a nice quiet lie down."

"Blankets?!" I gulped, half laughing, half crying, "It's over 30 degrees!" But I let myself be led back to the bedroom, where I lay down and turned my head to the wall. Men! Their lack of empathy! Their impulsiveness! Their pigheadedness, their lack of imagination! But despite these bitter thoughts I did fall asleep.

By the time I woke up it was afternoon. The kitchen had become reasonably accessible again. The television had been switched off and the children finally showed a little interest in their new baby brother. Gerard put his arms around me and mumbled a whole litany of incomprehensible apologies. At which I declared that I really was happy to have a new kitchen, clean white walls and a new pantry arch.

Three months later. It is a dark, heat-wave day. A thunderstorm is brewing. Above the bay at the bottom of our hill the sky is the colour of granite. Every now and than a gust of wind rushes past, bending the treetops double. I am standing on the veranda and nervously wondering how long it will be before the lightning starts. I don't like Australian thunderstorms. In Sydney, I once saw lighting bolts erupting from four sides at once out of a sky turned a monstrous black and green, and a fireball bouncing through the streets. Lindy has just started to go to kindergarten. She and Janneke aren't home yet.

Someone comes round the corner of our house, Patsy. She starts to climb the stairs slowly. She sees me. "Hi! I've been in town, but it's dreadful there, so humid and hot. There's going to be an almighty thunderstorm, the ferry was rocking madly." She has reached the veranda: "Can I stay here this afternoon? Heinz has night duty, so he's sleeping all day." She is looking a little pale, her green eyes are dull, and her red hair is limp. She looks older, thinner.

"Of course you can stay here, would be nice. I just hope the children get home before this storm starts. Shall I make tea?" She follows me into the kitchen and sits down. She brushes the sweat from her forehead. "Lovely. How is the baby?"

"He's angelic. I just need to check whether Paulie is still sleeping." I turn to go.

"I'm pregnant," she says abruptly.

I stop and turn back. "Oh Pat, how wonderful. Congratulations!"

"I don't know whether I'm so happy about it," depressed, "I wanted to get pregnant, I tried hard to. But now that I am…"

"Oh love, you're just a bit depressed, that's normal, it's so very hot."

"Mummy, Mummy, Mummy!" Paulie calls from the front of the house. Patsy follows me into the baby room. She lifts him up out of his bed. She plays with his wiry curls while I change his nappy. "So darling. When you have a child…it's something of your very own."

When we get back to the kitchen we hear Janneke, Katie, Sally and Lindy on the veranda stairs and then Josie's voice. "Agatha! We're all coming over to shelter from the storm at your house!" And once she is on the veranda: "I've brought something for you. Ice cream in a tin, a whole gallon. It's the latest thing. Great for people like us…Oh hi, Pat!"

Outside the world has become pitch black. A vast streak of lightning tears the sky apart. The first thunderclap erupts above our heads. It starts to rain, slanting sheets of water. The veranda floor is immediately drenched. The children run inside screaming. I shut the kitchen door and switch on the light. We usher the horde of children into the living room where Josie and I hand out plates of ice cream.

"No TV until the storm is over!" Josie orders, "Everybody understand? Here," she fishes two worn packs of playing cards out of the pocket of her sundress, "Let's see which of you can build the tallest house of cards."

When a little later the three of us are sitting in the kitchen drinking tea, trying to ignore the quick succession of thunder, Patsy suddenly says: "Things aren't good between Heinz and me. It isn't working."

"Oh, Lord," says Josie. The rain clatters on the roof, a quieter drumroll in between the crashes of thunder.

"I think I have made a huge mistake. The boy needs a mother not a wife."

"You just need time to get used to each other," I say.

"It isn't easy if you've been on your own for a while," says Josie.

Patsy shakes her head decisively. "That's not it. When we met each other, the way he talked then. He seemed so sure of himself, so wise, so experienced. For us there was only one kind of relationship possible, he said, everything or nothing. And I really thought he had thought through the consequences, even better than I could. I had no idea…Can you imagine what it is like having to educate someone from the very beginning?"

"Yes, but Pat…"

"He's as spineless as jelly. He is so passive. In everything! And he is scared. He is scared of me, scared of women if you ask me. He has no idea what goes on in a woman's head. And yet...he clutches on to me. He makes me feel as if I'm suffocating. I can't breathe in that flat. I can't breathe when I'm around him."

"Oh boy!" says Josie.

Patsy presses her fists to her mouth and rocks to and fro. "Oh God, oh Christ! What have I done? What am I going to do?" Outside there is a brief silence, only the drumbeat of the rain. I am speechless.

"So what about his great talent?" Josie asks caustically, "Remember? You were going to cherish and support his great talent?"

Patsy lowers her hands and places them in her lap. She looks at them. "I have done everything wrong. We should never have got married."

"Well, I'd still try to make the best of it, if I were you," says Josie, coolly, "Now that there is a baby on the way you don't have any choice. How you could ever have been so stupid, at your age and with your experience, is a mystery to me."

Patsy lifts her head. All of a sudden she is as straight as an arrow. "Well, what about you?! You with your shallow, frustrated, repressed life and your second-hand emotions. You just feed off what others experience! You watch other people stick their necks out, but you don't dare take risks yourself. You wouldn't have the guts!"

"How dare you?!" Josie cries, "You're selfish through and through! You destroy other people. You use them and then you break them. And everyone still runs around doing your bidding and feeling sorry for you and finding you oh so pathetic."

"Ah, and there is the green-eyed monster," Patsy voice is icy, "You've always been jealous of me and you still are. Are you enjoying yourself now? Isn't it wonderful to wallow in someone else's misery? God, I have never known a more hollow, empty person than you."

"Oh stop it, stop it, both of you!"

Josie jumps up, her eyes are like glowing coals. "I'm going home, you two can sort it all out together. Just let her weep on your shoulder all she wants, your naive idiot."

"Josie!" I run around the table but she is already gone. The outside door stands wide open. A gust of wind rushes into the kitchen and I try to grab the doorknob. I see blue and yellow streaks of lighting shattering the corners of the sky and watch Josie disappear into a curtain of rain. I shut the door. Patsy's mouth is a narrow, hard line.

"Oh, how dreadful! Why did you have to say that to her? You hurt her deeply."

"What about me? Do you think she treated me with care? I destroy people!" And then, gently: "I know I do, that's the whole point. I will destroy this boy if I stay with him. There will be nothing left of him or of me. He is turning me into a monster! By being who he is he brings out the devil in me. Look at me: can't you see how much this hurts me? I'm standing in a desert, completely on my own. I'm expecting a child and all I feel is pain, emptiness, fear. I can only see ruins around me." There is something primeval in her green eyes, something very old and very wild. I have no answer. "I have waited for so long and searched so hard," she says, "This seemed to be such a revelation, something bigger than me."

"Mummy!!" Janneke yells, "Sally is playing with the TV! And Paul needs to go into his playpen. Mummy, he knocked all my cards down!" Paulie begins to scream. The living room is a battleground. The floor is covered in cards. Paul is crying loudly in the middle of them, his face a fiery red. Katie is standing next to him, balancing on one long leg, holding the ankle of the other behind her back. Lindy is standing on the couch clutching her dolls in her arms and Janneke is lying flat on the floor next to a pile of cards, crying furious tears. Sally is near the TV, looking at the kitchen door over her shoulder.

Once peace and order have been re-established, and I am giving Bobby his bottle, with Patsy looking on in silence, I say: "Why don't you give it a chance, love? You barely know each other; give him time to grow up. In a little while, once the baby has arrived…"

It doesn't sound very convincing, even to me. If I had been Laurel I would have been able to find the right words.

Patsy gets up: "Now you sound just like Josephine," she says mockingly, "By the way, it is true that she has a jealous nature. She's also jealous of you. Jealousy has always been her biggest problem."

"Jealous of me? That's absurd. I don't have anything to be jealous of! Josie is a dear friend, she has always been such a great support to me."

Pat opens the backdoor. It is light again outside, and a watery sun has even begun to shine. "It's a lot cooler," she says.

Shortly after this incident, we throw a party, for Gerard's birthday, I seem to recall. "If Pat comes, I'm not!" Josie threatens. But she does come, and so does Pat. Patsy comes on her own. She is carrying an overnight bag. "Can I stay the night tonight? Heinz has a weekend shift. And I hate having to ask for a lift late at night." "She can have my room," Phons says immediately, "I'll sleep on the couch."

That evening we meet Nina, Jane's younger sister. Jane had produced a son a few weeks before, with the greatest ease. This was her first outing since the birth. She comes in happily, dressed in a yellow robe printed with green ferns and with enormous butterfly sleeves. She has become even more beautiful. Her eyes seem bigger, her cheekbones more prominent, her skin more translucent. She is followed by Nina, who carries the sleeping baby on a cushion. Behind her is Peter who has brought along a self-made totem pole for the occasion, and carries it like a staff. His beard is twice as long as usual, and he now resembles one of the apostles.

Nina has the same build as Jane, and is extremely slender. She has long, heavy, reddish hair and deep blue eyes. To start off with she is endearingly shy. She clearly regards the baby as her responsibility. She pays more attention to him than Jane does. She finds a place for him to sleep, goes to check regularly whether he is crying and gives him a bottle at a certain point, with Phons keeping her company.

Nina immediately acquires two devoted followers, Phons and Paul Gundry White, who both spend the evening hovering around her, first together then separately. She treats them both with a reserve worthy of a much older woman.

"I just spent a long time talking to her," Phons whispers to me, after the bottle-feeding incident, "She's really an exceptionally intelligent girl."

"Remarkable young woman," Paul comes to tell me, much later that evening, "How old is she again?"

"I think she just turned nineteen."

"Remarkable," he repeats, with shining eyes.

It was a strange party. I was painfully aware of the fact that Josie and Patsy avoided each other carefully. That Josie made too much noise and laughed too loudly. That Patsy, dressed in a far from festive tunic dress, spent most of the evening distancing herself from the party and simply observing; that Kenny was listless and Tony was behaving madly. Hiek and Jan were there too, but left early. I don't think they felt comfortable.

I drank too much. When I lay down in bed around four I could feel the earth spinning, and when I got up at six to heat Bobby's bottle it was still spinning, at a nauseating rate. Thank God the children were unusually quiet and I could go back to bed.

Coffee on the veranda in the afternoon, which had come far too quickly; we were all decidedly fragile. "Never again," I said from the bottom of my heart, "We're never giving a party like that again. And I am never touching alcohol again."

"I'll remind you," Phons grinned, "I'm off, people."

"Huh? It's Sunday, where are you off to all of a sudden?"

"I'm going to visit Nina," the grin spreads from ear to ear, "Making hay while the sun shines is what they call it."

"Good for you, mate," says Gerard.

"Oh," I say, "Er, and what time do you want to leave, Pat?"

"I'm not in a hurry, I'll see how it goes."

"I could drop you at St Leonards," Phons offers.

"Oh no, no, it's far too early. What would I do with myself in that empty flat?"

"Ah well. I don't think I'll be gone long. See you, kids."

That Sunday seems drained of colour. It is only by the evening that I begin to feel a bit normal. Patsy stays and stays. She does not talk about catching a particular ferry. She keeps the children occupied all afternoon. Helps to put them in the bath, helps me make dinner. And then Phons returns, clearly pleased with himself. When we are all having dinner together Gerard announces that he is going to bed at the same tine as the kids, "The years are taking their toll!" We wash up. Gerard disappears. I make coffee.

We are sitting in the kitchen, Phons, Patsy and I. It has been dark outside for some time now. I am having trouble keeping my eyes open. "Okay, kid," says Phons, "Don't you think it's time to hit the road? Shall I get the car?"

"Oh God!" Patsy cries, "Oh God, I don't know what to do!" and she bursts into wild tears. I am suddenly wide awake. Phons looks appalled, intensely shocked. She cries and cries. She places her head on her arms and weeps, long, hysterical moans of grief. I stand up and put my hands on her shaking shoulders. "There now, quiet, don't cry," as if I am comforting Janneke, "What's the matter, Pat? Try to calm down."

She lifts het wet, twisted face: swollen red eyes and a tragic mouth, an old, old woman.

"I can't go back. I can't. I have told him I won't go back. I can't stand it there. That boy is driving me completely insane. I'll murder him one of these days. Do you know what I did yesterday? I threw the teapot at him, and the ketchup and some eggs. Oh, God, what am I going to do? I don't have any money, not a cent; there isn't anywhere I can go. I don't have anyone."

"Christ almighty," mutters Phons.

"It's all my own fault!" weeps Patsy, "It's all my own, stupid fault. But I can't go back. Please don't send me away, I can't face it."

"Of course you don't have to go back straightaway," I say, "Certainly not tonight. You know what, why don't you stay with us for a little while? And you aren't completely on your own. You have us, we're here, aren't we, Phons?"

"Of course she has us!" Phons says, suddenly taking the situation in hand. "I can sleep perfectly well on the couch. I did it for years, and I'm fine with it. You can have my room, Pat, for as long as you want."

"But that wouldn't work," she weeps, "Gerard…"

"Gerard will be fine with it too," I say, even though I am far from sure he will. "You're staying here till you've recovered a little. Tomorrow everything will look different, you'll see."

"No!" another torrent of tears, "No, no!" almost screaming, "Not tomorrow. Never. I'm never going back there, never again. It's over. I never want to see him again. I will have to make it on my own somehow."

"Hush, hush; we'll think of something. You need to get some sleep now. We're all exhausted. I'll make you a glass of warm milk and then you need to get to bed."

Phons takes her arm and pulls her up. "Come on, kid. I'll bring you to my room. I'm very good at calming hysterical women, ask Agatha!"

Gerard took the news better than I had expected the next morning. Admittedly, he had no sympathy for Patsy and very little understanding for her predicament, but he agreed that I couldn't have thrown her out onto the streets. "She's going to stay here for a little while," I said carefully, "Phons has given her his room."

"Oh God," said Gerard, "Oh well, it's up to you two. I just hope she won't stay too long." At which he left. His use of "you two" made very clear he wanted to distance himself from the situation and have as little as possible to do with it.

Josie on the other hand was furious. I decided, once Phons had also left for work and the children had gone to school, that I had to pre-empt any unexpected confrontations between Pat and Josie, and ran over to Josie's house. "You're nuts!" said Josie, "You've no idea what you are getting yourself into! Let her solve her own problems. Do you really think she is the only one with troubles? That girl makes me sick. What if we were all like her, if we all ran away at the first disappointment? As long as she is staying with you, I won't come around."

"I'm sorry about that," I said crossly, "But you can't make me believe you would have thrown her out on the streets if she had come to you."

Pat slept late that morning. When she finally appeared she refused to eat anything. She sat silently and with a white face on the veranda, her hands folded together, staring at nothing, with an untouched cup of coffee beside her. I tried to talk to her. Did Heinz know where she was? Shouldn't she ring him? Wouldn't he be worried sick?

"He knows I'm not coming back," she said coldly.

"But Pat, he'll grow up one day, won't he? Don't you think that in his own way he is trying his best?"

"He has no core," she answered absently, "No backbone. There is nothing to hold on to. I feel like I am drowning. If we stay together we will destroy each other. Oh, let's stop talking about it."

I stopped. I cleaned nappies and made beds. I vacuumed and washed and went shopping, leaving Pat to babysit. I went to see Laurel. "Women!" she said, "My heart breaks when I think about how vulnerable most of us are, in all respects, emotionally and materially."

"I really don't know how to deal with this. I'm seriously worried. If only you could see her! I wish you would try to talk to her."

"No-one can do more for her than you have already done," said Laurel, "You have let her into your house. I think it is too early to talk. Let her calm down first. But you can bring her along here tomorrow if you like. It might do her good."

Patsy came along. The three of us talked about books and writers, as if there was nothing going on. After about ten minutes, Pat came to life, and started to talk enthusiastically. Two days later Laurel rang to invite Patsy over for coffee. She went. She stayed away till late in the afternoon and came back a changed person. "It's time for me to take practical steps," she said, smiling "I need to find a job, that's the first priority. And then somewhere to live. I can't go on abusing your hospitality."

"Oh, finding somewhere to live isn't urgent," I said relieved, "Just take your time."

"No, I mean it. As soon as I have an income, I am looking for a room. It won't be easy," she added, "And my old boss won't want me back, nor my old landlady, she was glad when I left, it meant she could raise the rent. Oh well, I'll cross that bridge when I come to it. I need to start by getting all my stuff here."

That same evening she had a long talk with Phons. The result of this was that Phons and I together drove to the Turramurra flat the next day. I protested about this at first: "You can go with Phons yourself, can't you? You and Heinz need to talk about a few things."

"Oh no," decisively, "We've already talked all we need to. It's over. I really never want to see him again. You don't understand. Seeing him would be bad for me." Large tears filled her eyes and her voice became higher and higher. "It was bad enough having to ring him. There is nothing to say. I need to forget him as quickly as possible. I need to forget this whole episode. I want to get a divorce as soon as possible. He has to organise this immediately, he just has to." By this time she was almost screaming. It cost some effort to calm her down again. Phons convinced me we should do what she wanted: pregnant women and all that!

Christopher/Heinz was waiting for us. All Pat's clothes were packed in two suitcases and her weirdly few personal belongings in two cardboard boxes. "I'm glad she is with you," he said. And: "We will both need to go our own way." Not a word about the baby.

I tried to be as normal and relaxed as possible.

"Will you look after her?" he asked as we were leaving ten minutes later. "She doesn't have anyone else."

"I'll do my best," I said, feeling extremely uncomfortable. I was hugely relieved to get back into the car. "Oh, wasn't that horrible? Do you think he is very unhappy?"

"No," Phons said drily, "You've just relieved him of a huge burden. I mean, he's barely twenty! It's a good thing it ended so quickly."

"Yes, but what about the baby?"

"Ah well....", said Phons.

I ran into Christopher/Heinz again many years later. I have forgotten where and why, but I remember that he was pleasant and seemed happy. He was married to a young Russian girl who adored him, and they had three children together. He did indeed write pieces of great value, later. His name can be found in literary anthologies of young Australian writers, though his talent never flowered to its full glory. He died young, of cancer.

1962
Met Hich Anvik   Patsy in de achtertuin

CHAPTER 21

The locust tree

26 JUNE 2001. *It is suddenly summer, the height of summer. It is 30 degrees today. The sun shines; the shadows are sharply defined; outside my window everything bursts with colour.*

This should make it easier to write about Australia; right now, just for this moment, Holland and Australia share a certain similarity. Living here usually means wearing layers of clothing. But now, miraculously, that is no longer necessary, just like over there. Wearing fewer clothes gives such a sense of freedom, a kind of lightness.

But I don't feel light. I am having trouble with where I am now in my story, April 1960 or thereabouts. I keep telling myself I don't have to record anything I don't want to, that there are no rules. And at the same time I wonder whether I shouldn't try to explain more, try harder to unravel how things really were. I am working on a kind of jigsaw puzzle. Twenty years ago I thought if I just ploughed on, threading incidents together, that a clear pattern would emerge. But I am no longer so sure of this. Writing a different version of the same events leads to a different conclusion. There is a subtle shift in perspective, of lighting.

It is so difficult not to let myself be influenced by how it all panned out – assuming anything ever does, something I am also no longer sure of. And to what extent can I trust my memory? I try to record as precisely as I can who said and did what, or rather what I hear and see when I open a door in that endless corridor called "memory." I did that 20 years ago too and, I sometimes think, better than now. The images were clearer then. And yet...

Take for instance that vague feeling of unease I felt after Phons and I had picked up Patsy's things. This didn't only arise from Pat's sole reaction on our return – a chirpy, "Oh, how wonderful! Now I can get dressed up properly again!" Not "How was Heinz?" or "I'm so grateful, that can't have been easy." Though she had in the meantime thoroughly cleaned my kitchen, which shone.

I think it arose more from helplessness, from being forced to accept a fait accompli, and my confusion about Gerard who kept a deliberate distance from everything that was happening. He came and went without any comment, and seemed to be so far away from me.

And Josie. I didn't for a second believe she was jealous of me as Pat had claimed. I was jealous of her! Oh, those long, brown legs and laughing, brown eyes and that unbridled energy. Was it my fault that our old intimacy seemed to have disappeared? Having Patsy suddenly living with us didn't help, of course, but could this have such an impact? Not that I allowed myself much time to ponder these things; I was far too busy. But the unease – I can find no better word for it – remained.

That Sunday, Janneke fell out of the locust tree. Locust trees have many spreading branches, ideal for children to climb in. They flower once a year, pretty pink flowers, and yield small fruits that are edible but which none of us liked. I remember sweeping up the squashed, flat, brown fruits from the veranda stairs.

Gerard had left very early that Sunday. He had to go to a medical conference. And Phons had left early too, for a barbecue lunch with Nina, he had told me. I had bathed the baby and then put Paulie, who had "helped," loudly protesting into the playpen on the veranda; a horde of squealing children were playing wildly in and around our locust tree. I had already told them a few times to calm down. I was trying yet again to tie my recalcitrant ponytail when I heard Janneke crying. She came up the stairs:

"Mummy, Mummy! Katie pushed me and then I fell. My arm, my arm!" Her blonde plaits were dripping with earth and leaves, and her face was black. She held her right arm with her left hand; there was a strange dent in her forearm. I stared dazed at that small, brown, round, broken arm.

"I fell out of the tree and it's Katie's fault! She pushed me. Oh, my arm hurts!"

"It's clearly broken," Patsy said, "You'll have to ring the doctor." She put her arms around Janneke and hugged her. "It's alright, sweetheart. The doctor will make everything better again. Come and sit with me, and hold tight onto your arm, that's right." And "Everyone go home now!" as she shooed away the horde of children who had followed Janneke up the stairs.

She sat down, pulled Janneke onto her lap, and ran her hand over Paulie's head who was still protesting loudly: "Hush, Paulie, darling, quiet now," at which he actually did calm down. She gestured with her head to the kitchen door: "You need to make that phonecall!"

I ran. I dialed Maine's private number with shaking fingers.

"Okay," he said "Don't worry. Bring her straight to the practice. We've just bought our own X-ray machine, so I can make a photo there."

Things were quieter on the veranda by the time I returned. Janneke was still whimpering, but had her head on Patsy's shoulder. Patsy held her tightly, while cleaning Paul's tearstained face and gently talking to Lindy who sat at her feet, crying silently. This was a completely new Patsy.

"We don't have any transport," despite the heat I was shivering.

"Your new neighbours, I know they're home. Quick, go over and ask them!" Our new neighbours had only moved in recently. We had met them briefly the day after they arrived, Ken and Moira Tolhurst. He was tall, blonde, skinny and wore glasses; she was small, dark and a little vague, I thought. They had five children, a lot older than ours. And had a station wagon parked outside the house. I ran through the corridor, out the front door, and through the gate of the twin house next door.

"Ken will drive," Moira said immediately – why had I thought her vague? Five minutes later Ken Tolhurst was driving me with Janneke on my lap through peaceful Sunday Mosman. Maine was waiting for us together with his two partners, all three in white gowns.

The photo was the worst thing. Janneke screamed and I felt her pain in every fiber of my body. I bit my lips so hard they bled. Afterwards Maine gave her an injection. It turned out to be quite a complicated double fracture that needed setting, but she felt nothing of this. She slept. There was no concussion or any other complication Maine assured me.

"In about six weeks she'll be as good as new. Just wait till she has woken up and then you can take her home. Good luck, little mother!"

Ken who had waited for us all that time carried a white and drugged Janneke, whose arm was in a sling, into the car. Once we were back in Middle Head Road he carried her inside and put her in bed. That was the beginning of a wonderful new friendship.

In the meantime, Patsy had firmly taken over the reins of the household. The children had eaten, including the baby. The house had been tidied up and there was tea. She warmly admired Janneke's plaster. "Oh wow! I wish I had such an interesting arm! Tomorrow, when the plaster is hard enough, we can all write our names on it. Would you like that? Oh, and Katie wants to come by later, she's so sorry she pushed you, she really didn't do it deliberately." Janneke brightened visibly. So did I. I have rarely been more grateful for anything than for Patsy's presence in our house that day.

"I'm getting rid of that tree!" Gerard announced, when he had inspected and cuddled his eldest daughter, "It just clutters up the garden, and causes a mess and I wouldn't be surprised if it were dying anyway. It's dangerous!"

"Fine," I said, "But how? It will cost a lot to have it removed, and we can't afford that right now, with the doctor's bill…"

"Oh, we can do it ourselves," Phons said cheerfully, "Just a matter of getting enough muscle together. All hands on deck! And Peter Adler did forestry, didn't he? He'll know how it should be done and I've chopped down many a tree in my time. Shall we say next weekend? We'll turn it into a party."

A cool autumn afternoon: our garden has become a miniature open-air theatre and our veranda stairs are the grandstand. Halfway up the stairs sits Jane in jeans and a t-shirt. One rung above her is Nina, auburn hair glowing in the sunshine, a light blue cardigan elegantly draped over her shoulders. Patsy, in a green tunic dress, sits two stairs higher, studying Nina thoughtfully. I sit right at the top, with Paul on my lap, and both our girls leaning against my shoulders.

"Why can't we go down? I want to go to Katie!" Janneke complains, but I am adamant. "You're staying here, it's far too dangerous." Katie and Sally are down below, standing behind the garden fence together with their mother (in her inevitable white tennis shorts), who has head-shakingly rejected a waved invitation to come up and join us. Ken and Moira and their children are hanging over the balustrade of their veranda, which borders onto ours. There is a lot of commenting and laughter.

Below us four men are working hard. They have all four taken their shirts off, and a range of hairy, muscled and sinewy chests are on view. Peter has brought along a huge axe; Paul is struggling with a thick rope; Phons has rustled up a gigantic saw from somewhere, and Gerard is working with a smaller saw, which comes from our own, decidedly measly set of tools. I can't imagine he will make any impact with this, and he indeed discards it as soon as Josie offers him an axe from their toolbox. Our locust tree isn't very high, but it is sturdy and thick, and sports thick, arm-like branches.

"It needs to fall this way!" calls Gerard, from the garden fence, "So we'll have about a foot leeway."

"Okay, okay!" Peter grins, white teeth in a black beard, clearly assuming the management, "We'll make sure we don't hit the veranda stairs, but we first need to cut off some branches."

Phons climbs agilely into the tree and catches the rope Paul throws him. This is followed by the saw, which he uses to cut off a first branch. Once it falls, Paul and Peter drag it away; then another branch and another. Gerard and Peter attack the roots; splinters begin to fly and white roots become visible; the tree groans.

"Phons! Rope round the trunk!" Peter orders. Phons waves, fastens the rope and jumps down, and then the men throw their full weight onto the rope. The tree tilts slowly.

We spectators hold our breath, and watch in tense silence as the tree tilts and tilts, and suddenly topples as the men jump away. The crash seems to reverberate through me. Shouts and applause erupt from our veranda and that of our neighbours. My daughters tumble down the stairs and within minutes the fallen tree is crawling with children.

"Well, that's a job well done!" Gerard says, with great self-satisfaction.

"Was a cinch!" says Phons, grinning up at Nina who has stood up and calls "Well done!"

"Drinks all round, something cool!" I hear the men calling as I finally let go of a squirming Paulie. In the kitchen I find Patsy, Jane and Nina busy with drinks and food. I had baked a *krentenbrood* (raisin bread) for the occasion – a recipe of Hiek's – and Jane and Nina have brought along homemade cakes. Pat waves me outside again: "We can manage in here, there are already too many of us."

I can't remember what we did with the felled tree. All I can recall is the image of everyone celebrating on the veranda that afternoon. What I also recall is that the tree episode changed my ambivalence about Patsy's presence in our house. I began to enjoy her company. She was sweet, funny and inventive. Her depression of the first few days seemed to have gone for good. She usually got up as early as I did and we wordlessly shared the work of looking after the children and the household jobs. The children adored her. She laughed with them, sang to them, made up little plays in which she also took part; she created wondrous costumes from old rags; she told stories.

When she received a letter from Christopher with a cheque in it she gave it to me as her contribution to the household expenses, telling me "He will keep on paying this until I have found a job." We talked. I began to realise that it was indeed impossible for someone like Patsy to be married to a man like Christopher. "Once the baby has been born maybe I will be able to get my old job back," she said, "I have finally accepted that I am on my own and will stay on my own. I'll be fine. I need to learn to live in the here and now, to stay in touch with reality. No hope, but also no despair. Do you know what I mean? I need to focus on events when they happen and only for as long as is necessary. Not look forward or back."

It sounded so brave and clever. We were, moreover, just like Laurel, whom Patsy also visited sometimes, fascinated by the glimpses of the outside world we caught. These were the sixties; there was a revolution going on: hippies, the beginnings of feminism, the importance of an own identity. It became an inevitability that Patsy would stay with us until the baby came. And yet, there was ambivalence...

Sometimes it was as if I was watching how Patsy pulled Phons towards her, like a spider using a delicate web to reel him in, very slowly, very carefully. Or was I imagining things? Was this just the inevitable result of the relationship they had had? Was it Phons who slowly and willingly let himself be enchanted again?

He stayed home more often, he became quieter, he began to pay more attention to everything Pat said. Pat in her turn listened fascinated to his every word. Moreover, her old talents began to emerge. She sang for us, accompanying herself on her guitar. One evening she even danced for us, mocking her ungainly figure, which did not mar the elegance and professionalism with which she moved. And Phons watched with an enigmatic look in his eyes. She was unchangeably sunny and gay. She and Phons took walks together. They started to have long and intense conversations, sometimes until very late at night, usually in the kitchen. Every now and then they would retire to her bedroom. And then came the morning that I discovered the couch had not been slept on.

I barely saw Phons that morning. He drank a quick cup of coffee and left. Patsy only appeared after the children had left for school. She looked like a little girl herself, with her two plaits and her large eyes. "Oh, love, I'm so happy. He's so gracious, so male, so normal. I finally feel like a woman again. I'm alive: this is the first day of the rest of my life. The world has changed. He loves me; he has always loved me, me, and no-one else."

Phons came home unexpectedly early that afternoon, and did not look all that happy. Patsy had gone to visit Laurel. He sat in a chair at my kitchen table. "I guess you know, right? Patsy and I...She doesn't expect anything from me, she doesn't want me to feel tied down. Nina and all that... Of course I love her. I actually never stopped loving her. It's just that I wonder... Oh God, can I handle this?"

I was silent. He stood up and paced the room. "I could adopt the baby. It should have been my baby. It would have been if things had gone normally. Who cares who the biological father is?"

"Phons..." He looked up and his eyes were full of pain. "She is so open, so trusting, and so alone."

"Yes, but what about you? What do you want?" He straightened his shoulders. "There is no question of making choices now. I made my choice, last night. From now on, I am going to look after Pat. I am going to find a flat, somewhere in the neighbourhood. As soon as the divorce comes through we're getting married and I am going to adopt the baby."

It felt right. It felt like the natural solution to this complicated, impossible situation. It put an end to all my doubts. At that moment I only felt huge admiration for Phons and relief for Patsy. I threw my arms around him, "Oh Phons, I hope you'll be so happy together!"

That evening Phons took Pat out to dinner, and the next day he brought a bottle of champagne home. He seemed taller, broader, and beamed with self-confidence. "We have something to celebrate, guys. I needed to do a lot of talking, but she has agreed. We're going to live together, we're officially engaged!"

"Isn't life miraculous?" said Patsy, "Whoever would have thought that the four of us would become a family – at least, that's what I feel that we are. The four of us belong together." At which Phons put his arms around her and grinned: "Good thing Paul is 300 miles away! He wouldn't understand this at all."

Gerard drank champagne politely and congratulated Phons, but later that evening when we were on our own he told me his mind in no uncertain terms: "The fool! The idiot! He's like putty in her hands. She isn't the kind of woman he should marry. She's an arch opportunist, he's getting himself into terrible trouble."

"Oh, that's not true! Phons isn't a child anymore, he knows what's good for him. Don't you remember how much he was in love with her?"

"And look what that brought him! My God, I thought he had learned his lesson then."

"Whether we like it or not this is his decision and we're just going to have to support him. He's our best friend."

Within a week Phons found a furnished flat a few streets away. "Couldn't be better," Patsy reported. "All the mod cons you could wish for. And I can come and visit you whenever I want, you and Laurel. It's only a few minutes walk away!"

"You'll help her, won't you?" Phons asked me, "You'll make sure she isn't alone all day when I'm travelling? She mustn't have any time to brood. She needs you as much as she needs me..."

CHAPTER 22

For better or worse

6 JULY 2001. *We have just had a heat wave, followed by a violent thunderstorm. Rain and hail have caused a lot of damage – many fallen trees and flooded tunnels. Today is Paul and Hanneke's 18th wedding anniversary.*

Our little, always smiling, adventurous Paulie, who delighted in seeking what was around every corner, who found the most inventive ways of escaping from the garden and going on walkabout when he was only two...

I have decided that, though I will impose no other rules while writing this book, I must write about events in the correct chronological order. Which means that I have to at least record the fact that in the early sixties Gerard and I went through a crisis. This coincided more or less with the Phons and Patsy saga; perhaps it was related to it somehow. Everything is interconnected, after all; all those people, all that interaction – impossible to unravel. Looking back now, the word "crisis" seems too big; after all these years it is no longer remotely important. That immense thing that dominated my life at the time has receded into nothing. I don't really care why this should be; perhaps I have repressed it, a fashionable term nowadays, but it makes no difference.

It was, however, a watershed in my life. After this, my life was fundamentally different. When Bobby was a few months old I discovered that Gerard and Josie were what we then called "involved." There was a single, shattering confrontation. They both declared that the affair was over and would never be repeated. I can no longer remember any other details. All I can recall is the silence between Gerard and myself, the emptiness, then. It took a long time before something resembling trust returned, before we could communicate again. I can remember too that I briefly saw this as a kind of perverse but just punishment for what I had, once upon a time, done to Charles.

We had four small children. The one thing I never doubted was that Gerard loved our children as deeply as I did and that children are always better off with two parents, a mother and a father. I still believe that, as long as the situation is not impossible for the children, as long as there is no implacable hatred between the parents or physical violence.

Josie announced to me that she had got a job. She was picking up her old profession of nursery school teacher. I barely saw her. There was nothing left of our friendship. About a year later, they moved. Years later I heard that she and Monty had had a fourth baby; and much later, that they had divorced and that Josie had gone to live in the house in the Blue Mountains, following her mother's death. If my most recent information is correct (March of this year), she is still living there and has changed her surname back to Neville.

And then there was money. Even if we had wanted to, we could not have split up. We were only just managing to keep our heads above water as it was. When Phons and Patsy moved out I decided that we could no longer rent out one of our three bedrooms. We needed a girls room and a boys room. I tried to compensate for the loss of income myself. I asked for more typing work from Hiek. I started to type manuscripts for an author of romantic novels who turned out to live in our neighbourhood. Peter Adler, who had been commissioned by an adult education institute to put together correspondence courses, also gave me work. I remember that we created a journalism course together. He regarded me as an expert as I had been a journalist. The end result can't have been all that bad: his superiors accepted it.

Laurel. She was always there. She listened. She gave me books. She took me to plays. She somehow guided my thinking. It was crucial to think, to find rational solutions for problems, to jump off the emotional merry-go-round, to take your destiny into your own hands.

I decide to apply for Australian nationality and am granted it. I do this, Gerard doesn't. He wants to remain a Dutchman. It feels like my first independent act. I also do a few mad things, like visit an old pub in the city (The George: wasn't it the headquarters of the beat generation in Sydney?). I tie my hair in a topknot. I wear a black sweater and black trousers, and clattering bracelets. I don't go on my own: Peter Adler comes with me, as do Paul and Nina, and Ken Neville, who acts like my personal watchdog. It's a Saturday afternoon – how did I manage an outing into town on a Saturday afternoon?

The George is a dark cavern of brown, smoke-stained wood, with a long row of tiny windows, which look as if they have never been opened. There is a long mahogany bar scarred by beer bottle stains and cigarette burns. It stinks of old beer, cigarettes, unwashed bodies and something sweet I can't place. Everyone is sitting or lying in groups on the floor: boys with shoulder-length hair and beads and medallions and dirty headbands; and girls with even longer hair, ankle length skirts and shawls. A guitar is being played in a strip of sunlight, but there isn't a lot of singing or even talking. Everything is done in whispers. No one laughs, there is a strange lethargy, an air of defeat. I'm here out of curiosity. I want to understand the time that I am living in. I had counted on seeing starry-eyed, young people, bursting with a desire to innovate. Champing at the bit. But, once again, I have clearly misunderstood.

Paul Gundry White declares he is fascinated by his surroundings. Nina strikes me as slightly bored. Peter talks about bourgeois angst and being different. About people who reject the rat race. And then Seth Frith shuffles by, clearly a little drunk and as clearly, completely happy. He is trailing a gypsy-like creature whom he calls "an old girlfriend of mine." She has vacant, black eyes and is distinctly dirty. "Bloody tourists," she says by way of making conversation, and then disappears. How did it go: don't trust anyone above thirty? And I am way beyond that. I'm hopelessly late; I am one of the enemy.

We meet a whole set of new people through Ken and Moira Tolhurst. Academics. Ken is a lecturer in economics at the University of Sydney and Moira, who has just resumed her interrupted studies in zoology, has a part-time job there. Their friends are all older, more experienced, more well read and more articulate than we are. And they all love to talk, to talk a lot. They analyse, categorise and discuss everything they feel, think and do in meticulous detail and with great openness. And they don't only theorise, they put their theories into practice, they experiment. They play a complicated game of which there are no rules but which is part of the "Me age," the desire for personal freedom and the current social revolution. They meander aimlessly and happily from partner to partner and from project to project. It is the time of flower power, Beatle mania, hippies, and phrases like "the rat race" and "the human condition" are scattered through every conversion.

Haven't we become each other's prison guards and forced ourselves into a straightjacket? Aren't we wandering in a wilderness of empty rituals that we have unthinkingly adopted? What about the self? Who can claim to genuinely have an identity of their own? Being married means a life spent floundering at the end of a chain, each of you pulling in opposite directions. In the final instance we are all alone in an empty universe, completely reliant on ourselves...

Blindly trying to cope in our particular black hole, we are easily sucked into this maelstrom. I feel like a child just learning to walk. There is a lot of talk about "open marriage." Can we do that? No, we can't. For better or for worse, all we can do is muddle along in the old pattern. Which is exactly what we do do. And yet, this witches' cauldron of people and experiences gives us a few very good, lifelong friends.

And in the meantime there is Phons, in our living room, working on a huge jigsaw puzzle, all night long. This is spread out on our living room table, a view of Sydney. It is Pat's jigsaw puzzle. Patsy is giving birth to her baby in a brand new (vegetarian and avant-garde) hospital a few suburbs away from us. She had spent the last few days with us while Phons was on a trip. Phons fits a piece into the puzzle every now and then. His face is grey with exhaustion, but he refuses to even consider going to bed until everything is over.

At four o'clock in the morning little Julie is born. At ten past four we get the news and Phons leaves for the hospital. By then the black night is becoming grey and only a few of the cicadas that have kept us company all night are still chirping.

The images I remember are like video clips, especially the images from the years that Bobby was a baby, a toddler. Why I remember what I remember is a mystery, but not important, I think: when I look back I see an immense black expanse lit up suddenly and randomly with bright video clips.

Balmoral Beach, the morning after a party at Ken and Moira's house: golden sand, green, shimmering water, glorious sun. I am lying on my stomach and can feel the earth pressing into me. Behind my closed eyelids sparks dance and explode against a red background. Around me are strewn last night's company. I hear them arguing: Moira with Jane; Tony with Patsy; Joel Margolis with Peter Adler; Maureen, Joel's girlfriend, with a man called Adam, whose surname I forget. They are arguing about Bach. The others are discussing Gestalt therapy, techniques for self-awareness, the newest theories in genetics and the very first computers that fill a whole room. I also hear the undertow: the flirting, the posturing. The eternal male/female game of challenge and retreat, attraction and rejection continues to be played on the beach the morning after every party.

I get up. I count all the chubby, brown toddlers, babies and children that belong to us: Janneke and Alison, Moira's youngest, are splashing around in the water with Joel's flippers and snorkel; Michie, Joel's little girl from his first failed marriage, jumps up and down excitedly on the edge of the water, twisting her little body into impossible shapes; Lindy and Paul are building a sandcastle, with Jane's little Phillip, his thumb in his mouth, looking on; Bobby, his little round head silver in the sunlight, is playing under our parasol with something that looks like a tiny crab. Next to him is the basket in which

Patsy's Julie is sleeping. Next to the basket sits Phons, with Gerard lying beside him. I know that Phons will keep an eye on all the children. I lie down again. All I want is to feel the sun on my skin, nothing more.

Patsy, Janneke and I are running down the long hill to Balmoral Beach. It is six o'clock in the morning. The hot summer's day is still very young. Pat and I have devised a new exercise regime. Before breakfast we race down for a ten-minute swim and then race back home again. Our men look after the children in the meantime.

"Don't you feel how healthy this is?" pants Patsy, "Under all this fat there really is a slim, elegant skeleton, believe me. She'll appear one of these days!"

She is passionately trying to get her old figure back after Julie's birth and I could do with losing a little weight too. Janneke is allowed to come along because she enjoys it so much and is perfectly safe in the water. She is a better swimmer than I am.

Balmoral in the early morning: a mother of pearl ocean under an eggshell sky and not a soul in sight. The waves gently lap against the virgin beach. The sea embraces us. Janneke's high voice echoes over the water.

Laurel and I are in an espresso bar in the heart of town. We are talking about a play we have just seen. Brecht? Noise buzzes around us, the bar is packed. All of the wooden cubicles are overflowing with people. We have managed to get a tiny one to ourselves. It is late at night. I will have to catch the last train, but I don't care. We are drinking black coffee with a small topping of milky foam, and smoking one cigarette after another. Oh, the luxury of hearing, seeing, talking and feeling without any sexual politics, without having to watch your words, without pain.

And then suddenly Henk van Eendenburg dies. Just like that, without any warning: a heart attack. He was only 38 years old. We knew that he had a stomach complaint, but as far as we were aware neither he nor Winifred took that seriously. We see them only rarely these days. (Have I mentioned that when Henk and Winifred got married, Gerard was best man at their wedding?). Gerard moved heaven and earth to get to Henk's cremation on time. He was on his way home from one of his country trips, but sadly arrived too late. He still tells the story that as he was approaching the crematorium he could see smoke coming out of the chimney and realised that it was probably Henk...

CHAPTER 22

A few months later: I am standing next to a hospital bed in which Hiek is lying. The wall behind her bed is olive green. The screen around her bed is a faded green. Transparent plastic tubes run from her arm to a bottle of blood that hangs from a shiny contraption set up next to her bed. Behind the screen is the noise of a hospital ward full of visitors: the shuffling of feet, coughing, talking, laughter. Here, within the confines of the screen, the air smells of disinfectant, of illness.

"A lump in my breast," she had told me airily a week before, "It probably isn't anything to worry about. The doctor doesn't think it is, but he wants to remove it anyway."

It is malignant. Hiek is very ill. She has a high fever. Her face is dark red and swollen. Tears stream down her cheeks. "They took away my right breast and all sorts of glands under my arm. Oh God, Oh God! I wanted so much to visit Holland again! I'll never see it again now. You'll see, I never will and I don't want to die here. I don't!"

It feels as if the ground has collapsed beneath my feet. As if a huge cavern gapes below me, holding all the horrors of hell. Chance – that black, irrational force that always lurks, that rules our lives. Why Hiek? Why must this happen to Hiek, who is so sweet, caring, patient? She rolls her head from side to side. She groans and weeps. "Oh God, oh my God…"

I am full of powerless rage. I would like to scream and curse. I would like to destroy everything around me. It is so vile, so unjust. "You are going to get better," I say, with clenched fists, "You are going to beat this, do you hear me, Hiek? And you are going to go to Holland after you do." I don't really believe what I am saying. All I can see is chaos, a terrifying, undulating emptiness, ruled by vicious, invisible, incomprehensible forces. "Don't give up, Hiek," I whisper, "Don't you dare give up!"

And then suddenly my old Hiek looks at me, smiling a watery smile. "Don't take it so to heart, love. I'm so sorry I let myself go, but every now and then I just can't take it anymore. It could have been much worse, the doctor says. I'm lucky they found it so early." This breaks my heart.

"I've had chemotherapy and they'll give me a prosthesis so that I will look normal. There's no reason why I can't get well again. They are so nice here. They explain everything so carefully. Oh love, there are people here who are much worse off than me."

Gerard and I that evening: talking – talking for the first time in a long time, about Hiek: "Cancer doesn't need to be fatal," he says, "They may have nipped it in the bud. It may never come back, as long as it hasn't spread…I think they took away those lymph glands preventively." He gives me a long, calm, scientific account and that helps me. It helps because this monstrous thing acquires a shape; it is tangible and so can be fought. It has a face and a name, and is no longer a malevolent force crawling out of the sinister crevice of fate.

"I wish there was something we could do for her," I say, "If only we had money! None of us ever have enough money. She so much wants to visit Holland. Wouldn't it be wonderful if we could give her a holiday there once she gets better?"

"What if we start a Hiek fund or something like that?" Gerard says, slowly. "If everyone we know donates a few pounds to it...we can all spare a few pounds. Shall I find out what a return trip to Holland costs? I bet we could get the money together!"

I look at him. For the first time in a long time I really look at him. I see a tired-looking, blonde man with deep furrows along his nostrils, long lines crossing his forehead, and a kind, gentle, concerned face; a familiar, dear face. And suddenly the "we" feeling floods back.

I take a deep breath. "Okay," I say, "No, not just okay – that's a fantastic idea!! The trip alone will do her world of good! Six weeks on a boat with nothing to do but get better. I'm going to make a list of all the people we can ask. And you should find out how much we'll need as a minimum. We could make it a birthday present. That gives us eight weeks. That should be enough time!"

And then there is an old shoebox on the mantelpiece in our bedroom with piles of pound notes in it, which I regularly count. Five pound notes, ten pound notes and even a few cheques...All our friends chip in spontaneously, whether they know Hiek or not.

Hiek's birthday in Seaforth: she is sitting on the couch; dry, limp hair flecked with grey above a thin, white face. She is holding a long, narrow envelope in her hands. "How is this possible? How is this possible? How on earth did you...?!"

"Just a little magic trick," Gerard says smugly, "You're going on holiday. You can't leave till March, but you are going, and you can decide yourself what your return date will be. You need to ring the shipping agent once you're in Holland."

"You have to stay away for at least four months," Jan says, "That'll give me enough time to finish our new bathroom and then you won't ever need to use that awful outside dunny again." He has already managed to finish the living room ceiling and put in a new window with a typically Dutch windowsill on which stand, in very un-Australian fashion, a row of plants in red copper pots.

"Once you're gone the boys and I will really set to work. It's much better that you won't be in the way." Hiek bursts into tears.

"You do want to go, don't you?" I ask, anxiously, "You will enjoy it, won't you?"

"Oh, love!" She is laughing and crying, "Oh love, I can't believe it! It's like a dream. Do you think the doctor will let me go?"

"We've taken care of that," Jan tells her, "I've already talked to him. Exactly what you need, he thinks."

"So you were in on it too? Is this a kind of conspiracy? Do you want me gone so much?" blowing her nose, then to me: "So now I really will have to have that prosthesis, won't I? Oh well..." And then, dreamily, "It will be spring in Holland when I get there." And looking at Jan: "Do you really think you'll be able to cope here for a while without me?"

A whole crowd of us goes to see her off when the time comes. No battered immigrant boat this time, but a cruise ship, gloriously white against the blue of the early evening sky. Cheering people throwing handfuls of coloured streamers: the ship is connected to shore by fragile, multi-coloured ribbons. High above us at the railing stands Hiek – laughing, waving, throwing kisses. Her hair is brown again. She looks just as she did when we left Holland.

CHAPTER 23

Weddings, divorces and babies

BREDA, JULY 2001. *I have just spoken to Janneke in Medowie by phone. Last night, in the middle of the night, I suddenly heard a door slam. This can't happen in an apartment like ours, unless the front door and balcony door are both open, and the wind is blowing. I got up to check, it was 1.30 am, but there was nothing wrong. Was it a dream? The sound was so real and so close. Was it because of the letter that arrived yesterday, from Phons? He isn't doing well: heart problems, migraine. Or was it the conversation I had yesterday with Jane? Jane is moving back to Australia in September after 20 years of living in Holland. Two of her children live there now. We don't speak often, Jane and I, only once or twice a year, usually by phone. But when we talk the past is suddenly very close. Jane's aura hasn't changed, that air of readiness for a crisis that will require her immediate attention – or rather, the conviction that life is a succession of crises, never peaceful, small and predictable.*

Shortly after Hiek's birthday, Jane rang me with the happy news that she and Peter had bought a house in Chatswood, along our old North Shore train line; something to do with an unexpected inheritance. They had already moved and were counting on us coming over to take a look, with the children, on Sunday afternoon.

A dapper, freestanding house with a neglected front garden in a quiet, broad North Shore street lined by high, dark trees. Jane is standing in the front door dressed in a long, yellow kaftan. She looks as if she has been partying all night. She has dark circles under her eyes. "We're camping out in the back for the moment," she says.

We walk through a broad, high corridor flanked on either side by huge, dusty, empty rooms, the walls of which are flecked with damp. "Loads of space. We're going to do it all up." "In the back" turns out to be a huge kitchen with patio doors opening onto a large back garden, their glass panes grubbied by countless fingers. Like the garden at the front of the house, the back garden is a wilderness; amongst bright yellow, knee-high weeds stands a lonely gumtree with bulging bark and twisted branches. In the middle of the kitchen is a vast wooden table covered with pieces of old iron, large sheets of greenish copper pots with poisonous-looking fluid and assorted hammers, chisels, saws and screwdrivers.

There is an old typewriter at one end of the table with a large pile of tightly typed pages alongside it. I can't see chairs anywhere. Along the back wall of the kitchen run wooden racks, on the top shelves of which perch countless little glass pots; the lower shelves are packed with books. The stove, washbasin and fridge are housed in a narrow alcove. Next to this sits Phillip in a high chair, sucking a piece of bread. Behind the table stands Peter. He is wearing a leather apron, busily hammering a sheet of copper. Splinters of copper twinkle in his beard. "His latest passion!" Jane shouts above the din.

Peter gives the copper a last bang and looks up. His grin is slightly malevolent.

"He's full of new creative vigour," Jane says in the calm that follows, "Only it doesn't pay the bills. My bourgeois employment agency jobs do that."

"Like hell they do!" cries Peter, "I do my bit!" making a sweeping gesture towards the row of pots on the shelves behind us. I look around at them and freeze with horror: the pots are inhabited by dead and living spiders: funnel-webs.

"Caught them myself," Peter explains cheerily, "There!" with a gesture to the garden. "It's overrun with them. I sell them to Sydney Uni. They're using them to develop an antidote. It's called a socially responsible hobby and it brings in good money." His black eyes are sparkling. His teeth shine white between red lips emerging from his beard. It finally dawns on me that we have walked in on an anything but subterranean marital quarrel.

Our children, who, like us, have watched in stunned silence, suddenly come alive. I am surrounded by eagerly grasping little hands. "Don't touch anything!" I cry sharply, "Peter is doing dangerous work here."

"Can we play outside then?" Janneke asks reasonably.

"Of course you can!" says Peter, grandly opening the garden doors onto that wilderness full of lethal funnel-webs.

"No, you can't!!" I squeak, slightly hysterically. Not in a million years!

"There's a paddock behind our garden," Jane intervenes, hurriedly "And there's a sheep there. Why don't you go and have a look, kids? But you have to walk along the garden path. You're not allowed into the undergrowth. If you follow the path, you'll find the sheep."

I control myself with an effort and let them go, Paul holding Janneke's hand. But I clasp Bobby tightly in my arms. He wriggles, squirms and protests. Peter starts to hammer again, explaining to Gerard in the meantime what he is doing. Jane lifts Phillip out of the high chair. "Come on, Agatha. You're not really worried are you? They can't come to any harm back there. He's exaggerating about the spiders. We've only found two so far in our garden." As if two isn't more than enough!

She leads me into a small room, adjacent to the kitchen. We are standing in front of a large unmade bed that almost fills the room. In the folds of a harlequin quilt nestle two large cats, a fat ginger cat and a thin black one. Bobby crows with delight and he and Phillip crawl along the quilt, tumbling over the cats. Jane scatters a pile of old colouring books and pencils on the floor, and settles down on the edge of the bed, 'God, I'm almost ready for the lunatic asylum."

I sit down carefully beside her; the hammering in the kitchen continues. "Does he do this every day?"

"This and making collages. And I keep on hoping he'll come up with something we can sell, but so far nothing. Oh, and he has developed a passion for psychotherapy."

"What?"

"He sees himself as a budding psychotherapist. He has discovered he is irresistible to neurotic women."

"Jane, you must be joking!"

"If only! Do you know what happened yesterday? He brought a claustrophobia patient home. The silly woman can't handle sitting in trains or something. So he thought he would cure her by taking her home by train from Wynyard. She had hysterics and tried to jump out! So he then brought her here in a taxi – a taxi, for God's sake! Paid for by us! And here I am trying to make every penny count! I was so furious. So I rang her parents, who had been trying to find her for days. There was such a scene outside our front door. Screaming and yelling, but they took her home. At least I managed to nip that little affair in the bud."

She rubs her hand over her eyes crossly. She is thin, so very thin underneath that kaftan, like a lost child. She looks at me, her brown eyes shining with tears. "I really don't mind being the breadwinner. He doesn't have the temperament to work in an office. He could never work for an employer. I love him. I want to give him the time he needs. But there is a limit, isn't there? The way things are going now I simply can't handle it anymore."

"Shall we go?" Gerard is standing in the opening of the door. The look in his eyes as he surveys the bed, the cats, and the chaotic open wardrobe behind us makes more than clear that staying here all afternoon is out of the question. He has his medihaler in his hand; he puts it to his mouth and inhales deeply twice.

"Animals are so good for kids, don't you think?" says Jane chirpily, "You just shouldn't let kids grow up without pets." All signs of desperation have suddenly disappeared as if an iron had smoothed her face. All at once she looks ten years younger, which of course she is, about 12 years younger than we are. She jumps up, "Surely you still have time for a cup of tea?"

"I'm going to call the children," Gerard says. He wasn't keen on this visit in the first place. He doesn't seem keen about anything anymore. He comes along if I suggest we go somewhere, but that is about it. I pull Bobby towards me: "We can't talk quietly now anyway. It's better if we go. I'll come back soon or better still, you should come to me."

Of course I can't separate the two Janes anymore – the young Jane and the Jane now, after a long life of fighting and never giving up. Building an independent career with a determination for which I have always had the greatest respect. But with whom, despite her vast, clever, witty vocabulary, it is difficult for me to communicate. Our frames of reference are so very different. They were when she was much younger too, but I was less aware of it then. Then I had no idea that actions could be misinterpreted, that agendas could be hidden or that growing up in a particular environment could leave an indelible mark. I did not know then how incredibly difficult understanding another person could be.

About four months after that Sunday, Jane took Phillip and moved in with her mother, and the Chatswood house was suddenly put up for sale. Peter lived for a little while in a room in Paddington – now one of the swankiest and most expensive suburbs in the heart of Sydney, but at the time the cheap refuge of choice for poor artists, beatniks and the homeless. A tempestuous reconciliation followed, and they lived together again for a very brief period, renting a cheap flat somewhere in Sydney. I don't remember where it was. What I do remember is Jane telling me about physical violence and that everything was now irrevocably over between Peter and herself. And that she was desperately looking for a better job. At which Hiek suggested that her old job might be suitable for Jane. I hastily passed this on and two weeks later

Jane was indeed working in the North Shore office where Hiek had worked for so many years.

And then we received a wedding invitation – an invitation printed in Gothic font on embossed cream parchment – to attend the wedding of Mr. Paul Gundry White and Ms. Nina Jones. Patsy and I thought the invitation bizarrely conventional.

"All that old English landed gentry blood will out!" Pat smirked, "And at Garrison Church no less, the sanctuary of the upper ten. That will mean hats and gloves. Whoever would have thought it? I'm going to have to rent a morning suit for Phons. Paul has asked him to be his best man. We'll go as a foursome, right? Let's make it a glorious fancy dress party!"

Which is what it indeed became, although the day did not begin so gloriously. I remember Phons, in beautifully tailored tails, coming through our back door only to collapse in a heap on our sofa, tears of helpless laughter rolling down his cheeks. Gerard was standing in his light blue underpants at the ironing board, solemnly pressing the dripping trousers of his only dark suit. He had got up very early to wash them by hand, despite my dire warnings not to: "Dry clean them? Much too expensive! They're washable, that's what the label says!" Unfortunately, it was a rainy day and the trousers were still resolutely wet, so Gerard was drying them with the iron. He kept on ironing till the last possible moment, but the result was not a happy one. He first stuck to the car seat and then to the church pew, and the trousers made a gentle sucking sound every time he stood up…

Nevertheless, the four of us do our best to exude what we hope is slightly amused, calm self-confidence. I am wearing a black cocktail dress, which I have bought especially for the occasion. I have never owned such an elegant dress before. I am also wearing a big black hat that Patsy found for me. Pat is a vision in green with long, elbow-length white gloves and a little white hat. She nods benignly to left and right – the packed church is a sea of black and white and pastels – her left hand resting lightly on Phons' black sleeve. And then Phons stands with his broad shoulders next to the bride and groom at the altar and produces the ring at the right moment. He does it with panache, as if he is an old hand at this.

Nina looks touchingly young in a cloud of white satin and Paul is as straight as an arrow. "For better or for worse, in sickness and in health, till death us do part." To my complete surprise, the words bring tears to my eyes.

My most enduring memory is of Christopher/Heinz. He appears out of nowhere after the ceremony has finished, as we, making our way to the reception in Jane and Nina's mother's house, are trying to get into Phons' car in the pouring rain. Phons and Patsy are already seated. Suddenly he stands next to me, his dripping wet hair stuck to his forehead. He holds my black-gloved hand and says something. What? And why does this image endure and not, for instance, what the historic church in Argyle Place looked like? It was the venue of choice for society weddings at that time, that famous Garrison Church, built in 1840 and so called because the troops stationed in the garrison of Sydney went to church there every Sunday.

Jane and Peter are at the reception, impeccably attired, Jane with a long cigarette holder between her carefully manicured fingers. They stand next to each other, shaking hands. "For Nina's sake," Jane hisses as an aside to me. And then Nina and Paul stand at the top of the stairs and Nina throws her bouquet; they drive away in a car with old shoes and tins rattling behind them and a Just Married sign attached to the back. And I am suddenly flooded with all-encompassing melancholy. Too much champagne? Probably, but also because I can no longer believe in "happily ever after."

Not long after the wedding Phons and Patsy came to tell us that Pat was pregnant again and that Phons had managed, despite the overwhelming waiting list, to speed up Heinz and Pat's divorce. Phons was the driving force behind this, not Heinz, and not Patsy. And Phons – as the guilty party – was also the only one who was summoned to appear in court. Pat spent that morning with me.

"How did it go?" I asked hesitantly, when Phons wandered in through the back door around twelve. His face was anything but happy.

"A nasty experience," he said, "It all sounded so different from what really happened. I had to sign an official declaration that I would take care of both children. As if I ever meant to do anything else!"

"Oh well," Patsy shrugged, "It's all nonsense anyway. What do all those people have to do with us? Forget about it." She sounded far too careless, I thought.

"Well, it'll only be a few more weeks," Phons said, "And then we can finally get married."

"We should really just continue as we are now," Patsy said pensively, "Why do we have to agree to all these labels? Let society determine how we live? Who we really are can't be defined by a category anyway. I hate all these conventions!"

"Well, this time you happen to be carrying my baby!" said Phons, with a sharpness I had never heard before in his voice. "And I happen to want my baby to have my name."

Patsy shrugged again, "Men! Here, will you carry Julie? We need to go shopping. Are you coming?" I silently watched the three of them leave. Something, somewhere didn't feel right, didn't feel genuine.

A white hot day: a day like a gong that loudly announces the end of the short Sydney spring. Summer! And the overwhelming feeling of joy it brings. I still get that wonderful feeling of summer on the very first hot day, even here, in Holland, where everything is always so much less intense. Then, over there, it was always blindingly obvious that something new had arrived. And even though you knew that later, when the heat became unbearable, you would long for the cool, for rain, for change, at that moment that hard newness was pure delight.

I feel awash with energy, as if anything is possible: a fresh, new beginning. I get out all our lightest clothes, and run into the laundry together with Paulie and Bobby to unearth the somewhat reckless, but now very welcome sale item we had bought a few months ago: a round, inflatable kiddies pool, consisting of two fat blue rings and a bright yellow floor. It needed to be inflated (I wasn't even aware of the existence of pool pumps at that time) and we did not have a garden hose. So the only solution was to fill buckets of water and carry them over to the pool, but I didn't mind at all and my little boys helped.

Just as they have climbed, excited and impatient, over the sides of the pool and water is beginning to splash everywhere Patsy appears with Julie in the pram. "My God, it's hot!"

"Hi Pat, you're just in time. Leave Julie here, she can play with the boys. Come on upstairs, it's cool there."

Patsy and I survey the summer idyll in my back yard from the shade of our upstairs veranda. We look down on two little, round, blonde heads and a delicate one full of black curls; on two sturdy little boys' bodies and one frail little girl, splashing around gleefully amid a selection of colourful plastic ducks. "Isn't this fantastic? I adore summer," I say.

"I don't," Pat sits, one hand resting on her large belly. And then without warning: "I don't think I should do this, marry Phons."

"What? Patsy, you can't be serious!"

"I am. We don't fit well together. He has no idea what goes on in my head. I can't be myself around him. Just by being who he is he forces me into a straightjacket, can't you see that?"

"Oh, good God!" I say, "Will you stop?! The man adores you; he would do anything for you. He is moving heaven and earth to make you happy. There are very few men around who would do for you what he has done."

"That has nothing to do with it."

"Nothing do with it?! He loves you; you mean everything to him! And what choice do you have? You're almost six months pregnant, you have Julie. Are you just going to split up? How on earth would you support two children on your own?"

"Can we leave the practical side out of the discussion for the moment?"

"Leave it out? You can't leave it out! Once you have children that is all that counts."

"For you! That is the way you are!"

"Well, isn't it the way you are too? For God's sake, Pat, I remember… Oh but, no, it was pure romance then; you had never been so happy. You had finally found him, a real man."

She covered her eyes with both her hands. "Oh, Agatha, stop. I can't bear to think how I fooled myself then. I must have known deep down that it was a compromise. I just ignored that. I wanted so very much for it to be real, I threw myself into it, surrendered myself completely. I really did give it my all, hence this baby. But it was wrong, all wrong. I should have been stronger. I shouldn't have denied my deepest instincts. I should have listened much sooner to this voice inside me. Don't you understand any of this?" with big, tragic eyes.

"No, I don't! Do you really think that perfection exists in a relationship? All you can hope for is to find something resembling it a little. And what about accepting the consequences of your actions? Willpower, it just takes willpower. Your kids…"

She is furious now: "Oh, all you ever do is harp on about the kids! This is the first time I have tried to put into words what I feel, to have the courage to take a hard look at myself and be honest. You are my best friend and all you have to say is: think about the kids! My God, that is all I ever do! I tell myself day in day out that this should be enough: a good husband, a normal family. But it isn't enough. I know I am going to suffocate. Am I supposed to spend the rest of my life pretending that there is nothing wrong?"

I close my eyes. When I was small I had a recurring nightmare. I dreamed I was climbing a dark staircase. At the top of the stairs it was light, but where I was climbing it was dark. The distance between the steps grew larger and larger. The last stair was so high that I couldn't possibly reach it. I tried, weeping, to pull myself up by my fingers, but my fingers slipped off the edge again and again. My arms were too short to get a good grip on the top stair. The light was so close yet so unreachable and below me was a precipice. That same feeling washes over me now. Was that because Pat was causing my own convictions, the certainties to which I held fast, to topple?

"Just go on," I hear myself say and it sounds like a prayer, "All you can do is go on. Accept things as they are. You have so much. We both have so much."

"Make a virtue of necessity, you mean? I despise that expression, it is so cowardly."

"Cowardly? Not to look down, not to turn around, to keep on trying even if it is hopeless? You could also call it very brave." I try to be calm, "Why don't you talk to your doctor? Some women suffer from depression when they're pregnant. Maybe that is what is wrong with you."

"Jesus! Is that the best advice you can give? Doctors, tranquilizers? Reduce what you feel to an everyday physical complaint?"

"Well then, why don't you talk to Laurel?"

"There are some things," Laurel tells me later, "it is dangerous to give a name to, to talk about, because it gives them a shape. Talking about something makes it important. You can give a specter solid form that way, create something that did not exist before. It's like turning an innocent stream that can be easily bridged into a raging torrent that destroys everything. I can't help Patsy, no-one can, she has to help herself. She has discovered that she has to make a choice, between "me" and "the babies and Phons.""

The stream did indeed become a raging torrent that swept us all helplessly before it. Patsy did not talk to their doctor, but Phons did. Not Patsy but Phons contacted a psychologist, on the advice of their doctor, and managed to persuade Patsy after lengthy discussions to meet with him.

"A psychologist!" Gerard said, "She deserves to be whipped! What the hell does she think she's doing? If Phons doesn't watch out this will destroy him. Listening night after night to her talk about her ridiculous hang-ups. And then she falls asleep and he has to get up, look after Julie and go to work."

"Pat is a very special woman," I said weakly, "It's all more complicated than you think."

"Rubbish! She should be thanking her lucky stars she managed to catch a man like Phons. Any other man would have left her a long time ago. I'm worried about him, not her!" And he was right. Phons became visibly thinner, his sideburns suddenly turned grey. His eyes were dull and he now permanently wore that look of pained incomprehension, which I had first seen the Sunday afternoon Patsy announced her marriage to Christopher.

The psychologist told Patsy she was living in a fantasy world. Her response to this was days of weeping. Phons kept on telling her that he loved her, that he loved Julie, that he loved his unborn child. That she could find herself as much as she wanted after the baby was born...

They got married on a dark, thunderstorm afternoon in a Catholic church. It was a very short ceremony. Twelve days later the baby was born. It was a little boy and they called him Luc. Shortly afterwards, Phons changed jobs. He became, just like Gerard, a medical representative, which meant he no longer had to be away from home so often on long country trips. Moreover, he found them a new house, through one of his business contacts. A freestanding house close to the wharf where the Mosman ferry moored, at the bottom of a steep street called Avenue Road.

Second-hand furniture was found from far and wide. Patsy underwent a metamorphosis. She began cheerfully to decorate her new home. She achieved miracles with what she had. Her children seemed to give her great joy. She behaved like every normal, devoted mother. There was no time for obsessive talking and we heard nothing more about the psychologist.

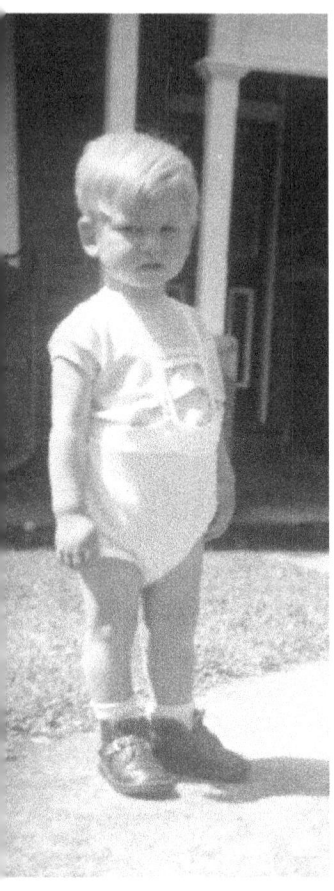

CHAPTER 24

Paul

BREDA, AUGUST 2001. *Another break of a few weeks. We have just spent two weeks in Paul and Hanneke's house in Oisterwijk while they are on holiday in Italy together with Jill.*

Paul. I have repeatedly postponed what needs to be written now. The Oisterwijk break contributed to this postponement. I still find it so very hard. For many years, I could not even talk about it. It literally made me ill. When I wrote about it for the first time twenty years ago I hoped that this would put an end to it, that this would be a kind of catharsis. But it wasn't.

I have just re-read my report from long ago. I am not going to change it. I will include it now, unchanged.

Patsy and I are in a small, experimental theatre somewhere in the middle of town at the end of a winter's afternoon. We are taking part in "a happening," about Indian dance, preceded by an Indian meal. Patsy had read the announcement somewhere and declared she absolutely had to go, no matter what, and that I must come along. We are both interested in Krishna Murti and his teaching on "reflecting like a still lake." Total serenity. We have talked and read about karma and reincarnation and the mysterious Indian culture. This is our chance to experience it, to view it with our own eyes.

It started at six o'clock, an impossible time, in my view. But Phons had decided that we should go (Patsy's self-realisation had priority above all else) and had arranged with Gerard that he would come over to our house with Julie and Luc. They would together bathe all the children, feed them and put them to bed. Easy peasy. Pat and I needed a treat, to get out. We so rarely went out...

Pat and I wander through an exotic, gold shimmering dream, past rows of sizzling, spicy dishes set out on long, wooden trestles. The light is dim. The dancers are sprinkled with gold dust. They wear enormous headdresses. They have tiny, graceful hands, which lead a life of their own. There is a round, red dot on their smooth, satiny foreheads. Sitting behind odd-shaped drums are young men, with shaven heads, brown, polished torsos, gleaming shoulders and narrow, long, brown feet. They are sitting on the ground, cross-legged. The smell of incense hangs in the air, of dust, of ivory stored for many years.

Suddenly Gerard materialises in front of me: "I've come to get you."

"You're much too early," I say surprised, "This is only the first break. The main event hasn't started yet."

"Something has happened."

"What has happened?" Patsy asks sharply.

"It's Paulie," says Gerard, "He's in hospital. There's been an accident. But he's alright, he's alright."

Something inside me rears up, lurches, stops, and then climbs into my throat like an ice cold, hard mass. "What?" I ask, suddenly hoarse, "What?"

"Just come with me," he takes hold of my arm firmly. We are outside. Patsy is holding my other arm. "Calm down, he's okay. Gerard says he is doing okay."

"I am calm!" I hear myself say, shrilly, "I want to know what has happened, what exactly happened?" The mass of ice has slipped back down to my chest. My ribs hurt. Patsy pushes me into the car. "We're going straight to the hospital now. You'll be able to see him for yourself."

"Here," says Gerard, "I have a tablet for you, it will calm you down."

I push his hand away. "What happened? Please just tell me what happened?"

"Just take it," Patsy says, "It's small. You can swallow it easily. Just take it."

To stop their nagging, I take the pill. It is raining, it is raining hard. The windscreen wipers move madly. "Where is he?" my voice is strangely high. My mouth is made of copper, and completely dry. "Which hospital?"

"The Mater," says Gerard, "We'll be there soon." And then he begins to tell his story. Paul. Little Paulie in the bathroom, on his own, with the door locked, and the matches near the boiler. "We didn't notice that he had disappeared. We broke open the door. His pyjamas were on fire."

"Oh no!" I cry, "Oh no, oh no!" again and again, the same thing, an endless litany.

I don't want to hear anymore. I don't want to know any details.

"He's in good hands, he'll be okay," says Gerard, "He isn't in pain anymore."

We fly through the wet night. I can feel Patsy's hands on my shoulders. We are standing in a sharply lit wooden cubicle. A nurse offers me a glass of water. I push it away.

"Where is he? I want to see him. He's not even three." My voice is hard. I am not crying, There are no tears. Only that lump of ice that has now grown to cover my whole chest.

"He's asleep," someone says, "He's asleep now, it's the best thing for him."

And then I see him. He is lying in a children's cot with high white bars and around the bed a kind of mesh cage has been erected. He is lying on a sheet, on his back, his legs pulled up. He is wearing only a nappy. His little chest, his arms, his little neck and whole of his top torso is an open, raw wound. His face is untouched. It is red and flushed, but untouched. His eyes are shut. His thick, red blonde curly hair is dark and drenched with sweat. He is not moving at all.

"He's sleeping, you see, he's asleep," says Gerard putting an arm around my shoulders, "He's sleeping. He isn't in pain. They follow the most modern procedures here. No bandages, no creams. He's being sprinkled every hour with sophramycine. They just have to make sure there is no infection…"

I stand and I look. And I know what it means to be engulfed in flames. What it feels like. "He's going to die," I say, absently. I feel the flames licking my arms, my chest, my neck. Terror of death, horrible pain. I have to stand still. I need all my attention just to stand still now.

"He isn't going to die!" Gerard's voice breaks, he shakes me, "He isn't going to die, do you hear me? He has suffered serious burns, but he is going to get better. He isn't disfigured. He is just sleeping. He is just sleeping now!"

Patsy takes my hand, "Come on love. Don't you want to talk to the doctor now? The doctor can tell you exactly what the situation is. We mustn't wake him."

"I have to stay here," I say, dully, "I have to stay here."

"Of course you have to stay with him. But you need to talk to the doctor first. You can do that more quietly in the corridor. Come on."

I let myself be led away. I am facing a tall, dark man in a white coat. "I fully realise how horrifying it must to be see him lying there," he says, "But it really isn't as bad as it looks. It's only the front of his body. His chest, neck, arms. And this is the very best treatment for burn victims, the open air. He really is just sleeping, madam. He'll stay asleep till tomorrow morning, believe me. We've made very sure of that."

"Pain," I say.

CHAPTER 24

"The worst pain is over. I promise you on my word of honour he will not suffer any more pain. We are watching him day and night. He is being cared for round the clock. You really can go home for a little while now."

"Home?" The man must be out of his mind.

"Home," Gerard repeats, "We need to get a little peace first, get some sleep. Tomorrow morning when he wakes up we'll be back."

"Sleep?" I stare at him. I can see tears in his eyes, "Oh God" he says softly, "Oh God, My little Paulie." The ice in my chest expands to my hands. My fingers become stiff. My teeth begin to chatter. The doctor is now holding a glass of water and another small tablet. "You need to take this, ma'am." He pushes the glass against my shaking teeth, "Drink up. Well done. You need to have faith in us. We really will take very, very good care of him here. You can help us best by going home quietly for a little while. And then tomorrow morning as early as you like…"

I am firmly pushed out the door.

"I'll drive," Pasty says when we are outside. Gerard and I sit in the back together. He holds onto me tightly, his head leaning on my shoulder. "I would give my life for him, you know that," he whispers, "I would give anything if I could bear this for him. Oh God, I should have watched him better."

The cold has taken hold of my whole body now. My feet are numb. I am shrouded in a blanket of ice. "Ssh," I say from somewhere far away, "Hush now. He's so quick and very clever. It could have happened to any of us." So reasonable, so cold, so icily alone. I stroke his hair with frozen fingers, as if he is an amiable stranger. I should never have gone with Patsy. I should have been home. It is my fault. It is my fault.

I spend the rest of that night waiting. Dry-eyed, lying awake in the dark and waiting, for hours. Until, once it is light, we are standing beside that little white bed again. He wakes up. He looks at me with hazy, feverish eyes. He focuses and his bottom lip begins to quiver. "Mummy, mummy!"

At the same moment a young doctor appears alongside the bed with a white mask over his nose and lips and with an injection needle in a gloved hand: "Don't touch him, ma'am!" At his side appears a nurse, also masked and gloved. The man opens the mesh cage carefully and bends over Paul. "Just a tiny pin prick, little man. So. Well done! Hush now. Mummy's here. And now we're going to have a little drink."

The nurse places her hand under Paul's head and lifts it up a tiny bit. She has a cup with a little spout that she places against his lips. "No, no, don't move, don't sit up. Just drink. Good boy. Good boy." Paul drinks. He swallows. Thick tears fall down his cheeks. "Mummy, mummy."

The mass of ice inside me melts. I become fluid. I hear my own voice. "Hush, darling. Go back to sleep. Mummy will stay with you. I will stay with you." The doctor holds me back. "Don't come closer, ma'am." The nurse shuts the cage again with great care. "We need to keep him as sterile as possible. You absolutely must not touch him. We will keep him sedated for a few days, he really can't feel a thing."

I nod. I can feel my willpower rear up, leave my body and slip into the cage. I need to will him to go back to sleep. He sighs. His eyes drift shut. And finally I can cry. I do not let myself be ushered out any more. I am adamant. There is no day and no night anymore. There is no Gerard and there are no other children, there is only an all-encompassing concentration on this child: an unyielding vigilance. He sleeps.

How long this lasted I no longer know. A day? A night? Time had no meaning at all. I know I remained sitting there until a specialist came to reassure me personally that there was absolutely no further threat to his life. That he was responding well to the medication. That he was going to get better.

Later. A children's ward with long rows of little beds, with high, light windows, with lots of toys and picture books everywhere, and Paulie, his arms and hands bandaged, and bandages on his chest, in little white pyjamas sitting straight up in bed, fiddling busily with a small airplane with the few fingers sticking out of his bandages. He is laughing and chattering animatedly.

He cries unhappily when we have to leave. The hospital imposes strict rules. If I remember correctly visiting hours to the children's ward were in the afternoons from two to three, longer on Sundays. Only parents are allowed, no brothers and sisters. The stay in the hospital is free, as is the treatment. We are eternally grateful for this.

We are also very grateful for the fact that Paul has acquired a special friend, a young nurse called Fran. She tells us that our little Paul looks exactly like her little brother who lives at home on a farm, deep in the interior. She pays extra attention to Paul. She comes to talk to him every day, even when she is not on shift.

Paul is operated on. Skin transplant. Skin from his upper right leg is transplanted to his right wrist and underarm. "He is so very strong and healthy," Fran reassures me, "He'll be as good as new, you'll see!"

And then he starts to walk again. Bent double like a little old man, he shuffles step by step through the ward with his upper right leg bandaged from top to bottom and his right arm in a sling. "Look, Mummy! I can walk! And tomorrow I'm allowed to go downstairs with Fran. To the shop. We're going to buy sweeties!"

For eight long weeks I go every second afternoon by bus and train to the hospital. Sometimes Gerard manages to come along too, but he usually has to restrict himself to the weekends. And for eight long weeks Patsy is my other self. She arrives when I have to leave. She looks after Bobby, Julie and Luc at our house and she is there for the girls when they come home from school. She always has tea ready when I get back home after many hours of travel and listens with sincere concern to my stories. I am still deeply grateful to her for this.

After eight weeks we are finally allowed to take Paulie home. "We are very proud of him," the surgeon says, "There isn't the slightest reason why he won't be able to lead a normal life. Those scars will disappear slowly but surely. They won't vanish completely, of course, but he will be able to do everything other boys do. My advice is let him take part in lots of sports, it will help those underarm muscles to recover more quickly. It's lucky he's such a lively little chap. And he doesn't stop talking for a second either, does he? He really is a remarkable little boy." I locked that man in my heart forever.

"Why can't Fran come home too?" Paul asks, "I want Fran to come home with me!"

"I'll come and visit you," Fran promptly promises, "I'll come to make sure you are doing your exercises properly. You won't forget them, will you? You have to practice every day."

"Like this," says Paul, stretching his arms up high and then bending his elbows, his little balled fists at ear level and stretching his arms straight in front of him, "And this!" He pushes his hands out and opens and closes his fingers a dozen times in a row. "Very good! Every morning and evening. And you must think of Fran every time you do them!"

That night, when I put him in the bath again for the first time, I saw the scars properly. From the point of his chin to his navel fiery, puckered skin. Thick folds under his right arm and equally thick folds on the inside of his wrists. On his left thigh a stretch of what looks like very thin newly developing skin.

The surgeon turned out to be right. It took years, but the physical scars slowly disappeared almost completely. I thought then that there was no trace of a mental scar. He still was and stayed the same sunny, enterprising and inquisitive little scamp that he had always been. He threw himself enthusiastically into everything, with heart and soul. Especially sports, whether it was swimming, rugby or later tennis. And music…

PART 2

CHAPTER 25

Globe Commercial

"*N*OW" IS 30 *August 2001. I have just turned 74 years old. Lindy is visiting Australia at the moment; she is in Canberra, and will be back in Sydney where she will see Janneke in three days' time. And I am reading Bill Bryson's* Down Under, *which is so wonderfully witty and well observed. I am enjoying every page. He notes his pleasant surprise at coming across a book that describes daily life in Australia in 1959/1960. Our time! And how happy people were then whenever they managed to acquire a fridge, a radio, a washing machine. "Oh, to live in a world in which the ownership of an electric jug is a source of pride!" So true. We did live in a world in which small conveniences were regarded as luxuries and were therefore valued hugely. We lived so close to what felt like the poverty line....*

I did not know that I was going to call this section Part 2 until I sat down to start writing just now. Then it suddenly seemed inevitable. I have reached a turning point in my story. Our lives are going to change drastically...

It began with a phone call from Jane. "Agatha. Do you feel like earning a quick thirty pounds?" I am crouching near the phone, which is still situated on the floor in our bathroom corridor. "Thirty pounds! Are you joking? How?!"

"Come and work here." I sit down, back against the wall, knees drawn up. "What do you mean?"

"I want to take two weeks holiday, as of next week if possible. Would you be my replacement here? It might even become three weeks. There are loads of things I need to do. In that case you would earn 45 pounds. Would you consider it? We need to keep this job in the family, love!"

There is a cool breeze blowing through my hall. I hear a bedroom door slam. "Oh, Jane, I couldn't possibly do it! I've never worked in an office in this country."

"Of course you could do it! It's a cinch, believe me. A little bit of typing, watching the stencil machine, smiling at the customers. Nobody will hassle you. You'll be as free as a bird!"

"Stencil machine? I don't even know what a thing like that looks like!"

"You won't need to work it. There are assistants for that. All you need to do is organise things, give a little bit of leadership. Typing stencils is much easier than normal typing work. I thought you could do with the extra money."

Of course we could do with the extra money! A while ago I had taken over the running of the household accounts because Gerard was so careless with bills. I would come across them in the strangest places. I also thought that at least one of us should know exactly what our financial situation was, an idea that caused Gerard to shrug. "What does it matter as long as we manage?" We rarely paid a bill until we had received a final warning, a habit I hated with a vengeance. Final warnings gave me palpitations.

I recalled the pile of bills in a drawer under our bed, as well as the motley array of necessities that had been worrying me, like the new shoes Paul needed, the girls' school uniforms that were becoming too small, the thinning sheets hanging on the washing line and the children's sweaters. I usually pulled these apart when they were too small and knitted them together again to make a new one. Thirty pounds was a fortune! All the things I could do with that...

"But the boys are still so little. If they were going to kindergarten..."

"You could ask Pat to help for three weeks?"

"She wouldn't be able to, not for whole days."

"There's an excellent crèche here in North Sydney, very close to our office. You could take them there. Why don't you think it over? Ring me back tomorrow morning. I need to go now. But I think it would be such a waste to let this opportunity go."

I hang up. I stay sitting on the floor. Work? From nine to five? Thirty pounds! Maybe even 45? I ring Laurel.

"I think it's a great idea," she says calmly, "It will be good for you to broaden your horizon a little. And it's only for three weeks. Talk it over with Gerard. It should be doable if he helps out a little. And call that crèche!"

"I'm afraid to," I admit, sweat starting to break out on my forehead, "I mean, I'm afraid to take this on. I have so little work experience. And I have no idea what it is like to work in an office here."

She laughs. "You can do a hell of a lot more than you think. Just be yourself, use your common sense. Give it a try, that's all. Let me know what you decide."

I scramble up. I feel as if I am being pushed up a steep slope against my will with no railing to hold on to. Why couldn't there be more time? Why did a decision have to be made immediately, now, today? And there was actually no decision to be made. It would be criminal to let 45 pounds slip through my fingers.

Clothes! What on earth should I wear to work in an office? I run into the bedroom and nervously open the door of our wardrobe. It isn't very full. A skirt and blouse, I decide, together with a neat cardigan that I happened to have bought recently. It would do. I go back to the veranda. It is a sunny winter's morning. The boys are playing down in the garden, Paul with the little blue car he can sit in himself and which we had bought for him when he came out of hospital; it has reached the stage of car wreck now. Bobby is running a few dinky cars along the bottom rung of the veranda stairs. I look down on them, biting my nails.

I return to the phone and ring the North Sydney crèche. To my surprise, my voice sounds cool and businesslike: "Full days, yes. From nine to five."

"We always give our children a warm lunch," the lady on the other end of the phone tells me. "And after that they usually take a nap." She sounds genteel, quite nice, in fact. I have forgotten how much it cost, but it can't have been too bad as I recklessly promise that we will come by the next afternoon to take a look.

Gerard's response that evening was a bit indifferent. "If it's what you want..."

"But we need the money so badly!" I said sharply, "We still spend more than we earn and I don't know how I can economise more than I'm already doing. Will you help? I can only do it if you help." At which he pulled out his diary. "Okay, I have an appointment at five tomorrow, but I can shift that. I'll make sure I'm home before five so I can come along with you to the crèche. And with a little bit of luck I should be able to drive you and the boys to North Sydney every day. But you'll have to pick them up yourself in the afternoons and take them home by train. What will we do with the girls? Don't they get out of school at three?"

"I talked to Moira," I said, "She'll keep an eye on them. I'll give Janneke a key. It will only be for three weeks."

"But only on condition that we like the crèche!" I told Jane the next morning.

"Atta girl! Will you drop by on Friday afternoon to meet everyone? I'll introduce you to the boss. He really won't bother you – we only see him once a week when he brings our money."

The crèche turned out to be situated in an old Victorian pile directly opposite the Pacific Highway, close to a busy, six-laned crossroads called Victoria Cross. The access road to the Harbour Bridge started there and Mount Street ended there, the street on which Globe Commercial was situated, the office supply shop where Hiek had once worked. Just driving around to work out where it was proved impossible. It was rush hour. A vast river of cars thundered towards the bridge and an equally vast one thundered in the direction of North Sydney. All six lanes were jam-packed. It seemed impossible to get through.

We were received in an echoing, tiled hall, which led to a stately, sweeping staircase. The owner, a small, round lady with stiffly permed hair proved to be very genteel indeed and quite kind, though businesslike. A tour didn't take too much time. Upstairs there was a high, light room with low cupboards full of toys along its walls; in the middle of the room were small tables and chairs. A slight, dark girl was busy helping a toddler into his jacket, other than that the room was deserted as it was almost half past five.

"You'll be working in Mount Street? Excellent. That's very close by. If you give us the number of your office…We ring our mothers immediately if there are any problems. And you can ring us at any time too of course."

"Look, Paul, a train!" Janneke crowed, inspecting the store of toys, "Wow, a whole lot of trains! And look at the dolls, Lin!" The cupboards were neat and the toys tidily stacked.

"Do you think you will like it here?" I asked my eldest son, nervously.

He nodded obediently. "I won't!" said Bobby, in his clear little voice, "I don't want to go to school!"

"It isn't school, silly!" said Janneke, "You're allowed to play all day here."

"And Paulie will be with you," I added, "You'll be together all day, just like at home. And there will be lots of other children too, it'll be fun." The lady proprietor smiled stiffly: "It usually takes them a day or two to settle in, madam. You have nothing to worry about. Shall we register these two? From Monday morning onwards? You need to pay a week in advance."

Gerard wrote out a cheque.

"It's bound to be a good place," I said when we were back on the pavement, "It's very clean, also upstairs. Don't you think?" trying nevertheless to ignore a vague feeling of unease, of doubt, of guilt.

"Hm," said Gerard, "Let's hope so. They certainly aren't cheap. How much will you have left after you pay for your travel costs?"

"Enough!" I am suddenly intensely irritated, "I'm not doing this for my own enjoyment, you know!"

Friday afternoon came far too fast. Gerard came home early again, as agreed, and I set off on my own to take the bus to St Leonards, where I transferred to the train to North Sydney. I felt like Marie Antoinette going to the guillotine.

North Sydney station was an underground station. Broad steps led to a deep cavern between high rock walls that obscured any view. Behind those walls was a muted, monotonous roar, like huge waves crashing on a beach: the traffic of the Pacific Highway. Ascending from the cavern I encountered the torrent of cars we had seen before. A traffic light. I waited patiently until the tidal wave of metal and noise stopped briefly and crossed.

I walked past the thick, sandstone wall of an old office building, jutting into the street like the prow of a ship. The footpath was very narrow, but I quickly turned a corner and entered Mount Street. At that time Mount Street was a narrow, one-way street. On a Friday afternoon it was choked with cars racing up the hill to Victoria Cross. Mount Street was also a kind of mini shopping centre. I passed one shop after the other. Globe Commercial was wedged between a wool shop and a dry-cleaners. A blue and gold billboard featuring a globe hung above a wide shop window, which was packed with merchandise; a glass door split the window down the middle.

Inside I found a high, glass counter with two girls standing behind it and five or six people jostling in front of it. The glass shelves underneath the counter were full, as were the glass cupboards along the walls. In a corner behind the counter girls, standing on the first step of a staircase, I saw Jane. She was holding open a dark, brown curtain. She motioned to me. I moved past the counter, mumbling apologies to the customers. I went up the dark and dusty staircase that ended in a high corridor with here and there an open door.

"Hi!" said Jane, "Over here. This is our office. Nice and light, huh?"

There was a broad window that overlooked the street. In front of it were two old wooden desks; they had been moved together so that they were facing each other. The room also contained two long tables, a low cupboard, a filing cabinet, an extra chair and in the middle the stencil machine, a large, black monstrosity.

"Globe Commercial Duplicating Service!" said Jane, with a broad sweep of her arm. "And this is Robin, our machine operator. She is worth her weight in gold." Robin was small, blond and vaguely square; she reminded me irresistibly of a friendly Pekinese. "Robin was trained by Mrs. Anink. She's been working here for seven years, haven't you?" Robin nodded shyly, "Shall I make tea?"

"Good idea. We'll give Winthrop a cup too." And to me: "I'll show you the ropes."

Globe Commercial was a subsidiary of a large office supplies store in the city and was managed from the city. North Sydney was up and coming as a centre of commerce at that time. More and more fledgling businessmen and especially architects who could not afford an office in the city were settling there. The duplicating and typing service where Hiek had started once upon a time had been devised as a sideline by Winthrop to help these local customers with small offices. Said architects would not dream of acquiring a hugely expensive stencil machine of their own. Some did not even have a secretary. But people still needed to have their building specs and designs typed and copied, and photocopiers did not exist at that time.

"You know what specs are?" Jane explained, "Those tomes that explain what goes into a building? So many meters of piping, so many taps, what kinds of materials etc. You type their stencils. You just type exactly what they say even if you don't understand a word. Then Robin runs off a dozen or so, or whatever number they need. Sort, staple and you're done. Oh, and our best customer is quite a large, established architect's office. They send us already typed stencils. We just copy those, but it brings in quite a lot of money. They can be huge documents, sometimes over two hundred pages. And we take on normal typing work too, of course. Here's your price list. And there's the intercom. They call you from downstairs when a job comes in."

"Oh," she added, "and if customers turn up who want better quality work, you take them on too. Opposite us is an offset printer and we have an arrangement with them. They do typing for us on an electric typewriter and they also do printing. They give us a hefty discount and we add 25% to the price. Do you get it?" I didn't, but I kept quiet.

"Here is your invoice pad. There needs to be an invoice with each order and you put the copy in this file. Once a month the accountant comes by and sorts everything out. You don't need to do any accounting yourself. Oh, it'll all work out and Robin can give you all the help you need. She'll help you get through the first few days. Well, Winthrop should be here about now. He comes by every Friday to give us our salaries and see how things are going. He doesn't care how things are run as long as they run. Relax, kid, this is a job in a million!"

She was so carefree and easy-going. I envied her from the bottom of my heart. All I did was nod and make the occasional note in a pad. I didn't really take in anything at all. "We have our own toilet up here and a small kitchen, very private. And there is a storage room up here in addition to the storage spaces downstairs…"

Footsteps on the stairs: Winthrop was a tall, gangly man of around forty. He wore a dark raincoat and a grey trilby. He did not take his hat off. He had a small head for such a long body and pale blue eyes. He shook my hand, weakly, and deposited himself on the only remaining chair. He then pulled two brown paper pay packets from the pocket of his raincoat and gave them to Jane. "Here. Sign for them please. Thanks. Everything okay here?"

"Fine!" said Jane with her most sparkling smile, "Mrs. Melman will start on Monday as we arranged and I will definitely be off for three weeks."

"Okay," a fleeting glance at me. And then he got up again. "No, no tea, Robin. I'm in a hurry today." And then directly to me: "If there are any problems you can always ring me. See you next Friday."

I watched him leave, completely bemused. I don't know what I had expected, but it was certainly not this. Didn't he want to know who I was? Where I had worked before? Didn't he need any proof of my competence?

Jane giggled, "He thinks you look very reliable. I praised you to the skies, believe me. And he trusts me. Oh well, best of luck with your temporary job. I hope you'll enjoy it. Here are your keys. This one is for the front door of the shop in case you're here very early or have to leave very late and this one is of our room. Robin also has a set. I'll introduce you to everyone downstairs, there's just enough time."

There were three shop girls, it turned out; they were friendly but a little harassed. They wanted to go home. Once we were outside Jane pointed to the other end of the street where I could see a glimpse of something blue glistening. "I have to go that way. The bus! See you!!" She started to run. I slowly walked back up the hill, to the station. "If Jane can do it, so can I," I told my shaking limbs firmly.

Monday morning. The girls went to school a little earlier than usual, Janneke carrying the house key, dangling from a ribbon around her neck. Gerard dropped the boys and I off outside the creche. I herded my two inside, and all went swimmingly. There was not a peep of protest; they trotted upstairs like tame sheep.

I walked past what looked to my eyes like a vast hyper modern mall, the downstairs floor of which was called the MLC building. Then came Victoria

Cross. Seven minutes later I was sitting at my desk, a model of efficiency, sorting the mail.

"The cheques go in that cupboard there," Robin said helpfully. "And that's the specification Mrs. Adler was working on. It needs to be done by Friday. And in this pile there are a few more jobs. Every job has a job sheet, you see? It shows you exactly what needs to be done and when it needs to be ready. I'm finishing off this one and then it will need to be billed. Shall I first make us a cup of tea?"

During that first cup of tea, she chatted endlessly. She had been working since she was fifteen. First as an assistant in the shop downstairs, a kind of general dogsbody, and then with Hiek as a machine operator, a job she still regarded as a gift from the heavens. She came from a large labourer's family with a father who used his belt as his primary method of education.

The kitchen at the end of the corridor was her domain. She kept it spotlessly clean. She also scrubbed the toilet almost every day and mopped the office floor every evening before she went home. The duplicating machine was her baby. If she had nothing better to do she polished it until it shone. She managed it with deft fingers and spoke to it comfortably every now and then. She knew all its whims and quirks, and never let it get the better of her. When she had finished a job she checked, counted and sorted the result, and shook the piles of printed sheets into stiff blocks. She then turned them into neat packages. If necessary she also picked up work or delivered it.

She monitored our paper stores and warned me if any supplies needed ordering. It was my task to order paper or any other necessities that were running low. I was also responsible for drawing up and typing the bills, making quotes, and deciding what was urgent and what had less priority.

We were still drinking that first morning tea when a call came from downstairs. Sporting my job sheet pad and price list I went downstairs. One of the girls who was wearing a red dress directed me smilingly to the corner of the counter where a dark man with a weathered face was standing.

"You're new here, right?" looking at me enquiringly, "Globe Commercial takes care of our monthly club magazine. Here are the texts. When can I pick up the magazines?" I stared at him helplessly. He frowned. "We need them in ten days at the latest," he said with emphasis.

I smiled amiably. "Eh, Wednesday week then? At the end of the afternoon, would that be alright?" "Okay," and he was gone.

"Don't let them pressure you!" The red dress piped up, "Everyone just has to wait their turn. It's no disaster if it takes a few days longer."

"Oh, I don't think it will be a problem," I said airily and scuttled back up the stairs. Upstairs I gave the pile of handwritten pages to Robin. "That was someone from the lapidary club. Do you know anything about them?"

As it happened I actually knew what lapidary meant: the cutting, grinding and polishing of gemstones. But I had no idea how to produce that club magazine.

"Oh, yes I do," Robin told me, cheerfully, "It's a bit complicated. The text needs to be typed the length of the stencil so that you end up with two half pages. That will cost you at least a whole day. And you need to take care with the numbering of the pages. We fold and staple the booklets. Get it?"

What I got was that I first needed to make a list of all the jobs that were already in house and assess how much time they would take. "Don't make the estimates too tight," Robin warned me, "We need to fit any Basset jobs in. They always have priority, no matter what."

"Basset jobs?"

"Basset is the larger architects firm Mrs. Adler mentioned, remember?"

So I assigned every job an ample amount of time in my schedule, asking Robin's advice every now and then, and fervently hoping I could type as quickly as Jane.

I must have made appeared decisive to the next customer who turned up downstairs, a rather shy young man, who brought me my first (tiny) building specification. Not till the end of next week? He seemed perfectly happy with that.

I started typing stencils. Robin's machine purred. The sun shone behind the large window and the roar of the traffic even began to sound a little familiar. I found the smell of paper and ink quite pleasant.

The phone rang. "Globe Commercial Duplicating Service," I said for the first time. A woman's voice: "Basset Architects. We have three hundred stencils for you. Thirty-five copies and we need them back in two days' time, by lunchtime. Can you do that, do you think?'

"Oh yes," I said, mindful of Robin's instructions.

"I'll have them brought over, that will save you some time."

"Thank you," I said.

"And good luck," which sounded ominous I thought.

"Robin," I said anxiously, "That was the Basset people: 300 stencils, 35 copies. They need them in two days."

She sighed, "No option, right? As long as you can help me?"

"Of course I'll help."

"I'll finish this, I have to. Then all the other jobs will just have to be pushed back, there's nothing else we can do."

I grabbed the schedule and Robin looked over my shoulder.

"That job isn't urgent. Move that to next week."

"But it says here there is a deadline, tomorrow! That was on the job sheet, and it was on the job sheet for that one too."

"Oh, don't pay any attention to that. They'll wait."

I decided to ring up the customers in question. I discovered that no-one minded a two-day deadline shift and that they were pleasantly surprised at being warned about it in advance.

By the afternoon every available table surface was covered in piles of folio pages and I moved amid the long rows with rubber coverings on my thumb and index finger, picking up page after page and sorting them. I never became as fast at this as Robin was, but did develop a respectable speed in the course of time. At five o'clock we shut the door of the office behind us, still packed with piles of paper. "Tomorrow's another day," Robin said, with admirable calm "We'll make it." And we did.

On Wednesday evening when Robin was printing the final stencil and I was still running up and down among the tables, madly sorting the pages, the Bassett lady rang again. I informed her, slightly out of breath, that everything was going fine and that I would greatly appreciate it if they could pick up the completed job. It would be difficult for us to deliver it just at this time. I then typed, with some pride, my first substantial invoice.

Friday: my first pay packet. The tangible evidence that I was worth money! Winthrop stayed a little longer than the first time. He flicked through the file with invoice copies and glanced at my schedule for the next week. "You've been busy, I see. And this looks pretty healthy. Great."

And that was that. I nevertheless felt as if I had been awarded a medal.

On the third day of the third week Jane suddenly appeared at my desk. She looked fantastic. Tall and slender in a brown skirt and jacket with high heeled brown shoes and a matching brown handbag. "I've been offered a new job, secretary for a market research firm. Also based here in North Sydney. I can earn a lot more there. What do you think, do you want to stay on here?"

"Stay?" I couldn't believe my ears.

"Why not? It's going well."

"Oh, please stay!" Robin begged,

"Yes, but I can't just decide that... there's home and the kids... I need to discuss it at home first."

"Oh, nonsense," said Jane, "Everything's arranged on the home front, isn't it? You told me yourself it's going fine. There's no reason why you shouldn't continue. Leave Winthrop to me. I'll call him now." I watched her, in stunned silence, sitting on the corner of the desk, talking on the phone. She assured Winthrop that I was perfectly prepared to take a permanent position. "There!" she said, putting the phone down, "It seems you're doing an even better job than I was. He's wildly enthusiastic. He'll bring a contract along for you on Friday. I bet he'll give you a raise. You must ask for one in any case! You can even ask for travel expenses."

"Actually, it would be great if you could manage it for a few years," Gerard said that evening, "We might finally be able to get out of this financial mess. And you enjoy it there, don't you?"

"We'd never have to be afraid of bills again," I said dreamily, "And things aren't so bad here, are they? It's all going very well."

We had developed a new routine in the past weeks. In the mornings we all left the house at the same time after the breakfast table had been cleared and the washing-up done (by Gerard) and the beds had been straightened (by me). When the girls came home from school in the afternoons they rang me and I listened to all the latest school news. Exactly at five fifteen I arrived at the creche door and then hurried along with the boys to the station. The train was always packed, but Paul and Bobby regarded the trip as the highlight of their day. They wriggled with determination between the arms and legs of fellow passengers until they reached a window where, glued to the glass like flies, they would cheer as we steamed out of the tunnel. At St Leonards our bus would be waiting for us, and we would get home just after six.

While I cooked, Gerard supervised the bathroom and while he washed up after dinner, I loaded washing into the washing machine and sorted the dry washing, which Janneke and Lindy had taken off the line when they came home from school. I made the lunch box sandwiches for the next day every evening before we went to bed and did any necessary daily shopping at lunchtime in North Sydney. Every Saturday morning, while Gerard did the weekly shop, I cleaned the house thoroughly, and on Saturday afternoon our weekend started.

Somehow the weekends seemed longer than before and our lives were calmer than they had ever been, also emotionally. When you are so taken up with the practical exterior of life the emotional interior goes underground. And you have no time or energy for excavation. You don't even want to go digging. All you want is to be left in peace. I don't know whether that is good or bad. It is just a fact and I don't think that in the long run it did us any harm.

I can't remember how I coped, in those early days of my office life in North Sydney, whenever Gerard had to go into the country for a week or when a child fell ill. I can only remember our routine at such times in Turramurra, when the children were older. If one of them was ill I took a day off and Gerard took the next day off; by then the worst would usually be over and Janneke (unless she was ill herself) would stay home for a day and play mother, which she enjoyed greatly. We always managed. Country trips were a hassle, but did not disrupt our routine too greatly. The six weeks of school holidays were difficult. We each only had two weeks' holiday, which we took in succession so that for four weeks there was always one parent at home. For the last two weeks of the holidays we had to find a minder. This was never easy, but we had good friends and helpful neighbours, and we always found a solution.

CHAPTER 26

Norman

I SEE MYSELF standing at the top of Mount Street. I have discovered that the street runs through Victoria Cross and doesn't end there; it continues steeply upwards, hence the name, of course. My section is only half the street. Sometimes when I turn the corner into Mount Street and glimpse that ribbon of blue below (the water of Neutral Bay) I stop briefly. I feel as if I can fly. The world is at my feet, wide and open.

I am happy. I belong here. I now know every shop and every shopkeeper. I know the yawning butcher's boy who sweeps the pavement in front of the shop. I know the vivacious Frenchwoman who cleans the window of her shop daily. She always has exactly the clothes I like and which suit me. She has taught me all about the lay-by system. She puts whatever it is I want aside and I make a small down payment to her every week until the full amount is paid. I can then take home my new purchase triumphantly without that anxious feeling of having spent an exorbitant amount of money. In this way, I have acquired an office wardrobe that I am very happy with. I know the little old ladies in the knitting shop next to Globe Commercial. I sometimes buy new knitting wool there, which still feels like a luxury.

I know the Greek in the dry-cleaners; every morning he stands in the sun in the open door of his shop in a shapeless pair of trousers, held up with braces. When I talk to him, he makes himself understood with exuberant gestures. And he bows with panache every time I hand him a pile of clothing. I also know the Italian owner of Torino, the restaurant on the corner. And the girls in the deli opposite Globe where I get my lunch every now and then, usually a salad sandwich, a complete meal between two slices of brown bread. And I know the lady florist who opens her door wide very early each morning. And she knows me. They all know me.

CHAPTER 26

Globe Commercial Duplicating Service has grown since my arrival. Our group of customers has expanded. My own view is that this is because we always keep our promises. Robin now works overtime quite regularly, but she doesn't mind. She gets paid double for overtime and she actually prefers to go home at 7 instead of 5 as I, tied to créche hours, am obliged to do. We have both been given a good raise. I can now pay all our weekly household expenses from my salary. We pay the mortgage, clothing and any extras from Gerard's salary. And there are no longer unpaid bills lying around.

Before starting my office day, I glance through my window at the opposite side of the street: a row of shops (butcher, hardware store, chemist) and a narrow side street.

I have just discovered – by consulting the Sydney Gregory's street directory we have in our bookshelf (dating from 1984, a nostalgic gift from Roger) – that this street was called Denison Street. The North Sydney map the Gregory's contains, even though out of date now, is already eons away from my Mount Street time. Denison Street here is no longer a small side street leading to a few alleyways and a courtyard. And Mount Street is a busy thoroughfare with a bridge over the Wahrringah Freeway (six lanes); it leads to the Bradfield Highway that takes you along the Harbour Bridge into the city. We went to look at Mount Street 8 years ago. The little shops had disappeared, we found only tall buildings of glass and concrete, and an enormous covered mall. The street was unrecognisable. Even the pub on the corner of Walker Street with its yellow, tiled outside walls had disappeared. In my time this is where all the men who worked in Mount Street went on Friday evenings to celebrate the end of the working week and where women were even allowed to drink along, on occasion.

Close to Denison Street, almost opposite us, there is an offset printing shop owned by Norman Waters, a man who intrigues me. He too stands in the open door of his shop every now and then, enjoying the sun, in a way that strikes me as irresistibly Eastern or at least Mediterranean. I have only met him a few times, and each meeting has been odd.

The first time a printing assignment came in I crossed the road to the printing shop myself, mindful of Jane's instructions. The shop window had been completely covered with white paint; behind it sat a man in a small office. He had a shining, yellowish, bald head, haloed by luxuriantly curling black hair, a large nose and a long, black moustache. He was short and very overweight and had, I discovered later, penguin-like feet. He was without a doubt the ugliest man I had ever seen. But his eyes were liquid, deep black and melancholy, and his voice was warm and friendly (he was talking on the phone when I came in). He was sitting at a desk, overflowing with rainbows of coloured paper, packets of negatives, photos, sketches, innumerable pens, pencils and two full ashtrays.

I stopped, hesitant, in the doorway. The black eyes took me in from top to toe. He smiled. He had large white teeth. He lifted a plump, gold-ringed hand and gestured to a chair in front of the desk. I sat down and was forced to listen to what was an unmistakably British voice. He put the phone down. Leaning back in his chair, playing with his pencil: "Well, well, well. The new manageress of Globe Commercial Duplicating! What can I do for you?" not making the least move to get up.

"I have a printing job here. I'd like to have a price quote and a delivery date," I said politely. I too remained seated but at the same time tried to move my pile of pages towards him.

He didn't take the papers, but started to laugh gently. "Really? I thought you had finally dropped by to make my acquaintance! We're neighbours, after all. It's important to be on good terms with your neighbours, don't you agree? Of course, you already know who I am, just as I know where you come from and that you live in Mosman and have a bunch of kids. We're one big happy family here in Mount Street. Everyone knows everything about everyone. How's business on your side of the street?" All this with laughing eyes.

There was no space on his desk for my pages, so I kept them on my lap. "Excellent," I said frostily. Clearly, the man had no manners at all and regarded both me and the job as a kind of joke, which incensed me. "And here?" trying to adopt the correct, somewhat distant attitude, which he found extremely amusing.

He now laughed out loud. "Couldn't be better! Offset is the industry of the future. It will be cheaper and better than any other type of printing one day. And we're in the best possible spot here. North Sydney is going to become very important. You must agree with that," still in the same teasing, amused tone.

"Oh, um, yes, certainly," I said, not amused at all. "I promised this customer that I would let him know what this would cost. Can you give me a quote?" flapping my pages again.

"Well, what do you think it should cost?"

"I have no idea," I said, with candour, "I haven't been involved in any printing work so far. It needs to be typed on an electric typewriter. And then he needs at least fifty copies, maybe more later."

"I'll teach you," finally reaching out his hand for the pages, "Look, a page like this is photographed and a plate is made of it. Making a plate costs four pounds. Of course you know what the price of paper is. Add to that typing and machine costs and of course labour costs. Make it about three times as much as you would normally ask. Thirty percent profit on top of the whole thing is normal. What would you say to ten for us and twenty for you?" I calculated as quickly as I could.

"Don't worry. Let me know what quotes you give your print customers. I promise my price will always be 20% lower. Happy now?" I stared at him. He seemed serious now. I took a deep breath and nodded.

He got up. "Come and meet my foreman. He's the one we're going to have to persuade to fit your little jobs into his schedule." Torron Printing's printing room was a narrow, stuffy space filled with noise. Standing amid this cacophony, with rolled-up sleeves, was a slight, red-haired young man in a dirty overall that must at some point in the distant past have been white. I remember his muscled arms, covered in reddish hairs and innumerable freckles, and the concentration with which he watched the paper-belching offset press, only interfering whenever necessary every now and then.

"Norm! I want you to take a look at the Heidelberg! It's playing up again." A gentle, slightly husky voice, and unmistakably Australian. He had light eyes in an anxious, friendly, tanned and freckled face. Alan Livingstone and I would later become friends for life.

"Alan. This is Globe Commercial Duplicating Service in person." I was beginning to find Norm irritating and juvenile. "You'll give her priority, right? She has four whole pages. You can manage that, can't you?" Alan looked at me and grinned, which for some reason I found encouraging.

"Could this be ready in three days' time?" I asked shyly. "Okay," said Alan and that was that. I fled.

Norm Waters: I can still see his broad smile and mocking eyes, which brimmed with vitality and a boundless self-confidence. He must have been in his mid-forties when I first met him, but he was always ageless. He generated a kind of magnetic field, and I was not surprised when I found out years later that he had been a hypnotist when he was young. That he had been on the stage. That he had led a colourful and restless life. He had been born in London and had emigrated to Australia when he was 24. He had been an actor, stage designer, advertising artist, copywriter, printer and photographer, all with varying degrees of success.

Yet Norm had one enormous talent that outshone the rest. No matter where he went or what he undertook, he had the knack of surrounding himself with people whose loyalty to him was absolute. Who were prepared to toil for him, who trusted him blindly and whose devotion to him was almost religious. He recognised them instinctively, those diligent salt of the earth slaves, the kinds of people who enjoyed being needed. For whom loyalty and working hard were second nature. He reeled them in and enlisted them in his team of bodyguards. I suspect Napoleon would have been proud of him!

About a week after our first confrontation, I bumped into him on the street. He immediately took me by the elbow. "We're going to have a coffee at Torino's. We'll be able to have a quiet chat there." I was too overwhelmed to protest. I went along with him and sat opposite him like a fascinated bird caught in the gaze of the proverbial snake.

That didn't last long. This time there were no mocking eyes or silly jokes. This time I was with a wiser, older colleague who appeared to be genuinely interested in me and my ideas. Who wanted to hear what I thought of life in Australia and especially of being involved in a small business in Australia. I talked as I hadn't talked for years. I didn't even know I had opinions about the Australian character or way of doing business. But I did. Or were they only formed as I spoke to him? Was I trying to impress him? I heard myself complaining about the "no worries, mate" attitude and "what we can't get done today, we'll do tomorrow." The holiday atmosphere. Exactly those traits I later learned to value. They are rare nowadays, and I do not have them myself. I toil and I worry, and in those days I was also incredibly naive. I had no idea I was being assessed carefully for my future usefulness.

Norm asked about my background, about what I had done before, about our current situation. He radiated sincere empathy and he understood the art of listening. When I discovered that almost an hour had gone by and jumped up to rush back to the office, he stuck his hand out: "Friends?"

"Yes, of course," I said, touched. I had not seen Norm since that first meeting, but I had seen Alan who, with great amiability, had received and completed, within the agreed time frame, my unimportant little print jobs. Alan was my kind of person, I realised even then.

December brought commotion on the opposite side of the street. An enormous truck was parked in front of the printing shop, loading up a vast, old printing press and unloading a smaller, more modern one. There was much excitement in Waters' printing shop, we heard; there was some kind of reorganisation going on, there was a new owner, he had sold everything...

CHAPTER 26

So close to Christmas there were no new print customers, so there was no need for visits across the street. But there was a lot of extra work for us. Everyone suddenly wanted vast quantities of stencils typed and multiplied. And I was very busy at home as well. I forgot all about Norm Waters and any changes that might be occurring across the street.

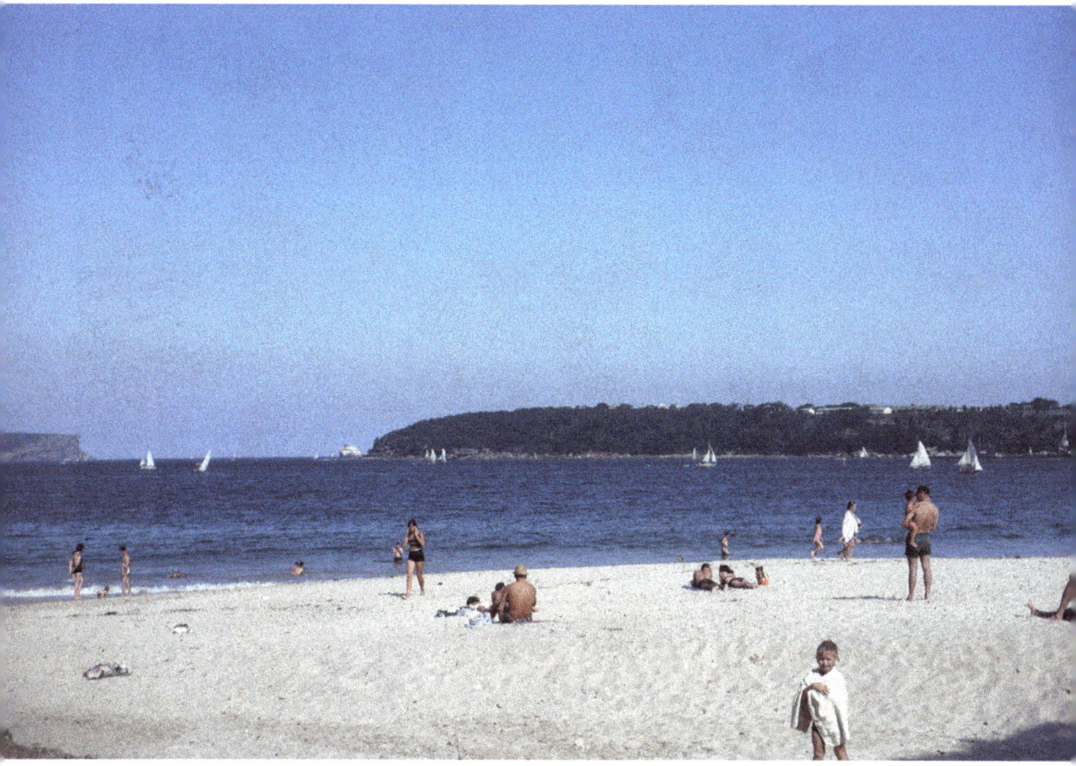

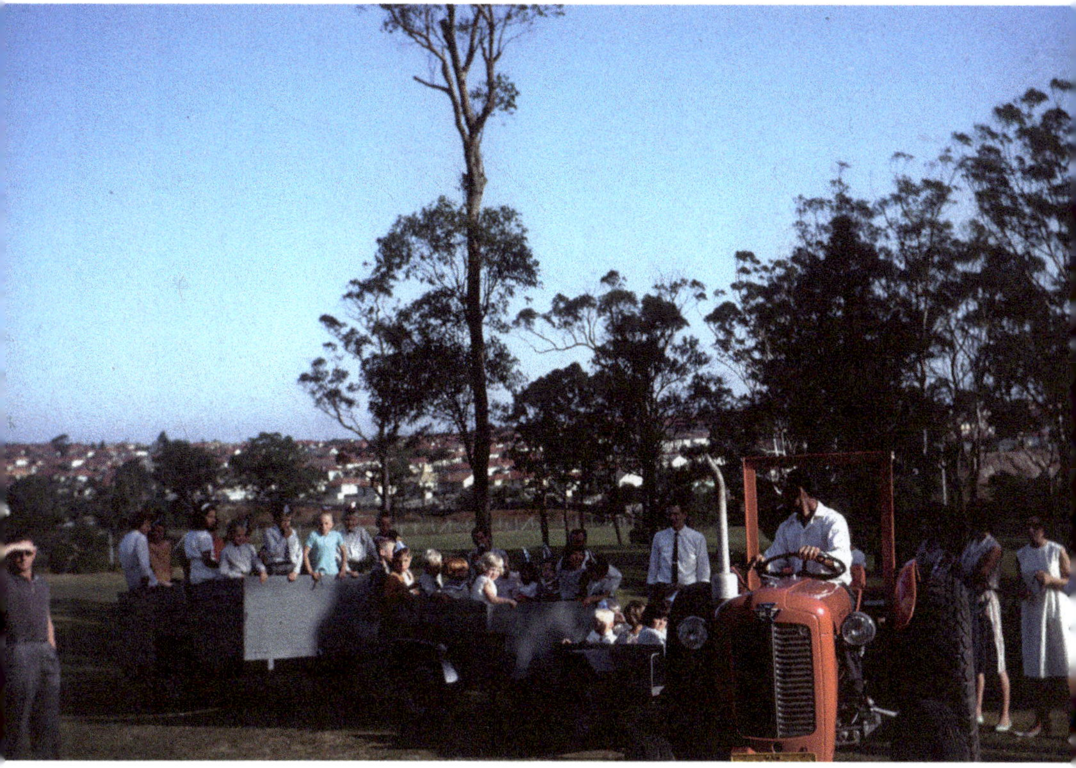

CHAPTER 27

Christmas and a new home

25 SEPTEMBER 2001. *Exactly two weeks ago two planes smashed into the Twin Towers of the World Trade Center in New York. Paul was in New York for a medical conference at the time, but is safely home now. It has also been two weeks since I worked on this manuscript. When a disaster like that occurs there is no space for old memories that are of importance only to me. On 11 September the world changed irrevocably and a new era began; we have yet to learn how to deal with it. The horror in New York cannot be fathomed, cannot be understood. I feel as if we are standing on the edge of a sea of sorrow and pain, and fear that these waters will drown us all. We are so impossibly vulnerable.*

I have suddenly become sharply aware of how much time I need nowadays just to read, just to absorb things – even unimportant, everyday things. How much longer it takes me to understand. I feel as if there is now a time gap between whatever I read, see or hear and my ability to gain a clear picture of it, to really comprehend it. And I also now know there will be things that I will never comprehend. The huge change our world is undergoing is one of them. Our old world is gone. What will take its place is literally incomprehensible to me. Paul is home, but Lindy is still in Australia. She is now with Janneke.

My first Christmas as a member of the Australian "work force." North Sydney seems awash with paper garlands, balloons, carnival hats, beer and employers bestowing festive kisses. All this in temperatures that regularly hit the thirties; there was no air conditioning at that time. Upjohn, where Gerard works, is also throwing a party. They have organised a barbecue for the staff and their families.

We are driving through a scorching, golden, late afternoon to Rydalmere where the head office and laboratory are situated amid an immense, well-watered area of parkland. A good hundred adults and children fill the lawns; there are rows of stalls with red and white striped awnings and wooden tables. Barbecue smells abound; steaks, lamb chops, sausages, salads, bread, wine and lemonade are in plentiful supply. An orange tractor is driving around, pulling along a row of small, open carriages containing jubilant toddlers waving coloured flags. Our four can't contain their excitement.

Later the same tractor brings a heavily perspiring Santa Claus with a long beard that curls all the way to his knees. He has a present for every child there that, miraculously, meets each child's wishes. Our children cannot stop talking about the fact that Santa knew exactly what they wanted! Janneke declares she has never experienced such a wonderful party as this one.

And then it is Christmas Eve and Gerard and I set up the Christmas tree at home. It is a meager, skinny tree with sharp needles protruding from its branches, and it does not remotely resemble a Dutch pine tree. But once it is covered in silver garlands and lights it glitters as bravely in the warm summer's night as any European tree in a Dutch winter home.

On Christmas morning, all four children turn up at the foot of our bed. It has just turned light. "Can we go and see what Santa brought us?" They have all been given summer things. New bathing suits and trunks; mini surfboards for the girls, inflatable swimming rings for the boys, beach balls – but also other toys and things they have long been hoping for. We try out the new swimming gear immediately. Christmas Day is a beach day. Late that afternoon, still glowing from the sun, we sit around a decorated table. We eat cold chicken with salad, and watermelon and ice cream for dessert.

We go to bed early that evening, as we are all exhausted. I hear the high chirping of the cicadas in the summer night as Gerard and I together go quietly from open bedroom door to open bedroom door; the light from the corridor spills in. It is still very warm but they are all four soundly asleep. Janneke is lying neatly on her back with the sheet pulled up to her chin. A cuddly, blonde angel, she is sleeping peacefully; she has displayed all her new possessions neatly on the windowsill. Lindy is lying on her side, without a sheet. She is holding her new doll and her pillow tightly in her arms. She is frowning and restless, as if struggling with a difficult task. Her long, honey blond curls are damp and spread wildly across the pillow. Paulie, his back a mass of tiny freckles, has rolled himself up into a fluffy ball, from which one arm protrudes. The scars on his little wrist pull at my heart. Bobby is lying on his tummy. Next to his little silvery head on the pillow are three tiny cars.

"This is what we do it all for, don't we?" Gerard whispers. He is right. I suddenly know that nothing in the world is more important than this. It is as if a gauze curtain has been lifted, as if after having been half blind for a long time I can suddenly see my children again. Really see them. Is this why this particular Christmas has stayed in my memory so clearly?

On Boxing Day, Phons and Patsy and their children come to visit. Patsy is depressed, yawning, impatient. She tells me she has decided to rent out a room: "It's the only way to make a little extra. We can't manage on what Phons earns alone."

It is oppressively hot. The sun is shrouded in a thick layer of clouds but there is no sign of rain. We decide that, like yesterday, Balmoral is the only place that will bring some relief. It is always cooler on the beach. The children are in complete agreement. A group of old friends have clearly had the same idea and we form a sleepy group together. We talk, swim, relax.

That day we make the acquaintance of Alice and Dick Fitzgerald. Alice and Dick are friends of Jane's. They have recently moved to Mosman. Alice is small and dark with a strong American accent, and reminds me of Hiek: the same warmth, the same smiling determination not to let anything throw her. I warm to her immediately. She had studied biology and had been married to an anthropologist with whom she had spent some time on a remote island in the Pacific. That is where her eldest child was born. I can't recall how or why she ended up in Sydney but it only became clear to me later that her anthropologist was a well-known Australian.

Alice writes, draws, and designs children's clothes. Her current husband, Dick, is at least six foot tall, with sunken cheeks and sunken eyes. He is an accountant and has a job in the city. He talks with passion about the "rat-race" which he wants to get out of as soon as possible. He would like to sail away, out of the harbour with his wife and children. He and Alice have an 18 month-old son and Alice's eight year-old daughter lives with her mother. It doesn't matter where they sail to, as long as it is not to another big city.

At the end of the afternoon we all somehow end up at a spacious house in Mosman Junction, Dick and Alice's home. It feels like a large bird's nest full of brightly coloured rags. The enormous living room is empty except for a pouf, a pile of coloured cushions and a few low tables. Along the walls are low, wooden, clearly homemade bookcases filled with books, toys, paper maché figures, shells, stones, dried flowers, an empty bird's nest and sundry other objects. There is no television. On the bare wooden floor someone has drawn a sketch of a ship (an actual design to scale). Dick is building a fibreglass boat himself in his back yard and has used the floor to sketch out his plans. This is the boat he wants to sail away in!

We are stunned by all this, but our children immediately feel at home. This is a kind of magician's cave where everything is allowed. On the walls of the living room, kitchen, bedroom and hall are drawings – children's drawings – together with a few large, white sheets with finger paintings on them. In no time our children, Patsy's children and Alice's children are busily dragging around cushions, blankets, dolls, toy animals, bits of wood, paper, hammers, nails – singing and chattering – and no-one tells them not to, on the contrary. Alice makes encouraging noises. She is the epitome of calm. She pours out glasses of milk for the children and makes tea for us. I am speechless with admiration.

Our men have been shepherded into the garden by Dick. They take turns scrambling up the prow of the ship under construction. They are intensely interested, and tools are inspected and discussed.

I talk to Alice about books and discover a soulmate. She lends me books. I am wildly enthusiastic about her though must admit that Patsy is right when she later remarks, dryly: "You can't fool me into thinking you could live like that! They are born gypsies, those two!" Nevertheless, I feel as if Alice is a member of my tribe, someone I recognise, and we keep in touch.

Christmas meant a few days off for me, and the start of an annual vacation for Gerard. It also meant the beginning of the big school vacation for the girls and even though the crèche was still open, the boys did not need to come along to North Sydney for three weeks because Gerard was at home. Back in Mount Street, I began to view Globe Commercial as a pleasant, somewhat sedate and predictable backdrop to my daily life, which also – oh joy! – generated money.

Hieke returned from Holland, looking surprisingly well and plumper than she had ever been. We listened to stories about a Dutch winter with snow and ice. About a new European road network, about urban renewal and a new, resurrected Holland. And about the incomprehensible luxury of holidays in Spain, Yugoslavia and Greece that everyone could afford. "Young people trek through Europe all summer these days," said Hiek, "With a backpack and a tent; you should hear the stories my nephews and nieces tell!"

We admired Jan's new bathroom and learned that the house in Seaforth would very soon be linked to the city sewerage system, a reason for great joy.

We talked about family ties and I believe this was the first time I can recall Gerard mentioning being sorry his children had no uncles and aunts, nieces and nephews close by. How much easier life would be if in times of need you could fall back on your family.

I did not agree with this. I mentioned the network of loyal friends that supported us, the immediate, spontaneous help we had always received, how well we understood each other because we all shared more or less the same experiences. Hiek agreed with me that it was impossible to explain in Holland how we lived in Australia and how much enjoyment we derived from what were regarded there as hardships.

Patsy came to tell me she had found a paying guest, though I can no longer recall how. His name was Guus Zaat and he was a young, single, Dutch engineer who had studied in Delft and had come to work in Sydney for a while. Guus, or Gus as he was called then, was introduced to us as a new friend who would have fit into our old discussion group beautifully. Patsy found him fascinating and talked about him with animation: "He is so intelligent, so cultured and his English is excellent!" Which was true. But I found him arrogant, dogmatic and appallingly young. I suspected that behind his brash, student-like exterior was an insecure young man who did not know how to deal very well with any of us. Phons liked him. "A decent chap." And Jane's comment was: "He is so gorgeously conservative. I didn't know men like that existed any more!" And then, thoughtfully: "He's exceptionally handsome, don't you think?"

I can't recall whether Jane and Peter's second child, Miriam, had been born by then, or whether that happened much later, after Jane had moved to Melbourne. Jane and Peter tried various times to live together again, and Miriam was the result of this last attempt. It did not work out and even before her birth they had separated, and Jane declared this was definitely the end. What I do know for sure is that Jane met Guus at Patsy's house and that, many years later, after a complicated and painful divorce, she married Guus Zaat.

After the Christmas holidays, Gerard started showing signs of restlessness. It took me a little while to notice that something was wrong. He grumbled a lot. He did things with obvious reluctance; he was always tired. And he kept on pointing out the obvious flaws of our home, our old Mosman house where I felt so comfortable. He came up with a whole litany of problems: the crack in the wall above the kitchen door, the rotting wooden veranda deck, the impractical laundry area under the stairs, the bathroom which – as we had discovered – was so dangerous, the stuffy, dark living room which resembled a prison cell...

"But we live here perfectly well!" I said surprised, "Balmoral is at out feet and there is a good connection to town. All those other things aren't important."

"We live in a hovel!" said Gerard, "It isn't even worth renovating. You should compare it with the houses that are being built these days. If we were sensible we would sell the house now. The value of the land here has gone up."

"Sell?!" I couldn't believe my ears, "And where would we live? This is such an ideal spot. We know the neighbourhood so well and the girls' school is so close by."

"Will you try not to be negative before you have heard me out? In the first place, we could make a serious profit now; house prices have gone up. And in the second place..." He had discovered a new, revolutionary building project, a modern suburb under construction. It was going to become a kind of model village and it had been designed and would be built by a company called Landlease, a subsidiary of a Dutch company called Brederode, the headquarters of which were in Utrecht. So it was bound to be trustworthy! In Turramurra, close to Wahroonga. Didn't I remember Wahroonga? That upmarket suburb? The project consisted of a series of unique, individual bungalows, built a considerable distance from the road, and each on a large plot of land. Space, there would be huge amounts of space around each house. We would be living in open parkland with gardens without fences and enclosures. "And they will be gorgeous homes. Ultra modern. I have seen a few of them. They have set up a few model houses on a piece of land near Ryde. You can't believe your eyes! The luxury and comfort. You should come and take a look with me!"

I could see my well-oiled, peaceful routine going up in smoke. "Oh, don't let's do this! Things are going so well now. Couldn't we wait for a little while? Why can't we just go on as we are and build up our savings a little?"

"But we have to act now!" said Gerard, "Those houses are selling like hotcakes! Even before they are built. This is the chance of a lifetime. If we don't act quickly we'll miss out. We can handle the cost. We earn a good income together. And it would be so good for the children. What do we have here? The beach and that's it. We live on top of each other here, in a packed, old suburb. Over there we would be living outside, you can breathe out there. It's time we left here, believe me. Phons thinks it's a brilliant plan too. He would do it like a shot himself too if he had a house to sell like we do."

Phons? My old support and refuge, the trusted big brother I had always longed for as a child and who had turned up out of nowhere in Australia? Phons, who was so good at listening and who never changed and who was as reliable as a rock? It almost felt like a small betrayal. "It's easy enough for Phons to approve," I said furiously, "He doesn't have a choice. But I think it is far too risky. We should save, we should build up our reserves so that we'll have something to fall back on if we need to."

"That would just be a petty, false economy! Will you never learn? This is a golden opportunity. We'll never get a chance like this again!"

I talked to Laurel and began to look at the idea from a different angle: leaving Mosman would mean leaving its sometimes painful history, starting something new together…

The next weekend we went to look at the model homes in Ryde. We looked critically at the cheapest. "You see? Large, modern, sliding windows in aluminum frames. No more painting! And look at the kitchen: an electric cooker, safe and clean, built-in oven, stainless steal counter, double washbasin, breakfast bar – all included in the price. Sliding doors in the living room, creates so much more space. And wait till you see the bathroom!"

The bathroom struck me as worthy of a film star. Built-in bath, separate shower, the toilet in its own, tiled niche; a double washbasin in an imitation marble table that spanned the length of the wall with rows of little bathroom cabinets underneath, and above it a mirror that covered the width of the wall too. The floor and walls were tiled, white mosaic. I felt my resistance melting away. A kitchen and bathroom like this – a kitchen you could waltz around in!

The large, light living room had double wooden entrance doors that led straight out into the carport. Outside the tall front window, which was the width of the wall, was a large wooden veranda. There were three bedrooms, all with large windows.

"We can't possibly afford this," I said glumly, "It's far too luxurious. What are they asking for it?"

"It's only brick veneer," said Gerard, "A wooden frame and only one layer of stone. But it looks pretty solid, don't you think? You don't need thick walls in this climate. If we can sell our house at a profit – and we can – we'll have the deposit. The financing is being arranged by the builders. The monthly payments will only be a little higher than what we are paying in Mosman, we can afford them easily."

After Ryde, we drove to Turramurra, to look at the actual land on which the houses would be built. We turned off the Pacific Highway into a shady, undulating road called Kissing Point Road: an old road, flanked on either side by old, picturesque bungalows amid large gardens. Masses of flowering, yellow wattle and huge, purple jacaranda flowers. After about a mile we came across a stretch of new, virginal, blue asphalted road with white sidewalks that twisted and turned, and rose and dipped through the bush. "The Connemarra Parkway," said Gerard, "And here to the left is the beginning of our village. Look, the streets have already been laid out and that little hut over there is the office. We can get information there." As if he didn't already know everything there was to know!

We got out of the car. We stood on the ridge of a hill. Below us were the copper tops of legions of eucalyptus trees. On the ground next to us were lead-coloured boulders, large hunks of yellow limestone and the traces of tractor wheels in the red earth. Gerard pulled out a design. "This street here is called Parkinson Avenue. They're going to build about twenty houses here. They've almost all been sold, but number 13 is still available. Shall we take a look?"

We ambled after the children who ran whooping down the hill. Parkinson Avenue dipped sharply and nr. 13 was halfway down the street: a triangular piece of land cordoned off with little wooden stakes. A sloping block, it was narrow on the street side but ballooned out further up the hill. In the middle of the lot stood a lone, whimsically shaped gum tree. At the front, along the street, there were two pine trees and further away in the distance, marking the boundary of the back garden, a whole row of pine trees. To the left of the gum tree was a large, shoulder-high block of granite, about the size of a small van.

"The trees will remain," said Gerard, "This is where the house will be built, the living room will be just behind the gum tree. Darling, our backyard will be as big as a football field!" He looked as if he was slightly drunk. "Our neighbours' house will be a lot closer to the street. Can you visualise it a bit? Can you see what it will be like when the gardens are done?"

"Our garden? Our neighbours?"

He put both arms around me: "Can't you feel the peace here? The peace and quiet?" And turning me around: "Isn't it indescribably beautiful here?" Bush. Dark hills against a gentle, shimmering, blue sky; a red, golden sinking sun; the sweet, sharp smell of summer eucalyptus and the chirping of cicadas.

"What about the sewerage system here?" I asked, trying for a business-like manner, and mindful of Seaforth. He began to laugh, "For the moment we won't be linked to the city system, but each house will get its own septic tank in the garden, which means you'll have a normal toilet, don't worry."

"And how far are we from the station?"

"Very close. It's opposite Kissing Point Road on the Pacific Highway, direct connection to North Sydney. Better than in Mosman."

I closed my eyes. I stepped into the abyss. I put my signature next to Gerard's on the request for financing.

"Are we going to live here?" asked Janneke when we left the office.

"How could we, silly?" chirped Paul, balancing on a rickety plank placed over a hole in the ground, "There aren't any houses here!"

"Oh, but there will be!" said Gerard, "Big, beautiful houses. When it is the winter holidays, we'll start living here."

"But what if we can't make a profit on the Mosman house?" I asked anxiously.

"Of course we will make a profit! Phons and I will smarten the place up a bit" (forgetting completely that he had said our hovel could not possibly be renovated….). The next evening he came home with pots of plaster and paint, and he and Phons set to work on the crack above the kitchen door: "That's an extra 100 pounds, old man!" Then the veranda was fixed, and then the walls of the corridor.

Three different estate agents appeared, knocking on doors and walls, making notes, and with giddying speed they produced potential buyers, who started knocking on walls themselves. Four weeks later we had sold the house. "We have the deposit," Gerard told me, complacently, "And there's a little moving money left over too. The only problem is we need to leave by 30 June."

"30 June? Will our new house be ready by then?"

"Well – maybe not completely…. But as soon as it is reasonably habitable we'll move in. We can't reject this offer, it's by far the best we have had and time is pressing." The papers were signed; the sale was a fact. From then on we drove to Turramurra every weekend. We saw how the foundations were laid and the first poles appeared in the ground. We watched our house grow, every week a little bit more. We took Hiek and Jan with us, Patsy and Phons, Alice and Dick; they were all as enthusiastic as we were. We scrambled over piles of planks, and mountains of stones and sand, and picniced on our own piece of land. The children enjoyed themselves hugely.

We investigated schools. Just around the corner on Kissing Point Road was a primary school, a so-called public school, which was free. Unfortunately, we – and therefore our children – were used to Catholic, and therefore more expensive private schools. We discovered a nuns' school in Pymble and a school bus that started at our door and drove all the way there. And at our introductory meeting we were told that we could send our boys there too after the winter vacation – both of them, even though Bobby was still a year too young. Because I worked. We were very relieved.

And then it began to rain, remorselessly: Monsoon rains. It rained day in day out; it rained in the mornings, afternoons and evenings; and it continued to rain for weeks on end. Every weekend anew we would stand, dripping and aghast, surveying a silent, empty wilderness full of gurgling brooks and muddy lakes amongst which half-finished skeleton houses stood. These did not change, week after week. All work on the building site had ceased.

Our deadline began to loom large and we could no longer be given any guarantee about the delivery date of our house. "What are we going to do?" was my monotonous question every weekend as we squelched through the water-logged site. More to myself than anyone else: what were we going to do if the house wasn't ready by 30 June?

"Your girls can stay with me," Alice reassured me, "For as long as is necessary."

"Our spare bedroom is almost finished," said Hiek, "One of the walls is still plastic; but it's dry and you can certainly sleep there if you need to."

"Gus is going away," said Phons, "He needs to go to Tasmania for a week and then on to Melbourne. You can all move in together, we've got plenty of room. You can sleep in Gus's room and the kids can sleep in the playroom. You'll have to bring your own beds! We don't have enough beds. And we'll store the rest of your stuff in the garage, you don't have all that much anyway!" this with a broad grin.

Gerard jumped at this last offer. We agreed on a rent, and that we would share the costs of food and other supplies. That Patsy would cook during the week, and I would cook in the weekends. Patsy seemed reasonably keen on this plan too. And yet...

"Do you think she will be able to handle this?" I asked Phons, nervously.

"Of course. It'll be good for her. She needs some distraction. This is much better than splitting the family up."

"With a little bit of give and take..." Gerard remarked sunnily. But I remained a little dubious. Patsy was not easy to be around at that time. She was irritable, listless, depressed and this time she wasn't pregnant. We knew that Jane and Gus were involved, and I suspected that Pat did not like this, although she claimed she was happy for Jane. "I just hope she won't make the same mistakes I did," she said, "We all tend to repeat the same old patterns endlessly."

I decided to stop worrying about Patsy. I had more than enough to worry about as it was. Phons' proposal was the only more or less satisfactory solution. 30 June arrived and our new house was not remotely finished. We moved together with all our things to Avenue Road. For the first two weeks, everything went smoothly. The children seemed to regard it all as an adventure; Gerard and Phons clearly enjoyed each other's daily company hugely. Patsy and I were far too busy to do anything other than talk about everyday arrangements.

I raced off every morning together with Gerard and the boys and returned tired every evening, extremely grateful that the evening meal was being prepared by someone else. The girls told us that the walk to school from Patsy's house was much shorter than from our own. Evenings were relaxed. We all tried hard to make the situation as pleasant as possible for everyone and we succeeded. Weekends felt like mini-vacations. We ate together, but otherwise went our own way. My sense of unease disappeared.

The rain stopped and the foreman assured us that our house would be ready in about four weeks at most. The crisis, when it came, was completely unexpected.

CHAPTER 28

Upheavals

ON THE THURSDAY morning of the third week Jane rang me, at the office. "Could we have lunch together later? I'm buying. I have something to celebrate!" When I entered Torino's around one she was already sitting at a table with a glass of red wine.

"You too?" and when I hesitated, "Oh, go on, be a little reckless for once! We're going to toast the future!" She looked beautiful, dressed as if for a magazine photo-shoot. Her clothes and accessories were carefully colour-coordinated, and she exuded a sophisticated, glamorous sheen. There was no sign of the old Jane who hung out with the "Push" crowd or of the lost child in her yellow kaftan.

"You've found an even better job," I said, accepting the wine, "And the divorce has come through."

She laughed: "Wrong. Both wrong! I think it will be another two weeks before I can call myself a free woman. And as soon as all that is over I'm moving to Melbourne."

"Melbourne?"

"Uh-huh. Now that Paul and Nina are living there, Mum wants to move there too, and Gus will be living there soon as well."

Her eyes suddenly became, briefly, very young. "Agatha. This is the real thing. He has asked me to marry him, and I've said yes."

"Oh, that is great news!! Congratulations!"

"I just need to make sure Peter doesn't find out too soon. He would start making even more problems than he already is."

"He won't hear it from us," I promised, "We don't have any contact with him any more anyway."

"I can't tell you how wonderful it is to have found someone who wants to look after you. Who believes in old-fashioned, conventional marriage. He wants to adopt my children and we want a whole bunch of our own. You'll see, we'll become one of the last, large families of the century! Oh Agatha, I'm so happy!"

That evening back home in Avenue Road, the news was met in a variety of ways. "I can't see that happening very quickly, that marriage," said Patsy, "I bet he proposed out of loneliness. He must be feeling so isolated out there in Tassie. They come from such completely different backgrounds. He is so intelligent, once he starts giving it some thought…when he gets back to Melbourne and they see each other again he could well change his mind. He'll suddenly see her in a completely different light."

"Not a chance in hell!" said Phons, "Guus isn't the type to take rash decisions. He knows perfectly well what he's getting into. And he is a man of his word, someone you can build on. I hope Jane realises how very lucky she is. If she hadn't met Guus…"

"Good for Guus!" said Gerard, "Jane is a great girl. She deserves a little happiness. I think she'll make an excellent wife for him. Those two will be fine."

The next morning, completely out of the blue, and as if six months had not passed since we had last spoken to each other, Norm Waters rang: "I need to speak to you urgently. Come to Torino's, I'll be there at one o'clock sharp," and that was that.

He was sitting at a table for two near the window, just like Jane the day before. No wine in sight this time. He stood up and pulled out a chair for me, which I found oddly chivalrous of him. He came to the point immediately: "I have a job for you. I want you to set up a new duplicating service for me."

"What?!"

"Doing more or less the same as you are doing now, but then for me, on the opposite side of the street. Do you see that empty shop next to the butcher? I bought it. I'm going to start a new business there, a duplicating service. And I want you to be my manageress."

"Oh," I said inanely, "But… what about Globe Commercial?"

"Globe Commercial? What do you mean, what about Globe Commercial? There is more than enough work in this neighbourhood for two duplicating services; and a little bit of competition will spice things up! We live in a free country. If I feel like starting a duplicating service I will, and if I want to offer you a job I'll do that too. I'd like to see you spreading your wings a little.

The job you have now is far too limited. We're going to handle things very differently. What's your term of notice? A week?"

I felt as if I had been cast adrift on a raft in a wild ocean, and tried to brush the water from my eyes. "I can't, I can't give them a week's notice, I can't do that to them."

He shrugged. "Okay. Three weeks then – four, if necessary. I'll pay you five pounds more than they do. You can furnish your office however you want. I'll give you a junior as a machine operator."

"Norm!' I said, "Norm, wait! I haven't even said yes yet!"

"All right. Ten pounds more. You can't say no to that! Winthrop would never pay you that in a million years." Ten pounds more? That would mean we could easily live off my salary. That we would have money left over every month despite the new house! "All right," I said, "I'd like to come and work for you, actually. But I can't just quit. We're moving house, at least we will move as soon as our new house is ready. We're staying with friends at the moment. We're in between homes. And I have arranged to take the whole of the month of August off, I have to!" I looked at him, a little regretfully.

He frowned. He pondered. "Hmm. Pity. Okay, well, actually September 1st isn't a bad date to start. It'll give us time to do a little bit of advertising. Let me know what your thoughts are about that. What can I order for you? An omelette?"

"Just coffee," I said, feeling distinctly seasick. "Norm, what happened to the printing shop? A while ago there was a lot of gossip about it."

The black eyes lost all expression. He looked at his watch. "Never listen to gossip about things that don't concern you. As soon as you've moved, ring me. Agreed? I have to go now." He gave me a warm, almost affectionate smile, "We'll show them, you and I!"

"Go for it! Go for it!" Gerard crowed enthusiastically when I came home with my story. "That's a huge salary for a woman!"

"I have," I answered, "I told him I would do it. It's just that it's all still so unreal. And how am I going to tell Winthrop? I didn't dare say a word about it this afternoon; there wasn't any time anyway. But I'll have to tell him next week. Ugh, how awful."

"Nonsense. That's the way it goes in business. If someone made him an offer like that, he'd jump at it himself too!"

Phons was equally positive. He laughed loud and long. "Well, well, well, what do you know? Little Mother Melman! Whoever would have thought you'd become a successful career woman? People will be fighting over you soon. This calls for a bottle of wine tonight!"

"Unfortunately, I'm exhausted," said Patsy, "I have to get an early night tonight." At which Phons, Gerard and I emptied the bottle of red wine between us, and opened another, if I recall correctly.

The next morning. Saturday. Breakfast. All the children are sitting at the large, round breakfast table. They are being very noisy. I try, half-heartedly, to maintain some kind of order. Phons is feeding Luc, who is sitting in his high chair drumming with his little hands on the table in front of him and blowing into the spoon of porridge Phons holds up. The porridge flies everywhere. Phons sighs. "Pat is staying in bed a little longer," he tells me, wiping porridge off the high chair. "She doesn't feel well. Hasn't had a good night." Phons looks slightly ashen too, I notice; too much wine last night? I don't feel exactly on top of the world either.

Julie bursts out laughing. She is throwing pieces of bread at Bobby who is sitting opposite her, pulling the most appalling faces – challenging, provoking. Paul, next to Julie, lets the jam jar slip from his fingers. A red trickle of jam flows slowly over the plastic tablecloth. Bobby sticks two fingers into the sticky mass and licks them with great enjoyment. Julie immediately follows his example, crowing with glee. She uses both her hands. I can see jam in her curls. In the meantime, Janneke, sitting beside me, is grumbling about the dress she is to wear for her confirmation tomorrow and Lindy complains that she really, really doesn't want to wear a hat tomorrow.

"That's enough, all of you!" I snap, suddenly losing my patience, "Outside, this minute: go outside and play in the garden. You too Janneke, off you go!" I pick up Julie who is now sticky from top to toe, "But you wash your hands and face first" and steer her in the direction of the sink.

Janneke pulls open the back door, whinging and cross. She slams it behind her. Paul and Bobby, pushing and teasing each other, laughing loudly, copy her. There is a strong wind blowing outside. I can see the leaves of the high bushes behind the kitchen window dancing wildly. Julie, now hiccoughing uncontrollably with laughter, tries to run after the boys without washing herself. I grab her. "Oh no, you don't!

And then Patsy stands in the doorway, her robe open, her face white, contorted, her green eyes flashing. "Have you all gone round the bend? This noise is unbearable! This is *my* house and I can't get any rest at all. I have to rest, I have to – do you hear me?!"

"The kids..." Phons starts to say.

"Sorry, Pat," I say remorsefully, "I forgot you were still sleeping."

She turns sharply towards me. "You! This is your fault. It's all your fault! Ever since you arrived it has been a total mess here. You think the whole world revolves around you. Oh, you're always so on top of things! So smart, so efficient. You make me sick. Get out! I want you out of my house today! I don't want to see your face here ever again." Her voice rises higher and higher. She staggers. She grabs the table. Her fingers find the jam jar. She flings it through the kitchen. The jar smashes into a thousand pieces on the floor. "Here!" she screams, "And here!" A plate follows. The fragments scatter wildly. I stand as if rooted to the ground with a wet tea-towel in one hand and a wailing Julie in the other.

Phons quickly gets between me and Pasty: "Pat, stop! Pat, control yourself!"

I see that Lindy has slipped onto the floor and is cowering in a corner of the room. Wide, panic-filled eyes in a little, white face. Luc screams. Pandemonium. I drop the tea-towel. I let Julie go. I kneel down next to Lindy and pull her into my arms. She is shaking as if she has a fever. "You don't need to be scared, darling. Patsy is sick, that's all." Julie pushes her head against my shoulder, sobbing. I hold her with my other arm.

Phons propels Patsy who is now wailing hysterically into the hall. "You are going back to bed. Come on!"

My heart is hammering in my chest. Gerard who has sat in stunned silence, now gets up and begins to clean up the dirty breakfast plates, shaking his head. "Why don't you go and play outside too, Lin?" he says calmly, "There's nothing wrong, sweetheart. Grown-ups sometimes do strange things when they're sick."

And then a wave of fury washes over me. I get up. I am shaking with anger. As soon as Lindy holding Julie by the hand is out of the back door, I explode. "She is insane! How dare she let herself go like that in front of the children?! You don't think we are going to stay here a minute longer, do you? You and your bright ideas! We are leaving, we are leaving today! I'll think of something."

"Okay, Okay," says Gerard, pushing a piece of toast toward Luc and so putting a stop to his wailing.

Phons returns. "I'm so sorry, guys. She isn't herself. She's over-tired," nervously.

"She is mad!" I say, "And she is dangerous."

"It's just jealousy. She's home all day with the kids and you get to leave every morning. You're in contact with the outside world. You're doing exciting things. You represent all her missed chances."

"Excuse me?!"

"She feels as if life is passing her by. That she is growing old before her time. That she has no future ahead of her anymore."

"Does she think I am working for fun?! I can't afford not to work!"

"Calm down," says Gerard. "Things are tough enough for Phons as it is. We just need to take things more calmly. She'll come round again."

"We are leaving!" I cry, "I am not staying here one minute longer. I'll ring Alice and Hiek."

Phons looks deeply unhappy. "Okay…maybe it would be for the best. I'm so very sorry things have gone this way."

I had no idea then that depression – real, medical depression – was a physical illness. That your brain could become ill. That depression could cause indescribable pain. It would take me thirty years to discover that. Only then did I begin to wonder whether any of us ever understood what Patsy had been going through, possibly for many years. I can't remember whether she took valium or lithium, the standard antidepressants in those days. If they ever came up in conversation it was as a joke: unhappy housewives of a certain age took valium… I realise now my presence must have been a constant irritant to her. I was completely absorbed in my own cares: my job, my house under construction, the children. Whereas Phons and Gerard were always having fun with each other, I wandered around worrying about things, always anxious, always distracted, and at the same time trying to remain alert, at least with respect to the children. Not capable of relaxing and certainly not of paying attention to Patsy.

We left the next day, after Janneke's confirmation ceremony. We took mattresses with us, bedding, pillows and clothes. Patsy remained invisible. Phons helped us with transport. The girls went to stay with Alice and Dick, and Gerard and I together with the boys went to Hiek and Jan's, where we slept on the floor in the half-finished room with the plastic wall. We wore sweaters over our pyjamas, it was winter and seriously cold at night. Nevertheless, it was lovely to be with Hiek. She turned every day of our sleepover into a party. The girls were less happy, but I was eternally grateful to Alice. She was all calm understanding.

After this crisis, informing Winthrop that I would be leaving on 1 August and would become the manageress of a new duplicating service across the road was as easy as pie. He didn't even seem upset.

Around two weeks later we can finally move to Turramurra. The winter holidays have begun. We arrive from three different directions. Gerard turns up from Avenue Road, together with Phons, in a rented van. Jan brings the boys and I, and Dick transports the girls. All our things are divided amongst the three cars – or rather, four. When Gerard goes later to pick up his own car, he brings another load of stuff.

It is a sunny winter's day. The house next to ours turns out to be inhabited already. There are elegantly pleated white and brown curtains hanging in the windows, the garden has been landscaped and from the front door a neat stone terrace leads to a short, improvised drive.

Compared to this, our house still looks very incomplete. There isn't even a hint of a drive. Our front door is still about half a meter above the ground. The garden is a moon landscape full of craters; there are pieces of wood, mounds of dirt and piles of construction waste lying around everywhere. When Jan and I arrive with the boys, we find Gerard and Phons busily constructing an improvised ramp out of wood and stones to enable us to get into the front door.

Phons gives me a huge hug: "There's water and electricity! What else do you need?"

I climb into our front door. The wood stain on the door still feels a little sticky. The floors in all the rooms consist of rough, wooden planks, except in the kitchen where the floor is made of concrete. The kitchen has a glass outside door that opens onto a long, high, narrow balcony. The outside door of the laundry, which is next to the kitchen, opens onto the same balcony. A narrow stone staircase leads down to the ground. The left side of our bungalow, where the front door is situated, is on ground level; the right side sits on top of high stone pillars.

"We have masses of storage space here," Gerard tells me as he shows me around, "Over there in the garden, where it slants down so steeply, I'll need to build a support wall. I'm going to make the back garden into a series of terraces, do you see? The floors still need to be sanded, stained and finished, but we'll do that ourselves. I've already rented a sanding machine, it's coming tomorrow. And come and look at the linoleum I chose for the kitchen. A steal!"

He shows me an immense role of mustard yellow material. "The bottom layer is cork, it's indestructible. It will need to be glued on though; that's the first thing I'm going to do."

He is glowing with purpose. For the last few weeks Gerard has devoted every free moment to planning the furnishing and interior design of our new house, and buying whatever was necessary. I am perfectly happy with this. I am sure he has more insight into this than I do, and a far better overview of everything that needs to be done.

The mustard yellow linoleum doesn't look at all like linoleum, but more like a futuristic carpet. It isn't smooth, but rough and patterned – very striking and durable, but I will later discover that the ridges in the pattern retain every morsel of spilled food, every speck of mud, sand, dirt and whatever else is walked into the kitchen. And that to keep the floor clean a weekly scrub with brush and soap will be necessary, every Saturday anew. But it did look lovely.

Paul pulls at my sleeve: "Where do I sleep? Where do I sleep?"

"The man from the phone company has arrived," Phons reports, "Where do you want the phone?"

"Where do I put these mattresses?" Jan pants, dragging a mattress on his back.

"Shall I dump the girls' stuff in the back room?" Dick asks.

"We're hungry!" Janneke informs me, "Can we eat our sandwiches now?"

And then a slender young woman with strikingly large front teeth and a Scottish accent suddenly appears. She tells me her name is Anna Smith and she is our new neighbour, and that she is so happy we have arrived because she has felt so lonely amid all these half-finished houses. She also tells me she has a small baby and has prepared a large pan of soup. Do we feel like a bowl of soup?

She looks around her with curiosity. "Don't you have any mosquito screens yet? You really need to screen off the windows here, it's an absolute necessity!" No, we don't have any screens yet; we also don't have any carpets, sofas or curtains. We're just going to camp out a bit and sort things out as we go along. But we're in party mood, all of us. We're back together again! We have a roof over our heads! We have a home.

We sleep on mattresses on the floor, all of us together in the same room, until the floors have been stained and sanded. We change rooms together every night. I only begin to consider cooking once the eight-meter long and four-meter wide linoleum has been laid, which takes Gerard and Phons a day and a half of considerable effort. Gerard is regularly forced to step over surfaces that have already been glued, with pieces of paper stuck to his bare feet. He does this with varying success, while Phons standing on the sidelines wipes the tears of laughter from his eyes.

We barely sleep that first night, even though we are exhausted. We are terrorised by buzzing and zooming, and the next day we are all scratching. Anna Smith is right. Turramurra is a paradise for bloodthirsty midgets. So we order them after all, those huge, tailor-made and very expensive screens for every window and door; they are an integral part of houses like these and had already been prepared. We have to pay for them in installments, as we pay for the linoleum, the dryer, the new washing machine, the new fridge, a shaded floor lamp, a rug for the living room floor, a new easy chair, two electric heaters (it is cold inside) and wardrobes for the children's rooms. I have given up trying to calculate what we can afford. Gerard decides what we need and I place my signature next to his, and accept yet another little installment payment booklet together with the article in question.

The sanding machine appears on the scene. It is a huge green monster that is almost too heavy to lift and emits heartrending cries when it is switched on. It continues to screech for almost a minute after it has been switched off. Gerard's first attempt at sanding (in what is to become our bedroom) is not a success. The machine bites greedily into the wood, "Just need to get used to it," he says, a little shocked, "Good thing I started in this dark corner. I think I just need to adjust it!" After a certain amount of trial and error, he produces a reasonably smooth, flat surface. But now he and the machine disappear into an almost impenetrable cloud of red dust. And then the asthma demon raises its ugly head. Gerard gasps and squeaks almost as loudly as the machine itself. Streams of sweat draw lines down his red-dusted face.

"We'll have to have it done," I tell him, anxiously, "You can't handle this."

"Of course I can! It would cost too much to have it done. Just let me get on with it." He drapes a wet handkerchief around his head, which I regularly replace, and fashions a kind of mask from another wet handkerchief for his nose and mouth. It helps, but not enough, I think. He nevertheless refuses to quit. He hangs onto the handle of the machine as if it is a lifebuoy and sands for two full days.

I am allowed to apply the first layer of stain. After this, another round of light sanding is needed, and Gerard applies the top layer, panting and groaning. In this way room after room acquires a beautiful, gleaming, new floor. When we are finally all sleeping in our own beds, in our own rooms, Gerard has lost at least five kilos and looks as ashen as Phons sometimes can. But he is beside himself with pride and rightly so. And the asthma demon disappears again from view.

We buy material for curtains, and do inexperienced battle with sewing machine and curtain rails. And then finally there comes a night that the children, deeply contented, are sitting on the ground in a row in front of our television set in the family room – a section of the kitchen to which the original plans of the house had assigned this name – while we stand, arms around each other, looking at the way the light of our new floor lamp reflects off our homemade, red, living room curtains and our self-framed Renoir poster (The Blue Girl) which is our only wall decoration. We are deeply happy.

"And now I need to sort out the garden," says Gerard. The garden. It will take us over a year to create a glorious pleasure garden of which we are very proud. Our neighbours all use garden architects, and from one day to the next the neighbouring gardens are magicked into respectable parks by means of grass sods, and flowering bushes and trees. Gerard watches all this carefully. We then pull up a few sections of grass from roadside verges and place them with care and at a small distance from each other on our hill. We water them with devotion and after some time we too acquire a somewhat bumpy and erratic lawn. Not the gentle, green carpet Anna and Peter Smith have, but we are happy with it.

Gerard begins to bring home huge slabs of natural stone, which he finds along the road on his work trips around New South Wales. He uses them to build a support wall. He then builds a stone terrace under and in front of the front veranda, and even better, at the back of the house, including a large and extraordinary barbecue which looks like a prehistoric, stone, sacrificial altar.

Once the heavy rains start again our support wall promptly collapses. After a night of heavy rain we discover that our house is standing on the banks of a mountain stream that is speckled with chunks of natural stone; in the deep ravine between the rock in the front garden and our bedroom window now gurgles a subsidiary brook. The rain stops eventually and Gerard begins fearlessly building anew.

A loudly bellowing asphalt machine appears, which spurts a scalding hot black brew, and is accompanied by bronzed men in leather aprons. Our drive is being constructed. Four mud-spattered, little schoolchildren perch on the very edge of the front door threshold throughout, enjoying themselves hugely and breathing in the soggy, tar fumes.

Our children enjoy the best winter vacation of their lives. They have already thoroughly inspected every half-finished house in the street. They know every section of bush, rock and ravine in the neighbourhood. They are constantly covered in scratches and bruises. They dress in irreparably torn old trousers and sweaters, and regularly turn up begging me to tend to bloodied knees and stubbed toes. I have long ago given up every attempt to try to keep track of them.

Hiek's eldest son, Frank, comes to bring us a gift of a puppy. A joyfully licking, black and white mongrel, whose ancestry is extremely colourful. I fleetingly hope he will become a second Lassie who will help me track down children busily occupied in the bush, but Timmy turns out to be a different character altogether. He does run, happily barking, a little way behind them when they set off on their adventures, but then returns home as quickly as he can to keep me company. When I ask, "Where is Paul, Timmy? Go and find Paulie!" he looks at me with compassion, places his pointed head on his front paw and shuts his eyes. He does bark whenever someone sets foot on our property. But if either friend or foe perseveres, he becomes all tail-wagging affection.

Frank had also made a kennel for him, which I place next to the rocks under our carport. Every evening when the children go to bed I motion to Timmy to go out to his kennel, where there are warm blankets. This results in mournfully hanging ears and deeply indignant eyes, and loud protests from the children. I nevertheless remain unrelenting. I explain to them that dogs should be outside. That Timmy – when I am back at work and they are at school and so gone all day – will have to spend the whole day outside and on his own. Not that this helps much. Every night there are deep, aggrieved sighs. In no time, Timmy has become a beloved member of the family.

On our third Sunday in Turramurra, Phons rings. "Would it be okay if we dropped by this afternoon?"

"Will Patsy come?" I ask.

"Of course she'll come. She'd love to see how the house has come along."

"Oh, alright." The scene in the kitchen seems a million years ago. The sun is shining. Outside where the morning mist has disappeared I see the children playing Tarzan in the back garden amid our pine trees with an old removal box and a piece of rope. They are swinging from branch, to box, to the ground, making Tarzan-like noises. On a morning like this all you can do is be happy.

When Phons drives up our brand new drive the whole family comes running out, jubilant. Julie tumbles out of the car and runs towards Bobby. Phons lifts Luc into Janneke's arms. Patsy kisses everyone and Gerard pats every back he can reach. The men disappear chatting animatedly into the back garden. Patsy and I look at each other.

"Well," she says calmly, "Do you expect me to apologise?"

"Nonsense," I say nervously, "Abnormal circumstances and all that. Let's forget it, shall we? Do you want to have a look inside?"

She is cool and composed, and slightly condescending. She does not share Phons' enthusiastic involvement at all. We talk about superficialities. Pat seems to have nothing in particular to tell me. The connection that once existed between us, the natural exchange, the confiding in each other, is gone. Will it ever come back? I don't know. I discover that I don't really care, that I do not experience this as a loss, on the contrary. It feels as if I have been given permission to distance myself from a responsibility, to let go of a burden. The afternoon turns out to be quite fun and relaxed.

When we have waved goodbye to the Albers family I ask Gerard what he thinks about Phons and Patsy. "She's destroying him," he says bleakly, "There really is something wrong with her. She never leaves him in peace for a second. She criticises everything he says or does. He is in a very, very difficult situation."

"I thought things were goiing so much better now. She seemed so calm."

"Forget it. He doesn't talk about it much, but if you ask me she is busily tearing him apart."

"They'll have to sort it all out together," I say, "There isn't anything that we can do."

"No, of course not. But we are not going to abandon Phons. No matter what happens."

BBQ, terrace + oleander

CHAPTER 29

Turramurra and Torron

BREDA, 29 OCTOBER *2001: a row of golden trees lines the street at the back of our apartment building. I haven't touched this book for two weeks.*
First, there were the grandchildren who demanded all my attention and energy. We have just had Marloes and Bart to stay (autumn holidays, and Bob and Stans are renovating their house).
Then there was Lindy's return from Australia. She has been gone for two months. We counted the days and sighed with relief – at least I did – when she had landed safely back in Holland. The instability of our world, like Afghanistan that we watch every night on the news; the growing antipathy for America – unjust in my eyes. There have been whole swathes of now-ness that have pushed out the past.
I am not satisfied with what I wrote two weeks ago, but I am powerless to improve it. A narrative like this creates a beginning, middle and end. But in life there is no such structure. Imposing a shape on the endless messiness we all live in is impossible. I know this, and yet I want to keep writing, if only to help myself understand. I know that I can never really tell the full story of Phons and Patsy. I know too little about it for one thing, I can only record what I experienced and how I reacted; what I saw, with my restricted field of vision, and what others like Gerard and Laurel saw.
Looking back, I realise that the chasm between Patsy and I had been growing for a long time, and was not caused by particular events. In those days, I believed in accepting what you can't change, in keeping hidden conflicts hidden and in simply getting on with life. But Patsy hated compromise. She refused to accept, to submit; she sought and found confrontation all the time. But why she felt this need to oppose and whom she was fighting I do not know. Her past? Herself? She fought ceaselessly with every weapon she could find. She lashed out wildly without any heed for the victims she made along the way.

Our Turramurra was very small. There was a tiny shopping centre at the end of Kissing Point Road we could reach easily on foot using a small path that ran behind our back garden. A few neighbourhood shops where you could buy most essentials, and that was it. We used these shops until Gerard found Franklins, the much cheaper shopping centre on the Pacific Highway, opposite Kissing Point Road and almost next to the station. From then onwards we shopped there every Friday afternoon, our weekly shop, and bought fish and chips for the whole family from the shop next door.

The heart of Turramurra consisted of a tiny business centre clustered around the station. Other than that, there were primarily homes for older residents. Turramurra lay along the North Shore line, adjacent to Wahroonga, and just like Wahroonga was very close to the bush; it edged onto vast stretches of virgin bushland that would later be developed for housing. But in our time, other than the few new asphalted roads running through the bush, there was no sign of this. There were only ambitious plans for the future. Our Turramurra was still all rural peace and virtually untouched flora and fauna. Laughing kookaburras would perch on the railing of our veranda and in our trees in the mornings. A blue-tongued lizard lived under the rock in our carport and would regularly sunbathe on the drive. Kangaroos would appear, shy but alert, at the end of Parkinson's Avenue, and wombats could be found in the bush.

It is Saturday afternoon, the last week of August. I am in the train. Gerard has dropped me off for the first time at our little Turramurra station. I am on my way to North Sydney, to a meeting with Norm Waters about the set-up details of the new duplicating service, which I am to manage. I am trying to muster my new, second identity. Somehow I am going to have to come across as a cool businesswoman. We definitely need two incomes if we are to live in Turramurra.

Yesterday I had worked out how many installment payments we had signed up to and for how many years we would be burdened with those booklets of coupons. I gave myself an awful nightmare as a result. I dreamt that an army of repossession men had turned up, taking away the dryer, the washing machine, the new screens, rolling up the new carpet as they went. I heard my children sobbing. I woke with terrified sweat on my forehead recalling that the newspapers were full of such stories every day.

And now I am in the train and dying a thousand deaths. What if I can't do this? What if I don't have the skills? I keep telling myself I know everything there is to know about the duplicating business; that there will be more than enough customers; that Norm sounded so kind on the phone; that nothing would go wrong. But I don't really believe a word of this, and so much depends on this job....

After half an hour in the train, I have become thoroughly depressed and walking into a desolate Mount Street doesn't help. It is a Saturday afternoon so the street is empty and the shops are closed. Behind the window of Norman's new shop, I see a group of people standing around. The shop is in fact an old, narrow house. The open front door gives access to a broad hall at the back of which is an ornate wooden staircase. There is only one door leading off it.

I walk into my new office. Pushed against the window along the side of the room are an old, metal desk and a whole set of metal filing cabinets. In the corner, opposite the door, stands a large, new, bright blue duplicating machine. It is running. Next to it stands Alan in his inevitable overalls and next to Alan is a young, blonde girl of about sixteen, who is catching pieces of paper, her cheeks pink with effort. Norm is warming his hands at a petroleum stove and next to Norm stands a delicate woman of about fifty with carefully styled, jet black hair. She is Norm's height.

"You've lost weight," is Norm's only, slightly disapproving greeting.

"Hallo," I respond cheerfully, "So this is it?"

"This is it. We've bought a few things already and you're just going to have to live with them. That's what happens if you stay out of touch. That thing over there is the most state of the art duplicator on the market. And this is Brenda," nodding his head in the direction of the blonde girl.

"Hi Brenda," I say, with a smile.

"I'm Rachel Waters," the dark woman says, putting out her hand, "I'm glad to meet you at last."

"She understands how to do it now," says Norm to Alan, "She can go home," and to Brenda, "So you'll start here on 1 September," at which she mumbles something unintelligible and dashes out.

"Sit down," orders Norm, gesturing towards the desk.

"How did the move go?" asks Rachel, pulling up another chair. Alan shuts the lid of the duplicator and comes to sit on the edge of the desk, with a pile of papers in his hand and Norm sits down in the chair behind the table.

My memories of that first meeting are erratic – snippets of conversation, odd images of Norm, Alan and that hollow room. But what I recall most vividly is how naive I felt, how unreal and stupid. And that I wondered why, when I had had the chance, I had not found out more about the how and why of this business venture. Now it was too late. Norm lets me know in no uncertain terms that he is depending on me, on my compliance, my ability to adapt, my unconditional loyalty.

The pieces of paper in Alan's hand turn out to be leaflets that need to be circulated, door to door: advertising for the new duplicating service which will carry the name "Torron." Rachel explains to me, smiling, that the name is made up of her two son's names, Victor and Ronald. Norm tells me I will be working for Rachel's business. That officially he will have nothing to do with it, other than act as a consultant if needed. He explains that Rachel has her own office in a building at the back. She runs the Sydney branch of an international Zionist movement from there. She will also do admin for Torron – that is, she will support me with accounting, signing cheques and such matters. Which will not curtail my freedom, however. I will be the manageress of the business, and I will decide what is necessary and when. My name also appears on the leaflets.

"We're counting on you contacting your old customers," Norm says cheerfully. And suggests I make an additional list of customers who do not live close by so that we can send them a mailing; a personal note from me should do wonders.

I discover that Torron will also offer offset printing, and that the old printing shop has been transferred together with its staff to new owners. Which means that Alan is still foreman there. Torron will become a tiny competitor. Torron has hired a room in Rachel's office building and placed an offset printer there, which will do all the work I acquire. Alan will work for us in the evenings, freelance.

Norman says, laughing, that he is perfectly capable of working the machine himself too if necessary, and that his consultancy will cover a lot of areas. He suggests that Alan and I design Torron paper and that we print it ourselves. He invites me to look at the rest of the building. Upstairs are two empty rooms that have been rented out. On 1 September a one-man advertising company and small market research company will move into the building. He shows me the kitchen and bathroom, which are for general use. We go downstairs and walk outside, past the door of the butcher's shop and stand in front of our printing facility. Later, the butcher would close and the shop would become part of our office and printing works.

Alan pulls out a key and we go inside, past the press, the storage space, the dark room, and end up in an alleyway. Opposite our back door is the back door of Rachel's office. This turns out to be a high, light suite of rooms with carpet on the floor and curtains in the windows, three luxurious desks and a glass cabinet full of books. There are electric typewriters on two of the desks.

"Anything that needs to be typed on an electric typewriter can be done here," says Rachel, "You should make sure we get lots of work!"

I am given a copy of a monthly magazine with a respectably laminated cover, *The Jewish Hope*. "Torron will be printing this from now on."

"This is your first steady customer," says Norm, "The copy will be sent from the US. As soon as the text arrives, you consult with Alan, he'll make sure Ramon does the layout."

Ramon? Layout? Alan explains that Ramon Araullo also works at the printing shop, that he is an artist and does text layout. It seems that Ramon too is prepared to give up his free time to help Torron get started.

Norm decides the introductions are over; he and Rachel clearly have other places to be. He hands me a bunch of keys. "See you on September 1st."

Alan and I stroll back to my new office. I remember that Alan appeared to know exactly how I felt. "I'll give you a lift later," he said kindly, "I need to drive through Pymble anyway. And don't worry. Everything will be fine. We're going to start small, there isn't a great deal that can go wrong. Norm is an experienced businessman. He has vision and he has the gift of the gab. Just let him get on with it. What he can't get done the first time round, he'll achieve the second. You'll see."

When I asked him what had happened to the printing shop, he shrugged. "It's all got to do with high finance if you ask me. We're now part of some kind of conglomerate. I don't think anyone really cares whether we make it or not. No-one seems to be paying any attention to us. Ah well, I'll stick around for the ride. As long as it puts bread on the table."

Only then did I realise Norm Waters was pulling off a kind of magic trick; that a mysterious game of which I was a tiny part was being played. And that for my own sanity I shouldn't try to understand it in too much detail. Was it something vaguely shady? Well, it wasn't any of my business. I decided that the best thing I could do was keep my eyes firmly on the fact that I needed this job, that I was going to be well paid, and that neither I nor Alan, who was clearly not burdened with any of the scruples I felt, had any understanding of this side of the business anyway.

At the same time, I realised that this vague mystery was exciting; it felt as if we were buccaneers. Something I found appealing. It reminded me very slightly of Charles, and his gambles on the future. There was an enormous challenge ahead of us, Alan and I, and the third unmissable member of our team, Ramon, whom I met a week later. Ramon came from The Philippines and was a talented artist. He could do anything, from photography and dark room work, to typesetting in any and every font, and if necessary artwork.

He was, moreover, a cheerful and witty man. And like Alan, seemed tireless. There was always space for another quick job. And he too, like Alan, and like me, was a devoted disciple of Norm Waters.

Alan assured me that I should run any real decisions by Norm, not Rachel. Rachel was just a front man. Norm was the real power behind the throne. He also told me that poor Rachel suffered from regular migraine attacks, which laid her low for days on end. And that before I started a small, wooden counter would be built between my desk and the door, to keep customers at a suitable distance.

September 1st was a Monday. My first customer was the man from the lapidary club, who looked around him with curiosity. "We want you to keep on producing our magazine. You've given us a few good ideas in the past and you know exactly how I want things done. Much nicer and easier if we keep on working with you."

He was followed quickly by an architect whom I vaguely remembered. He had an enormous spec in one hand and our leaflet in the other. "You've started your own company, I see," he said approvingly, "Very sensible." I didn't make the slightest effort to disabuse him. I just accepted his job, beaming. And the jobs kept pouring in. It was a madhouse that Monday. And in the meantime, a painter was busily painting *Torron Duplicating Service* in large letters on our window.

Brenda was no Robin, but she proved very willing. I trained her, and eventually she began to achieve the kind of standard Robin had worked at. And miraculously the jobs kept coming.

I didn't see Norm all week, but Alan dropped by occasionally to eat his sandwiches with me at lunchtime and also to find out whether I was coping. "You're not feeling lonely here, are you?"

On Friday afternoon I paid my first visit to Rachel in her Zionist building at the back. She studied my pile of invoices with surprise. "This is much better than I expected!" which was also what I thought. She handed me two pay packets, one for Brenda and one for me.

On the first day of the second week, Norm appeared. "So where's my coffee? Come on Brenda, make us some coffee!" Brenda promptly fled upstairs. He put a hand on my head: "How are you feeling, young lady? Happy?" And I did. I still felt as if I was balancing on the edge of an ice floe, which no-one could guarantee wasn't melting (a feeling I would have for years). But it was an exciting, even a fun sensation, especially now that the boss himself had arrived, so positive and sure of himself.

He sat down on the edge of my desk. He pulled some forms from his breast pocket and some tightly typed pages. "A surprise for you. I need this stenciled and this offset. Two new clients. I want you to contact them personally. There will be a lot more work from them. And things are going well here, aren't they?"

"Very well."

"I told you there were opportunities in North Sydney. You and I are going to move mountains. I'll do the acquisition for the moment, but you can get out and about too, once you have a little time. We need to follow up on that mailing. You need to push offset. Duplicating is bread and butter; offset is jam. To start off with you could remind our duplicating customers of the offset facilities we have to offer. Make them realise they can call on you for all their needs!"

I ask him to explain to me exactly which facilities Torron had to offer. Offset printing needed a camera, a dark room and plate-making equipment. As far as I was aware we only had a small printing press at our disposal. Who was going to do all the photographic work and how would it get done? "I will, said Norm, "At home. You can ring me at any time," tapping the phone, "All you need to do is calculate. Quote for the jobs. And give Alan and me a little bit of extra time in whatever schedules you agree."

I began dutifully to offer offset printing and to point out to our customers that we were cheaper than the big printing shop next door. We only took on small jobs, black and white and suitable for a small press, but we were good, accurate and very reliable. We always did what we promised.

Our turnover grew by leaps and bounds. Our group of customers expanded. Alan worked night after night in the little room in the Zionist's building. No deadline was impossible for him to meet. Week after week, Norm deposited extra work on my desk.

About ten days before Christmas he summoned me to a second Saturday afternoon meeting in my office. This time Rachel did not join us. Alan did, looking as if he was sleeping on his feet, and an older man, with a skinny face and restlessly roaming eyes. The press officer of a large computer company situated in North Sydney. His name was Johansson. Norm introduced me as "our manager." Johansson presented me with a huge pile of offset jobs. "These need to be ready before Christmas. Would that be possible? I'd like a quote on my desk on Monday."

"Of course," said Norm even before I could open my mouth.

I waited until he had shown the man out. "Of course not!" I said, looking at a silent Alan, slumped on my desk. "We have God knows how much work already and it all needs to be done by Christmas."

"We don't have any option," said Norm, "This is the beginning of a whole lot more work. This customer is going to become essential for Torron. Once we have reeled him in… I'll help. We can take shifts at the press. Alan, for God's sake, go home and get some sleep!"

"Not sure what that is anymore," Alan said, disappearing out of the door.

"So let's work out the costs." Norm said to me, "Atta girl, let's see what you're worth."

"Norm, we are biting off more than we can chew!"

"Relax, things are going to change around here soon."

"Oh?"

"The printer next door is closing. They aren't making enough profit. I can rent their space. Alan and Ramon and whoever else we need can come and work for Torron. Torron Duplicating will become Torron Printing and Duplicating. We're going to expand. Our office will remain here. You'll continue as before, but things will get busier."

I stared, speechless, at his laughing red mouth, gleaming white teeth and pirate's moustache. He actually was a magician, pulling white rabbits out of countless top hats. "I warned you: we're going to fly! But let's get those quotes done."

I calculated, with Norm at my elbow, adding all sorts of printing costs and requirements. When we were done I had a page fall of notes, which I typed into respectable quotes for Johansson.

"Perfect!" said Norm, "He can't say no to that. And now we're going to get a cup of coffee at Torino's. My treat, with cheesecake! Did you know our Torino's makes the best cheesecake in Sydney?"

CHAPTER 30

Torron success

NOVEMBER 2001. I *have just gone through a box of old Australian mementos, untouched for years, and found a copy of our first marketing leaflet. Even now, thirty years later, it still strikes me as a gem of graphic design. It was made with such care. The colours are still bright. The photo of the painting of a printer and press on the inside and the "work in progress" sign printed jauntily on the back are still brilliant in my eyes. And the text – which if I recall correctly, Ramon and I wrote – is still inspiring: "A good idea is good business and it deserves the imaginative attention of craftsmen." And "From design to finished product your ideas are developed and shaped by our team, efficiently and economically." And then a list of the services on offer: Graphic Arts Department, Printing Department, Binding Department, Typing Department, all with full details listed under each heading. Impressive and true. We could do all this and we did. When this leaflet was printed and circulated, Torron Printing Pty Limited, 88 Mount Street, North Sydney, was about two years old.*

Our breathtakingly swift metamorphosis from humble duplicating-cum-printing shop to professional printing company with office duplicating services is impossible to describe. All I can do is sketch snapshot moments from the time after that metamorphosis was complete. By then, Norm, like Zeus on Olympus, had withdrawn from his creation and had begun devoting himself to other things. This was the period in which Alan, Ramon and I formed the tripod on which Torron – that in my eyes still seemed a fata morgana, a mirage, a magician's trick – rested precariously. We were all three aware that our own prosperity depended completely on the success of the business; that a profit needed to be made and fast; that somewhere beyond our field of vision was an enormous bank loan that had been granted on the grounds that Torron would become a success and which paid our salaries.

Why Torron's predecessor had not succeeded had never become clear to me. I did not enquire too deeply into this, but every now and then I was still overcome by a feeling of profound panic. Yet somehow this balancing on the edge of the abyss was also fun. Ramon, Alan and I did it with a great deal of laughter.

I see myself sitting at the window of the shop. I now have an intercom on my desk with which I can contact Alan in the printing works, which saves me frequent trips out the front door. I can also reach Ramon via the intercom. He is now situated in the empty room upstairs, where the light is excellent.

Ramon is a small, slim man with jet-black hair and the hands of a Balinese dancer. He is the father of a large, Spanish-speaking family, but speaks English perfectly, albeit with a distinctly Latin rhythm. When he speaks – and he speaks a lot – you can hear the clicking of castagnets. He is quick, witty, erudite, perceptive, and he has an infectious laugh. Sometimes he holds forth with passion, a small brown cigar between his lips, dark eyes glittering, hands expressive, although usually these continue to work. He adores Norm. His faith in him is limitless, even though Norm is in every way his opposite. Ramon is not assertive; he dislikes change or anything unexpected, and hates to take risks. His manners are excellent. He is unchangeably polite and very gallant. It is lovely to talk to him – he enjoys the absurdity of life – and he often comes up with brilliant ideas. I usually run up the stairs if I have something to discuss with him, and we confer a lot. Just like Alan, he starts work at a barbarously early hour and works until late at night.

In our factory area now stand the little press from the Zionist building, an enormous, new, colour offset press, the ancient letter press machine which is known as "The Heidelberg," a new paper guillotine, and in a corner next to the dark room, a large, state-of-the-art camera, which has countless possibilities. Alan is assisted by an apprentice printer called Jimmy, who is about sixteen. A tall, gangly, silent lad, he serves as general dogsbody. And then there is a small, grey, bespectacled lady called Kathleen, who stoically does the bookkeeping. She has been working in the business for years. All the changes that have taken place – that we are now called Torron, that Norm, then those city types, then Rachel is her boss – seem to have washed over her without affecting her in the slightest. She does what she is asked to do and also functions as coffee lady. If she isn't too busy, she brings me a cup of coffee at eleven o'clock every day, which I greatly appreciate.

I deal with all the customers. I supply price quotes and offer advice. I work out the schedules, of course in consultation with Alan and Ramon. I plan, coordinate, juggle, change priorities and strictly guard our maxim that a deadline that has been definitely set has to be met. I also correct proofs. Every piece of artwork passes through my hands and every job is checked by me. In between, I also still type stencils. We are always madly busy and in need of extra help, which we cannot afford.

These days Rachel comes to me, every Friday afternoon, carrying pay packets for all of us. Only at the end of each month do I visit her with a list of our turnover figures. I sometimes run into Norm there and fill him in on how things are going. Norm is still clearly the main puppeteer, even though he has other things on his mind. He agrees with me that we need more help. He promises to take care of this personally. Alan receives assistance, first part-time then full-time, from an experienced printer: a very tall, blonde, young man with huge muscled arms called Brian. He laughs a lot and works like a slave. Kathleen is assisted by a mousy junior, who follows her about like a shadow.

And then electric typewriters are bought and we make the acquaintance of Alexa. Our offset master sheets are typed by Alexa from now on. She is installed together with her machines in Ramon's spacious studio. Alexa is American. Her waist is tiny, her wrists fragile; she has a pointed face with beautifully eye-lashed dark eyes – natural eyelashes, not made up – and wears her black hair in a bun. She looks as if the slightest puff of wind could blow her off her feet, but she types faultlessly, very fast and is unshakably serene. Nothing causes her to panic. She believes in alternative medicine and acupuncture, in the influence of the stars on human lives and that regular fasting is healthy. She is a vegetarian.

"I'm sharing my studio with a rabbit!" Ramon complains to me, "She eats salad leaves for lunch, with raw carrots for dessert. She sits nibbling in the corner for half an hour – it's unsettling, believe me!"

"But she's a darling," I laugh, "And she handles so much work. She is worth her weight in gold."

"Well, that isn't a great deal! Have you seen her boyfriend? He's more mind than matter too. Where on earth did Norm find those two?" Alexa's boyfriend comes every afternoon to pick her up. He is not much bulkier than she is. Ramon discovers that he also believes in an alternative lifestyle and shares all Alexa's opinions. We had no inkling then that our dear Norm was building a new career in that area...

My new assistant is called Jan. Brenda had suddenly announced that she was leaving to get married. Jan has no connection with Norm. I select her myself from the train of gum-chewing, heavily made up girls who to my surprise turn up in answer to our ad. She comes from a country family and has a fresh, round, happy face, and wears no makeup. She sees life in Sydney as a dream come true, and the city streets as paved with promise. She lives in a tiny flat, which she shares with two other working girls. She turns out to be quick, clever, neat, down to earth and irrepressibly sunny. Soon she is picking up the phone, teaching herself to type stencils and ordering me to take a proper lunch-break. She talks to customers at the counter, makes sure that interruptions are kept to a minimum if I am working on a complicated quote, and whenever possible she sings. In this way, I learn all the songs from the current hit parade. Moreover, she is popular and gets on with everyone. In other words, Jan is the perfect assistant.

Australia transfers to decimals. Pounds, shillings and pence become dollars and cents, and yards and inches become metres and centimetres. These are golden times for printing companies. Our client base continues to expand, and so does our turnover.

And day after day, Alan slaves away in his dark cave to the rattle and roar of his machines, amid the smell of oil, ink and terps. Alan is gentle, quiet and kind, a true comrade who always has time to listen, whose patience seems inexhaustible. His greatest hobby seems to be surfing, at the crack of dawn in the mornings and in the weekends. The sea, the ocean is his great love. (He still lives near the ocean, in Avalon. The view from his veranda is breathtaking. But swimming is no longer an option. He needs to protect himself from the sun: he regularly undergoes treatment for skin cancer).

He is married to Hilary, young, blonde, pretty and dissatisfied with her lot. They have two little boys. Hilary likes luxury. She wants more money. She wants to rise on the social ladder, and reproaches Alan for not being ambitious enough, something Alan does not know how to deal with. A few years later Hilary will disappear to New Guinea with a new husband. But at the time I am writing about, this was in the distant future.

And at that time Alan and I never discussed personal matters, until the day I had to go and talk to him – our careful, accurate Alan – about a job he had delivered, which contained mistakes. He is standing by the guillotine. He places a shining block of paper on the metal plate. The knife rises and falls, and he pushes the unwanted snippets of paper aside. Then all of a sudden he starts talking about home. About Hilary and what she expects of him. About how impossible it all is, about not being able to be himself, about how some people couldn't be happy with what they had. I want so much to put my arms around him then, ink-stained overalls and all. But at that moment Kathleen appears. "Can you spare Jan for an hour or so this afternoon? If I don't get any help we'll never finish binding that computer book on time."

"You need to order more paper," Alan says, suddenly businesslike again, "I've finished my quarto bond stock and we need more black ink."

Back in my office Jan pushes a pile of typed pages towards me, "Alexa brought these. They need to be proofed as soon as possible. And Ramon wants to talk to you. He needs more time for the flower brochure. And Mr. Johansson rang, he needs you to ring back. And a giant spec from Clement and Associates just came in." She stops to take a breath, the phone rings. "Torron Printing," she says, "One moment please," and to me "Price quote" at which I grab pen and paper, and take the phone.

That was the day Johansson asked whether we could supply his computer books a day earlier than we had agreed – that is, that evening – just a few advance copies, surely that would be possible? At which not only Jan, but Alexa, Ramon, Jimmy and I dropped everything we were doing and helped out in the binding department.

It was also the day that Oscar popped his head round the door, just as we were preparing to go home. Oscar was a six-foot tall, painfully shy Australian, with a hare lip, who owned the marketing office upstairs. He regularly gave us work. He was blushing profusely, and came to tell us that Norm had told him to give our number to his best clients so that we could take messages for him whenever he needed to be out: "Only temporarily. I'm going to get a secretary."

"As if we don't have enough to do already," said Jan, after he had left, "Mr. Waters must worry we are getting bored!"

The next morning, as if Jan's remark had released the genie from the bottle, Norm appeared, a rushed Norm who seemed totally uninterested in the daily affairs of Torron. He came to tell me that he intended to open a homeopathic consultancy in the empty office upstairs at the back. That I would be getting a second phone, a separate line, an extension of his phone upstairs, so that I could take messages for him.

"So now it really will become a madhouse here," was Jan's dry comment, "Ah well, no-one could call this a boring office! We never know from one day to the next what is going to happen. What on earth is a homeopathic consultancy!?"

Alan told us that Norm had been involved with homeopathy for years. That people visited him at home for health advice, and that he now wanted to take it to a more professional level. We also acquired a new client: The Society for the Promotion of Homeopathy, which gave rise to regular discussions among Torron staff about the pros and cons of homeopathy.

In the meantime, a consulting room was created upstairs. A Persian carpet covering almost the entire floor was installed. A vast mahogany desk was placed in front of the windows so that when you entered the room you were confronted with an imposing black figure without a face, as the light streamed in from behind him, with a halo of black curls clustered around his shining, bald head. Tall mahogany bookcases were set up full of tomes about homeopathy, and a narrow table, covered in plastic, with a small pillow at one end was placed in the middle of the room. In a windowless alcove glass shelves were placed to house countless bottles, jars and packets, all without labels. The alcove smelled of dried herbs. Every now and then a hefty lady with wild, grey curls would spend hours in the alcove, working in the light of two bright lamps. Later, when Oscar had moved to a larger office in the city, she moved into his room and opened a kind of herb store there.

"What on earth is he doing?" I asked Alan, "It's a kind of quackery."

"Well, it's his business, not ours. You know Norm. He isn't happy if he isn't dabbling in at least ten different things at the same time. It's not a bad thing that he is so absorbed in this – at least he leaves us in peace."

In the beginning, Jan would keep careful track of whoever went upstairs once Norm's "practice" was officially open for business: an unhealthy looking young man with waist-length hair; a little, bent, old lady who could barely get up the stairs; a sophisticated woman in a spectacular outfit and wearing heavy eyeliner; a man on crutches. But we soon lost interest. Though an Alice in Wonderland atmosphere remained, at least for me; I felt like a character in a story someone else had written.

I also need to mention Giuseppe and Maria, the owners of the large advertising agency in the spacious room opposite Ramon's studio, called Intersect. It was thanks to Giuseppe and Maria that we could make our trip back to Holland at the end of 1968 on the (later, infamous) ocean liner, the *Achille Lauro*. And they got us a hefty discount on the tickets. Giuseppe was Italian; Maria was American. They were both middle-aged. He was tall and dark, but already greying; she was small, plump and blonde. They had no staff then, but did everything themselves. They seldom left the office before midnight and often worked in the weekends. They brought us a lot of printing work. They would later move to the city, to a large glass and steel office with staff to do their bidding.

There came a day that Maria, talking about Italy – her spiritual home, she said – about the Renaissance, about art, told me her life story. She was a history teacher in Texas and had gone on holiday to Rome where she had met Giuseppe. They had decided to start a new life together in a new world, to set off on their own personal Romeo and Juliet flight. But they both still viewed the Italian way of life as the ideal way to live. Which did not mean that they did not believe passionately in hard work and the so-called American dream: from newspaper boy to millionaire! A dream they managed to make a reality.

We visited them at their home once, Gerard and I. Maria had invited us to come and taste how wonderful an Italian spaghetti meal could be. At her insistence, we took the whole family. I can recall that Maria draped an Indian sari around Janneke, which she had picked up on one of her trips, before the beginning of her Italian adventure. And couldn't I see how beautiful Janneke looked?

They lived in an old, quintessentially Australian house, which they had renovated together. The high veranda was draped with vines full of bunches of yellow grapes. The backyard (somewhere below it, the ocean glittered) consisted of tiled terraces, which moved down the hill, surrounded by masses of bougainvillea and jacaranda plants. Cleverly situated lamps lit the red and purple flowers when it became dark. There were also rose beds in all sorts of shades, pergolas dripping with roses, graceful little white balustrades and white, glazed, wrought-iron garden furniture.

Inside everything was white. The walls, doors and floors were all white, which created a sense of light, air and space. There was little furniture but what there was, was clearly antique. Underneath the house Giuseppe had created a wine cellar complete with Italian arches. We walked amongst the racks of ruby red and golden yellow bottles, resting between blocks of sandstone. Gerard swore that he too adored the Italian way of life! And the spaghetti was indeed delicious.

We also once went to Norm's, or rather Rachel's house in Castle Crag, without the children and together with the Torron staff for a barbecue. Castle Crag was then, and probably still is, a very elite suburb ("How the other half lives!" Gerard called it). It was an enormous, modern house, but I only remember the under-floor heating, which impressed me hugely at the time and was very unusual in Sydney. I believe I discovered then that Rachel was Norm's second wife and that her two almost grown up sons were her children, not his.

I am listening to Rachel who is telling me that Torron is doing very well, but that we can certainly grow more. And to Alan, who is unusually depressed that evening. He is afraid that Norm is transferring Torron income to his new practice. I am too tired to worry about this. I am not particularly interested in the financial structure of the company anyway. Just as long as our salaries are paid, I have no problem with how the company is organised.

Moreover, I am feeling particularly grateful to Norm. Shortly prior to this, when I had hurt my black and could barely walk, Norm arranged an appointment for me with a personal friend of his, a manual therapist, in his own private hospital. I spent a day and a night there, and this man straightened my back under anesthetic. We were never sent a bill for this. I have never forgotten this treatment or Norm's generosity. My back problems (lumbago, according to our GP) started just after we had moved. I can remember vaguely that I had to lie flat for days then. But after the treatment Norm arranged for me, I had no more problems for years.

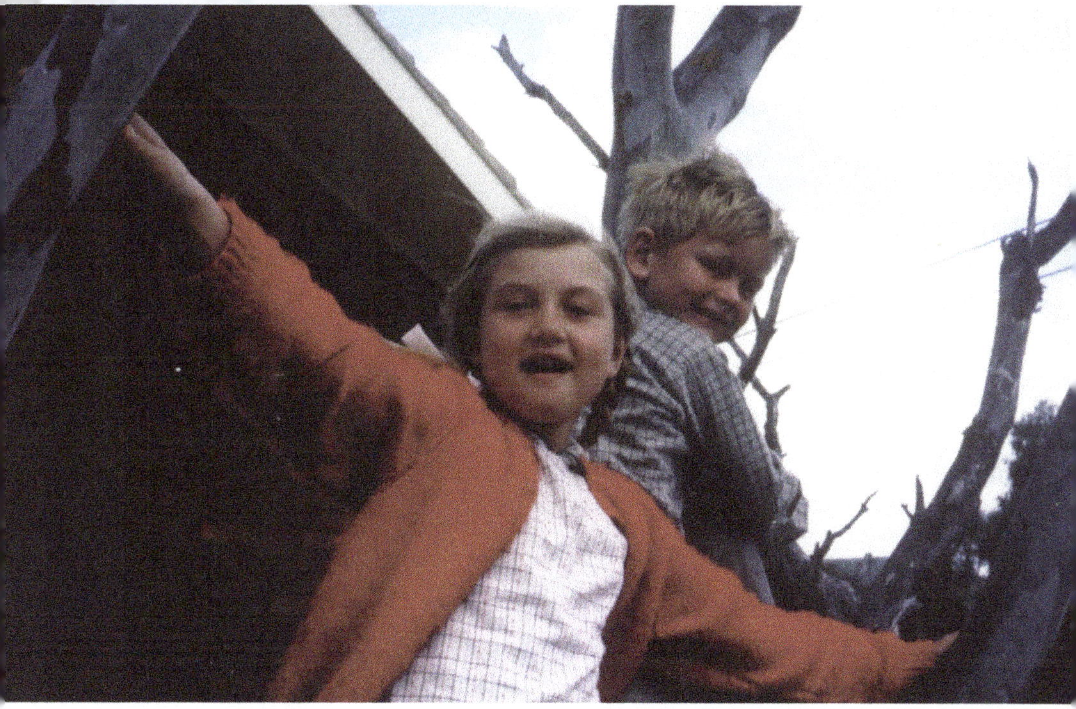

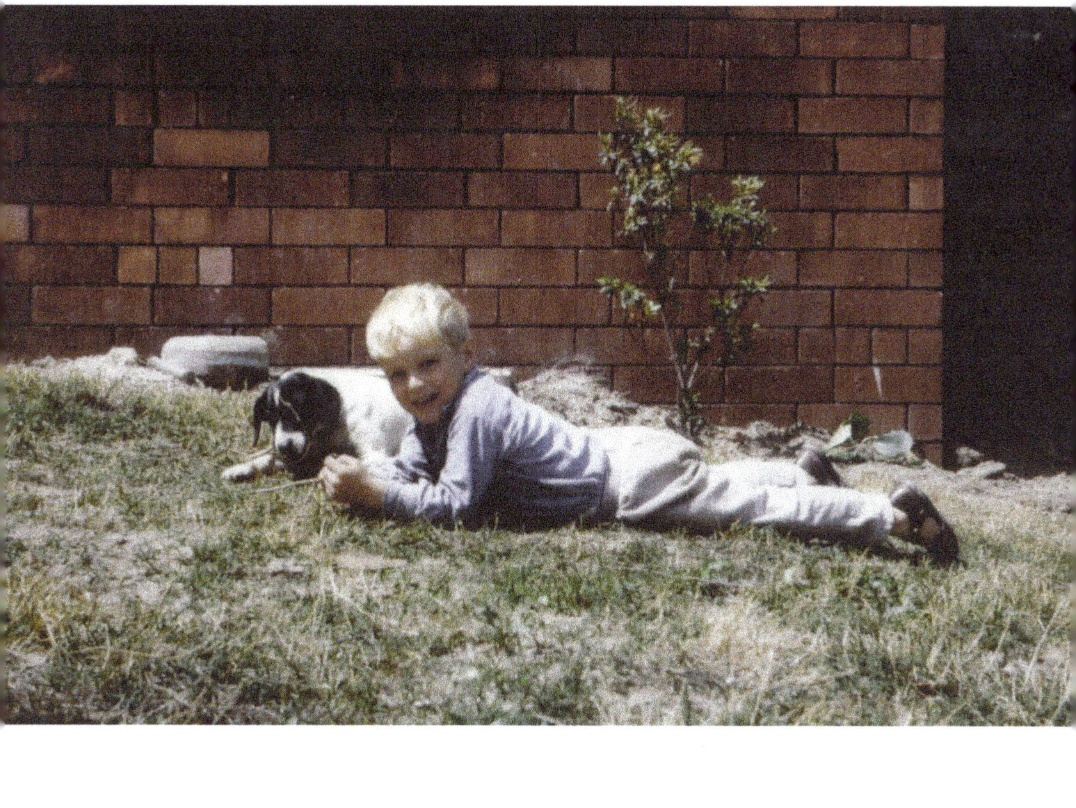

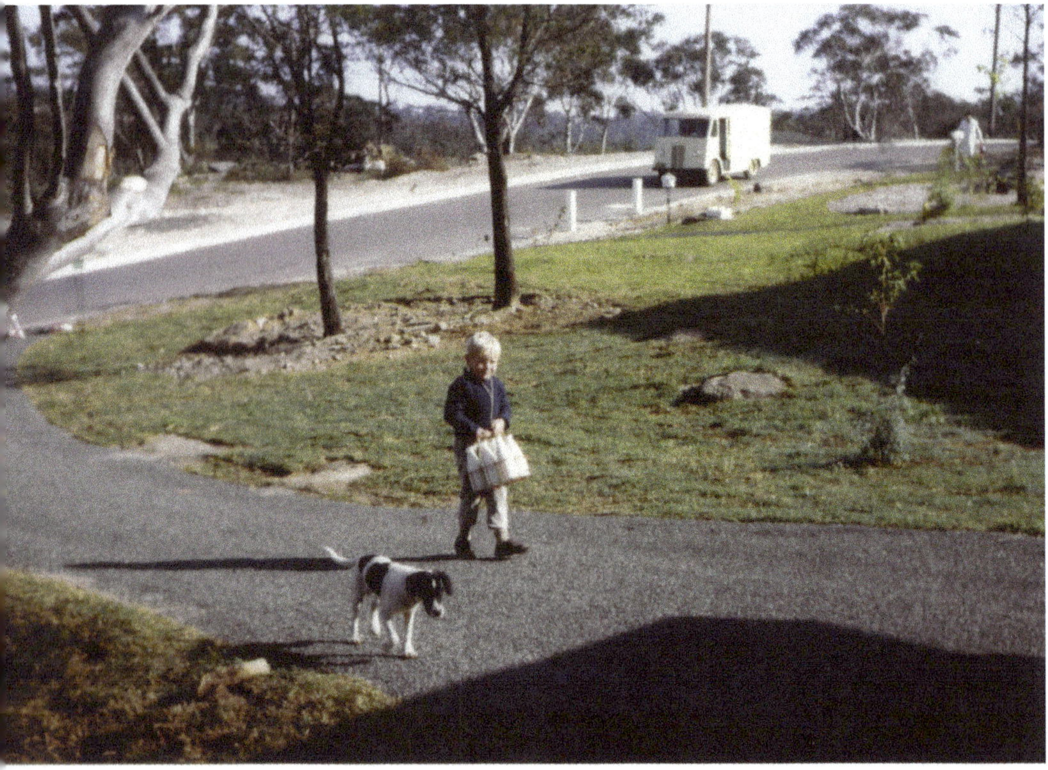

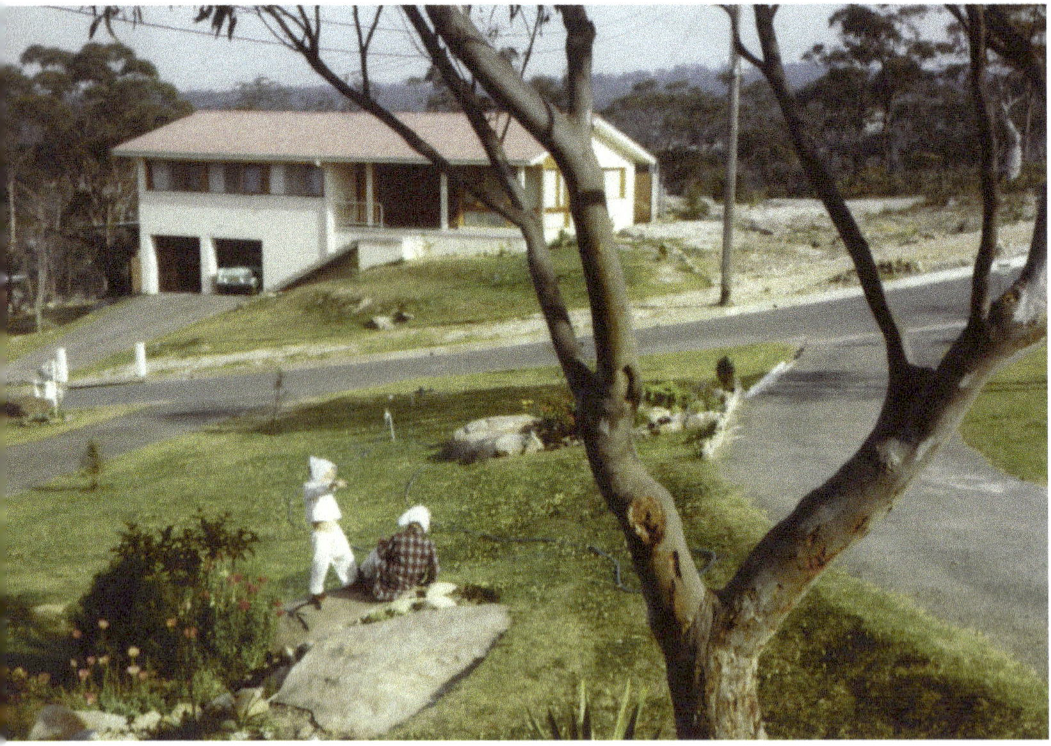

CHAPTER 31

Life in Turramurra

THAT A COMPUTER *is an inanimate object, a soulless piece of equipment, I know perfectly well. And yet – unlike an old-fashioned typewriter, it makes demands of you. It imposes its will on you as if it were a living being. You can't just up and leave it for one thing, you need to save your work first otherwise mysterious things happen to it. And if you do not follow the computer's rules, if you ignore its protocols, it punishes you. It is like a strict father figure, at least to me. And then there are the unpredictable things that can happen. It can lose your work, pick up a virus, crash altogether. It can completely refuse to do your bidding. Of course, I know I should make more effort to understand it better. Perhaps then I might have some sense of control. But I doubt whether I am capable of that, and, moreover, I don't have the time. What time I have I want to devote to finishing this book.*

Time. Time past – it is such a strange expression. Is it the same as lost time? An even stranger expression: how can time be lost? It is always here and it is always now.

Turramurra on a winter's day: a day like today. It is almost eight o'clock in the morning. I am plaiting Janneke's hair in the family room as fast as I can. "Don't make it so tight, Mum! It's too tight. You're pulling it too hard!" She is wearing a dark red school uniform with a row of gleaming red buttons running down the front. She is holding dark, red ribbons up for me to use. She hops impatiently from one red-socked, ten-year-old leg to another. "Hurry up, Mum! Where's my lunch? Lindy! Where's my lunch?"

"Stand still!" I command, "Your lunch is on the table. Where's your hat? You haven't left it at school again, have you?"

Lindy comes running in, struggling to carry two school bags and two school hats with broad brims, her hair cascading around her shoulders. She wears an identical uniform, but a few sizes smaller: the uniform of Mount St Bernard, the Catholic girls' school in Pymble. "Here's your hat, Jan."

I start a second set of plaits; thankfully, Lindy stands still. Will we make the eight o'clock school bus? Will I miss my train? "Put on your blazer, it's cold!" I call to Janneke, who is already half out of the door, "Where have the boys got to?"

"They're outside," Lindy tells me, "Bobby forgot his cap. There it is."

I run from door to door, checking that everything is locked. I hear Timmy barking. I hear Gerard honking the horn, impatiently. I grab my handbag and Bobby's cap. I run outside, following Lindy. Paul is on his knees next to the car, he has his arms around Timmy. "You can't come, Timmy, it isn't allowed. We have to go to school!" Next to him Bobby is twirling himself around, his little school bag held away from his body, humming like an irritated wasp. I grab him and put his cap on his head. The boys wear brown uniforms: dark brown shorts, light brown shirts and a tie, dark brown sweaters, and caps, of course, also dark brown. "Hurry up, boys, run!" The bus stop is on Kissing Point Road, which means a run up Parkinson Avenue to the corner, about two hundred meters uphill.

"No!" cries Paul, "We're allowed to drive today. Daddy says we can come in the car."

"Hurry up!" says Gerard, holding the car doors open. It is a windy day. We sit on top of each other in the car until the bus stop is reached. The bus full of chattering schoolchildren is about to leave. There is no time for goodbye kisses. I push my children onto it and wave. And then Gerard and I race to the station. Miraculously, I arrive with a whole minute to spare! I stand on the platform amid crowds of commuters. My raincoat flaps in the wind. The tree tops wave wildly. In my head, I am making a list of the shopping I need to do at lunchtime: meat, bread, cereal...

The train: men hidden behind morning newspapers; a group of girls going to work, twittering like a cage full of birds; a small army of boys in school uniforms with fuzz on their top lips, flat straw hats on their heads, blue school blazers with sleeves that are too short and scratched school bags. One station after another flashes past the windows. And then we are in North Sydney and I dive through the traffic of the Pacific Highway as usual and turn the corner into Mount Street.

Every afternoon at four o'clock I stop being the manageress of Torron Printing and Duplicating for a little while. At four o'clock I speak to my children, by phone, and Jan makes sure no-one disturbs me. One after the other they all come to the phone to tell me what has happened to them that day, and I rejoice or sympathise with them, and settle any arguments along the way. This is afternoon teatime at home. The children eat something (usually cereal), drink something (milk), play outside (stay close to the house!) and watch television (cartoons). I may be a full hour's travel time away but in this way I can be there for them when they get out of school.

That afternoon the unimaginable happens. The first thing Janneke says is: "Bobby's gone, Mummy."

"What do you mean – Bobby is gone!? Where is he?"

"He wasn't in the bus and Paul doesn't know where he is either."

"Put Paul on the phone," my mouth has suddenly gone dry.

"Bobby wasn't there!" Paul complains, "And now Janneke is cross with me! I looked for him and he wasn't there and so I went home."

"But how could that happen? Is he still at school?"

"I don't know."

Janneke comes back to the phone, "When Lindy and I got onto the bus there was only Paul."

"I'm calling the school," I say, "Go and look at the bus stop. Maybe he came back on the second bus." The school does not pick up. I wait a few minutes and ring Janneke again. She is back, panting and now crying a little. "He isn't there! He wasn't in the second bus. What's happened to him, Mummy? It's almost dark."

"Daddy?" I ask, hopelessly. Gerard is almost never home before dark. And I have no idea where to reach him, "Is Daddy home?"

"No, of course not. What should we do? Where's Bobby?"

"Calm down. I'll try the school again and if that doesn't work I'll ring the police. We'll find him. I want you to stay quietly at home, okay?"

The school still does not pick up. I call Turramurra police station. I explain what has happened and they promise to warn a patrol car in our neighbourhood straightaway. I give them the Torron number.

And then there is nothing more I can do. I sit at my desk, biting my nails. My heart is hammering. My throat hurts. Kathleen comes in. Jan whispers something to her. She disappears. Alan comes in. He pats me on the shoulder: "Do you want to go home?" I shake my head. I can barely see him. A nightmarish yellow mist surrounds everything around me. Our lights are on but that doesn't help. "I have to stay here," I say dully, "I have to stay at the phone. There is no point in going anywhere."

And then the longest half hour of my life begins. The minutes drag by. And I sit and I wait. The phone rings twice, clients. I try to get rid of them politely, promising to ring back.

The third phone-call is Bobby: "Why did you have to ring the police, Mummy? You knew I'd come home! I had to walk." He is five years old.

It feels as if a giant hand has just pulled me back from the edge of a monstrous abyss.

"Walk?! All the way from Pymble?" Along the Pacific Highway! Miles and miles of madly rushing cars in gathering darkness; a little boy in a dark uniform, walking along the edge of the road where there were almost no footpaths. He is crying. "The sister threw my marbles out of the window! I had to find them and then the bus was gone."

"Did you find them?" I ask, fighting back tears and laughter.

Heartrending sobs. "They're gone! All my marbles are gone!" And then suddenly he is calm and says with obvious pride: "I knew how to walk. And then Peter Barnes came. He's got a new racing bicycle! And he took me on it! He brought me home."

Peter Barnes is the 15-year-old son of one of our neighbours and my boys admire him hugely. Oh, angelic, sensible saviour, Peter Barnes! "You are never, never to do that again, darling! No matter what happens you have to go home with Paulie."

Janneke takes over: "I told him off, Mum. He won't do it again. But Paul was very bad too! He should have waited for him."

"Sweetheart, we'll talk about all of that when I'm home. Now you have to be nice to each other. Why don't you give Bobby a bath and then you can all watch television?"

"But Mum, I think... You mean we can watch all the cartoons we want? Can we watch as long as we want?"

"Just this once."

"And that is the absolute limit!" says Gerard that evening when he hears the story, "We're taking the boys out of that nun's school! We'd have to do that anyway once they're too old for kindergarten. We'll put them in the school on Kissing Point Road. It's just around the corner. All the neighbourhood kids go there. I've heard it's an excellent kindergarten and primary school. And it'll save us a lot of money."

Both Paul and Bob accept this change without demur. They find themselves in a new environment with new rules, but they know many of their new schoolmates already. I seem to recall that Paul told me about a Mr. Grey (head of the school) who was very strict and threatened punishment with his ruler. And that Timmy accompanied them to school one day, trotting all the way into the classroom; Paul had to take him home again because he refused to leave. The brown uniforms became (much cheaper) grey uniforms. And Paul now went to school with the front door key hanging on a string around his neck just like Janneke, which was a great source of pride to him. And my children's half hour in the office was split into two. Just after three Paul would ring, and an hour later, Janneke.

Paul was always in a great hurry to get off the phone. There were so many fascinating things he needed to do, so many important tasks that required his attention, so many friends waiting for him. "We're building a billy cart, Mum. I'm helping Peter and Wayne! Here's Bobby." Bobby was often even briefer: "I gotta feed Timmy, Mum."

When Janneke got home she would usually give me a conscientious report of what the boys were doing at that moment: "Everything's fine, Mum. They're outside. They're trying out the billy cart with a whole group of boys. It goes really fast!" in a reassuring tone. At which I would do my best to banish from my mind visions of how things were going out there on Parkinson Avenue hill. A wooden cart on old pram wheels, careering wildly down the hill – hitting the curb, hitting a tree, ambulance sirens, blood everywhere... None of this happened. I never again received a horror telephone call like the one following Bobby's disappearance, an incident that still makes my palms sweat and my heart beat faster as I write about it.

For the boys those years in Turramurra were a huge adventure: they had space, freedom and endless possibilities for play. There were places in the bush they regarded as their private property, to which they gave secret names. Admittedly, Bobby went through a period in which his favourite pastime was to sit in a large cardboard box on the drive, completely on his own. But he also made determined attempts to teach himself to jump as high as the carport roof or onto a convenient tree branch where he could perform daring feats. And of course experimenting with the billy cart was another favourite game. Paul loved even more to experiment and tried to be as brave and as enterprising as his real life heroes: Peter Barnes and Peter's pal of around the same age, Wayne.

I discovered one Saturday, sometime after the billy cart had begun to lose its appeal, that the older neighbourhood boys were building a hut among the branches of a giant eucalyptus tree in the bush at the bottom of our street. The tree had nestled its roots into a crack in the rocky floor of a shallow gully, and overlooked a kind of miniature ravine.

Peter and Wayne are hammering and sawing busily up in the tree. They had already built a kind of platform. They had pulled themselves and the smaller boys up there by means of a long rope. Bobby had politely declined an invitation to be hoisted up, but Paul had grabbed the opportunity with gusto.

He is sitting precariously on a rickety plank stuck between two branches when I arrive. My heart almost misses a beat when I see him. My panicked command to him to come down at once is met with deep indignation from him and utter amazement by the hut inhabitants. "All my mates are working up there!" he protests as soon as he reaches the ground. (The mates have now disappeared strategically among the leaves. All the hammering has stopped.)

His t-shirt is torn and covered in green stains. Twigs and leaves are sprinkled through his wet hair and his freckled face is black. Along his bare legs run long, bloody scratches. "I'm never allowed to do anything!" is his bitter complaint at my insistence that he stay safely on the ground with Bobby.

"You're allowed to climb trees that aren't overlooking ravines! Why don't you build a hut on the ground? Here, among the bushes?"

"Oh, Mum!" I can still hear the bitter disdain in his voice at my lack of understanding.

Looking back, I realise I wanted very much to be a perfect mother, full of wisdom, attention, utterly calm, which I certainly was not. But life consisted of juggling work and home – housekeeping, children, the endless battle to stay organised, to keep in touch with what was going on when I was not at home. And then trying to see friends, though the latter could be combined more easily with my working life. So I would constantly feel that I was failing as a parent.

There was one thing Gerard and I always agreed on completely, and that was the fact that we could only really give our children immaterial things. We needed to make sure they were fully developed people. So Janneke received violin lessons at school, because we had been told she had a great aptitude for music and perfect pitch. She also took horse-riding lessons and tennis lessons.

Lindy went to an acting class. She showed great acting talent and had a rich imagination. So we enrolled her into a youth acting club, which was associated with The Independent Theatre. Paul loved sports so when a youth rugby club was set up in Turramurra we made him a member, at his urgent request. And Bobby? Bobby preferred to be an onlooker. He wasn't too keen on sports and certainly not on group activities as a child (yet years later in Holland he would insist on going to the sports academy, and has become a tennis coach and physiotherapist).

Turramurra acquired a brand new library, situated at the crossing of Kissing Point Road and the Pacific Highway. We became regular customers. We borrowed mainly children's books. Books to read aloud. Lindy loved reading. The boys certainly did not; Janneke was undecided. But they all adored being read to...

A warm, early, Sunday morning: we are on our way to the beach. No longer Balmoral, but Mona Vale, which is now closer by and is moreover an ocean beach with surf, which our children find much more exciting nowadays. We are in a traffic jam on Mona Vale Road.

It is already hot in the car. In the back squirm our four bathing-costume-clad children.

Bobby is trying to wriggle onto the ledge underneath the back window where till recently he fit easily. Paul is hanging out of the window, his chest bare, waving noisily at other children in other cars. Lindy is trying to create order among her toys. She always takes a great many things with her whenever we go anywhere – a few dolls, a box of beads, a book, a favourite, old swimming ring. Janneke, leaning forward between us, is counting cars and complaining loudly. "I am so hot! I am boiling!"

"Why don't you sing?" I suggest, at my wit's end. They sing and we sing along with them. First a whole lot of English children's songs, then *Waltzing Matilda* – all the verses – then theme songs from their favourite television shows, and then, thank God, we start to drive again. The glitter of moving cars, asphalt and white dust hurts my eyes. And then, at last, ahead of us is the beautiful Pacific Ocean. Colossal waves rise and break into vast fields of foam. Only experienced surfers ride those waves. The beach is already busy; there are lots of families with small children. We find a wide, open spot on the warm, red sand. We put up our beach umbrella and spread out our towels.

Janneke has already disappeared into the water. She jumps into the surf and dives. I see her wildly swimming along with a wave, which comes speeding into shore. Janneke is our best swimmer. Lindy is almost as good but she is more careful. They were both members of a swimming club in Balmoral where they learned to swim and where Janneke took part in competitions every now and then. Now that we live in Turramurra all that is over. The boys are just learning to swim.

Lindy and Paul race at the waves, but jump back just in time to avoid the water. Bobby is playing with a car at a safe distance from the surf. Gerard and I lie under the umbrella. I envision vast, green, glass walls crashing; I am afraid of this kind of surf.

Suddenly there is a loud, high-pitched siren: shark alarm. The sea empties quickly, as if swept clear by a vast magical broom. The children dance excitedly around us. "Here come the lifesavers!" Half a dozen bronzed young men with red and yellow bathing caps push a surfboat into the surf, jumping in as they go. The boat plunges like a cat amongst the waves, taking one breaker after another until it reaches quiet blue water. We wait. A helicopter circles high above our heads. Minutes later the boat – now tiny in the distance – waves a yellow flag and the all-clear siren sounds.

A mass of swimmers plunges back into the sea, Janneke and Paul amongst them.

Lindy hesitates, dawdles. "The lifesavers really have chased the shark away," I tell her, reassuringly. "I'm going to play with Bobby," she decides.

When we drive back home late that afternoon we come across a bushfire. Bushfires are part of every summer, but you cannot comprehend fully what a bushfire is until you have experienced that blood-red, shimmering column of fire ahead of you: a fire snake that raises itself up high, spirals wildly, and curls down, then jumps up again into another treetop. Until you have smelt the acrid smoke, heard the growl, hiss and spit, broken by an occasional explosion and felt the indescribable heat even at a distance of well over a hundred meters. Until you have seen firefighters with blackened faces, slashing away at brushwood and digging ditches, amid the vicious sparks. There are houses close by. We see men standing on their roofs with garden hoses, trying to keep them wet.

The fire is only raging on one side of the road and we are told that it will probably not jump to the other side. The wind is blowing in the right direction. We can drive on therefore. I want to get away as quickly as possible, but Gerard and the children are fascinated, and don't want to leave. We stay for about ten minutes, watching.

Tomorrow the earth here will be covered in a thick layer of blackness with here and there a blackened tree stump emerging. It is impossible to imagine that when the time is right leaves will begin to appear on those stumps, that the crippled bush will begin to grow again. That in a year's time all signs of the fire raging here will have disappeared. These are the mysterious natural laws of this country.

But I am not thinking about next year. Fire fills me with terror. It is the greatest horror I can imagine. I remember those walls of fire following a bombardment in Nijmegen – that all-destroying, uncontrollable violence.

Another hot Sunday, but this time we stay at home. We are picnicing in our garden, dressed in swimsuits, underneath the beach umbrella. Lindy devises a cooling down game for the boys with the garden hose. They run screaming straight through the stream of water, they dance underneath it. In the meantime, Gerard is mowing the lawn with our ancient lawnmower, which he has managed to get hold of at a rock-bottom price. His eyes are red-rimmed with hay-fever. Every few minutes he stops to use his inhaler. Asthma is also part of every summer, even though he claims to know exactly how to control it now. He is now an experienced asthma veteran and thinks the garden is much more important. He mows and sprays, plants, prunes and builds rock walls, and even stairs, if necessary.

The whole of Turramurra hums with lawnmowers on Sundays. Everywhere garden refuse is being burned and relaxed neighbours chat, unless a fire hazard warning has been issued. In that case no fires are allowed and even barbecues are vetoed, which happens regularly in the summer.

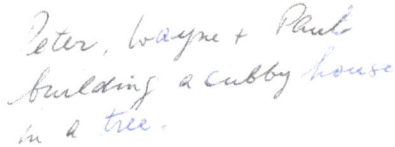

Peter, Wayne + Paul building a cubby house in a tree.

Mum + Phons watching

CHAPTER 32

Hill End

BREDA, 3 JANUARY *2002: four weeks have gone by since I last worked on this text. And once again I feel I have to fight to get back to that other world. I know it is there. I know that "then" and "now" are two sides of one coin, but to flip that coin costs a great deal of effort and I am tired. I don't know whether I can still do it.*

First, just before Christmas, I had back troubles again, which meant I could not sit normally. By the time this had passed, it was Christmas. Christmas Day in Paul's house: masses of presents, excited grandchildren and a wonderful Christmas dinner. But Hanneke was sick and spent the day in bed. Then there were Gerard's palpitations and his heart procedure here in Breda.

It is very cold today; last night the temperature dropped below zero. All the cars in the parking lot below our kitchen window are covered in a layer of frost. But the sun is shining; it will be a beautiful winter's day. In the meantime, vast bushfires rage in Australia, in the area around Sydney. Janneke tells us about temperatures of 38 degrees and a strong, scalding wind. The fires have almost reached Turramurra.

Against a wall in our living room stands a piano; it is the first thing you see on your left as you come in through the front door of our house in Parkinson's Avenue. Paul is standing next to Gerard while he is playing. I hear his high voice: "I like that Daddy!" Was it Beethoven's *Für Elise* or Mozart's *Turkish March*?

The piano was Patsy's. We were borrowing it for a little while. I think it was because Phons and Patsy were moving to Melbourne. Phons had been promoted. He was being made a supervisor in Victoria. He passionately hoped that he and Pasty would start a new life there, that a page would be turned. Which did indeed happen, but not in the way Phons hoped: Phons and Patsy separated in Melbourne.

Melbourne also reminds me of Jane who suddenly turned up one weekend. Was this because of her divorce proceedings? I can't remember. I do remember that she had definitely divorced Peter at long last. She came to tell us that Guus was in Karachi and that she would be going there soon too, together with her children. Guus and Jane were married in Karachi.

But I really want to go back to the things we did with the children. We only went on holiday once; that is, we went away from home together for three days, during the winter holidays – an exciting and unusual occurrence. We went to Hill End, an abandoned gold-rush town about 300 km from Sydney, which in the time of the gold-rush around 1880 had boasted over 4000 inhabitants. We went, after much urging from them, to visit Dick and Alice who had moved there and who now ran the only general store in the surrounding area.

Because I was too caught up in Torron affairs, I had missed the launch of Dick's boat in The Spit. Gerard and Phons had been there. They gave me a colourful account afterwards of how the boat had turned out to be less watertight than expected. Urgent repairs took place, and then, all of a sudden, the boat was sold. Dick and Alice had decided to escape the big city by moving to the country. They bought the general store in Hill End. "We're hoping to find a bit of the real Australia left there," said Alice, "There are 47 people living in the town. But all the famers in the surrounding area depend on the general store, so we should be able to make good money." They bought a secondhand truck, filled it with their few belongings, and left.

Alice writes to me often. She writes me long, witty letters. The shop is booming. She has become a member of the country women's association. She describes meetings in the school, located next to the graveyard, with weather-beaten famers' wives and the schoolteacher who must have been about sixty and teaches at least six different classes single-handedly. Tiny classes, admittedly, but still. Alice helps to organise an arts and crafts fair, she takes a first aid course, she becomes a correspondent for *The Bathurst Courier* (Bathurst is the closest city, about 40 km away. The bus there goes twice a week). The old truck is indispensable, she writes. Doctor, dentist, hospital – they are all in Bathurst. She describes a night drive with a toddler running a high fever and a drive with a neighbour's boy who had broken his leg. And of course she helps out in the shop. She and Dick run it together. "You should come and take a look! In the winter we have a second house at our disposal. You can all stay in a bungalow opposite us for free. The climate here is so healthy. It freezes at night and we sometimes get snow!"

By this time we had excellent arrangements in place for the school holidays. Gerard and I both had one week off in August and two weeks in the summer. We alternate taking time off, and for the weeks that are left we can call on Jan's younger sister who is now studying in Sydney and is always looking for ways of earning extra money. She is 17 and her name is Anne. She can cook, is sensible and reliable, and our children adore her. She is their holiday mother.

But even she cannot compete with possibly seeing snow and visiting Alice. We are united in our wish to embark on this adventure. I collect sweaters and blankets, milk and coffee, sandwiches and fruit. I try to make Timmy realise that Anna Smith will be looking after him for a few days. Timmy gets carsick and so cannot possibly come along on the trip. He sadly watches us leave, one black ear hanging down despondently.

We need to drive over the Blue Mountains. It is bitterly cold. The sky is an icy blue. The wind howls through the rock masses. The light is white. The rocks are like rows of grey teeth and the immense mountains throw huge, black shadows. Our children huddle together on the back seat, blankets pulled up to their chins.

Bathurst was founded in 1815. It lies on the southern shore of the Macquarie River, 2200 feet above sea level. It has 17.000 inhabitants and two cathedrals, and seems – to us – to be all empty, windy streets so wide that a herd of cattle could be herded through them easily. We then bump and rattle down a hard-baked, dirt road, through a surreal, flat, grey-yellow moon landscape. The road runs straight through a riverbed, where piles of slate lie crazily on top of each other surrounded by small pools of water. The car climbs up the other shore with difficulty. Was that the Macquarie River?

The road becomes paved again. We come across a weather-beaten sign: Hill End, 20 miles. We drive through a bushfire forest. There are skeletal, black trees standing sentinel along the road. The light here is grey. There is not a blade of grass to be seen. No birds sing. Even the wind holds its breath. Everything is dead and black – a ghost forest.

Then suddenly we enter normal, green, living bush. The road twists and turns. The sun has now sunk low and is orange red. And finally we see along the right side of the road a low, rectangular building, made in part of corrugated iron, in front of which stands a bright red petrol pump. Next to it, on a piece of land surrounded by a fence, stand two rusty water tanks, among knee-high weeds. A little further away are a car wreck, half a motorbike, a very old tractor and Alice's truck. Between two wooden poles hangs a freshly painted sign, which reads *Hill End General Store*.

Alice and I hug each other, the children jump up and down excitedly, and Gerard surveys his surroundings with raised eyebrows. "Where *is* Hill End?"

"We're in it!' Alice laughs, "The village is beyond the next bend in the road." She is browner, rounder and more compact, a small, energetic lady with black curls and very clear dark eyes. She is wearing a large, flowered apron over a thick, sheep's wool sweater and a worn pair of trousers.

We follow her in single file into the barracks. We are standing in a badly lit supermarket, which is filled to the rafters with merchandise. Near the entrance is a counter, which also serves as the bar of a milk-bar. Behind it are racks and shelves, packed with goods, with narrow paths running between them. Groceries, tinned food, yarn, material, tools, nails, screws, pens and toys: whatever you need, Alice says proudly, we stock! And she knows where everything is stored too, which impresses me greatly.

All the way in the back, in a chaotic office sits Dick, amidst newspapers, magazines, files, dusty piles of bills and dozens of cardboard boxes with mysterious contents. Behind him stands an enormous olive green metal safe. "This is where my gold is stored," he says, patting the thick safe door, "Do you want to see it?"

Dick is even skinnier than before and has become paler instead of browner. His Adam's apple protrudes far too much, I think. He has dark stubble on his chin. He is dressed in an old army jacket, old khaki trousers and muddied boots. He fishes a rusty-looking key out of his pocket and opens the door of the safe, which squeals in protest. Alongside an untidy pile of banknotes stands an open shoebox full of coins, and next to that is a whole row of leather pouches. "That's gold dust! I buy it from our local prospectors. There are still a few old diggers living here. They make a living by hunting for gold. And here's a nugget that was found here. It was included in the purchase of the house."

Gold! I hold the thing in my hand. It is not much bigger than my thumb, but very heavy. It doesn't even shine. It is a copper-coloured, dull, pockmarked lump.

"It's worth a lot of money," says Dick, "But I'm not selling it. I'm keeping it here. I've grown very fond of it."

"That isn't exactly a solid safe, mate," Gerard says, "A strong can opener could rid you of your gold pretty quickly!"

"It won't get stolen," Dick says, nevertheless closing the safe securely, "Do you know how we bring our takings to the Bathurst bank every week? I give them to the bus driver. I put the whole lot – money, gold dust – into a cotton bag and place it next to his feet every week before he drives off. He drops it off for me at the end of his trip. That's how things work here."

"Let's go home, gang," says Alice, "Who wants to drive with me in the truck?" All four children do of course, so I go along too. Gerard follows in our own car. Hill End lies in a bowl, surrounded by dark, ancient hills. We drive past pale yellow, treeless fields and undulating, dark green meadows. Here and there stands a house. We drive onto a dusty country road and pass one or two horses, a few pigs and a mass of clucking chickens, all roaming freely. "This is a common," Alice explains, expertly turning the steering wheel of the large truck. We drive very slowly, "A communal field. Don't be surprised if you find a cow looking through your window tomorrow morning. Fun, don't you think? I love it."

The road begins to move gently upwards. Alice's house stands against the edge of the bowl and amongst high trees. It is brown, a square wooden hut. And opposite it on the other side of the road is a small, white, wooden house on stilts. "That's where you'll be sleeping: four bunks and a double bed. Oh, and kids," to the children, once we have all got out of the truck, "Be very careful with water. Only flush the toilet when it's absolutely necessary. There's a drought here. Our water-tank is only half full. It should have rained a long time ago, but there hasn't been a drop for months."

She shows Gerard and I a deep hole and mounds of earth in their back garden. Dick is digging there in his spare time, searching for a well, which according to local legend should be there. "Once we've found it, our water problems will be over. We'll have our own water supply."

It is cold in Hill End. It is intensely cold everywhere, both inside and outside until Alice lights an enormous wood fire in the area that serves both as living room and kitchen. The flames leap into the chimney. The fire not only supplies warmth, it also supplies light once darkness begins to fall. There is no electricity. There are petroleum lamps. Alice cooks on butane gas, but creates a delicious meal for us.

"We live like gods here," says Dick, "You can see that, right? None of that 9 to 5 insanity. We're our own boss. We can run the shop however we want. We don't have set opening hours, and everyone is fine with that; really friendly people here. Who needs Sydney?!"

We go to bed early. We shuffle through the ink-black, icy night to the opposite side of the street. Gerard carries an oil lamp and I have a torch. There is no light anywhere. The trees around us groan in the sharp wind. The stars glitter; they are very close, fiercely cold. We pull sweaters on over our pyjamas. Our little house creaks and whispers and rustles all night long. Once the lamps are out, the darkness is so profound it is almost tangible.

But when we wake up everything around us shimmers. There are frost flowers on the windows. The grass is white. Trees and bushes are covered in a layer of hoarfrost and the sun is a delicate yellow. The children are speechless with ecstasy. When on top of all this a small herd of cows with tinkling bells around their necks wanders by just as we are leaving the house, their joy knows no bounds.

Alice's house smells of frying bacon. She gives us plates full of bacon and eggs, and the fire crackles exuberantly. Around eleven o'clock, when the sun yields some warmth and the frost has melted, we set off into the hills with Alice as our guide. "Stay on the path!" she warns, "There are loads of old mine shafts around here and if you fall into one of them no-one will ever be able to get you out. Some of them are hundreds of meters deep."

And it all looks so innocent! Charming little paths amidst bush overrun with blackberry bushes. Alice pulls a blackberry bush aside and shows us a circular hole in the ground, about three or four meters in circumference: a mine shaft which drops straight down into the depths of the earth. She throws a stone into it and tells us to listen. Only after a few seconds do we hear a soft thud. "That's how deep they are. Wherever there are blackberry bushes, that's where the mine shafts are. Nobody knows how many tourists have already disappeared down them." And we are surrounded on all sides by blackberry bushes! I keep a firm grip on the sleeve and collar of two loudly protesting boys.

We climb up to the top of a hill. We look out over vast, grey, bulging mountains that roll gently into the blue distance. They resemble giant, sleeping, prehistoric animals. "That's what gold country looks like," says Alice, "Tomorrow we'll go to Summer Hill Creek where the first gold was found. We can pan for gold! You can still find some there. Today we'll go to the old town."

We go back down into the valley: a ghost town, grey and dusty, nestling in a grey and dusty landscape. There are bumpy streets that are only paved here and there; they run amid rows of little square houses made of clay, propped up by crooked wooden beams: one-room houses where whole families lived. Some are still standing; some have been pulled down. Some streets consist only of rubble.

"Once upon a time there were 40 pubs here," Alice says, "And of course huge tent camps close to the mines." We visit the only pub that has survived. A small sandstone building that is not only a pub but also a museum. We stare at scales, ranging in size from miniscule (for gold dust) to man-high, with matching copper weights. We admire pickaxes, wooden buckets, cleavers, portable iron ovens. We peer at sepia photos of bearded men in leather, with wagons and horses. It is strange to find ourselves outside again in the light, silent emptiness surrounded by somber hills. There should be gently moaning ghosts floating around, but there is nothing but silence.

The next day we are all infected with gold fever. On the way to Summer Hill Creek we hunt avidly for lost nuggets. There are broken chunks of quarts lying around everywhere, glittering in the sun, some even containing so-called fool's gold. Alice shatters our illusions: they are worth nothing. Sadly, we don't come across a real nugget.

The creek is so shallow you can stand in it easily (we are all wearing rubber boots). The water is crystal clear and fast moving. A gold pan looks like a huge metal soup bowl without an edge. You scoop up mud with it and then shake it through the water. The water washes away the sand and what settles on the bottom should contain gold dust: easy peasy, or so we thought. We crouch intently, a few meters apart from each other, on slippery stones in the freezing, rushing water. We shake our pans and stare hopefully at the residue. Not the least sign of gold dust. All we end up with are disappointingly ordinary pebbles. We keep moving slowly, panning as we go, stream upwards.

After a while the children (all six of them) give up on the gold and try to catch little fish instead, which proves equally unsuccessful. So Alice begins to hand out the food she had taken along. Gerard and I are not interested in food; we keep on panning with determination. Until we meet, in a bend of the river, a legendary Australian swagman sitting on a rock. He must have been very old. His face is chestnut coloured and adorned with grey stubble. On his head is a green felt hat with a row of old corks hanging down from it, the bushman's method of keeping off the flies. He is wearing a fraying green sweater, an ancient leather jacket, and very muddied waders. He grins from ear to ear when he sees us. He has very few teeth.

"Hi Bill!" says Alice cheerfully. We have found a real-live prospector, one of Dick's suppliers of gold dust. I can't understand a word of what he mutters, but I get the impression that he finds my attempts to pan highly amusing. He gets off his rock. He takes the gold pan out of my hands. He crouches down; he scoops and shakes. And lo and behold, something shiny appears on the bottom of the pan. Gold dust! As minuscule as nail clippings, but gold nevertheless.

I rejoice. The children suddenly cluster around us. Paul and Bob push their pans towards the swagman in unison. Good old Bill crouches and fishes for each child. The communal catch is placed on a piece of paper in the sun to dry. Alice produces a small glass phial into which she carefully pours the gold dust. She closes it with an accompanying cork.

"You can take this home with you, kids. Hill End gold, which you found yourselves! You'll have to show it at school!" We still have that glass phial of gold, half a thimble-full, with a label attached to it: *Alluvial gold*.

We share our sandwiches with Bill and when we say goodbye Gerard gives him a dollar bill: "Buy yourself a drink, mate." The dollar disappears under Bill's hat and Bill shuffles into the bush, grinning and mumbling.

Alice announces it is time to stop. We are chilled and half frozen, but I continue to walk slowly through the churning water, staring down to see if somewhere there isn't a forgotten nugget waiting to be found. We climb up a hill of quarts, along a narrow path. I study the quarts wall beside me. All I need is a tiny vein of gold! Only when we reach the road do I begin – with a sudden rush of guilt – to count children's heads again.

On the last morning of our three days in Hill End the valley takes on a completely different aspect. No night frost, no shimmering grass and no sun. Dark clouds hang above the massive hills. Is it going to rain at long last? The wind howls like a drunkard, but there is no rain all morning. The last thing I see when we drive away is Alice with a little girl beside her and a little boy holding on to her trouser leg, staring up at the sky, while waving goodbye to us. And behind her I see the ghosts of many other women, women in long skirts and with shawls around their shoulders in exactly the same stance. Rain, oh God, please let it rain.

Alice: so talented, so versatile, so strong. One of the special people we came into contact with and about whom I understood so little at the time, whom I had so little time to get to know properly. We kept on writing, but the periods between letters grew increasingly longer. Later, the periods would become years.

The Fitzgeralds stuck it out for about three years in Hill End. Then they separated; the reasons why I have forgotten. I remember that Dick lived in Melbourne for a while where he had family. And that Alice moved to Cairns in Queensland (by this time we had returned to Holland). I also remember that Alice became a Baha'i – a faith about which to my shame I know very little. She even went as a Baha'i missionary to a Pacific island where she lived for some years.

I recall that she and I had long discussions about religion. We felt that we were both "searching," even though I allowed our children to be brought up as Catholics; since we had started out that way I thought it would be wrong

HILL END 309

Gold panning: Paul and Mum.

to confuse them. Alice was Jewish, but not religious. She told me she would take her children to a church every now and then, a different one each time. She felt that they should learn about all the religions that existed, without distinction, so that if they later felt the need to join a religious community they could at least make an informed choice.

About eight years ago I received a short note from Alice's eldest daughter telling me that her mother had died, in Cairns, where she had lived her last years, alone.

CHAPTER 33

Losses

I CAN STILL hear Laurel's voice: "You and I belong to the same tribe." And I believed her. Of course I believed her, she was my mentor. She moulded me, at least as far as my literary tastes went. She introduced me to an endless stream of great writers and philosophers whom we explored together and whose wisdom we felt was relevant to our own lives, though nothing was further from the truth.

I had only just started to work at Mount Street when she suddenly came to tell me that she had sold her house in Mosman. After our move to Turramurra I used to meet Laurel in North Sydney, usually for lunch or more rarely after six o'clock. She told me that the house was making way for a block of flats, and that she intended to live in one of them. But before that, she was going on a six-month-long trip, to Greece, to start off with and then to London and Paris, and possibly Italy. Gidley was not going with her. He was going to move in with his sister for the intervening period. "I've waited for this chance for such a long time," she told me, "I can now finally do it. The children are at university; they don't need me anymore. It may even be good for them if I'm not around for a little while."

Had she already had her facelift by then? Laurel and a facelift – in my wildest dreams I would not have combined the two. But it did happen. I remember that I thought her face mask-like when she allowed people to visit her again after having been incommunicado for weeks. Her eyes were still the same, thank God: those strikingly clear, dark eyes that reflected her undivided attention, always. I have a photo of her in Greece looking touchingly young with her smooth skin and warm smile. She must have had the facelift done before she left.

I see myself in the flower-filled cabin of a Greek ship bound for Piraeus. I am part of a group of men and women who appear in *The Herald's* society pages: friends from Laurel's other life. She takes my hand: "When I get back we'll pick up the thread again, but in the meantime, you must just go on" (a quote from Samuel Beckett's *Waiting for Godot* that we had spent many evenings discussing). I look at the light in her eyes and I nod. I suddenly feel intensely lonely.

When she returned she did not continue living in Mosman for long. She bought a house in Stanmore, a suburb close to the centre of Sydney, which in our eyes seemed almost a slum area. Primarily poor Greek families lived there in long rows of houses, which had been turned into flats. Laurel's house was well maintained, but did not make a prosperous impression. Not in comparison with Mosman. All the houses stood shoulder to shoulder, divided only by dark, narrow alleyways. There were no front gardens. It was a noisy street. Lots of traffic and families who when it was hot spent the majority of their time on the pavement in front of their houses. Laurel was incomprehensibly enthusiastic about all this. She claimed that it reminded her of Greece. She adored everything Greek, she said; had never known what an affinity she would feel for that country....

Her house was split into three flats. There was a large flat downstairs at the front in which a young Greek family lived. Laurel herself lived downstairs at the back. She had a living room with open kitchen, a bedroom with a bathroom and a patio. She had rented out the top floor to two single Greek men, one of whom she had met when she was in Greece.

It took me a little while to realise that Gidley was no longer part of her life. She did not talk much about this to me. She did remark that neither of them wanted a divorce; that they were good friends but no longer wished to live together.

She very quickly became a kind of centre of the Greek community around her. She taught English to new emigrants. She became involved in neighbourhood affairs. She devoted herself to a new hobby, photography, but stayed faithful to her old love, theatre. She visited all the big theatres, close to which she now lived. She regularly came to report to me in North Sydney about the opening nights she had attended. She met Alan and Ramon. I remember a Christmas party at Stanmore. Ramon was there with his wife and children, Gerard and I were there with our children and Alan was there on his own. And the Greeks who lived upstairs were there. It ended with Greek dancing to Greek music played on the record player, in which we all, at Laurel's great insistence, took part.

Alan became Laurel's most faithful pupil – I think the word is appropriate – and friend. He learned a great deal from her, as I did. He was with her a few days before she died, when she was very ill. (Janneke too, as a matter of fact. She kept me posted, far away in Holland. That must have been in the late seventies).

I visited Australia on my own in 1977. That was the very first time since Janneke moved back there. Laurel was living in Manly then, close to the beach. I stayed with her for a few days. Alan came to dinner one evening. I remember the sea and that Laurel and I took long walks and how little there was to say then despite the deep affection between us. She was depressed. But her eyes were as bright as ever, still the eyes of a young woman. I no longer know how old she was when she died – younger than I am now, I believe.

Unchanging stability came from Hiek. Hiek was the only one who remained faithfully where she was, who was always there and who never changed. Every few weeks on a Sunday we would descend on Seaforth with our kids, on an outing to *Tante Hihi*. It felt like going back to an old, familiar haven. Hiek's house was a quintessentially Dutch home even though it nestled at the foot of an Australian rock. There was the inevitable Persian rug covering the wooden coffee table on which stood the small, copper barrel-organ tin, which functioned as an ashtray. There were the decorated soup bowls, the Dutch dresser with its glass doors, the book case full of Dutch books, and Dutch magazines lying around, and of course copies of *The Dutch Australian Weekly*, the newspaper of the Dutch club in Sydney. In Seaforth, we spoke half in Dutch, half in English. Janneke learned to sing the Dutch nursery rhyme "*Slaap, kindje, slaap*" there and "*Een karretje op de zandweg reed.*" And all the children learned to say "*Goed zo*" and "*Dank je wel*" and "*Welterusten*."

Did Hiek really never change? When did it begin to dawn on me that that first, green hospital screen could well be the precursor of a whole parade of future hospital screens? Certainly not when she had just returned from Holland. Nor in the period that we, homeless, slept in her half-finished spare room. Then, she was still plump and energetic.

Shortly after Torron Duplicating had become Torron Printing she even took a job again. Also in Mount Street, in the office building that looked so much like the prow of a ship. She became a secretary at a start-up advertising agency, a one-man company that unfortunately did not last long. At that time we met each other almost daily. We drank coffee and, giggling like young girls, swapped office gossip, and we talked by phone if we couldn't meet. It felt so good to have Hiek nearby.

About six months later she told me at Torino's that the little company wasn't doing well. That she would undoubtedly lose her job soon, a prospect she didn't really mind. "I think I'm just going to stay home for a while," she said cheerfully, "All that commuting makes me tired. Frank and Paul now both have weekend jobs, so financially things aren't bad at all. It would be fine for me to rest on my laurels for a while."

Only then did I suddenly notice how thin she had become and I saw shadows in her face that I had never seen before. "You should go and see a doctor," I said, "When's the last time you had a check-up?"

"Oh love, I hate all that pushing and pulling about. I feel fine. I'm just getting old. Happens to us all."

"You, old? Never! I still think it would be a good idea if you had a check-up. It can't hurt, after all."

She went. She was given pills "to pep her up a bit." She reported back that she felt a lot better. That she was hugely enjoying her job-less existence. That she was working in the garden, that she was going to make new cushions for the settee. How wonderful it was that she now had time to read…

On a bright Sunday afternoon, as we were leaving, she told me briefly that she had to undergo chemo again: "It's purely preventive. The doctor doesn't want to run any risks, and neither do I really. It's just so awful that it makes you so sick. And I had meant to start looking for another job. There's so much we still want to do to the house. Oh well, it'll just have to get done later."

My stomach lurched.

"It's spread," said Gerard, as we drove away.

"How can you know that?"

"They wouldn't do anything like this for nothing. I see this at work every day."

Another Sunday. Hiek is sitting on the settee, smiling weakly. She looks as if she barely has the strength to sit up. Her face is grey. "There's a big pan of soup in the kitchen, love, vegetable soup with meatballs. Would you warm it up? There's more than enough for everyone."

"Why didn't Jan warn us?" I asked aghast, "I had no idea you were feeling so ill. We shouldn't have come, it's much too busy for you."

"Oh no, don't say that. I'm so happy you're here! I see so few people these days. I'll feel better again in a little while. You'll see. It's like morning sickness. It comes and goes."

The same settee on the day of Frank's engagement party: it is a velvety summer's evening. Pop music in the garden and a long table full of lovely things to eat under the trees decorated with paper lanterns. A group of teenagers is dancing on the patio between the house and the bathroom/laundry. Janneke is jumping up and down with them.

Inside, the standing lamp is on. Hiek is lying against a pile of cushions. She looks almost transparent; her high forehead is bluish in the lamplight. "He's still very young, but he's determined to get married soon. He says she is the one for him. Oh well, Monica is a few years older and very sensible and such a sweet girl. And Frank has now found a good, full-time job. They have promised me they'll wait till I am completely better."

Her health did not improve for about a month and then suddenly things seemed to get very much better. She no longer threw up, she could eat normally, she became much less tired. She even did her own housework again. She began enthusiastically to make plans for the coming wedding of her eldest son. Would our girls like to be bridesmaids? Not that it was going to be a large, traditional English wedding. Something intimate, here in the garden in Seaforth....

And then Jan phoned me: "Hiek is in hospital. She slipped when she was getting in the washing. She broke her hip. How is it possible to fall as badly as that? She just slipped on the grass! Thank God I was home. She's in Manly Hospital, it's nice and close."

"Oh God," said Gerard, "I bet it was a spontaneous fracture, nothing to do with slipping."

Manly Hospital is situated on a peninsular surrounded by the sea. We find Hiek in a large bed in the corner of a spacious women's ward. A green curtain between her and the neighbouring bed affords a little privacy. She is on a drip. The needle sticks out of the top of her hand. She grins shyly when she sees us: "Ridiculous, isn't it? I feel like such an idiot. My leg just slipped and I landed in such a strange way." At the back of her eyes I see the same anxiety I feel, which must at all costs be ignored. We try to make her laugh, we chatter about everyday things. The ward is packed with visitors. There is a constant coming and going. Only two visitors per bed, a rule that is strictly enforced. We don't stay long. We know that Frank and Monica are waiting their turn in the hall.

Eight weeks later she is home again, sitting up in bed, laughing. I look at the bone structure of her face, which is now so clearly visible. The round jaw, the high cheekbones covered tightly with very delicate, almost transparent skin. Not a wrinkle to be seen anymore. Her eyes seem to have become larger; they are more deeply embedded.

"How on earth do you do it, Hiek? You look younger!" I say, hugging her.

"Oh, I feel so good. They fixed me up again beautifully. There is now a silver screw in my hip and I can walk a little already." She points proudly to her crutches, which are leaning against the wall next to her bed. "It's so wonderful to be independent again at last. I'll be hopping about like a robin soon, you'll see!" She did indeed become almost completely mobile again surprisingly fast. First she walked with crutches, later she no longer needed them.

Frank and Monica get married. I can't remember a thing about the wedding, but we do have a small photo somewhere of Frank and Monica on the settee in Seaforth with Janneke and Lindy on either side of them, clearly not at their ease. Behind the couch stand Hiek and Jan. Hiek's right hand rests on Jan's shoulder, and she is holding something hidden behind her back with her left hand: one of her crutches.

Another operation, again in Manly: the screw is replaced by a plate. I keep hoping that it will all turn out fine in the end. They wouldn't do something like this if there wasn't any hope at all? Gerard shrugs silently. Jan can tell us nothing about what exactly the matter is. You shouldn't bother doctors too much, he says. They know what they're doing. Hiek herself asks nothing either. She does not talk. She waits. It is almost as if she is completely on her own, bent over a small flame, which she must protect in the hollow of her two hands. As if she needs all her attention for that. Only when, on the advice of her doctors, she is sent to a nursing home instead of home to Seaforth, does she seem to look up and show something resembling resistance.

"The home is in St. Ives," Jan tells me over the phone, "Close to where you are. It's in beautiful grounds in the middle of a nature resort. She'll be able to get her strength back there." He sounds optimistic.

I need to take two buses to get there: first, a bus to the station; then change to a bus to St. Ives. The nursing home is situated in a large, old, stately home, with a red-pebbled drive between high, whispering trees. It is surrounded by beautifully kept parkland. It smells of summer herbs, of tropical flowers, of freshly mown grass. All the high, white-framed windows and doors are wide open. I feel myself becoming more cheerful. Hiek loves flowers and plants.

She is lying in a white bed in a four-person room, next to an ancient lady who is clearly no longer responsive and opposite two equally geriatric patients. One of them is sleeping, with rasping breath, and the other inspects me with dull eyes before turning her gaze back to the ceiling. Hiek looks at me, her eyes blazing, her fingers nervously plucking the sheet that is covering her: "They call this a convalescent home! What a joke! Everyone is dying here. There is far too little staff. And there isn't even a resident doctor. Of course they don't think one is needed, it's an unnecessary extravagance. How dare they put me in here? I'm not dying! I want to live and I'm going to keep on living. I just wish there was someone here who knew what was going on. I'm getting the strangest bruises on my arms and legs, and no-one knows what they are. Or they won't tell me. It makes me so angry!"

The panic in her eyes is more than I can bear. "It's lovely outside, don't you think?" I say timidly.

She perks up: "Oh yes, let's go outside! It's allowed. Do you see that wheelchair over there? If you help me I don't need to call a nurse. We can sit out on the veranda; that would be lovely. Will you hand me my dressing gown?" She quickly pushes the sheet aside. I help her with her dressing gown. I lift her with shaking hands into the wheelchair. She is as light as a feather, as light as a four-year-old child. Oh, those tiny wrists, those thin, white legs. I push her outside.

On the red-tiled veranda are wicker tables with matching chairs. There is no-one about. Suddenly, a young girl in a white uniform comes running up the veranda stairs. "What a good idea, ladies!" she says cheerfully, "Would you like me to bring you some tea?"

"Yes, thank you," says Hiek, cool, prim, not Hiek-like at all.

I talk about the butterflies that dance in clusters among the bushes full of bright yellow flowers that frame the veranda. About the river rock that Gerard had found, which contains a fossil. About Paul's last rugby game, which resulted in a loose front tooth despite his gum protector. She becomes more peaceful. She tells me about her Paul's new girlfriend. And all the time a series of unspoken questions stands between us. Is this really the end of the road? What is going to happen? Is there no-one left who can help? What is the next step? How do you prepare for death?

When I say goodbye an hour and a half later none of these questions have been asked. Later I blamed myself bitterly for not saying anything real that last time that I saw Hiek, for not being able to comfort her, other than perhaps by my presence. On my way home I felt like a traitor because I am one of the survivors – those who shamelessly think, thank God it isn't me. And then go back to normality.

That was the last time I saw her alive. The very last time I saw her doesn't count. This was about three weeks later when she was back in hospital for a last operation the need for which I never understood, and she was in a coma. Gerard talked about hormone-dependant tumors, a last straw chance of survival...When I saw that shocking, shuddering little body, attached to tubes and bereft of all human dignity, I knew there wasn't the slightest possibility of a last chance. Hiek's eldest sister was there. She had just arrived from Holland. I stood dry-eyed next to this weeping old lady and I prayed. "Please let her die. Please let her go. Now. Please, please let her be free."

"Terrible," was all Gerard said as we left the hospital.

She died without regaining consciousness, in the early hours of the morning. Sunday morning. How do you tell children about death? Janneke wept loudly, Lindy sat staring out of the window, very quiet, her face white. She did not say a word. Paul sobbed, and Bobby looked wide-eyed from one to the other. "Where's Tante Hihi?"

"It's much better for her to be dead," I said, "Now she doesn't have any pain anymore and she won't ever have to go to the hospital again. I'm sure she's happy now."

"Will her soul fly to God now?" asked Paul, wiping his tears away with one brown arm, "Can we go and watch?"

"She's already with God," I said, "She went there last night. For Oom Jan and for Frank and Paul it's very, very sad but for Tante Hiek it's a good thing."

Paul sighed heavily, "I wish I could have seen her soul fly away. Do you think anyone saw it in the dark?"

"You can't see a soul," said Janneke.

"Yes, you can! When someone dies they fly away!"

Bobby slipped off his kitchen stool. "Can I wear your Black Prince, Paul?" In those days Paul wandered around with a cicada that had just emerged from its cocoon on his t-shirt. A huge, deep black cicada with glittering eyes like golden jewels who remained attached to the cotton, motionless, no matter what Paul did. A Black Prince was very rare, the boys had explained to me, and you could tame them. At night he was placed tenderly in a shoebox full of eucalyptus leaves and in the morning he glowed on Paul's chest like a brooch. Would he ever spread his wings and fly away?

"Okay," said Paul, and he carefully plucked the creature off his t-shirt and placed it on Bobby's shoulder.

"I'm going to play with my mice," Bobby said contentedly. He was the proud owner of a white and a black mouse who lived together in a little cage under the carport. Whenever Bobby was confronted with perplexing things he would let the pair run loose on the veranda and, lying on his tummy, would hold long conversations with them. The animals never tried to escape. They ran around a little and then sat on their hind legs and nibbled the tidbits that Bobby offered them.

That morning Bobby left his mice alone for a few minutes. A kookaburra flew onto the veranda and the black mouse disappeared from our lives forever.

Bobby wept and wept, and was inconsolable until Paul pointed out to him that Blackie was now with Tante Hihi.

Bobby stopped crying. "Tante Hihi is allowed to have him," he said.

Hiek is buried at the foot of the Blue Mountains, in a graveyard that does not resemble a graveyard. There are no headstones, only plaques that are placed flat in the grass with a name and two dates listed on them. It is a park with here and there a single tree and flower beds separated by small, blue, twisting paths. Innumerable sprinklers noiselessly produce silver arches of tiny water drops and keep the grass eternally green.

CHAPTER 34

An unexpected journey

WHENEVER ANYONE ASKS us why we moved back to Holland – a question that generally arises if the topic of Australia comes up and because we both talk about the country with great enthusiasm – I usually answer evasively. Along the lines of: "There's never one single reason for the things you do, there are always a whole lot of reasons." Which is true, of course. Gerard on the other hand will always say that the reason was his health. That he would often seriously worry about what would happen to the children and I if his asthma ever got the better of him. Which was also true.

At that time, Australia had few social provisions, and in the early sixties Gerard's asthma was a constantly present threat. Although he had it under control and we had all become used to it, it remained an uneasy backdrop to our lives. Gerard and his medihaler were inseparable and despite it he still sometimes had trouble getting up a high flight of stairs, and daily affairs were sometimes accompanied by a gentle wheeze in his chest. He often slept very badly. He claimed that he knew exactly when to take action, that he had become an expert in arresting an asthma attack, that he would never let things get as bad as in the early years when Janneke was a baby. But he was never completely unconcerned about it. We never talked about it. It was simply one of those things that we did not discuss.

In 1964 he changed his job. He left Upjohn and went to work for Schering. He earned more, but the job did not become more enjoyable. "All these regulations are madness! They want to know the tiniest details! They think they own you. And all that internal competitiveness, it makes me sick." I didn't pay a great deal of attention to his grumbling. I was far too busy. He stuck it out at Schering for about a year and a half.

CHAPTER 34

One late autumn day in 1966 he confronts me with a fait accompli: "I have just quit."

"You have just what?!"

"I'm leaving Schering. I've had more than enough of the insanity there. And I told them what I think of them too!"

"Oh, Gerard!" I can feel panic rising.

"Don't, oh Gerard, me! And don't worry. I can always go back to Upjohn. But first I need a bit of peace and quiet. I'm taking two weeks off. I just have to get some rest." Only then do I notice how terribly tired he looks. How he has aged. How thin he is. New lines have appeared on his face. He takes short breaths. This is the worst possible time of year for him, all that pollen in the air, the colds going around. One day it can be boiling hot, the next can be icy cold...

"Do you really mind so much that I'm taking a few weeks off?"

"No, no, of course not. I didn't mean it like that."

"It really was impossible for me to keep working there. I'll finish this week. I have to hand in my car on Friday, so we won't have transport for a little while."

"Okay, we'll manage. Just put it all out of your mind now. I can take the school bus to the station, why not?" But it is still a bit of a shock.

One morning around 7.30 am, a week into Gerard's "holiday," we received a completely unexpected phone call from Holland. I can't recall that we had ever had one before. What I do recall is that the usual morning rush had started. The girls and I needed to catch the eight o'clock bus. I think Gerard had just spoken to his eldest brother's eldest son. Or was it to Bertus himself? In any case he had been told his mother was very seriously ill and that the family had booked him onto a KLM flight leaving Sydney for Amsterdam late that afternoon. Gerard was the only one of the 15 children living outside the Netherlands.

He was devastated. "What can I do? I can't just up and leave you all here...!"

"Of course you have to go!" I said, "We'll be fine. And you have the time to go now that you're between jobs."

"But I'd be gone for at least four weeks. It can't be shorter than that. I can't leave you and the kids for that long."

"Don't worry, we really will be fine. We have to go! I'll ring you when I get to the office. Make a list of everything you'll need."

"I don't have a valid passport," he said, "It expired ages ago."

"Ring the consulate. I really have to go."

Throughout that long day Gerard raced around town – by train and bus (becoming suddenly intensely aware of our precarious financial situation) – keeping me posted about his progress every now and then by phone. The Dutch consulate was making a Herculean effort to get him a new passport. Shots! He needed to get shots from the Health Authority on the other side of Sydney. "A re-entry permit. I need to have one otherwise they won't let me back into the country."

I passed on every piece of news to the Torron team who were following developments with bated breath. Even Norm emerged from his ivory tower to enquire whether Gerard was going to make it. Around three he let me know he would be coming to North Sydney. "I need your signature. It's for the re-entry permit. You have to give your permission otherwise I can't leave the county. It'll also give me a chance to say goodbye. Shall I take a taxi? I'll never make it otherwise."

"I'll take him to Mascot," Alan said, "I can take an hour off."

At three fifteen Gerard ambled into my office. He looked dazed; his hair was standing on end. He was carrying a briefcase and had a raincoat draped over his arm.

"Alan will take you to the airport," I said, hastily signing the document he gave me, "Where's your suitcase?"

"Suitcase?!" He stared at me in amazement. "I don't have a suitcase. You don't think I had time to go home and pack, did you? Anyway, it's summer there. I won't need any clothes."

"Oh, no!"

"The man's right!" said Alan who had been standing next to me, following this marital exchange, grinning from ear to ear, "Travel light, eh old man? Come on, we need to go."

Our farewells were very brief. "They know I'm coming. The consulate called. I think they'll hold the flight for me," were about the last words I heard as he left the office. He rang me from the KLM desk at the airport, around five. The departure time was four. He had missed his flight. All the roads had been jammed full of traffic. Alan had done his utmost but it was hopeless. By the time they reached the airport the KLM plane had left. He had been rebooked onto an American flight that would leave at eleven the next morning. Everyone had been unbelievably helpful and were continuing to be. Alan had offered to drive him to the airport the next morning. The whole of Torron heaved a sigh of relief. "That's much better!" said Jan, "At least you'll be able to pack a suitcase for him tonight. Men!"

"I hope he gets to Holland on time," I said downheartedly. I was utterly exhausted as if I had been the one running from authority to authority all day. Gerard on the other hand was remarkably cheerful when he got back. His eyes shone with repressed excitement, he looked ten years younger. "I'm flying via Panama and Hawaii. Great fun! The extra few hours won't make all that much difference, I think. Isn't it fantastic that they found a seat for me?"

We travelled back to Turramurra together and travelled together again early the next morning to North Sydney. I did indeed pack his suitcase that evening while he talked to the children who were not happy at the prospect of his sudden departure. But they understood it and accepted it, especially Janneke and Lindy. Alan made sure that Gerard got to Mascot the next morning in good time. He arrived in Holland late in the evening and was driven straight to the hospital where his mother was waiting for him. He was in time to talk to her, and also talked to her the next day. She died the day after, very peacefully.

When Gerard returned from Holland he was no longer carrying the old valise he had left with but a large, brown leather suitcase. He was also wearing a brand new suit and shiny shoes: all presents from loving relations, he told me. From the suitcase emerged among other things flowery summer dresses for the girls and for me, Dutch sailor suits for the boys, a Dutch tablecloth and Dutch towels and tea towels. For some strange reason it felt as if I was being attacked. Of course I was happy with all the luxurious gifts, and yet..."I didn't have the heart to refuse them," said Gerard, "It gave them such pleasure to come up with things which we could use here. You have to admit that when I left I looked a little shabby."

"Oh," I said.

"You have no idea how high the standard of living is over there. The luxury they live in! It has become paradise on earth there. They call it a welfare state and that is exactly what it is. Wives don't need to work. And the social services! You wouldn't believe your ears. Everyone is protected from cradle to grave. Study grants for young people. Whoever wants to can go to university. No-one needs to worry about anything!"

"Oh," I said again. It made me a little irritated, all those superlatives. That small, prim, cold country that I happened to have been born in didn't matter to me in the least.

The stream of stories kept going for a day or two. How, after the funeral, he had travelled from brother to sister to brother, from Maastricht to Leeuwarden, from Leiden to Tilburg, from Oegstgeest to Den Bosch. How well kept the country looked. Not a trace anymore of the devastation of the war.

How solidly built and well designed the houses were, how incredibly luxurious the restaurants. And the most wonderful thing of all: he hadn't had any trouble at all with asthma over there, despite the emotion of especially the first few days. Granted, it was colder than he had expected. It had rained a lot, but clearly that kind of climate was better for him than the Australian climate....

Then the excitement waned. Gerard went to talk to Upjohn. They gave him his old job back. We had a car again, and the old routine was resumed.

When did I begin to notice that a kind of offensive had started? A few months later, I think. It is so difficult to unravel the synchronicity of events. I believe that this was the year Lindy did her entrance exams for the new Turramurra high school, which she passed with flying colours. So Janneke must have been at school in Chatswood for at least two years by then, the Catholic school there to which the nuns in Pymble automatically referred their pupils. We continued to be unimpressed by the quality of Catholic education so when a new public high school was set up in Turramurra...

Back to the conversations Gerard and I had at the time about Holland versus Australia. Not that we talked about this such a great deal, but it was a topic that began to regularly recur. A depressing subject, I thought.

Gerard: "We're working ourselves to the bone here! And where is it getting us? What have we achieved? Nothing. We can't make any progress at all. We still can't manage to save a penny. Yet we both have good jobs. Why can't we get ahead?"

Me: "We have achieved something! We have a house, don't we? It's our property. We aren't doing so badly at all!"

Gerard, with scorn: "Oh sure, we have a house, but it's brick veneer, a thin outer layer pulled over a wooden frame! It looks okay on the outside, but on the inside it's as ramshackle as can be." This remark would be accompanied by a light kick against the sliding doors between over living room and kitchen, which would promptly jump off their rails, an inconvenience we were all too familiar with and for which we never found a satisfactory solution. "Surrogate! Like so many things here. We freeze in the winter and are boiling hot in the summer in this house!" which was undeniably true.

Me: "We have four healthy children!"

"Yes and what is to become of them? The schools here! They only ever learn things about Australia and England, but the rest of the world doesn't exist!" which was also more or less true. "You need to be extremely wealthy to afford to send them to a good school here and let them study later. We could never afford that."

"Oh, that's nonsense, you can get a kind of grant here too, I've heard." But I had also heard that you needed to belong to the top students in your school to be eligible for it. I hastily tried to find another argument: "The climate is so wonderful here, the country, the people!"

"What good does that do us if one of us is sick? You know as well as I do that we would be destitute if one of us fell ill for any length of time. I worry about that terribly. What would become of us then? We have no family here. We don't belong anywhere."

"You're exaggerating hugely. There are God knows how many people who would help us!"

"For how long? We're so isolated here. What if something goes seriously wrong? My asthma, your back?" I had no answer for this. "There is so much freedom here," I said weakly.

"Freedom? If you have four kids to look after? You're joking!"

Why did I never succeed in persuading him to accept my views but did he always manage to get me to see things through his eyes? I began to look critically at our sparse furniture, our threadbare carpet, our bedroom with still only a bed, cupboard and chair in it, through Dutch eyes. I could tell myself a thousand times that it didn't matter, that we lived outside most of the time anyway, that a house was only a nighttime shelter. I began to doubt my own convictions. Had we achieved so much after all?

I could counter Gerard's: "Australians don't have any stability; they're nomads, they come and go. They don't have a real history, no solidity," with: "But they are wonderful friends! They are incredibly hospitable and loyal. And they are open, informal, easygoing." None of it helped. I heard in his words a yearning for past security, for old certainties, for predictability. I also heard an unspoken, possibly even unconscious disillusionment, which I did not want to share but which was contagious nevertheless. And then there was always and forever the asthma...

There came a point that I could no longer muster any new arguments. At which I felt only tired, utterly drained. It became very quiet for a little while. No more discussions about Holland. And then a day arrived that everything suddenly became crystal clear. When I realised that for the two of us together there was only one possible answer.

It is the end of a blistering heat-wave day. We are sitting on the front veranda, exhausted, waiting for the southerly winds that have been promised. There is no coolness anyway. Our lawn resembles a tough, yellow straw mat with here and there bare patches showing. Our bushes droop; they are parched and covered in dust. The whole of New South Wales has been suffering for some time now from a destructive drought. In the outback the dry earth is covered in deep cracks as far as the eye can see. We see it on television every day.

Here in Sydney strict water restrictions have been enforced. Cars cannot be washed. Garden sprinklers are forbidden, and watering by hand is limited to half an hour a day, early in the morning. Sometimes, especially at bathing peak times, only tiny rivulets of water trickle out of the faucet. Day in day out, the cloudless sky resembles a metal plate. The sun is merciless.

"Would it really be possible?" I say listlessly, "To go back to Holland? Do you think we could get enough money together for the trip? Six people..."

Gerard immediately jumps up: "Of course we can! If we sell this house we'll make a profit. I've been to a few realtors already. We'll have enough for the trip and some money to tide us over in the beginning. You know I wouldn't need to be without a job there for even a day? Jan in Leeuwarden." He had told me repeatedly that his brother Jan, who has his own business in Leeuwarden and no male heir, had asked him whether he didn't feel like coming to work with him. He had also told me his whole family was champing at the bit to welcome us with open arms and help us if we decided to come back, and that we would have a carefree future in Holland. That I would never need to work again, unless of course I wanted to...

At that moment a mighty wave of coolness blows over us. The southerly! The trees begin to whisper, a bird begins to sing. I take a deep breath. "If you are absolutely sure it would be possible..." He puts an arm around my shoulders. "I believe it would be for the best if we went back, the best for all of us. And that this is the right moment to do it."

"But you have to promise me that you won't do anything rash. I want to know first absolutely for sure that it will be possible. We aren't in a hurry, are we?" The air now sings. The wind sweeps over us in huge, cool gushes. The children run down the drive, jubilant. I can hear Anna, next door to us, pushing up a window.

"We'll take it very slowlu. I'll investigate everything down to the last detail. You really don't need to worry." He nods, so sure of himself, so convinced that this is the right decision, that I suddenly begin to consider quite a rash move myself.

"Shall I quit?" I ask. What is this? A gesture to indicate: "Here, you take back the reins?" Or a personal giving- up? A kind of, well, it can't be helped anymore, so why should I devote any more energy to it? I am so tired. So indescribably tired. I don't want to have to think anymore. I don't want to have to take any decisions.

"Of course you should quit! And as soon as possible. So we'll be able to lead a normal life here for the last few months. So you can get some rest too." I am sitting, leaning against him. The wind brings tears to my eyes.

Written down like this it seems as if that period of doubting was only very brief. That isn't true. There was at least a year between Gerard's visit to Holland and our decision to go back. Once it had been taken, Gerard changed jobs again. He had had his fill of multinationals. He found a well-paid job with a small Australian pharmaceutical company, called Protea, which was much less demanding and which did not require him to make trips into the country. His working area was the whole of Sydney. If I am not mistaken he told them from the start that we intended to return to Europe but that we didn't yet know when this would happen. This did not appear to be a problem for them. And in the meantime I did indeed take my leave of Torron.

Oh, the joy of no longer being a slave to the clock! I am a jobless housewife! I can go shopping whenever I want. I can, if I wish, wash and iron during the day. I can attend school meetings. I can go to the library at any time. I can have coffee with my next-door neighbour and I am home when the children come home from school. That rediscovery of our children; it feels as if I have not seen them for years.

Janneke is a teenager now. She has long, blonde hair, which she now wears in a ponytail. She is generous and bubbly, sunny and practical. She is always visiting our neighbour a few houses further down who has a six months' old baby. She adores the baby whose name is Christopher. She takes him for a walk almost every day. She knows exactly how to change a nappy and what giving him a bottle entails. And she has announced that she wants to be a babies' nurse in a big hospital when she grows up. Her other great love is Elvis Presley. All her school exercise books are covered in hearts with "Elvis, I love you" written in them. From the wall above her bed, Elvis' pasty face stares at you, in a variety of poses. When Christopher's mum gives her an old portable record player as a present her joy knows no bounds. All her pocket money is spent on Elvis records. Her favourite pastime becomes lying in the grass in the backyard with the wailing suitcase glued to her left ear. This is also how she does her homework, accompanied by Elvis Presley. Her school results aren't great and she no longer plays the violin.

Lindy has honey-coloured hair and a little, round face. She lives in her own dream world. She draws delicate fairy figures and fills exercise books with mysterious stories. Her great hero is Captain Kirk in Star Trek. She plays endless games together with a neighbour's daughter, her best friend, full of space ships and adventures in space featuring Captain Kirk in the main part and, I suspect, herself in a supporting role. Sometimes Bobby joins in. At the same time, Lindy is the only one of our children who comes home from school with astronomically high marks on her report cards, seemingly without making the slightest effort ("Oh, well, you know, Lindy...!" the others scoff, whenever we confront them with this).

She hates turmoil, chaos, loud voices and arguments. She is our great peacemaker. She is also always the one whom the other children dispatch on missions to acquire parental agreement – be it Janneke, Paul, Bobby or all three of them. She carries out this task with large, somewhat distant and slightly tragic eyes, which are almost impossible to resist. Gerard especially is like putty in her hands, and she is invariably successful.

The boys, whom we still call "the babies" and whom we treat like a unit, are actually no longer a unit at all. Paul, with his red, wiry hair, his large and noisy group of friends, his sports gear that constantly clutters the house, and his always flushed face, freckled and covered in droplets of sweat, throws himself into activity after activity without the slightest pause, singing loudly along the way. He has a pure, high soprano voice and loves to sing.

Bobby, whose hair is still satiny and white blonde, never sings. Nor does he like group activities. He is a loner. He is fascinated by Japanese Samurai and Ninjas, whom he sees throwing star knives on television. They feature in a popular children's programme, which, I suspect, does not offer a very accurate picture of life in ancient Japan. Little girls adore Bobby. He is naturally gallant. Every now and then I glimpse him helping a little neighbourhood girl down from the rocks alongside our carport. And once, when he is accompanying me to the shops, he is greeted blissfully from the other side of the street by a little blonde fairy, who is also walking with her mother. He responds to this ecstatic "There's Bobby! Hello Bobby!" with a small, blasé wave, as if gravely acknowledging that "she's sweet, but I have more important things to do."

Sometimes I wonder with amazement where they have come from, these four strangers. I know that I know them, but they remain a mystery. Extraordinary. Life itself is extraordinary.

Slowly but surely I recover from my constant rushing and exhaustion. A certain relief descends once the decision has been taken. I have always been able to do that – accept a decision once taken, support it fully, not look back, not give room to constant regrets. What is done is done. I decide that I need to teach the children Dutch, but this resolution is doomed to failure. They don't show the slightest interest, they are far too busy with other things. They barely pay attention whenever I try to tell them about Europe. I don't make a huge effort, in fact. It is all still far too far away. We don't even have a time line in mind. I allow myself to do nothing.

Leaving for the Achille Lauro

CHAPTER 35

Departures

THE SALE OF our house does not proceed as Gerard expects it to. Every now and then a few people come to view the house, but there are no enthusiastic offers. The realtor suggests we drop the price, which Gerard refuses to do. "We'll just wait," he says, "We can manage for a while yet." I agree completely. We still have some savings. We live frugally, very frugally, and we wait.

And then a long letter arrives from Phons. He writes only briefly about his personal life. Patsy is now living in Queensland with the children; he is living in a boarding house. But he writes at length about a newly arrived inhabitant of the boarding house, an American, called Don Jacquot: a businessman, an entrepreneur with brilliant ideas. Not a careful let's-test-the-waters-first type of man, but someone who likes to dive in on a grand scale.

In Melbourne, Don has set up a permanent, weekend flea market for the general public. It's called *Trash and Treasure* (brilliant name!). For a small fee everyone can set up a stall on an open air lot rented and protected by Don, and offer for sale whatever goods they wish, and everyone, again for a small fee, can come and shop there. "And it's a huge success! It's a gold mine, and such a simple idea!" Don is now working on setting up a whole chain of such weekend flea markets, on parking lots that aren't used in the weekends. "He wants to open one in Sydney. And here it comes: I'm going to become his Sydney manager and if things go well, his partner. This is a real chance, guys. This is the beginning of making it big, at last! Don and I are coming to Sydney very soon. I'm driving and he is going to fly a few days later. Can I come and stay with you?" Gerard rang him that same evening.

About a week later, late one morning, a dusty, cream-coloured van drove up our drive. Printed on both sides, in huge, multi-coloured letters surrounded by bright yellow flowers and broadly grinning black and red stick men with raised index fingers, was the name *Trash and Treasure Pty Ltd*. Behind the insect-spattered front windshield sat Phons. He looked grey with exhaustion, but despite this he thrust, grinning with delight, an immense flagon of red wine at me: "Here you are, darling! We have something to celebrate. Reunion booze! I did the trip in one night. Oh Lord, it's good to be here again! Let's pitch three tents here and all that, eh?" We hugged as if we would never let each other go.

"Oh Phons, you need to sleep. You first need to get some rest! You can sleep in Janneke's bed for now: first a shower, then bed. We can talk tonight."

"And tonight I'll sleep here, right?" said Phone, collapsing on our old sofa and patting it as if it were a horse. "Will be just like old times. Oh, I've missed this virtuous couch so much! God, life was uncomplicated then. You look great, by the way. Gerard told me you've stopped working. What on earth are you two up to?"

"Tonight! You need to get into the bathroom."

"Still the same old sergeant major! I'm going! I'm going! Oh, Don will be arriving tomorrow morning. Can we put him up somewhere in the neighbourhood?'

"There's a private hotel at the top of Kissing Point Road, I'll give them a call," I said, propelling him towards the bathroom.

That evening he drily described for us the Melbourne years. How his relationship with Pat had become more and more difficult, how bad this was for the children. How he had finally come to the conclusion that splitting up, which Pat had insisted on for a long time, would indeed be the best solution. But that he still hoped that one day they would find each other again. He told us that the children were doing well, that he had gone to take a look for himself but could not afford to do this very often.

He listened intently to our plans for the future. "Well, maybe this would be the best for you two. You couldn't have continued as you were for much longer. We're all getting older. And if a good partnership is waiting for you over there…It will be very strange not having you two around anymore. I'm glad you're not leaving soon. You're not going to let that realtor lower the price, are you?'

"Not in a million years," said Gerard, "We're not budging till we're offered our asking price. Even if it takes a few extra months."

"You really should talk to Don," said Phons, "What if he has an opening for you too, somewhere? What would you do if you got the chance to be your own boss too? Would you stay then?"

"Only if it were an offer I absolutely couldn't refuse," said Gerard.

"Wait till you see and hear him, old man!"

Don turned out to be a genuine, American cowboy, the kind we saw on television. He was at least six foot tall with powerful shoulders and elegant, narrow hips in tight jeans, which should clearly have sported a gun holster. He had a square chin, an interesting hint of grey on his dark temples, brown, weather-beaten skin, sharp grey eyes and a deep, gravelly, very authoritative voice. He filled our living room. Our chairs suddenly appeared dwarf-like. Our house became a doll's house and I became a Lilliputian.

All of a sudden the dinner I had prepared struck me as measly, even though Don praised it graciously that first evening. Feeling more insecure than I had for years I handed out coffee cups at the end of it and sat down quietly on the sofa next to Phons. Don Jacquot was sitting opposite us on the only chair he fit into, the Swedish bucket chair, which was years old and which Gerard and I had together refurbished not so long ago. Gerard had glued the legs on more securely and I had renewed the upholstery. The chair looked a great deal better.

Don was leaning back in it at is ease. His long legs took up three quarters of the available space in front of him. "That was a great dinner," he said, nodding at me, after which he continued his exposition about the difference between doing business in the States and Australia, emphasising the wealth of unexplored opportunities here.

There was something strange about the chair. To my horror I saw that the legs of my Swedish bucket chair were slowly but surely becoming wider. As if the chair were a sleeping spider which had awakened and was stretching itself in a leisurely way, gradually becoming wider and wider. I sat and watched this process, petrified, eyes wide with horror, unable to say anything or lift a finger to stop it. Don Jacquot was gently sliding, chair and all, towards the floor. Until with a polite crack my chair finally expired, legs sprawled wide on the floor. "God damn it!" roared Don in huge surprise, "I'm sitting on the floor!"

Gerard burst into helpless laughter; tears streamed down Phons' cheeks and I laughed hollowly too, out of sheer nerves and shock. I could see Phons' future going up in smoke amongst the legs of my collapsed chair.

"My wife," hiccoughed Gerard, "My wife just repaired that chair with her own hands! That was our show piece!"

"Christ," said Don, scrambling up, and looking at the mess on the floor, "Shall I buy a new chair for you?"

Another round of helpless mirth. "Not on your life!" said Gerard, "We were just trying it out on you."

"They're leaving anyway," Phons guffawed, wiping his tears, "They just figured if it could carry someone of your build, they'd take it along."

"So we won't!" Gerard managed to shout between bouts of uncontrollable mirth.

"You bastard," said Don, amiably, "You know what I like about you, Gerry?" giving him a hearty slap on the shoulder, "Nothing man, nothing!" with a thunderous laugh that shook the windows. From that moment onwards Gerard and Don were fast friends. They sat together on the floor, glass of wine in hand, leaning against the wall. They exchanged autobiographies. Don told us what it was like to be a young furnace operator on a torpedo boat destroyer during the last year of the war and Gerard told him about Indonesia. Don described wanderings through Mexico and California; how he had started an ironmonger's shop; a failed marriage and now, with quite a lot of money in his pockets, Australia. "There is gold to be picked up off the streets here! This country is still in its infancy. Just a matter of keeping your eyes open."

Our home became Don's headquarters. He only went to the little hotel at the top of Kissing Point Road to sleep. In between his business dealings he behaved like a rich uncle. He brought baskets full of goodies along. He brought presents for the children. He took us out to dinner to the newest and fanciest restaurant in Sydney right on the top of an office tower in the heart of the city; a restaurant that slowly turned around and so treated you, while you were eating, to constantly changing views – the harbour, the city.

With Phons' help he quickly found a few open-air locations, which could be suitable for his Trash and Treasure markets. But acquiring the necessary permits turned out to be a complicated business. Don and Phons were sent from bureau to bureau; none of the civil servants they encountered showed any enthusiasm, on the contrary. "It's much more difficult here than in Melbourne," Don complained, "There are far too many people here with a finger in the pie. And the people I speak to are anything but helpful. It's almost as if they've been appointed to stop entrepreneurs, rather than encourage them."

And then a strike broke out. We were used to strikes, of course. The harbour labourers were very skilled at striking and the civil servants were good at it too. I have forgotten the reasons for the strike. All I recall is that Sydney was suddenly without petrol; that no cars could drive and that public life came to a standstill. Gerard was given days off out of necessity. The girls, who were dependent on the bus, could not go to school, and the Trash and Treasure van stood idle under our carport next to Gerard's car.

Not for long, however. Don did not intend to twiddle his thumbs until the petrol shortage was resolved. "I've seen cars drive on methylated spirits, on kerosene, on God knows what in the good old days." What exactly he poured into the petrol tank I never discovered, but the van drove. It groaned, coughed and rattled, and it belched black smoke, but it drove. So Don and Phons again set out searching for permits and locations. Unfortunately, wherever they went they found surprised, sleepy individuals who claimed not to be authorised to take decisions. After which Don spent half a day on the phone, fruitlessly.

He finally resigned himself to the inevitable: "Our timing is wrong. Just bad luck. And this blasted town clearly isn't ready for us. It will be, one day. We'll be back. We'll try again in a year's time." He left the next day, by train (the planes were grounded in Sydney), Phons stayed with us until the strike ended. He then drove back to Melbourne in the Trash and Treasure van. Both Phons and the car made a defeated impression. The car continued to belch, and it seemed as if Phons' natural optimism had deserted him: "We couldn't have had worse luck! There goes my goldmine and all that!" Don had told him that he would be able to find something for him to do in Melbourne, that they wouldn't lose each other. That he shouldn't worry about money. But it wasn't what he had hoped for.

We continued to wait. The realtor became more and more pessimistic. Our bank began to make problems about our (modest) overdraft. Gerard took out a personal loan with a finance company against a high interest. We received a letter from a now seriously depressed Phons. He had a menial job and a low salary: "If only I could find a job in Sydney to tide me over. Then at least I would be there. So I could keep an eye on developments..."

To make matters even worse, Timmy became ill. He died two days later. The reason was a tick, which we had failed to notice. The children were inconsolable.

After the summer, Gerard decided to lower the asking price. We simply had no choice. The first winter rains brought the first serious buyers. An English couple, who had lived in Switzerland for four years. I have forgotten their name but believe he was an engineer. They came back three times. On the third occasion, the husband crept armed with a torch into the space between the roof and ceiling to carry out a personal inspection, checking for termites or other house-destroying vermin. He found none.

A preliminary sales contract was signed, which still allowed both parties to change their minds. This worried me greatly, as it meant that we were still not sure of where we were. But Gerard viewed things very differently. He rang Giuseppe who was now working in a glass and steel office in the centre of Sydney, together with Maria and a large staff, and was doing very well for himself. Giuseppe's biggest customer was the Italian Flotta Lauro shipping line. We were promptly invited to come and talk. Giuseppe was convinced he could arrange a large discount for us on the price of a passage to Holland. Jubilant, Gerard then went to talk to his boss. He proposed that Phons would become his successor.

Phons immediately came to Sydney. Don thought it was a marvelous idea! He could go back to being a medical rep for a while and in the meantime test the waters with the Sydney bureaucrats. And as soon as the permit problem was solved…Don still estimated that they would need to wait for a year or so.

Phons was indeed employed by Protea from the moment Gerard stopped working. I watched and heard all this with mixed feelings. On the one hand it was lovely to have Phons staying with us again. The children adored having him around. On the other hand all these somewhat loose arrangements did not give me a sense of security. It felt like our old, unsettled days in Mosman. Gambling on the future. Dancing on slippery ice floes – would we fall off or would be remain upright? "But what if none of this happens?" I pointed out, "That contract still isn't definite. What if those people withdraw?"

"Oh, don't nag," was Gerard's irritated response.

"Relax," said Phons, "It's almost impossible for it to fall through now. Those people really won't break the contract: they're getting the house at such a bargain. I think Gerry has organised things beautifully. He'll keep working until two weeks before you leave and then I'll take over. So you'll have a car at your disposal until the very last day, I promise. And once the last signatures have been placed, the bank will give you carte blanche."

"So shouldn't we have just waited for those last signatures?"

"Oh, Agatha, you have to take a risk every now and then! It'll be fine." Which it was. The signatures were placed two days later and the bank became a whole lot friendlier.

That weekend Gerard proposed a plan that in my view was appalling. Gerard and Phons had discovered that KLM was promoting a special deal, especially for young people. For the whole of the month of August they were offering spectacular discounts. If we were to send the girls ahead, by plane, immediately it would save us a fortune. It would more than make up for the loss we had had to incur on the selling price of the house. Moreover, it would be a great experience for the girls, said Gerard.

"You should go for it!" said Phons, "It will be good for their independence! They're 14 and 11, old enough to travel on their own."

"Are you both out of your minds?" I exclaimed, shocked, "I wouldn't consider it. We stay together, we're a family, we travel together."

"Listen," said Gerard, "My sister Jos lived in England for years. She has loads of room and they could stay with her. She even has a daughter at home still, a little older than Janneke, a nice kid. She grew up in England. So they wouldn't have any language problems. Yvonne is very helpful. I'm sure she'd help them find their feet. They would arrive during the school holidays in Holland and so could be there to start off a new year in school. That would be a huge advantage, wouldn't it?"

I stubbornly kept refusing: "No, it isn't going to happen. I want to keep the children together."

Gerard sighed. "This attitude really isn't contributing to what's best for Janneke and Lindy," he said mournfully, "The boat trip will take at least six weeks. We won't be able to leave till the middle of September, and won't get to Holland till November. That will mean months of missing school. Try to think rationally about this."

"Oh God," I said.

"Are you afraid they won't have a good time with Jos? They will have the time of their lives! I bet all my sisters will be falling over each other to look after them. They will be spoiled rotten. I'd be glad to ring Jos tonight, see how she feels about the idea. In my eyes there are only advantages. We'll save a lot of money and it will be a wonderful experience for the girls. Use your brain for a change! Stop thinking about your own peace of mind."

My counter arguments slipped like sand through my fingers.

That evening, Jos, who lived in Leiden, the town Gerard grew up in, was called and the joy at the other end of the line knew no bounds. Of course it would be possible! They would be met with open arms. The whole family was looking forward to our arrival and if we sent the girls ahead they would be helped from all sides. They had at least fifty cousins, aunts and uncles in Holland, after all! Some of them were the same age they were. Jos promised to find out about suitable schools…

Our girls were considerably less enthusiastic. Janneke was willing to consider it, but Lindy, from the moment I carefully explained the plan to them, looked exactly like a sick kitten. I tried, feeling as miserable as she felt, to describe the fun aspects of the idea. "It will be a real adventure! You should both keep a diary! You're going to really fly in an airplane! Just like Daddy did before. Lots of people never get to do that! When your girlfriends hear they won't believe their ears! And when you arrive in Holland, a whole lot of aunts and uncles will be waiting for you."

A light August day: we are standing on the outside terrace of Mascot Airport, Gerard and I and the boys. We are watching a silver KLM plane, which is shining blindingly bright in the sun. The grey runways are shining too. Everything glitters, flashes, dances in front of my eyes. I turn around. I can't watch anymore. I watched when they went through customs, Janneke eager, self-consciously the eldest, busily gesturing to her little sister while curiously trying to see what was happening behind the barrier. Lindy looking back, looking back....

The boys jump around me. Paul pulls my sleeve. "There they go, Mum! There they go! Now they're getting in! Look!" We are surrounded by excited girlfriends with mothers who have brought flowers. There is a lot of shouting, calling, jubilation.

"Now they're taking off!" I hear Gerard say, "Look, boys, the plane is taxiing, you see! In a minute it will take off." I remain doggedly staring at the glass door through which we entered or rather stepped outside.

For two days I wander around aimlessly and wordlessly. I cannot leave the radio or TV. As soon as one news bulletin ends – no airplane disasters, thank God! – I begin to wait for the next one. And then finally there is a phone call. Oceans of tears on the other end. I comfort and console. They are our pioneers; they are paving the way for us. They have an important mission. In about eight weeks we'll all be together again. Eight weeks won't take long. We will write and they can write to us. In every harbour our ship calls – the *Achille Lauro* (and I've given you a list of those, remember?) we can send and receive letters. And before we leave we can ring again....

This is the moment I transfer from one continent to another. It is over. The pain is over. In the two days that I walked around like a zombie I have gone through an amputation of which the scar will always remain and sting, but the acute pain is over. Saying goodbye is over. I have accepted that I will never fathom the mystery of my deep connection with this indefinable, fascinating, 50 million year-old country, and that the time for trying to do that is now over. There is so much, such a vast amount that I have never seen, never explored, never visited. I know so little about Australia. I have experienced so very little of it. But oh the light, the indescribable Australian light, and the summer singing of the cicadas, the dry rustling of the eucalyptus trees, the voice of the ocean. And the people, the amazing people.

We have a photo of an open red truck with the name Stephens Baggage Service printed in bright yellow letters on the side. Leaning against the kangaroo screen that protects the windscreen is a smiling young man. In the back are two chests: a large one and a small one. These contain everything we are taking to Holland. The truck is standing on the drive of our house in Turramurra.

I don't remember this moment. What I do remember is the last time that I pulled the front door shut behind me, late in the afternoon. I remember that the light was yellow and that the boys rushed past me, chattering like sparrows, and dove into what was now Phons' car. On our last night in Sydney we stayed with an old colleague of Gerard's who lived a lot closer to the centre.

I remember Circular Quay the next morning, the shimmering rectangles of water in which the ferries bobbed up and down. We had to queue for a long time in a harbour warehouse and then go up the gangway of a high white ship, the *Achille Lauro*. We have a four-person cabin with our own toilet and shower. "What luxury!" I exclaim, remembering the *Sibajak*. People come to say goodbye. I can recall flowers, magazines, chocolates, but no faces. I am not sad. I can't wait for us to be off. I feel as if I am twenty again. And Gerard? It is harder for him than for me. His chest wheezes and he is unusually quiet.

By the time we set off twilight has set in. We stand next to each other at the railing and watch all the colourful paper garlands break one by one. The stretch of water between the ship and the quay grows and grows.

I put my hand in Gerard's. "You'll see, everything will be fine," I say, "We're just going to start again." He holds my hand tightly. "Yes," he says softly. And then louder, with more conviction, "Yes, yes, of course."

I see the lights come on along the peninsular of North Sydney, thousands of fairy lights. Luna Park. On the receding quayside we see Phons, his raincoat over his arm: waving, waving. It is the 16th of September 1968.

Breda 6, February 2002.

On our way to New Zealand

www.ingramcontent.com/pod-product-compliance
Lightning Source LLC
Chambersburg PA
CBHW040320300426
44112CB00020B/2820